The Crimes of Empire

THE CRIMES OF EMPIRE

Rogue Superpower and World Domination

Carl Boggs

Foreword by Peter McLaren

PlutoPress
www.plutobooks.com

First published 2010 by Pluto Press
345 Archway Road, London N6 5AA and
175 Fifth Avenue, New York, NY 10010

www.plutobooks.com

Distributed in the United States of America exclusively by
Palgrave Macmillan, a division of St. Martin's Press LLC,
175 Fifth Avenue, New York, NY 10010

British Library Cataloguing in Publication Data
A catalogue record for this book is available from the British Library

ISBN   978 0 7453 2946 8   Hardback
ISBN   978 0 7453 2945 1   Paperback

Library of Congress Cataloging in Publication Data applied for

This book is printed on paper suitable for recycling and made from fully managed and
sustained forest sources. Logging, pulping and manufacturing processes are expected to
conform to the environmental standards of the country of origin.

10   9   8   7   6   5   4   3   2   1

Designed and produced for Pluto Press by
Chase Publishing Services Ltd, 33 Livonia Road, Sidmouth, EX10 9JB England
Typeset from disk by Stanford DTP Services, Northampton, England
Printed and bound in the European Union by
CPI Antony Rowe, Chippenham and Eastbourne

Contents

Foreword

In a nation beset by financial meltdown—stemming from the catastrophic decline of Wall Street and the global crisis of financial capital in September and October 2008—and marked by wildly undulating peaks and troughs within its moral history, this book might be something most American readers will studiously want to avoid. That would be a regrettable error of judgment indeed. This powerfully illuminating volume by storied leftist author Carl Boggs is precisely what is needed at this precipitous historical moment that reaches further than the shores of the Americas and encompasses the very heart of what we have come to call civilization.

The United States bears no small responsibility in fomenting the current climate of fear and repression. The crimes of empire of which Boggs speaks are not peccadilloes but reflect the quiddity of the American soul. This is a book about criminal behavior. Not the crimes that my grandmother used to read about in *True Detective* magazine, a Du Maurier cigarette smoldering on her lower lip. After all, these are not, for the most part, isolated crimes involving bank tellers, love triangles or clerks in the neighborhood liquor store shot over a bottle of malt whiskey and a *Baby Ruth*. The criminal behavior featured in this book illustrates a contempt of the law that runs deep inside the structural unconsciousness of U.S. society; so deep, in fact, that it remains unacknowledged as such, or even mistaken for its opposite—the protection of liberty and freedom, not just for U.S. citizens (although they appear to be democracy's preferred customers) but for all of humanity, including the United States' colonial valets.

These are systematic, widespread, and officially sanctioned crimes that are designed from the outset to kill and maim thousands of people in whatever theaters are deemed appropriate by the U.S. administration and military, employing what is unmistakably the most feared and powerful war machine ever created. The use of remote-controlled drone Predators that kill one enemy target for every 70 civilians killed; the use of bunker-busting bombs, cluster bombs, radioactive weapons such as depleted uranium shells, napalm, white phosphorous, and weapons of mass destruction that have over the last 50 years left millions dead; the arming and funding of death squads in places such as East Timor, Argentina, Chile, Brazil, El Salvador, Guatemala, Honduras (especially the CIA-created "Battalion 316"), Colombia, Bolivia, Angola, and Mozambique; "free-fire zones"; the massacres carried out by the infamous "Tiger Force" of the U.S. Army's 101st Airborne Division; the American-style death squads of Iraq's "Salvador Option"; the Chicago police dungeons, the practice of waterboarding that can be traced back to the U.S. conquest and occupation of the Philippines (1899–1902); extra-legal operations such as the CIA's Operation Phoenix (that assassinated between 20,000–40,000 civilian Vietnamese "activists" between 1967 and 1971); and, more recently, executive assassination rings under the aegis of the Joint Special Operations Command that engage in preemptive and proactive attacks on foreign nationals in their own countries—all of these actions taken by the United States over the past centuries send an unmistakable message to the world: The U.S. is ready and willing to employ vast arsenals of death to protect its geostrategic and financial interests around the world.

That the leading violator of international legality and prime perpetrator of international outlawry can view its own legacy with so few official admonishments is shocking to the rest of the world. To take just one example, it would require 69 walls the size of the Vietnam memorial to list all the Vietnamese who were killed in that war.

The hooded figure standing on a stool at the U.S. Abu Ghraib prison in Iraq—wires to administer electric shocks dangling from underneath a blanket draped over his outstretched arms, on whose broken figure the imprint of the depraved brutality of the U.S. military was so dramatically augmented—haunts the blood-splotched corridors of our national memory. Sheikh Mohammed was waterboarded by CIA "interrogators" 183 times in one month in 2003—a torture technique so heinous that it provokes the victim to gasp for air when being suffocated (it is considered a war crime under U.S. law and illegal under international agreements signed by the U.S.). We will remember these crimes that were not labeled as torture when undertaken by the U.S. military and intelligence agencies but were decried as such when used by other countries such as Japan and the Soviet Union (the U.S. convicted Japanese torturers for waterboarding U.S. troops after World War II). We will remember images of naked prisoners covered in feces forming a human pyramid for the amusement of U.S. guards, or a naked prisoner on his hands and knees being led around on a leash by a female soldier. We will remember the accounts of female interrogators wiping red ink disguised as menstrual blood on the faces of Muslim prisoners, or a naked detainee lying on a wet floor, handcuffed, and having objects shoved up his rectum. Or the coffins where detainees were confined along with insects described to them by their interrogators as venomous. We will remember these acts which were not designed to extract information so much as to strike fear into the hearts and minds of all those who would oppose U.S. interests, domestic and abroad. But we can have no memory of those who died during interrogations by the U.S. military, which according to John Sifton amounts to at least 100 post-9/11 detainees, whose alleged murders were left uninvestigated and prosecuted by the Bush Justice Department, even when the CIA Inspector General referred a case (see Sifton's article, "The Bush Administration Homicides"; available at: http://www.thedailybeast.com/blogs-and-stories/2009-05-05/how-many-were-tortured-to-death). Of course, the top levels of government had given its imprimatur, and it is likely that this also involved key Democrats as well. While U.S. military personnel participating in the torture of detainees are required, when necessary, to apply sub-xyphoid thrusts or to undertake tracheotomy procedures during waterboarding, Sifton reports that at least half of these deaths were deliberate homicides.

Many pundits in the U.S. media, for example Thomas Friedman, justify the torturing of Al Qaeda operatives because they represent a special cadre of fiends, whose martyrdom tactics require a special barbarism (see Friedman's article "A Torturous Compromise," *New York Times*, April 28, 2009; available at: http://www.nytimes.com/2009/04/29/opinion/29friedman.html). When, after the release of four formerly secret torture memos, President Barack Obama announced—"[I]t is our intention to assure those who carried out their duties relying in good faith upon legal advice from the Department of Justice that they will not be subject to prosecution" —it set up a terrible precedent that haunts the legacy of those World War II German soldiers who sought to be excused from prosecution for their participation in crimes against humanity because they were merely following orders and relying in good faith upon the advice of their superior officers—a defense clearly rejected during the trials of Nazi war criminals held at Nuremburg. Torture is clearly and plainly a crime against humanity. Granting immunity to torturers in the face of such crimes robs the U.S. government of its humanity as much as the prisoners it tortured.

True, some politicians have decried the recent torturing of "enemy combatants," but the words falling from their tongues have about as much moral gravity as roaches dropping off a laminated table cloth in a skid row establishment. Their remarks seem scripted and patently disingenuous, as they ignore the fact that U.S. war crimes have been undertaken and supported by U.S. administrations for centuries. What was so special about the Bush regime was that, more than any other administration before it, it attempted to codify and institutionalize such criminal behavior. And especially significant was the intense fascination with the images from Abu Ghraib on the part of citizens around the world, images that punctured viewers' imaginations and arrested their attention. So powerful were the spectacular effects of these images on the U.S. public that they temporarily released viewers from their ideological custody and removed the leg irons that the Bush administration had placed on their moral conscience. But that should not distract us from all the horror that occurred prior to the Bush gang's now infamous eight-year legacy.

The idea of the United States as a pro-torture society that egregiously violates both domestic and international law is as about as surreal to many Americans as the idea of entering a local Baptist church and being greeted by a pastor wearing bobby socks, a rainbow colored wig, Twiggy-like eye makeup and teetering toward them on stilts. It just doesn't fit the expected image. The United States of America has done a majestic job of fashioning itself in the eyes of its own population as the world's greatest defender of freedom and justice. Yet the main principles of the Nuremburg tribunal, adopted by the United Nations in 1950 and generally respected throughout the world, do not appear to apply to the United States. And for nearly half the country, the fact that the U.S. nurtures cadres of indefatigable torturers is something that is rationalized as a dirty but necessary business in order to protect the Homeland. Advocates for torture go so far as to argue that the "enhanced interrogation techniques" practiced by the U.S. military and intelligence agencies should never become a serious object of debate in the public square, because such a debate would only steel our enemies against us. Rather than sanctioning a public judgment or repudiation, with some legal consequences for the crimes exercised by U.S. military, many U.S. citizens would simply prefer to look the other way. With their heads inside buckets decorated with the Stars and Stripes, infuriated Americans have told us insistently that we are coddling terrorists. Their intellectual conceit allows them to ascribe to the meaning of "patriot" an identity and political role that enables them to judge patriotism as applicable to any action that will protect the Homeland. While debates abound in the independent and corporate media about U.S. torture practices, Congress was being asked to support a bill of $83.5 billion in supplemental funding in Iraq, Afghanistan, and Pakistan (these war fronts are costing the U.S. $12 billion each month).

The Crimes of Empire takes an enlightened look at the history of U.S. military criminality. It is unwaveringly critical in situating the problem of war crimes and outlawry generally within a systemic framework. What makes it especially important is its focus on the long legacy of U.S. imperialism and militarism, and hence its revelation that the Bush Doctrine did not really depart that much from the crimes that preceded it. The author has a profound understanding that more current examples of U.S. outlawry and criminality must be tied to the entirely of U.S. history, going back to slavery, the Indian Wars, early colonialism, and later imperialism. The outlawry and brigandism and aggressive U.S. militarism, along with familiar doctrines of national exception- alism, "humanitarian intervention," and "preemptive war," so evident throughout American history as a recurrent feature of U.S. global behavior, have been captured brilliantly in *The Crimes of Empire*. The present cannot be understood apart from this historical legacy, which remains very much with us. Unlike other writers on U.S. militarism, who provide shade-tree analyses of U.S. foreign policy, Carl Boggs' Argus-eyed focus on outlawry and criminality permits a broader, more contextualized, more radical treatment of such commonly discussed topics as terrorism, weapons of mass destruction, treaty violations, tribunals, torture, changes in the military-industrial-complex, mercenary armies, and contemporary geopolitics, resulting in a powerful conceptual and historical context for evaluating the Bush Doctrine. There are few places in any literature dealing with U.S. foreign and military policy in which one finds such a powerful contextualization. And especially in the absence of serious media, political, intellectual, or legal scrutiny this volume in a much-needed corrective.

The Crimes of Empire explores all aspects of the problem of U.S. outlawry and criminality—economic, political, global, racial, psychological—linking the ideological and institutional factors underlying such outlawry and doing so with unflinching verve and scholarly expertise. It is a book of epic scope and is sure to become a classic work of this genre.

When Walter Benjamin wrote about the Angel of History (Angelus Novus) in his ninth thesis from his essay "Theses on the Philosophy of History" he described the Angel with his face turned toward the past being swept into the future by a storm from paradise whose winds are raging with such force that the Angel can no longer close his wings. The storm—what we call "progress"—has only increased since Benjamin's day, blowing the wings right off the Angel of History so that he can no longer move of his own accord. War, genocide, and the culture of militarism have rendered history itself immobile and risk blasting us into the future at such a speed that time itself becomes obliterated and history is demolished. The future of humankind—what Marx referred to as the end of the prehistory of humankind—rests on creating the kind of world in which the deforming power of the culture of militarism no longer feeds the engines of progress. Boggs' new work is a vital step in creating such a world.

Peter McLaren
Los Angeles, 2009

Preface

In writing a book on U.S. outlawry going back to the earliest days of the Republic, the author predictably encounters a reflex hostility to a subject matter likely to be received by most Americans as outrageous, if not entirely crazed. After all, war crimes and other international bad deeds are impulsively understood as acts perpetrated by *others*, usually the evil foes of a democratic America: Nazis, Communists, rogue tyrants, terrorists, and the like. Even when U.S. military personnel have been identified as war criminals, as at My Lai in Vietnam or Abu Ghraib in Iraq, they are normally viewed as a few deviant sadists who violated military discipline and were then swiftly brought to justice, with no thought of holding upper-level government or armed-forces leaders responsible. Further, where the U.S. has clearly been guilty of wider criminality, such as unprovoked military aggression, the conventional wisdom is that all such misdeeds are by now ancient history, offering important lessons, and never to be repeated. In an era of modern warfare, moreover, is it not generally appreciated that the Pentagon will go to any lengths to avoid "collateral damage," minimizing the civilian deaths and destruction caused by U.S. weaponry? We are also routinely informed that the past blunders and excesses of U.S. military action, however unfortunate, must be viewed in their proper *context*: as the unfortunate side-effects of a benign superpower doing everything in its capacity to extend the virtues of democracy, human rights, and peace to a troubled, anarchic world. It follows that scholarly or journalistic work ought to confront the real sources of conflict—foreign evildoers using ruthless violence in the service of nefarious interests. Why should any reasonable investigator want to explore *American* criminality when the really threatening bad guys on the planet ought to be the all-consuming target of moral outrage and political dissection?

In surveying and analyzing the protracted legacy of U.S. outlawry, this book follows a quite different path, taking on the sacred myths through many chapters of detailed historical evidence. My central thesis is that the U.S. stands today as the most fearsome outlaw nation in the world, its leaders having contributed to a steady descent into global lawlessness. American political and media culture, it is true, remains saturated with images and narratives of horrendous war crimes, along with human rights violations, on TV, in movies, books, and magazines—but only when carried out by *others*, mostly culprits designated as U.S. enemies. A recent case in point: a group of Hollywood celebrities, preparing for the 2009 Academy Awards, organized a series of fundraising events to aid prosecution of war criminals—nothing related to Iraq or Afghanistan, of course, but instead to Bosnia, where Serb "ethnic cleansing" in the 1990s remains an uppermost target of criminal indictments. The group, including George Clooney, Elton John, and Cindy Crawford, were assisting the work of an international justice clinic at UCLA set up to deal with global atrocities occurring in such places as Rwanda, Darfur, and the former Yugoslavia. The culprits, of course, were to be found thousands of miles from American shores.

Another example: the 2007 film *The Hunting Party*, starring Richard Gere and Terrence Howard, a gripping *noir*-style story framed against contemporary world events, brought to the screen as a documentary-style drama based on four reporters' search for an at-large war criminal. Could such a story possibly be constructed around events in Vietnam? Iraq? Afghanistan? Panama? In fact, director Richard Shepard chose to focus on Bosnia, where Western searchers were tenaciously hunting down a number of demonic Serb outlaws on the run—those same "ethnic cleansers" who were meant to have been neutralized by three months of U.S./NATO aerial bombardments in early 1999. Advertised heavily by the U.S. State Department and marketed as "the story of a lifetime," the picture was described by Gere as a much-needed effort to "put the ghosts of that region on film." The movie ends as three of the journalists, outraged and ready for vengeance, finally locate a Serb war criminal and decide to inflict their own brand of justice. This formulaic plot perfectly fits the taken-for-granted American discourse on war crimes, the villains sure to be found in a geopolitical setting where U.S. interests are threatened by figures so dehumanized that audiences will instinctively identify with good guys against the bad guys—a motif with deep roots in Hollywood Westerns and combat movies.

Another recent example: in November 2007, the New York-based Human Rights Watch, energetic watchdog of rights abuses around the world, published its list of the most guilty violators—the Congo for its use of child soldiers, warlord crimes in Afghanistan, myriad atrocities in the Sudan, Egypt, and Uzbekistan. These violators no doubt deserve mention. But so to a far greater extent does the

United States, its ongoing military operations in Afghanistan and Iraq constituting a source of death and destruction far beyond these other examples combined—but we get nothing. To believe that such omissions might be simple oversight is to forget the remarkable power of the dominant mythology, fueled by the mass media, in defining contemporary discourse around global politics and especially war crimes.

Such parochial bias obfuscates understanding of international realities, further blocking the struggle for a peaceful, lawful order. Little progress along these lines is conceivable without a full accounting of U.S. lawlessness: repeated episodes of military aggression, large-scale attacks on civilians and their life-support systems, ongoing treaty violations, subversion of the U.N. Charter, stockpiling and use of weapons of mass destruction, support for client-state outlawry, training and equipping of terrorists and death squads, the practice of torture, armed threats against other nations. This legacy has produced, by conservative estimate, several million deaths since World War II, tens of millions wounded, and yet another tens of millions displaced (at least three million in Iraq alone since 2003). Public infrastructures in many of the targeted countries have been left in ruins. Environmental horrors have followed every large-scale U.S. military operation, the damage left to fester. And deadly consequences of an escalating U.S. militarism persist, while the power structure continues to locate ominous new threats. Since American outlawry has continued and in some ways intensified across more than two centuries, the phenomenon can only be understood as part of an enduring historical *pattern*.

Yet as the political and media cultures carry forward an ethos of strict denial, the stubborn actuality of U.S. global power remains difficult to ignore—military deployments in some 130 countries, control of international seas and airspace, unmatched surveillance capacity, stockpiling of more weapons of mass destruction (WMD) than all other nations combined, plans to weaponize (and possibly nuclearize) space. Americans remain fixated on the crimes of fascism, the Nazis, and Hitler—and of course the Germans did invade several countries at the outset of World War II, did commit crimes against humanity, and did kill millions in their push to dominate Europe. Such historical finger-pointing might be comforting to those Americans who want to feel morally superior (or politically complacent) in the face of present-day U.S. lawlessness. Implicit in such "comparisons" with historical fascism is the notion that, while Americans were guilty of terrible deeds at certain points in history, they have surely never been *that* bad. Hitler and the Nazis, after all, were irredeemably evil. But there is a question as to whether the Nazi barometer is a useful standard for measuring one's own national legacy of wrongdoing. Does the common murderer, or even serial killer, feel better or in some way vindicated when compared to Ted Bundy or Charles Manson? A more salient point, however, is that Hitler (and the Nazis) were quickly de-legitimated, fought, defeated, and driven from the historical stage, never to return. And subsequent generations of fascists and neo-Nazis have made little headway. The contemporary U.S. empire, on the other hand, has both retained and *expanded* its economic, political, and military power across the planet, emphatically so since the 1980s. Its imperial hegemony enjoys solid domestic legitimacy while its worldwide presence, at least militarily, has no serious rivals. Its capacity to bring death and destruction to any region of the world is unmatched. Furthermore, while the Nazis carried out their horrendous crimes over a period of several years, the American behemoth has conducted itself as a rogue power across two centuries (although in this book I focus mainly on the postwar decades). By the early twenty-first century the U.S. global agenda had become the single biggest threat to planetary survival, for reasons explored in later chapters.

Such arguments cannot be sustained without running head-first into an ensemble of myths shrouding American political life—especially in the realm of foreign policy—that remains powerful despite massive countervailing evidence. Iraq furnishes a nearly ideal case study in itself, yet the fiction that this or any U.S. military venture is driven by strictly noble, enlightened goals cannot be easily dislodged, even among the educated strata. The same goes for the belief that earlier U.S. criminality is best forgotten at a time when Washington is struggling mightily to bring freedom and democracy to a perilous world. Obsession with past history, after all, fixates on false standards and solves no problems. Other myths linger, including the belief that U.S. war crimes today are the work of a few thugs failing to heed standard military discipline. Could the behavior of U.S. armed forces ever be deliberately unlawful, a function of political choices, strategic vision and tactical planning? Perhaps, but such behavior must obviously be the fault of stupid or incompetent leaders—never systematic or planned, never produced within the framework of Pentagon agendas—and of course the wrongdoers are swiftly and severely punished. By this rendering, the (failed) invasion and occupation of Iraq was a simple miscalculation by the Bush presidency, already known for its political myopia and clumsiness, rather than a calculated operation with well-articulated economic and geopolitical objectives. As we shall see, these and related myths about U.S. foreign policy and military behavior can be easily demolished by an abundance of historical and present-day evidence.

In Iraq the deadly several-year record is visible for the world to see: an invasion carried out in flagrant disregard of the U.N. Charter and based on a series of false claims; a "shock-and-awe" campaign targeting urban centers; an illegal occupation giving the U.S. control of Iraqi resources and institutions; a death toll, mostly civilians, possibly surpassing one million; several local massacres; unlawful detentions and torture; the deployment of "private contractors" able to wreak havoc outside local jurisdiction; use of terror weapons like white phosphorous, napalm, and depleted uranium. (According to the London NGO Iraq Body Count, by early 2009 total Iraqi deaths—overwhelmingly civilian—resulting from war and occupation numbered between 800,000 and 1.3 million, leaving more than one million war widows and five million orphans.) Terrible as this debacle has been, it fits broadly within the pattern of earlier U.S. military ventures. In fact Bush's militarism, beginning with his "preemptive war" strategy, continues a legacy going back to the presidencies of Andrew Jackson, James Polk, William McKinley, Woodrow Wilson, Harry Truman, and indeed most of Truman's successors. Jackson, of course, became one of the most idolized presidents in U.S. history—his portrait etched on the 20-dollar bill, his name memorialized in thousands of schools, his enduring image that of a working-class champion, a man of the people. Yet it was this same Jackson who, in 1830, inaugurated the notorious Indian Removal project that drove Cherokees and other tribes from their homes so that white settlers could steal their land and resources. It was this same Jackson, moreover, who owned large numbers of slaves and who invented the modern "imperial presidency." Arthur Schlesinger's Pulitzer-Prize winning biography, *The Age of Jackson*, somehow managed to skip over the embarrassing topic of Indian Removal while glorifying a leader who today would be universally viewed as a war criminal.

My hope is that this book will contribute to widening public interest in questions of American criminality and outlawry, similar to what has taken place in Germany, Japan, Argentina, South Africa, and elsewhere, although a deep culture of national exceptionalism (and denial) militates against it. As the major superpower and dominant military force in the world, the U.S. possesses a unique capacity to militarily intervene across the globe, trigger new cycles of armed conflict, foster a renewed arms race, subvert global agreements, and spur general lawlessness—with planetary survival quite possibly at stake. American public awareness is crucial, moreover, insofar as people living in the midst of empire will, theoretically at least, have real political leverage over the course of events, which is the generally understood essence of citizenship in a democratic society. Citizenship obligates people to speak out and act, especially where grievous injustice or criminality is carried out in their name, but that in turn requires information and awareness. What happens in China and the Sudan is surely worthy of close attention, but American citizens have no power (individually or collectively) to confront those more distant evils—unless, as with Israel, the U.S. itself is deeply implicated through its financial and military support. At the same time, where it concerns the (actual or alleged) criminal behavior of others, Americans are best advised to refrain from taking the moral high ground, as their credibility shrinks in a universe where their own imperial state is by far the most frequent and destructive offender. Citizens of any nation, especially the most powerful, must first work to get their own affairs in order. The familiar recourse here to the spread of "American values" is fraudulent because it assumes what has never been demonstrated—namely that such values (democracy? peace? human rights?) effectively guide U.S. foreign policy as opposed to what can be proven empirically: that aggressive imperial pursuits, since the time of the Indian Wars, have been the truly operative "American values."

Pointing elsewhere when more pressing challenges are closer to home amounts to yet another form of collective denial. Dwelling on genocidal monsters and war criminals responsible for horrors *elsewhere*, Americans can breathe a sigh of relief while redoubling efforts to locate guilty parties in foreign lands, or in past history, while sidestepping one's own immediate culpability. It might be comforting to identify Stalin, Hitler, and Mao as totalitarian mass murderers—while also charging assorted present-day foreign tyrants and terrorists with assorted war crimes—as the protracted American criminal legacy gets obscured. U.S. politicians and the media routinely insist on recognizing the historical responsibility of others—Russians, Serbs, Germans, Japanese, and Chinese, for example—the presumed first step toward atonement and "recon-ciliation" in dealing with past crimes. Museums and monuments are erected as testaments to the awful crimes of others. But what of an American "reconciliation" process yet to be undertaken, or even considered? What about past crimes against Native Americans, Filipinos, Mexicans, Japanese, Koreans, Panamanians, Guatemalans, Vietnamese, Cambodians, Laotians, Yugoslavs, Afghans, and Iraqis? What about the terrible legacy of slavery and the slave trade? What about the flagrant outlawry of the second Bush administration? Sadly, the Washington power structure and its ideologues remain oblivious to past military crimes, having made no apologies, no reparations, no "reconciliation," indeed having built no monuments or museums toward such purposes. At no time in its violent history has Washington faced direct moral and political accountability for its actions, its leaders being seemingly immune from legal culpability or criminal punishment, given a free hand to continue their outlawry. Herein lies another rationale for injecting war-crimes issues into American public discourse: outlaw behavior, reaching the very summit of governing and military circles, should be named, delineated, prosecuted, and, where guilt is established, severely punished. My view, which seems hardly worth debating, is that principles of international law should be universal, applied evenly wherever violations occur—a view widely upheld outside, but rarely within, the U.S. Creating a machinery for this process, along the lines of the International Criminal Court (dismissed by Washington), is among the most urgent of global challenges. As Barack Obama took over the U.S. presidency in January 2009, issues regarding the culpability of Bush administration leaders for war crimes, other violations of international law, and even abrogations of the American Constitution began to surface—even within the political establishment. Representative John Conyers, for example, called for a Truth and Reconciliation Commission similar to those set up in South Africa, Argentina, and elsewhere. (The postscript to the present work contains a fuller discussion of this issue.) Serious efforts to hold U.S. government and military figures responsible for criminal activity, either domestically or globally, face tremendous obstacles of the sort discussed in later chapters.

The historical perspective employed in this book calls forth a *systemic* view of U.S. outlawry, with the distinctly *legal* component being just one part of a complex whole that incorporates history, politics, culture, and international relations. The crimes of empire should be viewed as neither episodic nor simple excesses of otherwise benevolent policies but as endemic to an imperial order legitimated domestically by a fierce national exceptionalism, superpatriotism, militarism, and racism, all with a strong resonance in the political culture. Stupid or incompetent leadership decisions occasionally enter the picture but hardly account for an established historical *pattern* spanning many decades.

U.S. outlawry takes many forms—international law violations, treaty abrogations, subversion of the U.N. Charter, crimes against peace, military atrocities, human rights abuses including torture, use of banned weapons, attacks on civilian populations, proxy crimes, rejection of an independent world tribunal—that constitute an unmatched record of lawlessness and criminality. Of course most Americans prefer to regard such behavior as a relic of the past, symptomatic of less "civilized" times, but now made obsolete by "precision" high-tech warfare that essentially solves the problem of "collateral damage." True enough, an evolving international moral consensus now stigmatizes and criminalizes military behavior once regarded as normal—but the U.S. has, with few exceptions, stubbornly refused this consensus, and remains prepared to follow its own dictates and set its own rules, with clearly disastrous consequences.

An Obama presidency is thought by many to promise new directions in U.S. foreign policy, suggesting that the paradigm of American outlawry explored throughout this book might give way to less militaristic and more engaging modes of international behavior. As I explain more fully in the introduction and elsewhere, however, such hopes—and they are indeed *hopes*—lack empirical grounding. Obama's own record, political statements, and opinions stated in books and articles—not to mention his cabinet appointments and initial decisions—all contradict prospects for any such paradigmatic change in Washington's global ambitions and strategies. The watchword is almost certain to be *continuity*, despite new departures here and there.

*   *   *

This book is the third part of a trilogy on U.S. imperial power that was conceived roughly a decade ago. First in the series, *Imperial Delusions* (2004), was intended as a multifaceted analysis of American global behavior, linking global and domestic (economic, political, cultural) elements of a power structure that I argue is increasingly addicted to militarism and war. This work grew out of an earlier study, begun under the auspices of the journal *New Political Science* and published as the anthology *Masters of War* (2003), with articles by such antiwar critics as Noam Chomsky,

Chalmers Johnson, Michael Parenti, James Petras, Douglas Kellner, and Peter McLaren. A second book, *The Hollywood War Machine* (2006), written with longtime collaborator Tom Pollard, explored the deepening convergence of militarism and media culture in American society, reflected most profoundly in the contribution of the Hollywood film industry to the war-making apparatus. Important motifs developed in the present volume originated in these earlier works.

In *The Crimes of Empire* primary attention is necessarily directed toward complex issues of international law, but within a conceptual framework that takes interpretation well beyond the paradigm of legality itself. It is commonly recognized that laws and norms of political behavior (international or otherwise) are perpetually shifting, subject to widely varying perspectives dependent on ideological outlook and cultural traditions, with evidence sifted and mediated according to time, place, and viewpoint. When it comes to U.S. outlawry, however, accumulated historical knowledge based on a large body of historical events, decisions, and outcomes is so conclusive and damning that no impartial observer could possibly ignore or refute it. While the developments in question span at least two centuries, the historical focus of the present book is limited mainly to the post-World War II era. There is nothing particularly obscure or secret about this record or the supporting evidence, nor has it involved sinister plots or conspiracies by government leaders, military planners, or other dark forces. It is surely possible to uncover frightening plots at certain moments in U.S. history, but such plots hardly go to the core of the problem, much less exhaust the task of historical analysis. American transgressions can be established on the basis of information available to any patient researcher—no "secret" files or elusive sources are needed. Here I document and interpret U.S. outlawry relying on historical materials drawn from extensive public sources: newspapers, magazine and journal articles, books, online sites, and various official and semi-official documents. I have learned from many years of study that most U.S. global transgressions (or *types* of transgression) can be identified and researched with little difficulty. Over the past decade or more there has been a steady outpouring of journalistic and academic work illuminating the dark side of U.S. international behavior. In this project my goal is to conceptually integrate and critically analyze the full range of conditions and issues related to

American lawlessness that, as I am forced to conclude, threatens the planet as does nothing else.

*   *   *

A special gratitude is owed my colleagues at National University in Los Angeles, whose support over many years has provided valuable intellectual and social inspiration, with extra thanks to Dean Maggie Yadegar and my collaborator on earlier projects, Tom Pollard. Clay Claiborne, George Katsiaficas, Peter McLaren, John Sanbonmatsu, and Milt Wolpin gave much-welcomed encouragement and counsel from the outset, recognizing the unique difficulties and challenges involved, yet also the great value a study of U.S. outlawry might provide. Katsiaficas also helped locate vital sources of information concerning U.S. war crimes in Asia. My deepest thanks go to Laurie Nalepa, who shared my travails and fortunes every step of the way.

Carl Boggs
Los Angeles, October 2009

Introduction

The experience of two calamitous world wars produced global commitments to a new era of international law that it was hoped would strongly alleviate if not abolish the worst features of human warfare, while also laying the foundations of peaceful cooperation among nations. This epic ideological shift was reflected in the post-World War II Nuremberg and Tokyo tribunals, the subsequent United Nations Charter, a series of Geneva Protocols updated in the late 1970s, and more recently in the International Criminal Court set up in Rome in 1998. It also found its way into hundreds of bilateral and multilateral treaties signed over the past several decades. Earlier precedents go back to The Hague Conventions of 1899 and 1907, stipulating rules of engagement governing warfare among states, and the 1928 Kellogg-Briand Act—a futile effort to outlaw warfare. As international law became more firmly grounded, it gave rise to a global consensus in which all political agents would be obligated to follow strict moral and legal principles, including those regulating how armed combat can be initiated and conducted. Thus the U.N. Charter prohibits military force as an instrument of statecraft except in clear instances of self-defense. Such a paradigmatic shift always depended on a global community of interests based on universality and reciprocity, where all states, subject to and protected by the same laws and rules, would have roughly equal (legal) standing.

Within this ideal world system it would be at least theoretically possible for any political or military actor to be prosecuted for crimes against peace, war crimes, or crimes against humanity. For several decades war-crimes discourse has unfolded in a milieu of radically shifting views about the very nature of warfare—a discourse embodied in legal doctrines that propose to transcend familiar left–right ideological divisions. Although Nuremberg was essentially a victor's tribunal set up by the Allies, its main principles were adopted by the U.N. in 1950, and today are widely regarded as universally enforceable. The principles state that any person found to have committed a war crime under international law must be held accountable, like those German and Japanese defendants found guilty of assorted crimes in the late 1940s. International statutes were seen as valid beyond national or cultural variations in laws, traditions, and ideologies, binding for all individuals whatever their place in governmental or military hierarchies. No heads of state, no political or military officials were to be allowed immunity from criminal prosecution. In the German case, the entire Nazi system was defined by Allied prosecutors as a massive criminal enterprise in which political and military leaders would be held legally responsible for their actions.

This fundamental moral and legal turn occurred quickly, within a span of several decades, a radical departure from centuries of international horrors that went unpunished and even unrecognized. In his book *The God Delusion*, Richard Dawkins refers to dramatic changes in the "moral Zeitgeist"—large-scale shifts in prevailing beliefs, attitudes, and norms from one historical period to the next. A case in point: two centuries ago anything resembling democratic politics stood in radical opposition to the authoritarian mainstream, while slavery, harsh patriarchal domination, sadistic treatment of prisoners, and flagrant acts of military aggression were all within the established (and fiercely defended) norm. Dawkins calls attention to how an evolving moral consensus shapes rules and codes of behavior across time and place. Thus if slavery was taken for granted a mere 150 years ago, today even minor hate-speech episodes can be severely punished in many parts of the world; laws have been passed against virtually every type of racial and gender discrimination. Only a few decades ago some of the most highly educated and respected personages—Presidents, celebrated intellectuals and artists, religious leaders—could go on public record with virulent racist outbursts, hardly fearful of repercussions. Figures like Theodore Roosevelt, Jack London, and H.G. Wells could offer ringing defenses of "white civilization," which they (like many others) viewed as under siege by menacing (red, yellow) hordes. Women could be beaten mercilessly and repeatedly by husbands with no fear of legal punishment or social censure. In just the past 50 years the world has seen dramatic changes in sexual attitudes and behavior to an extent that basic social institutions like the family have been fundamentally transformed, unrecognizable against the long shadow of patriarchal traditions. The modern welfare state, little more than a century old, is still embryonic when viewed across the wide expanse of human history. A new moral consensus often takes hold in such a way as to be nearly invisible, especially once a generation accepts it as something of a natural right. Dawkins suggests that "the *Zeitgeist* moves on, so inexorably that we sometimes take it for granted and forget that change is a real phenomenon in its own right."[1]

Large-scale changes in the moral *Zeitgeist* do not ordinarily result from single factors, and Dawkins makes no such claims. In the U.S., social transformations since the 1950s alone have occurred along many fronts, having little to do with changes one way or the other in the capitalist economy or religious traditions. (One of Dawkins' main tasks is to show how noteworthy shifts in the *Zeitgeist*, usually moving in progressive directions, are rarely if ever shaped by religious values that, in any event, are mostly derived from ancient texts—values shown to be fully consistent with such heinous social practices as mass murder, slavery, and genocide.) History seems to follow an increasingly enlightened (though uneven) path, usually synchronized across nations and cultures as it passes through local and universal discourses; as Dawkins comments: "How swiftly the *Zeitgeist* changes—and it moves in parallel on a broad front, throughout the educated world."[2] Building on Dawkins' schema, it is easy to see how progressively enlightened views coincide with changes in the moral consensus, and this would appear to be the case in such realms of life as race and gender relations, sexuality, the environment, and political arrangements despite enclaves of resistance here and there. In some realms—for example, the exploitation of labor—one is tempted to conclude that the *Zeitgeist* has changed little if at all.

Dawkins' framework makes particularly good sense when one surveys the trajectory of international relations across recent history; within little more than a century the stated and generally agreed-upon norms of global behavior have undergone wholesale transformation. Moral and legal standards governing the conduct of warfare, for example, have been effectively codified and institutionalized just since World War II. International law has been shaped and reshaped in the aftermath of global military conflicts bringing unspeakable death and destruction, repeated atrocities on all sides, and crimes against humanity. The new era purportedly upholds novel, more humane international norms—an end to military aggression, embrace of a strong human rights agenda, a move toward stricter battlefield rules of engagement, defense of national self-determination and sovereignty, a turn toward egalitarian relations among states. This particular *Zeitgeist*, as mentioned, found its way into the U.N. Charter, the Geneva Conventions, and myriad international as well as bilateral treaties and agreements. The world has moved ahead dramatically since ancient (and not-so-ancient) times characterized by endless and brutal wars, often remembered for sadistic massacres and other atrocities that were more frequently celebrated than castigated and punished. Horrendous acts of violence were likely to be enshrined in epic myths and rituals glorifying military heroism and patriotic valor. Until recent decades government and military leaders faced few if any external restraints on their conduct of warfare—one need only revisit the unbelievable carnage of the U.S. Civil War and World War I. The concept of human rights has barely outgrown its infancy, while punishment for war crimes and crimes against humanity (an offense recognized only at the end of World War II) was scarcely imagined even among the most visionary thinkers. That the world might witness global agreements embedded in a multitude of conventions, protocols, statutes, and tribunals is a recent phenomenon made possible by far-reaching changes in the moral *Zeitgeist*. Such an effort to reconfigure the parameters of world politics rests upon an ideological consensus the basic premise of which is the sovereign equality among nations.[3] No nation—regardless of power, resources, or military strength—is entitled to stand outside these arrangements or be allowed to make its own rules and laws.[4] It follows that prohibitions against military aggression must apply to all nations if the system of international law is to have political integrity, much less legal validity.

*   *   *

No moral consensus, of course, is likely to extend uniformly across the global or even domestic landscape; it is sure to be resisted or challenged at different points in time. In the case of international rules it is the United States that nowadays most consistently stands outside the enlightened *Zeitgeist*. Despite references to an expanding "culture of human rights" and worldwide spread of democracy, the pacifistic (some might say utopian) dream of a world moving toward respect for sovereign equality, arms control, and binding principles of military conduct has turned into something of a Hobbesian nightmare, as if the lessons of two world wars and the legacies of Nuremberg, Geneva, and the U.N. Charter had been forgotten. While the causes of this predicament are multiple, a central problem has been the ceaseless American pursuit of global hegemony on a foundation of expanding military power. While U.S. leaders dutifully uphold the rhetoric of democracy, human rights, and rule of law their actual conduct has been more congruent with imperial agendas that run counter to the requirements of a peaceful international order. In the actual world of corporate-driven globalization and U.S.

imperialism such requirements are ceaselessly subverted, leading to what Philippe Sands' defines as a "lawless world."[5]

Such policies and behavior starkly contradict the familiar American self-image of a noble, idealistic nation working tirelessly and generously to bring light to a world of darkness. As a matter of simple logic, generally binding rules of global behavior are unthinkable so long as the U.S. continues its drive toward world supremacy, so long as its power holds sway across the planet, and so long as the neoliberal order sustained by that power remains intact.[6] We have reached an historical juncture where the lawless flexing of American strategic interests works to undermine longstanding dreams of a peaceful world order—even as U.S. leaders would prefer everyone to believe that their own national strivings are synonymous with the global pursuit of democracy and human rights.[7] What has become known as the Bush Doctrine of preemptive war, involving outright contempt for the U.N., has already exacerbated the deadly cycle of militarism and terrorism—a development more fully explored in later chapters. Bush's strategic designs, actually consistent with the long tradition of U.S. exceptionalism, reflected the degree to which Washington refuses to tolerate any sustained challenge to its global power.

The consequences of U.S. outlawry for the future of world politics can only be described as nightmarish: an aggressive superpower with loosened restraints on its military conduct, the U.S. was able to step up its quest for world hegemony in the wake of 9/11, becoming more brazen in its disregard for laws, conventions, and treaties understood as constraining its national interests. As shown by its hostility to the International Criminal Court (ICC)—a nascent, struggling embodiment of legal universalism—Washington has so far remained unswervingly exceptionalist, outside the moral *Zeitgeist*, consistent with historical notions of a special American mission and destiny. Washington has arrogated to itself the "right" to carry out military aggression that, departing from the contemporary moral *Zeitgeist*, validates Noam Chomsky's point that "Contempt for the rule of law is deeply rooted in U.S. practice and intellectual culture."[8] Such contempt extends to those nations, cultures, and international organizations that stand outside of, or refuse to be manipulated by, American interests. Through the postwar years, moreover, steady expansion of the war economy and security state has brought renewed U.S. capacity to employ armed force to advance its global agendas, while the "war on terror" helps legitimate the ongoing struggle for Pax Americana. Every act of aggression, every subversion of international law, deepens the very chaos that anti-terror proponents claim to be fighting: spread of social and military strife, arms build-ups, proliferation of WMD, weakened global agreements, blowback in the form of insurgency, terrorism, and renewed national rivalries.

Not only has Washington been the leading violator of international legality, its nearly trillion dollar war machine (as of 2009) deploys bases in some 130 nations, has ambitious plans for space weaponization, possesses a most lucrative arms sales program, and continues a pattern of military ventures that makes it the most fearsome agency of violence in the world today. This enormous power has needed ideological justification in the doctrine of Manifest Destiny, in the "civilized" virtues of democracy, Judeo-Christian religion, and technological progress—motifs still alive at the start of the twenty-first century, a system of legitimacy rarely questioned by politicians, intellectuals, educators, and religious leaders, by any of the presumed gatekeepers of national morality. Such myths permeate a political culture that gives policy-makers a relatively free hand to pursue geopolitical ambitions. The license for international outlawry is enlarged to the extent that worry about political and media scrutiny diminishes. The idea that the most powerful state (and war machine) in history might be free to create its own system of rules has become an article of faith throughout American society.

At odds with its well-crafted political image, the U.S. has long stood opposed to a system of global norms that would limit arbitrary and unrestrained use of military force. Such outlawry not only contravenes all pretense of democratic values but seems inconsistent with a legal culture that is surely the most elaborate on the planet. No ruling elites proclaim the "rule of law" more loudly, and no society produces more lawyers, prosecutors, judges, legal theorists—and prisons. But this sprawling legal system goes no further than the *domestic* society; when it comes to international politics the U.S. routinely favors power over legality, often dismissing legality as a nuisance in the face of pressing global realities. A fixation on power, or "realism," and *Machtpolitik* reinforces an impulse to act unilaterally, or at least to forge friendly coalitions willing to embrace military options, typically in response to manufactured "crises." An imperial agenda presumes that superpower hegemony is, or ought to be, unchallengeable in an era when once-stigmatized defenses of Empire no longer require apology.[9] Consistent with a belief in national exceptionalism, *this* Empire is viewed as different from any before it—a benevolent giant working for democracy, human rights, and peace. But such claims are to nothing less than an Orwellian sleight of hand used to justify virtually any U.S. resort to military force, even where international law is thrown to the winds. The "superpower syndrome," as Robert Jay Lifton observes, is nowadays wedded to an ideology of nuclearism grounded in the accumulation of huge WMD stockpiles and a seeming readiness to use them as a tool of warfare. The very *discourse* of WMD is vital to imperial supremacy, but the *spread* of WMD represents an intolerable threat when it comes to nations outside the American orbit, such as Iran.[10]

Comparing American and European political cultures, Robert Kagan writes that "those with great military power are more likely to consider force as a useful tool of international relations than those who have less military power."[11] The author of seminal neocon treatises, Kagan believes that the United States' pursuit of its geopolitical aims simultaneously advances the common interests of humanity insofar as American force is said to restrain the chaotic tendencies of a Hobbesian world. For U.S. leaders the "language of military power" is functional to a peaceful world order—regulated and policed, of course, by Washington.[12] At a time of mounting anarchy marked by the intensification of a global economic crisis and the twin threats of militarism and terrorism, the U.S. is perched to combat such anarchy with every instrument at its disposal, affirming the efficacy of its own order-giving Leviathan. The U.S. "naturally seeks a certain freedom of action to deal with the strategic dangers that it alone has the means and sometimes the will to address."[13] Since the U.S. represents an "empire of liberty," its hegemony is to be welcomed by enlightened humanity as "the ambition to play a grand role on the world scene is deeply rooted in the American character."[14] Within this neocon illusion of grandeur, in which Bush's Iraq venture figured strongly, it follows that any global restraints on U.S. flexibility will be held deeply suspect. For Kagan and the neocons, nothing should interfere with the "language [or practice] of military power," so the U.S. "must refuse to abide by certain international conventions that may constrain its ability to fight effectively."[15] (Such rejectionism could apply to virtually *any* international agreement insofar as political contracts always necessitate a certain yielding of power and interest that the exceptional state might well resist.) The European preference for diplomacy, collective agreements, welfare-state allocations, and reduced arms spending appears nothing short of utopian when framed against the massive global responsibilities inherited by Washington. (Whether an Obama foreign policy departs significantly from this paradigm will depend on a complex mixture of domestic and international factors.) As the enlightened behemoth asserts its rightful claim to world domination, therefore, it should have space to set its own international rules—even as it insists that all others adhere to established legal precedents. In a world of perpetual crisis and dangerous enemies, only the U.S. is said to possess a sufficient combination of military power and political will to enforce peaceful stability. Like authoritarian systems of the past, the U.S. justifies its global supremacy on a basis of permanent war against evil threats: rogue states, terrorists, Islamo-fascists, insurgents, and the like.

*   *   *

If U.S. global power is improbably upheld as a remedy for chaos and breakdown, as a force to deter predatory monsters, then warfare is sure to be understood as an epic struggle for its antithesis— for democracy and human rights. The idea of "human rights intervention," first systematically embraced to rationalize the U.S./ NATO war in the Balkans during the late 1990s, gives the most powerful states license to carry out military actions against smaller, weaker, often defenseless countries. Weaker nations, it follows, are not permitted to rely on even modest force, as intervention goes only one way. Given this lopsided global equation, the notion of universality as linchpin of international law winds up torn to shreds, the limits to superpower maneuver stripped away to meet ostensibly higher purposes. As David Chandler writes, "the more the concept of human rights militarism is allowed to gain legitimacy, the greater the inequalities become between the enforcing states and the rest of the world."[16] A "new ethical agenda" championed by Western powers ultimately erodes the very fabric of international legality. Chandler adds: "The human rights discourse makes it difficult to place limits on the use of force by major powers allegedly acting on behalf of the vulnerable of the world."[17] In this context a new generation of moral crusaders has waged an ideological crusade against the presumably outmoded principle of national sovereignty (that is, for lesser states), inconvenient global agreements, and at suitable times the U.N. Charter itself. Such a political environment has made it fashionable to speak of the "limits" to international law, if not its obsolescence.[18]

In their fixation on the evils of "ethnic cleansing" and "genocide," moreover, human rights campaigners are known to exaggerate and even manufacture such charges, serving to deflect attention from the often more serious crimes of the Western powers. In Iraq, U.S. intervention had by spring 2009 led to as many as 1.3 million Iraqi deaths while having reduced the country to ruins, supposedly to liberate an oppressed people from a monstrous tyrant armed with doomsday weapons. After six years of war and occupation, Iraq has been turned into one of the great catastrophes of postwar history, the result of an outlaw intervention dwarfing any crimes laid at the doorstep of Saddam Hussein. Put on trial by an ad hoc tribunal created and largely financed by Washington, Hussein was surely enough found guilty of war crimes by "victors" once again sitting in judgment of the "vanquished." For the Bush administration, awesome military power justified by high-sounding moral claims gave rise to a comprehensive lawless whole, the same kind of criminal enterprise for which the Germans were prosecuted and found guilty at Nuremberg.

U.S. global power at the start of the twenty-first century is legitimated through a dense mixture of ultrapatriotism, a renovated spirit of Manifest Destiny, and a deepening culture of violence and militarism, with every Washington venture taken as credible by an American public well-conditioned by the corporate media. A "bipartisan" affair in which politics is said to vanish at the borders, U.S. foreign policy is presented by political elites, the media, and academia as "pragmatic," non-ideological, even while behavior is expected to conform to well-honed premises. Policies are driven by an economic and geopolitical consensus that now centrally revolves around a struggle for domination over the Middle East. As detailed in later chapters, many treaties and other global agreements have been reduced to so many scraps of paper, as shown when the U.S. invaded and occupied Iraq under false pretexts and in contravention of the U.N. Charter. If we follow the argument of Antonia Juhasz, for example, the Bush/neocon claim to be "democratizing" the Middle East was better understood as a cover for rapacious brigandage by corporations seeking greater control over immense petroleum reserves. The resulting business jackpot was made possible by (a) massive Pentagon spending, (b) expanded American control over natural resources, (c) the broadening role of private military contractors, and (d) the huge profits reaped by hundreds of U.S. and other Western companies investing in the "reconstruction" of a war-shattered society. The crucial Iraq venture is taken up in later chapters: here it is enough to cite the record profits accrued by Western corporations derived from the Bush agenda since early 2003: ExxonMobil, Bechtel, Lockheed-Martin, Raytheon, Blackwater, and Chevron to name only some of the most profitable, a phenomenon Juhasz fittingly describes as "corporate globalization through the barrel of a gun."[19] It follows that, if an unprovoked military attack on a sovereign nation is legally and morally indefensible *under any conditions*, then military invasion and occupation to advance such nakedly imperial objectives must be regarded as *doubly* illegitimate.

*   *   *

The legacy of U.S. outlawry has its origins in the earliest days of the Republic as the colonial destruction of Native peoples began in earnest—a process viewed by the white European settlers as a God-given mission of enlightenment and social progress. The settlers left a trail of systematic conquest, slavery, and warfare, all justified by some variant of the "white-man's burden," later to be identified as Manifest Destiny. This ideology fed not only the Indian Wars but the plantation slave economy, conquest of Mexican lands, and later U.S. expansion into Central America and Asia. Such conquest and expansion required a virulent nationalist ethos and militarism paying little attention to what is nowadays called "rules of engagement." An Indian population estimated to be as high as 15 million when Columbus arrived in the Western hemisphere was reduced to just a few hundred thousand by 1900, the result of Europeans' inexorable drive for land, resources, power, and religious hegemony. Through a combination of slave economy and westward expansion the white-settler strata had by the mid nineteenth century built a cruel regimen of exploitation and violence fueled by unmitigated racism.

   The idea of Manifest Destiny actually goes back to the pre-revolutionary period when the Puritans, animated by a mixture of religious zeal and Enlightenment ideals, moved to conquer new frontiers they believed were inhabited by primitive savages unable to properly develop the land they occupied. Early white settlers were colonialists in the fullest sense, motivated by a sense of inalienable rights which, at the time, meant entitlement to other peoples' territory. While upholding a new "empire of liberty," the Puritans saw themselves as harbingers of a liberal revolution that was destined to sweep away all obstacles to human progress—progress that, of course, would often have to be secured by armed force. Belonging to an anointed national and religious community and attached to a special historical mission, the first American settlers were expansionists to the hilt, without apologies, anticipating the later westward and global thrust of U.S. power. The characterization of settler populations as inward-looking or isolationist, fearful of new ventures, was a great myth even during the pre-Constitutional era.

The founding of the new Republic only deepened these feelings of exceptionalism, which increasingly depended on a fierce white racism endowing the settler population with unique possession of civilized virtues and historical destiny, reinforced by an ethos of material and technological supremacy (especially on the battlefield) that persists to this day. Those standing in the way of expansion were dismissed as subhuman, savage, Godless, fit for extermination. The privileged sense of entitlement spread outward, beyond national borders, to be legitimated by such pronouncements as the Monroe Doctrine (1823), imposed at a time when Latin countries were gaining independence from Spain and enforcing the dictate that Latin America would forever be a sphere of U.S. domination—a warning that American ruling interests had the right to intervene anywhere in the Western hemisphere to protect their aspirations, goals, and interests. Throughout the nineteenth century the U.S. carried out military operations in several nations more than 100 times, a prelude to later interventions in Central America and the Caribbean. Meanwhile, the U.S. moved to consolidate its position on the continent, wresting by force lands belonging to Mexico in the 1840s. Elected to the presidency in 1844, James K. Polk saw the U.S. as a rapidly expanding power with an absolute right to the Mexican lands it coveted, across to the Pacific. Provoking war while lying about imminent threats to American security, Polk was able to annex vast regions of present-day Texas, California, New Mexico, Arizona, and Nevada based on what today would be called a "preemptive war" strategy. With total contempt for the Mexicans, Polk argued that the U.S. was justified in attacking a foreign nation so long as compelling interests were at stake. The bloody war against Mexico, it should be emphasized, was supported by a patriotic frenzy across the political spectrum—just as the war against Spain would be a half-century later. Indeed the Mexicans, slaughtered by the thousands, were degraded as backward, ignorant, and undemocratic, hardly worthy proprietors of the land they had controlled.

Manifest Destiny was fueled by a white-supremacist ideology that could link exterminist practices with the civilized discourses of freedom, democracy, and progress, along lines established by European colonialism across the world. The conquest of new frontiers meant sweeping away all barriers to development, an ethos that would provide a symbolic frame of reference for American politics in the twentieth century and later. When President Andrew Jackson laid out his Indian Removal policies it was assumed across the political system that such policies represented unilinear progress from savagery to civilization, from barbarism to modernity. The dominant culture approached the Indians in terms of two extremes—as either helpless children or warlike savages. Indians were excluded from a social contract based on the possessive individualism of capitalist market relations, and they accordingly deserved whatever fate befell them at the hands of superior military force. Indeed Native peoples were the out-of-control terrorists of the period—bloodthirsty, innately violent, killers lacking any restraint. Jackson and other leaders called openly for a regimen of total Indian control or, where that failed, annihilation. Such hopes were realized as hundreds of Native villages were burned to the ground with the inhabitants expelled, murdered, or killed off by disease.

Indian savages symbolized a certain madness endemic to a Hobbesian state of nature spinning out of orbit—a madness needing to be tamed or eradicated. Moreover, it was never enough to destroy specific populations and their resources; it was imperative to stamp out their entire culture and historical memory. As whites entered into treaties with those few remaining Indian forces increasingly pushed into reservations, the federal government routinely and unilaterally broke those agreements once the land was discovered to contain desirable resources. Indians were systematically denied any humanity and thus any claim to rights much less citizenship in a society that championed liberal values. Contracts and treaties were entered into regularly as an instrumental ploy, to be broken at the slightest whim, as in the case of Cherokees whose villages, homes, and people were destroyed in the wake of Jackson's infamous Removal Act of 1830. Within this dictatorship Native peoples were punished when they failed to exhibit proper gratitude for any white benevolence that might be extended (for example, in providing safe journeys to the reservations). Even where contracts and laws regulating Indian life remained in force, they could suddenly break down or be overridden by military force. Given whites' attitudes of racial supremacy and national exceptionalism, it would be no difficult matter—in the nineteenth century or later—to suspend or dissolve agreements. The harsh authoritarian regimen and its murderous policies brought no agony to its architects who, after all, were the chosen beneficiaries of Manifest Destiny.

In 1890, with the massacre at Wounded Knee, the Indian Wars came to a merciless end just as the westward push was largely completed, leaving a system firmly rooted in authoritarian controls and propelled by a mixture of colonialism, racism, capitalism, and militarism. An ideology of ruthless expansion was incorporated into the political culture, shared especially by the upper circles of politicians, business elites, the military, and Christian institutions. As leaders like Theodore Roosevelt would quickly recognize, at the turn of the century the U.S. was in an enviable position—a nation conditioned to conquest and warfare—to accelerate its God-given mission of building a new civilization for the modern world. Indeed Roosevelt openly stated that the long history of Indian massacres added up to splendid legacy of righteous deeds that cleared the terrain for a modernizing, enlightened, civilizing project unlike anything the world had ever seen. This very ideology of messianic nationalism would be passed along to succeeding generations of political, economic, religious, and intellectual leaders convinced that the new civilization (the "first new nation") represented an epic triumph of progress over backwardness, good over evil. However, for such an ideology to become fully legitimated, to be inculcated into the popular consciousness, the history of colonial oppression would have to be somehow deflected or denied with the hegemonic discourses. Over time, in fact, that history would be roundly *celebrated*, as it is in Columbus Day rituals, the worshipful treatment given such leaders as Jackson and Roosevelt, and the proliferation of "Western" movies romanticizing the genocidal past. Not only did the most terrible crimes disappear through elaborate forms of historical erasure, but the prevailing image of American politics that emerged from the period was one of a revitalizing liberal democracy shaped by freedom, equality, and citizen participation—one of the most impressive propaganda achievements ever. It was precisely the legacy of imperialism, warfare, and outlawry that was carried into, and helped shape, later U.S. behavior in such targeted areas as the Philippines, Central America, Korea, Vietnam, and the Middle East.

*   *   *

While Bush and the neocons have, with the impetus of 9/11 and the war on terrorism, taken U.S. outlawry to higher levels, the historical pattern had in fact been clearly established. The subsequent trajectory of militarism and warfare, ideologically enforced by an ethos of national destiny, has taken multiple and overlapping forms, essentially as follows:

1. U.S. violation of international agreements, treaties, and laws has flowed from the historical trajectory, beginning with the first Indian wars. American outlawry since World War II, from Korea to Iraq, exhibits many parallels with the nineteenth-century attempts to pacify and destroy Indian resistance. Hundreds of treaties signed with Native tribes were abrogated or ignored, depending on the priorities of the settlers, the military, and the federal government. Spanning nearly two centuries, U.S. outlawry took many forms— crimes against peace, proxy wars, breaches of rules of engagement, indiscriminate attacks on civilians, aerial terrorism, support for death squads and torture, use of prohibited weapons, abrogation of treaties, overriding of the U.N. Charter.

2. Transgressions have typically been shrouded in moral claims about overthrowing tyranny, "civilizing" backward populations, eradicating weapons of mass destruction, carrying out humanitarian interventions to fight "ethnic cleansers" and "genocidal" villains, or waging a war on terrorism. Rarely have these righteous pretexts stood up to close scrutiny.

3. The human consequences of a long colonial and militaristic history—even if we go back no further than the postwar era— have few parallels in modern history: millions of deaths, tens of millions wounded, more tens of millions displaced, several ruined public infrastructures, and badly damaged environments in Asia, the Middle East, and Latin America. This legacy remains, unfortunately, very much alive today.

4. Such criminality has been facilitated by superior American economic wealth and military technology—that is, within a framework of modernity, not outside of or against it. With the development of technowar, increasingly refined by the Pentagon since World War II, military action has become ever-more calculated and rationalized, the province of technocratic war planners relying

on the advantages of science, technology, bureaucracy, and communications. Methods employed by the planners have included aerial bombardments and high-tech weaponry, advanced satellite-based communications and surveillance, and sophisticated innovations like robotics. Contrary to myth, technowar has largely served to *expand* the scope of civilian casualties under modern battlefield conditions.

5. The perpetuation of U.S. outlawry depends on the work of government officials, politicians, and a corporate media that, among other of its functions, instills public fear of menacing enemies. Such evil monsters have always been omnipresent within the political and popular culture, in the personae of Indian savages, barbaric Germans (World War I), and a garden-variety casting of Communists, tyrants, rogue states, drug traffickers, and (mostly Arab) terrorists—all imminent perils to freedom and democracy, usually Godless, always guilty of heinous atrocities, and all staples of literature, movies, TV, video games, and of course political discourse.

6. With few exceptions, such as Germany and Japan during World War II, the targets of devastating U.S. weaponry have been small, weak, poorly defended nations, mostly inhabited by dark-skinned people. The attacks have often involved wanton or indiscriminate warfare against civilians, in violation of the Geneva Conventions and other canons of international law. Strict rules of engagement mostly honored in Europe have commonly been ignored in cases where racist objectification is involved, as in Japan, Korea, Vietnam, Laos, Cambodia, Panama, and Iraq.

7. Since World War II the U.S. has been the leading reservoir of weapons of mass destruction—producing, refining, stockpiling, deploying, and (on two well-known occasions) *using* them as instruments of warfare. Washington has consistently held to a policy of strategic first-use of nuclear weapons, while refusing international moves toward nuclear controls and disarmament. The second Bush administration unveiled plans for state-of-the-art nuclear weaponry and delivery systems, including bunker-buster mini-nukes, while threatening Iran with economic sanctions and possible military action for maintaining a nuclear program that (so far as has been determined) adheres to the Nuclear Non-Proliferation Treaty (NPT) guidelines. The U.S. has contributed to nuclear competition, assisting friendly nations like Israel, Pakistan, and India while railing against proliferation when it comes to others. The U.S. has for many decades integrated diverse forms of WMD into its own battlefield repertoire, including chemical weapons, biological devices, ordnance tipped with depleted uranium, and high-powered

conventional weaponry such as bombs and incendiary explosives with WMD-level firepower.

8. Despite its undeniable history of war crimes, the U.S. government has never offered apologies or reparations to anyone, for even a small part of the military terror it has brought to millions of victims. Nor has there been any official *recognition* of such deeds. Meanwhile, Washington politicians, media pundits, and academics never tire of criticizing others (Japan, Germany, Russia) for lack of contrition regarding their past criminal behavior.

9. Aside from a few local episodes where U.S. troops committed well-known atrocities (My Lai, Abu Ghraib, Haditha), no Americans possibly guilty of war crimes—government leaders, military personnel, operatives in the field—have been charged, arrested, prosecuted, or punished for any offenses. At the same time, U.S. leaders have used their vast leverage and resources to put on trial designated enemies at special ad hoc tribunals (The Hague, Baghdad) where guilty verdicts are a foregone conclusion, even as Washington resists jurisdiction of the International Criminal Court, justifiably fearing the consequences of truly independent legal inquiries into war crimes for which the most powerful and militarily active nations might be held accountable.

10. As rogue behavior continues to shape U.S. foreign and military policy, its consequences are still met with silence across the public sphere—a point further developed in later chapters. The political, media, and academic cultures merge to create an ideological fortress concealing or explaining away American transgressions, kept off the radar screen by the fiction of a benevolent U.S. national mission. When it comes to the issue of war crimes, the American public remains firmly in the ideological grip of national denial.

*   *   *

Lawlessness has been integral to U.S. global behavior for so long that it has come to appear ordinary, routine, scarcely worthy of attention. Moral outrage? Political protest? Such responses cannot be located anywhere in the mainstream political spectrum. Despite rhetorical lip service to the "rule of law," such American indifference toward its own outlawry extends also to the reputedly "objective" or "scientific" realms of academic life. Hypocrisy and double standards leave their imprint on elite discourse as well as popular consciousness, both saturated with the entitlements of imperial power. No other state devotes even a significant fraction of what the

U.S. spends on its armed forces, no other state deploys large-scale military units across dozens of countries, and no other state claims to be defending its own "national security" and "global interests" hundreds and thousands of miles from its home shores.

Despite repeated U.S. violations of international law, we commonly face a business-as-usual attitude toward the consequences of such violations. To raise fundamental criticisms of this behavior in the public sphere has been largely taboo. Questions as to whether the U.S. should be managing a far-flung Empire, should have military bases deployed around the world, should be invading and occupying foreign countries, should be rejecting or obstructing global treaties— or indeed should be prosecuted for any of its criminal behavior—are never permitted to enter political discourse. When such issues do rarely surface, they are simply regarded as normal for great-power activity in the world. Superpowers naturally have urgent global obligations that other nations cannot imagine, as the opinion-makers have been quick to remind any doubters. If political divisions have narrowed in the U.S. since the 1980s, nowhere is this shrinkage more visible than in the realm of foreign affairs, where differences between Democrats and Republicans, never great, have declined to near invisibility.[20] Both liberals and conservatives uphold a view of the U.S. as "leader of the free world," as the driving force behind democracy, human rights, and rule of law in a world threatened by extremes of tyranny and anarchy. Mainstream politicians who so much as timidly question basic assumptions underlying U.S. foreign and military policy meet harsh and immediate backlash. Any second thoughts about American global behavior must be *instrumental*— that is, centered around matters of tactics and viability—an outlook that has even shaped the bulk of antiwar protests since the 1960s. The moral *Zeitgeist* informing the broad postwar international consensus has scarcely entered American public debate outside the left fringes. Few in government, the media, or academia have chosen to endorse the perfectly rational notion that the U.S., like every sovereign nation, should be willing to accept legal and moral constraints on its international behavior and should follow the same rules as everyone else.

As for the Iraq disaster, few American politicians or media pundits have even mentioned, much less criticized, flagrant U.S. violations of the U.N. Charter as the Bush administration unleashed its war machine on a nation already weakened by war, sanctions, bombings, covert action, and years of international inspections—a nation, moreover, clearly posing no military danger to anyone. The outright deceptions used to justify military aggression elicited nothing close to the kind of political response directed at others for lesser infractions—North Korea and Iran for their nuclear programs, Russia for its assaults on Chechnya, Serbia for its supposed "ethnic cleansing" campaigns, Somalia for its violent warlord combat, China for its human rights abuses, and so forth. Not until a disillusioned American public turned against an obviously *failed* and costly military operation, in mid 2006, did politicians and the media finally raise questions about the false U.S. pretexts for war.

The crucial role of the *New York Times* in supplying a political rationale for "Operation Iraqi Freedom," as it became something of a journalistic venue for White House and Pentagon propaganda, is especially noteworthy here. A reputedly liberal and balanced newspaper, with the *Times*' award-winning reporter Judith Miller taking the lead, started beating the war drums well before the March 2003 invasion, orchestrating an arsenal of false reports and justifications, much of it furnished by Bush operatives, neocon and right-wing think-tanks, and testimony from "defectors" like Ahmad Chalabi. In dozens of editorials pushing for war, never did the *Times* raise questions about U.S. violations of the U.N. Charter and international law—and of course the paper was hardly alone in this stonewalling. Indeed, the *Times* made little pretense to objectivity as its "news" was framed in this case overwhelmingly to meet the priorities of government, military, and corporate opinion-makers. The result was a one-sided picture of what turned out to be a grossly inflated Iraqi threat. Huge antiwar protests in late 2002 and early 2003 were marginalized in the columns of the *Times*' reputedly diverse news and editorial pages, essentially kept from view. Edward Herman writes that "Regrettably, we have moved into the age of the lap-dog, nowhere more clearly than in the case of the *New York Times*."[21] And when it came to repeated, flagrant cases of U.S. outlawry—far too visible in the assault on Iraq to be missed—the *Times*, supposed forum of objectivity, was reduced to an embarrassing silence.

By fall 2002 the *Times* had published a series of front-page articles, many by Miller, with phony tales of vast hidden Iraqi arsenals of biological, chemical, and nuclear weapons, at a time when inspectors like Scott Ritter and Denis Holliday (as well as independent journalists in the field) had already reported that the Hussein regime had dismantled virtually all of its WMD by the late 1990s and, in any event, lacked effective delivery systems and overall military capacity after years of U.S. operations. Following a decade of U.S.-engineered sanctions, bombings, inspections, and covert activity it should have been obvious by 2002, if not earlier, that Iraq posed no military threat to any of its neighbors, much less to the geographically remote U.S. The *Times* coverage featured obligatory parallels between Hussein and Hitler, much the same as those linking the Nazis with Manuel Noriega in Panama and Slobodan Milošević in Yugoslavia. In editorial columns the *Times*, with other media outlets following the lead, called for an increase in American military toughness to contain and overthrow perhaps the most fearsome tyrant in modern history. As became subsequently clear—and as critics argued at the time—this war-making crusade had no factual grounding from the outset; it was nothing but propaganda, with no foundation even in CIA and other intelligence data, most of it passed on to complicit or embedded journalists by White House and Pentagon operatives. The U.S. agenda had been set in 2001, even before the terrorist attacks, if not earlier. As Herman observes: "What is remarkable in their doing this is that the basis of invasion was so crude, the lies so blatant, the violation of international law so gross that you would think a hired press agency of the government would be embarrassed to have to swallow these and push for war. But the *Times* pushed ahead, not just disseminating propaganda, but propaganda whose central components were disinformation."[22] The leading newspaper's function as an ideological arm of U.S. militarism extended not only to news reports but to long features, editorials, op-ed pieces, and book reviews—a non-stop pro-war barrage giving sustenance to an illegal Bush project at every stage. Alternative views were jettisoned or ignored, with real debate over prospects for imminent war effectively ruled off-limits. One of the most egregious examples was the dismissive reception given to the crucial 2002 statement of Mohamed ElBaradei, head of the International Atomic Energy Agency, reporting that Iraq's reputed nuclear facilities had already been destroyed—precisely what Ritter and others had been saying for years. Most everything passing through the *Times* during the build-up to war was part of a deliberate, painstaking *strategy*—coordinated with the White House—to establish momentum behind an outrageous act of military aggression so transparently tied to U.S. economic and geopolitical interests. If so, those like Miller who were involved in such shameless propaganda must be viewed as complicit in crimes against peace, following the Nuremberg precedent.

What took place at the *New York Times*, unfortunately, helped set the ideological paradigm for American media and political culture in the wake of 9/11. By late 2002 and early 2003 the vast network of corporate media outlets obediently followed suit—leading newspapers, magazines, local news venues, TV stations, talk radio, think-tanks, and university institutes, all joining in one large chorus for war. The media apparatus became an adjunct to the Bush agenda, disseminating blatant lies and myths about Iraq, WMD, Hussein's ties to Al Qaeda, and U.S. plans to "democratize" the Middle East. As Chris Hedges writes, "the notion that the press was used in the war is incorrect. The press wanted to be used. It saw itself as part of the war effort."[23] Following a well-established pattern, the American media aligned itself with a military venture that became part visual spectacle, part superpatriotic catharsis, part infotainment—rarely pausing to investigate any of the pressing legal and moral concerns. As with earlier U.S. interventions in Vietnam, Panama, Iraq, and Yugoslavia, the media eagerly and blindly followed every official statement and handout, little attention being devoted to a critical assessment of U.S. imperial objectives. The idea that Washington might invade and occupy a sovereign nation to serve its own geopolitical ambitions was either sidestepped or, when grudgingly acknowledged, framed as a matter of superpower entitlement. Thus, at the outbreak of the 2003 U.S. attack on Iraq NBC anchor Tom Brokaw could nonchalantly say: "one of the things that we don't want to do is to destroy the infrastructure of Iraq, because in a few days we're going to own that country."[24]

As Bush and the neocons moved inexorably toward war, administration ideologues, their cavalier attitude toward international law more transparent than ever, now argued that Washington should prepare its own global rules, even in the face of hostile American or world public opinion. Within the anarchic universe constructed by writers like Robert Kaplan, Richard Perle, Robert Kagan, and Max Boot, a belligerent warrior ethic made perfectly good sense, especially with the U.S. having to face off against armed-to-the-teeth madmen like Saddam Hussein and Osama bin Laden. Legal "theorists" like John Woo, Eric Posner, Jack Goldsmith, Anne-Marie Slaughter, and Alan Dershowitz entered the picture, calling attention to the "limits of international law" while arguing that universal legal principles could be junked where (as in Iraq) they stood in the way of pressing U.S. military imperatives. For Dershowitz and others, moreover, the practice of torture—uniformly regarded as a violation of human rights—might under the new circumstances be considered a potentially useful method in the war on terrorism. Media figures like Rush Limbaugh playfully toyed with reports of

U.S. torture in Iraq, Afghanistan, and Guantanamo, referring to a much-needed "emotional release" for American troops working under great battlefield stress. The epic battle against an evil Islamo-fascism, moreover, was widely understood (at least in the U.S.) as giving the benevolent superpower a moral upper hand. Consider the arguments of Sam Harris in *The End of Faith*, where he shockingly refers to the U.S. as a "well-intentioned giant" that never aimed to harm anyone by its military actions since "as a culture, we have clearly outgrown our tolerance for the deliberate torture and murder of innocents, while much of the rest of the world has not."[25] Harris adds, referring to President Bush: "Whether or not you admire the man's politics—or the man—there is no reason to think that he would have sanctioned the injury or death of even a single innocent person."[26] That Bush or any U.S. leader could wage an aggressive war, that Washington could use "shock-and-awe" tactics to achieve geopolitical ends, somehow fails to strike Harris as a venture that might "intentionally" lead to excessive loss of human life. For Harris, despite all the unspeakable death and destruction in Iraq, despite the ruination of an entire society, U.S. behavior appears to satisfy some ill-defined, obscure set of moral criteria, meaning that the carnage is just a sad product of "collateral damage."

The contemporary wars in Iraq and Afghanistan reveal the extent to which U.S. outlawry has become taken-for-granted within the political culture. Far from being immune to this intellectual and moral inertia, the academic world embraces it at the very moment it affirms the virtues of open and critical discourse. In *Lawless World*, Philippe Sands remarks that even modest praise for the International Criminal Court, indeed for any independent global judicial body, at academic conferences invariably sends American scholars into fits of rage, apparently unwilling to contemplate limits to American power.[27]

When it comes to U.S. global behavior, the culture of national denial has a long and well-cultivated history, reflected in clichés such as the natural law of superpower aggression—the comfortable myth that great powers have always, and will always, behave just as they please in order to secure international advantage, with a license to plunder and destroy at will. (Of course this moral and legal latitude is never granted *other* powers.) Political and media references to U.S. war crimes, as mentioned, have always been noteworthy for their virtual absence, taken up only by a few (discredited) left-wing critics. One recent study of U.S. outlawry, though limited in scope, is Sands' *Lawless World*, the excellent work of a British scholar that was poorly received once it reached American shores. David Chandler's important contribution, *From Kosovo to Kabul*, is devoted mainly to the broader trajectory of international and human rights law. Diana Johnstone's hard-hitting *Fool's Crusade* explores war crimes and similar violations in the context of the U.S./NATO military interventions in Yugoslavia during the late 1990s.[28] In the U.S. only a few writers—Noam Chomsky, Edward Herman, Michael Parenti, and Gilbert Achcar most notably—have ventured onto this perilous and thankless terrain. Two recent books, Michael Mandel's *How America Gets Away with Murder* and David Model's *Lying for Empire*, provide much-needed research and analysis in this area, though neither fully explores the general historical and political terrain of U.S. outlawry, which is the purpose of the following chapters.[29] Carla Del Ponte's exhaustive book, *Madame Prosecutor*, systematically addresses war crimes in Yugoslavia, Rwanda, and elsewhere, but the promise of its subtitle "Confrontations with Humanity's Worst Criminals" falls predictably short of dealing with American or NATO crimes.[30] As for U.S. history, a political culture of denial remains fully embedded within hegemonic discourses, revealing more than ever a wide chasm separating the celebratory self-image of Washington officialdom and the real-life horrors produced by U.S. imperialism and militarism.

*　*　*

With the dreadful Bush administration relegated to history, a Barack Obama presidency brought hopes for a new turn in U.S. international behavior, toward a less belligerent and militaristic, more diplomatic and peaceful approach. Throughout his path-breaking campaign Obama called for a new kind of politics, including in foreign policy. The Democrats' breakthrough encouraged many liberals and progressives to see Obama as a source of new departures on the war in Iraq, the Middle East, global warming, the economic crisis, and WMD proliferation, among other issues. Although Obama's promises of "change" on the campaign trail seemed rather vague, hopes in early 2009 were nonetheless high if not euphoric. Regarding the main focus of this book—the long history of U.S. outlawry—it is surely worth asking whether an Obama presidency augurs far-reaching change, whether it is reasonable to expect a more lawful, less arrogant and militaristic Washington establishment, ready to play a more constructive and peaceful role in world politics.

As of this writing (March 2009), with the Obama administration still in its infancy, any firm generalizations are bound to be premature. At the same time, certain tendencies can be identified on the basis of Obama's political record, abundant statements, cabinet appointments, and initial policies—tendencies, unfortunately, that offer little cause for optimism. An Obama presidency is likely to represent continuity, with little evidence to suggest future U.S. global behavior will divorce itself from the same corporate and military interests that have dominated earlier presidencies. Obama's record is that of a cautious, middle-of-the-road, calculating politician who gravitates toward the political center, an "antiwar" candidate who routinely voted for Iraq war funding and whose promise to withdraw troops from Iraq within 16 months remained highly conditional. To be sure, Obama's presence on the world scene—his thoughtful approach to politics, his charisma, a stated emphasis on diplomacy and global exchange—will differ sharply from the outright provincialism and aggressiveness exhibited by Bush and the neocons. In real terms, however, everything points toward reaffirmation of longstanding U.S. global ambitions: more effective "world leadership," stepped-up resource wars, consolidation of American power in the Middle East, more troops deployed to Afghanistan, a continued NATO eastward push, unconditional support for Israel, increases in military spending. Prospects for full withdrawal from oil-rich and geopolitically crucial Iraq, where the U.S. has built several large "permanent" bases, seem uncertain at best. Speaking in late February 2009, Obama pledged U.S. withdrawal from Iraq, but indicated that between 35,000 and 50,000 troops would stay on indefinitely, to carry out training, security, and counterinsurgency tasks. The Afghan situation had already turned into a bloody, hopeless quagmire that, by early 2009, seemed to offer no meaningful strategic options—except withdrawal (ruled out by Obama). The President immediately deployed an additional 17,000 soldiers to Afghanistan, with more to be sent later. He also escalated missile strikes against Taliban and Al Qaeda targets in north-western Pakistan, with potentially destabilizing consequences.

The Gaza massacres carried out by Israel in January 2009 were met in Washington with deafening silence, hardly surprising given Obama's hard-line pro-Israel speech before AIPAC (America's pro-Israel lobby) the day after he won the nomination. There have been no signs of even slight deviation from longstanding, unwavering U.S. support of Israel, regardless of its ongoing violations of international law. During the murderous Gaza attack, Obama referred only to Israeli "security," pointing out that arms smuggling into the Palestinian territory should be blocked—saying nothing, however, about the steady flow of military arms and equipment into Israel from Washington that enabled the Israeli Defense Forces to carry out their atrocities. Consistent with the policies of Israel and the domestic Israel lobby, Obama also chose to ignore the elected Hamas government in Gaza, thereby turning his back on any viable political settlement of the Palestinian–Israel struggle that remains at the heart of Middle Eastern turbulence. When the issue of Palestinian self-determination surfaced once again at the U.N., in December 2008, a supporting resolution passed 173 to 5, with the U.S. and Israel leading the rejectionists—thus further closing off any chance of a just settlement.

Obama's cabinet appointments also reflected an ominously conservative, hawkish direction: the Republican Robert Gates for Secretary of Defense, Rahm Emmanuel as chief of staff, Hillary Clinton as Secretary of State, and Joseph Biden as Vice President. All of these politicians supported the Iraq war from the outset, voted massive funding for it, and strongly endorsed the Afghan escalation. All are closely tied to the Israel lobby. Obama's National Security Adviser, the hawkish James Jones, formerly served as a Marine Commandant. These appointments were cheered by such media establishment voices as the *Wall Street Journal* and the *New York Times*. With Obama's most important high-level foreign-policy operatives so closely tied to the orbit of the military-industrial complex, it would be difficult to envision an Obama departure from conventional imperial priorities. The promise to close down the already dysfunctional prison system at Guantanamo, with fewer than 250 inmates, hardly points toward a renovated foreign and military outlook. Once having entered the White House, moreover, Obama revived Bush's rather lame faith-based initiative, extended the CIA's infamous rendition program, moved to protect executive secrecy, allowed ROTC (Reserve Officers' Training Corps) programs back on university campuses, ruled out Pentagon spending reductions aside from a few limited "cost-cutting" measures, and, during an interview by Al Arabiya TV, said absolutely nothing about the U.S.-backed Gaza catastrophe. He also pushed, successfully, to extend massive Iraq war funding, seemingly undeterred by the tenacious economic crisis.

That Obama might actually initiate basic changes in foreign policy was, given his cozy relationship with corporate and military interests, an illusory prospect in the first place—no doubt a manifestation of collective wishful thinking in the wake of Bush's great failures. It is worth remembering here that postwar Democrats, wedded to the bipartisan consensus, have always followed the contours of Empire, the war economy, and the security state. Moreover, the notion that a single presidential election might itself reverse some 200 years of U.S. history, bringing to power a leader dedicated to a radical new course, contradicts the historical logic of American politics. Eight years of a dismal Bush presidency naturally gave rise to a public mood of anger and frustration resulting in desperate hopes for something new—and of course the new White House occupants did inspire expectations for just that. Any Obama-initiated change, however, is destined to fall short of altering the long historical trajectory of imperialism and outlawry explored in this book.

1
Crimes Against Peace

Even setting aside forms of intervention such as proxy wars, CIA-sponsored covert operations, economic and political subversion, and blockades, the U.S. record of military aggression waged against sovereign nations since World War II has no parallel. It is a record, moreover, that stands alone in its scope of criminality. Immersed from its very founding in an ethos of perpetual warfare, the American nation-state achieved early imperial status as it expanded westward and outward, later reaching global proportions with the growth of the permanent war economy in the late 1940s. The immediate postwar years witnessed little reduction in Pentagon spending, and no lessened interest in broader economic, political, and military pursuits. Across subsequent decades the U.S. has initiated dozens of armed interventions throughout the world, resulting in a gruesome toll impossible to fully measure: at least eight million dead, tens of millions wounded, millions more made homeless or forced into refugee status, and environmental devastation on a horrific scale. In the post-9/11 milieu, with the brazen military invasion and occupation of Iraq, there seemed no end in sight to U.S. imperial expansion. Every aggressive move was framed by the political and media establishment as rational and noble, vital to the national security if not to Western civilization. But with just two partial exceptions (the U.N.-backed Korean War and the initial Afghan operations) these actions could never be defended on either rational or noble grounds; they stand, rather, as clear violations of established principles of international law.

At the end of World War II the Germans and Japanese were tried for "crimes against peace"—that is, unprovoked military aggression waged against sovereign nations. Eventually, 15 German and 24 Japanese leaders were convicted of such offenses, with U.S. prosecutors most adamant in pursuing guilty verdicts followed by death penalties. The Nazis were prosecuted and convicted of planning and waging war against Poland, the USSR, Norway, England, Holland, Denmark, Yugoslavia, France, and Greece. The Charter of the International Military Tribunal at Nuremberg defined "illegal warfare" as "planning, preparation, initiation, or waging a war of aggression, or a war in violation of international treaties, agreements, or assurances, or participation in a common plan or conspiracy [for war]." Moreover, the Nuremberg statutes framed military aggression as "the supreme international crime differing only from other war crimes in that it contains within itself the accumulated evil of the whole," meaning the aggressor is criminally responsible for all offenses that follow with negative outcomes traced back to the first military decision to intervene. Drawing on the Nuremberg principles, the nascent United Nations banned the first use of force, stating: "All members shall refrain in their international relations from the threat or use of force against the territorial integrity or political independence of any state..." (Article 2.4). It is generally acknowledged that prohibitions against military aggression constitute a fundamental norm of modern international law and its prevention is the chief purpose of the U.N. There has been consensus behind rules that could ensure some measure of global stability, limits to military action, and protection of human rights. The U.N. Charter provides a definitive list of violations, including armed invasion, occupation, bombardment, blockade, attack on a nation's armed forces, using territory for aggression, and supporting local groups to carry out military operations. These prohibitions are contained in numerous treaties, conventions, protocols, and organized charters established in the several decades since Nuremberg.

FORGETTING NUREMBERG

At different times in its history the U.S. has violated every one of the above principles, generally holding itself above the most hallowed norms of international law. Its many acts of military aggression have for the most part been planned, deliberate, systematic, and brutal, with its increasingly high-tech firepower directed against weak, small, underdeveloped, and militarily inferior countries. Such acts have *always* been carried out in the absence of a serious military threat to the U.S. arising from those nations or groups targeted for attack; the U.S. took the first move, usually sidestepping or ignoring diplomatic initiatives. The American military—since 1945 the most powerful and far-reaching in the world—has conducted both selective and strategic (area) bombing, used weapons of mass destruction, wantonly attacked civilian populations and infrastructures, mined harbors, invaded and occupied foreign territories, set up draconian blockades, organized population relocation programs, and supported paramilitary groups for proxy wars on behalf of U.S. elite interests—and it has done so across the globe with virtual impunity. In some cases U.S. military aggression has been patently unilateral, while in others it came under cover of a U.N. or NATO coalition where U.S. military (and political) resources were decisive. Rhetorical justifications have been routinely offered for public consumption—including appeals to humanitarian agendas, human rights, national defense, arrest of drug traffickers, the fight against Communism and terrorism, support for democracy—none of which, however, have enjoyed much credibility outside U.S. borders. A more recent pretext has been the claim of halting the spread of weapons of mass destruction, especially nuclear weaponry. In any event, closer historical investigation shows that economic and geopolitical interests have most often driven U.S. military intervention from the outset, reflecting a long and deep imperialist legacy. A comprehensive list of U.S. acts of military aggression, prior to Iraq and Afghanistan, direct and indirect, large and small, can be found in William Blum's books *Killing Hope* (1995) and *Rogue State* (2000).[1]

Postwar military interventions that have brought U.S. leaders directly into conflict with international law include the following: Greece, Korea, Guatemala, Vietnam, Laos, Cambodia, Haiti, Grenada, Panama, El Salvador, Nicaragua, Somalia, Yugoslavia, Afghanistan, and Iraq. There have been literally dozens of operations that were covert or indirect, or involved some form of proxy war (to be discussed later). It will suffice to address a few such episodes here, concluding with the most recent violation, Iraq.

In the case of Korea, President Truman's undeclared war on the North (begun June 25, 1950, and referred to as a "police action") proceeded under the auspices of the U.N., although there really was no independent U.N. army, navy, or air force separate from the U.S. armed forces at that time. The operations, lasting nearly three bloody years, were framed as a U.S. response to North Korean invasion, but the political situation and the *context* of warfare were far more nuanced and complex. U.S. forces had occupied South Korea in 1945, setting up a brutal dictatorship under Syngman Rhee and dividing the country. In reality, the two sides had been clashing at the 38th parallel for several years before the outbreak of full-scale warfare; North and South could be said to have shared more or less equal blame. By 1950 there had indeed been hundreds of incursions from both sides, accompanied by sometimes heavy bombing. In a context where the South Korean dictator openly proclaimed his intent to reunify the nation by force and on his terms, and where the South had actually captured the town of Haeju in the days leading up to war, the question as to who precisely fired the first salvos turns out to be rather meaningless. Military conflict seemed to be built into the very logic of a harsh and arbitrary national partition. In any event, it was the Washington decision-makers who first initiated large-scale armed operations, having mobilized U.S. troops (stationed at dozens of bases in Korea and Japan) well in advance of a U.N. resolution facilitated by a Soviet boycott. U.S. armies invaded North Korea and pushed all the way to the Yalu River on the Chinese border where they were repelled by joint Korean–Chinese troops. The U.S. steadfastly refused any negotiated settlement, forcing a military stalemate costing up to three million Korean lives, and which was finally resolved only when both sides agreed to the original demarcation line—but not before Truman had considered using atomic bombs to break the impasse. Whatever the original context or pretext for war, the U.S. was unquestionably guilty of military aggression once its armies moved to the Chinese border and then sustained the bloodbath well beyond reasonable limits.[2]

Turning to Vietnam, U.S. leaders emphasized military action from the earliest postwar breakout of Indochinese nationalism, purportedly to halt the spread of Communism in Southeast Asia and beyond, part of the "domino effect." By the early 1960s President Kennedy and his enlightened liberal elites (Dean Rusk, McGeorge Bundy, Robert McNamara, Walt Rostow, Maxwell Taylor, et al.) had set forth an ambitious war plan according to which Indochina would be a major testing ground in the Cold War struggle between totalitarianism and democracy. The foundations of everything that would later unfold—large-scale troop mobilizations, aerial bombardments, strategic hamlets, free-fire zones, search-and-destroy missions, chemical warfare—were already firmly in place under Kennedy and his circle.[3] Warfare as counterinsurgency was immediately and energetically taken up as vital to U.S. national interests. The logic of military intervention meant rapid expansion of U.S. operations, starting with teams of "advisers," from South to North Vietnam by 1965 and later to Laos and Cambodia, ignoring diplomatic overtures spelled out in the 1954 Geneva Accords, not to mention U.N. Charter prohibitions against military aggression. The Geneva Accords stipulated that elections would take place within two years as a prelude to Vietnamese reunification, but the U.S. blocked both the elections and reunification in favor of a dictatorship (led by Ngo Dinh Diem) that turned the South into a besieged American colony. After Diem's harsh rule generated massive resistance, Kennedy approved military aid and intervention in 1961, explicitly abrogating the terms of the Accords. In 1964 President Johnson used the manufactured Gulf of Tonkin crisis to launch full-scale war in Vietnam, which eventually spread to Laos and Cambodia, where in 1969–70 the U.S. carried out the deadliest aerial onslaught in history, creating utter carnage over vast regions. What JFK and his technocratic planners set in motion was extended during the Johnson and Nixon presidencies, although war was never formally declared against North Vietnam, Laos, or Cambodia. For one of the most flagrant violations of international law ever, spanning a period of 14 years, three U.S. presidents and their war managers could and should have been held criminally accountable for crimes against peace, just as the Germans and Japanese were at Nuremberg and Tokyo. Christopher Hitchens has correctly identified Henry Kissinger as a mass murderer and war criminal for his role in Indochina, but Hitchens fails to explain why the list should stop with Kissinger.[4]

Turning to the Caribbean, the U.S. legacy of military aggression in the region is well-known, being the product of geopolitical interests going back to the nineteenth century. Leaving aside covert action and proxy wars, the past several decades have witnessed American warfare launched against five sovereign nations: Haiti, the Dominican Republic, Nicaragua, Grenada, and Panama. In April 1967 a popular revolt swept through the Dominican Republic, its goal the restoring to power of reformist Juan Bosch (earlier overthrown with U.S. help). The U.S. sent 23,000 troops to crush the rebellion and preserve the military dictatorship, never bothering to secure U.N. support. While the U.S. regularly waged proxy warfare in Central America, its operations took on a more direct character at times—for example, with the mining of Nicaraguan harbors in the early 1980s. Nicaragua filed suit in the World Court in 1984 asking for relief, whereupon the court ruled (in 1986) that U.S. leaders were in violation of international law, and should cease their intervention and pay reparations. The Reagan administration summarily dismissed the charges and verdict, refusing to accept the court's jurisdiction over American interests. In October 1983 the U.S. conducted a surprise raid on tiny Grenada, killing hundreds of people (including 84 Cubans) in order to overthrow the reformist Maurice Bishop government—ostensibly to "restore democracy."

A decade later, in Haiti, President Clinton sent U.S. troops to bring Jean-Bertrand Aristide back to power under the diktat (enforced by occupying soldiers) that he implement neoliberal economic policies. Judged by established canons of international law, these and related military ventures must be regarded as crimes against peace— especially given U.S. refusal to entertain diplomatic initiatives.

A more brazen U.S. attack came against Panama in December 1989, when 26,000 air and ground forces invaded and then took over the country, ousting supposed drug trafficker Manuel Noriega and installing a friendly regime at the cost of an estimated 4000 Panamanian lives (mostly civilians) and the destruction of many opposition groups. The working-class section of Panama City, El Chorillo, was largely demolished, with 14,000 left homeless.[5] The first Bush administration justified its unprovoked attack on several grounds—arresting Noriega on drug charges, restoring democracy, protecting American lives—none of which carried much weight relative to the pull of U.S. strategic priorities in the Panama Canal region. The actual problem with Noriega was not drug offenses but his increasingly defiant attitude toward Washington. In this case, as in others, President Bush never declared war, nor did he secure the backing of the Organization of American States (OAS) or the U.N.[6]

Little more than a year later, following the August 1990 Iraq invasion of Kuwait, the U.S. unveiled Desert Storm—supported by a coalition it had mobilized—as the first salvo in the Gulf War and in the post-Cold War assertion of unchallenged U.S. global power. The Bush administration had been prepared for military action to counter the Hussein regime, dismissing negotiating initiatives from Russia and other interested parties, including from Iraq itself. In early 1991 the U.S. used bribes and threats to build its coalition before carrying out its technowar blitz against Iraq, destroying much of the country's infrastructure and killing at least 200,000 people, including some 30,000 troops in retreat along the "highway of death" as military action was ending.[7] The U.S. was able to inflict more damage on Iraq than on any other country in the twentieth century, leaving aside Korea and Vietnam. (Although Washington bought the participation of coalition partners, for example by means of seven billion dollars of loans to Russia, *military* operations remained almost exclusively the province of the U.S., especially in the air, with some British help.) Anticipating the 2003 invasion and occupation of Iraq, Bush the elder justified the armed response by invoking Hussein's threat to Western interests, in particular his possible invasion of oil-rich Saudi Arabia. No evidence was ever furnished, however, to validate such claims. What Desert Storm achieved for the U.S. was a durable, large-scale military presence in the Gulf region serving as a prelude to further strategic ambitions in Iraq and beyond.

After the Gulf War the U.S. created no-fly zones over Iraq, continued regular bombing missions, and enforced draconian economic sanctions that U.N. agencies reported to have cost more than one million lives, almost exclusively civilian.[8] While the Security Council endorsed *political* efforts to deal with the rather implausible Iraqi foreign ambitions, there were no stipulations allowing the kind of *military* carte blanche that Washington was pursuing throughout the 1990s. War crimes visited upon Iraq during this period included some of the most ruthless and unnecessary in modern history.[9] Even with the blessing of U.N. cover in the case of Desert Storm, the U.S. was clearly guilty of planning and carrying out a war of aggression that historical evidence shows was entirely avoidable, and of sustaining it for more than a decade.[10]

The U.S./NATO intervention in the Balkans during 1999 came under cover of the first "humanitarian" war, said to combat the horrors of Serb "ethnic cleansing" and "genocide." Virtual non-stop aerial bombardments, lasting 79 days, demolished the Serb infrastructure, with Belgrade suffering thousands of casualties. Relying on the safety of high altitudes, planes attacked civilian targets, dropped cluster bombs, and delivered missiles and bombs tipped with depleted uranium (DU), disseminating tons of toxic chemicals and radiation into air, water, and crops. Justified as a human rights crusade, a small, poor, relatively defenseless nation of eleven million people was pulverized by Western air power. NATO commander General Wesley Clark boasted that the aim of the air war was to "demolish, destroy, devastate, degrade, and ultimately eliminate the essential infrastructure of Yugoslavia."[11] No only did these unprovoked military operations violate the U.N. Charter prohibiting armed aggression, they also flew in the face of the Geneva Protocols outlawing wanton destruction of civilian populations and objects. (Indeed President Clinton never even *sought* U.N. Security Council backing for this venture.)

Whatever the crimes of Slobodan Milošević in his desperate attempt to hold together an embattled Yugoslavian nation-state, they would pale in comparison to the carnage left by the U.S./NATO campaign of aerial terrorism. The Western propaganda campaign dwelling on Serb atrocities—and turning Milošević into "another Hitler"—was not too far removed from the narrative presented in Barry Levinson's popular film *Wag the Dog* (1998). The simplistic media conveniently ignored the role of NATO powers in the post-Cold War disintegration of Yugoslavia, U.S. support of the fascist Tudjman regime in Croatia, the tyranny brought by the Islamic fundamentalist Izetbegović regime in Bosnia, and rampant local terrorism practiced by groups like the Kosovo Liberation Army (KLA) that were organized and funded by Washington. Also sidestepped was the expanded NATO military presence in Yugoslavia after 1995, part of U.S. geopolitical interests in the Balkans including plans for the eastward expansion of NATO. To believe that the Serbs were the *only* villains within this conflicted political history makes no sense. Evidence shows that Washington chose to target the Milošević government not because it was criminal or authoritarian (it was in fact twice elected) but because it presented an impediment to U.S. domination of the Balkans, strategically connected to the rest of Europe, Russia, the Middle East, and the Caspian Sea—a region rich in oil, natural gas, and other prized resources. The NATO planners of military action were ultimately charged with war crimes in 1999, in a suit naming President Clinton as a defendant—along with Secretary of Defense William Cohen, Secretary of State Madeleine Albright, General Clark, and British leader Tony Blair. With substantial evidence at their disposal, including a record of sustained aerial attacks on distinctly civilian targets, the plaintiffs took their case to The Hague Tribunal, hoping to be heard by chief prosecutor Carla del Ponte. The case, however, was summarily thrown out in the wake of vehement American protests as the mystical (but seemingly ironclad) law of U.S. special immunity once again held sway.[12]

Other records of postwar military aggression, more limited in scope, ought to be mentioned—for example, the four aerial bombardments of Libya in the 1980s, troop deployments to Somalia in 1993, and military intervention connected to the war on terrorism in Afghanistan going back to October 2001. (The Afghan operation to destroy Al Qaeda base camps and overthrow the Taliban regime could be justified as a *defensive* response to 9/11, permitted under the U.N. Charter, but as of early 2009 the very length of the war there and its excessive costs in human lives—along with the resulting chaos and violence—raises compelling questions about *proportionality* as well as political motives.) In early 2002, a CIA-operated unmanned Predator aircraft struck a target in Yemen with a laser-guided Hellfire missile, killing six people in a civilian vehicle, part of an increasingly bold U.S. effort to fight terrorism. This and similar attacks, presumably fitting Bush's doctrine of preemptive warfare, wind up expanding the boundaries of permissible military action consistent with the "right" Washington has given itself to militarily intervene in any country, at any time, in whatever fashion it chooses, international law be damned.[13] In such cases a few generalizations stand out: casualty tolls are overwhelmingly civilian, the military option comes before diplomatic efforts have been exhausted, justifications are invariably bogus, reliance on technowar reduces U.S. casualties while creating more bloodshed on the ground, interventions come against small, relatively weak and defenseless nations that have challenged U.S. power, and the decision to attack stands in clear violation of international law.

SUPERPOWER ETHICS

After the first Gulf War the U.S. relied upon every device available to it—espionage, inspections, bombing raids, covert action, economic sanctions—to subvert Iraqi power while moving to secure its imperial supremacy across the region. As early as 1992 some neocon ideologues had called for a "remapping" of the Middle East, beginning with regime change in Iraq (a task left "unfinished" in 1991), while the U.S. set out to bolster its economic, political, and military leverage in the Persian Gulf and Central Asia. We have seen how the 2003 invasion and occupation of Iraq was designed to reorder that nation's governing, industrial, financial, and legal structures as a step toward controlling its resources. U.S. intervention followed several (often overlapping) phases: build-up to war, invasion, occupation in pursuit of hegemony, reconstruction, and final consolidation of control and governance. The first two phases were carried out swiftly and efficiently enough, although deceitfully, after desperate U.S./British efforts to win U.N. Security Council backing had failed. Media-centered public relations campaigns that demonized the Hussein regime were indispensable to success. Quick battlefield gains, however, turned illusory, masking enormous political and military disasters to come. The third phase—occupation—soon turned into a major catastrophe because of contradictions inherent in efforts by a foreign power to rule a nation mainly by force, especially where the predatory aims of the occupier were so transparent. As for reconstructing a society it had already essentially destroyed, the U.S. goal has been to maintain enough stability to permit Western corporate penetration of the economy. However, as of early 2009, the occupation could only be described as fragile despite the reputed gains of the military "surge" undertaken by Bush in 2007. More to the point, every phase of this operation has unfolded in flagrant violation of international law.

Without Security Council approval, the war was patently illegal from the outset—a reality understood around the world but typically obscured in the U.S. Article 2.4 of the U.N. Charter is firm in its prohibition against military aggression, the only exception being self-defense, which could never have applied where an already debilitated Hussein regime's capacity to harm even its neighbors, much less a superpower 6000 miles distant, was nil. The erosion of American political culture is so advanced, however, that legal and moral concerns about U.S. global behavior never get raised, much less debated. In late 2002 the U.S. Congress gave President Bush "authority" to use military force against Iraq, as if such a resolution affirming superpower interests might trump established principles of international law. The American political consensus was, and remains, that such rules cannot set limits to the pursuit of national interests, as reflected in Bush's statement on the eve of war, "I don't care what the international lawyers say, we are going to kick some ass."[14] The prevailing ethos among U.S. politicians, the media, and even most academics was that "preemptive war" against Iraq might be illegal but it was nonetheless *legitimate*, that is, fully appropriate given the mad dictator Hussein's threat as patron of terrorism and bearer of weapons of mass destruction.

Regardless of any Iraqi threat, moreover, Bush's doctrine of preemptive war—a military strike against a "possible" or "anticipated" but in fact totally conjured threat—still violates the U.N. Charter mandating Security Council approval. In fact the entire build-up to war was fraudulent: public statements clearly reveal that regime change in Iraq was on the neocon (and then official Washington) foreign-policy agenda going back at least a decade. This was the essence of the 1998 Iraq Liberation Act, which at the time mentioned nothing about democracy or Hussein's alleged connection with Al Qaeda or his possession of WMD. The strategy revolved around securing economic and geopolitical interests in the region. After the first Gulf War Security Council Resolution 687 demanded that Iraq dispense with its WMD and be open to U.N. inspections, but no WMD were ever found after years of searching, while it was generally understood that Iraq had been largely disarmed soon after Desert Storm. Nonetheless, with graphic images of an imminent Iraq WMD attack, replete with Condoleezza Rice's visions of "mushroom clouds," Bush, Cheney, and Rumsfeld energetically beat the drums of war in the aftermath of 9/11. The issue of an Iraqi WMD threat, not to mention patronage of terrorism, was nothing but a pretext for war cynically manipulated to persuade a gullible American public to go along with the larger Bush agenda.[15]

In November 2002 the Security Council adopted Resolution 1441, saying that if Iraq failed to cooperate with nuclear inspections and did not fully reveal its WMD programs, the regime would face "serious consequences." But nowhere did the resolution explicitly authorize the use of military force which, in any event, France, Germany, Russia, and China strongly opposed; military action should never have been a matter for the U.S. alone to decide. From November 2002 through March 2003 inspections continued but nothing was found, leaving the Bush administration with no recourse but to forge its own illegal "coalition of the willing" in arrogant contempt of the U.N. and its member nations. There was absolutely no legal basis for war.[16] No foreign leaders, including neighbors of Iraq, believed that a Hussein weakened by war, disarmament, sanctions, and bombings could possibly threaten *anyone*, much less to the world's most powerful war machine. Desperate for support, Washington set out to bribe leaders of several countries, just as it had done before Desert Storm, with mixed results. And no international lawyers outside the U.S. could find merits in the American case: Bush was simply never able to defend the imperative for war. The U.S. itself was not in a position to determine a breach of U.N. resolutions, or, more importantly, exactly how to punish Iraq if there had been one. Sheer military power was the only trump card that Washington possessed.

In September 2004, far too late to influence the course of events, U.N. Secretary-General Kofi Annan said he believed the U.S./British invasion and occupation of Iraq was illegal, a clear violation of the Charter. The pretext for war was entirely bogus. Most Security Council member states had in 2003 already rejected the U.S. case, and of course history shows they were correct and the Bush/neocon warmongers wrong. In justifying war the U.S. fell back on the claim that its own intelligence agencies had reported Iraq's possession of WMD, but it turned out the intelligence "data" had been systematically distorted to support the Bush agenda. In the end, the U.S. managed to sabotage international law at several junctures, its determination to initiate military action at any cost a major factor behind the mounting global ethos of lawlessness.[17]

The build-up to war was accompanied by a series of legal violations, illegal maneuvers, provocations, and a propaganda campaign waged to demonize Iraq as the world's greatest military threat, although its arms expenditures had sunk well below one billion dollars—inadequate for even a *defense* of the country. What bothered the U.S. most about Iraq after the late 1980s was not its possession of WMD (real or otherwise) but rather its growing independence from the West and perceived challenge to U.S. designs in the Middle East. Whatever its defects, the Ba'ath Party favored land reform, public ownership of national resources, socialization of industry and finance, a secular Arab nationalism, and support for the Palestinians. While "socialist" elements were in retreat during the 1990s, the U.S. was most agitated over Iraqi foreign policy and stepped up its crusade for regime change, long before 9/11 or the neocon ascendancy. U.N. economic sanctions were imposed in 1991, blocking many essential imports and precipitating a sharp decline in public services and standard of living, a policy strenuously championed mainly by the U.S., but devoid of legal or moral rationale. In May 1993 Clinton unveiled a plan to destabilize the regime and force the downfall of Hussein. Toward this end the U.S. created no-fly zones over Iraq, allowing the Pentagon to bomb targets with impunity, supposedly permitted by Article 51, chapter VII of the U.N. Charter, although nothing in that statute actually permitted *military* attacks by the U.S. or any other nation. The U.S., Israel, and Saudi Arabia collaborated in several efforts to assassinate Hussein, illegal according to several international treaties. A coup attempt sponsored by the CIA with Saudi intelligence help was aborted at the last minute in 1996. Such foreign intervention in the domestic affairs of a sovereign nation is understandably viewed as an outrage by every government in the world.

The above constitutes only a small part of the dreadful historical narrative leading up to war. The U.S. carried out ongoing espionage and sabotage activities in Iraq under cover of the U.N. inspections regimen (UNSCOM), much of it designed to identify military targets for the planned future armed intervention. Infiltration and covert action were stepped up after 1994 as the U.S. moved toward regime change, hoping to replace Hussein with a small coterie of pro-Western generals. By the late 1990s such illegal activities had steadily increased as CIA operatives financed and supported oppositional elements, none of which, it turned out, could mobilize any popular support outside the Kurdish population. As the U.S. demanded virtually unlimited access to sites across Iraq, seizing on that freedom to conduct surveillance and espionage, Hussein inevitably resisted and strengthened repression at least in part to counter foreign subversion.[18] The accumulation of intelligence data seemed to be a crucial function of the entire inspection process. As Dilip Hiro writes: "Having collected highly confidential information about the inner workings of Saddam's regime—most of it by infiltrating UNSCOM—the Clinton administration was eager to use it to impress on Saddam his vulnerability and to warn him of more punitive action."[19] Such intervention was both brazenly illegal and provocative, designed to force extreme crackdowns that would allow the U.S. to further demonize Hussein. However, while the CIA and kindred agencies deployed several thousand operatives to Iraq and its periphery (mainly Jordan, Saudi Arabia, and Kuwait), their efforts to destabilize the political system had largely failed, leading to more frustration in Washington.[20] When the U.S. Congress passed the Iraq Liberation Act in 1998, calling for regime change, it earmarked nearly $100 million to train, equip, and finance Iraqi opposition groups, with relatively little to show for it. Frustration led the U.S. to gravitate toward more immediate military solutions: in late 1998, for example, Clinton ordered extensive bombing of hundreds of targets, on the pretext of attacking Hussein's (alleged) WMD arsenal.

By the late 1990s the U.S. had already chosen a leader to succeed Hussein—Ahmed Chalabi, head of the CIA-invented Iraq National Congress (INC), a selection that had absolutely nothing to do with WMD, terrorism, or democracy. In May 1999 National Security Adviser Samuel Berger reiterated that the U.S. had a "determination to get rid of Saddam Hussein by the end of Clinton's second term."[21] When nothing happened while Clinton was still in office, the Bush administration just carried forward the same policy injunction, but now with a new sense of urgency owing to neocon influence and the events of 9/11. Leading figures under Bush—Cheney, Rumsfeld, Rice, Wolfowitz, et al.—rushed to embrace the INC as beneficiary of regime change, though now this bogus group was offered up as a "democratic alternative" to Hussein's tyranny. None of these plans to overthrow a sovereign government in order to satisfy U.S. strategic objectives were, needless to say, consistent with the norms of international law. Knowledgeable inspectors and observers, including CIA officials, knew that Iraq possessed no WMD, that it had no connection to Al Qaeda, and that it was a nation reduced to poverty and weakness, scarcely able to defend itself militarily. It was also widely known that the most sustained human rights violations emanated from Washington and London rather than Baghdad, although the Hussein regime was hardly guilt-free. The invasion was conceived and planned months and even years in advance, the product of criminal intentions spanning three presidencies and both major parties across more than a decade.

As James Bamford has shown, the road to war never followed on the basis of actual problems and threats related to Iraq, but was opened up by a lengthy, expensive propaganda campaign managed in great part by the Rendon Group and abetted by the corporate media. Beginning in the early 1990s, the Pentagon secretly awarded Rendon tens of millions of dollars in contracts to provide the ideological context in which regime change in Iraq could be effectively pursued—a project that worked beyond even the neocons' wildest fantasies.[22] Collaborating with the CIA and leading neocon operatives, Rendon was able to construct a public understanding of Iraq as the greatest menace to world peace, a dictatorial regime ready to unleash powerful weapons on an unsuspecting world. A self-proclaimed "information warrior," John Rendon was convinced that modern warfare depends crucially on public perception—how threats and enemies are viewed, what prices are worth paying, what methods of warfare are acceptable, and so forth. The Rendon Group has done business in no less than 91 countries, preparing the groundwork for U.S. interventions in Panama, Yugoslavia, Afghanistan, and Iraq among others. Addressing the 2003 invasion of Iraq, Bamford writes: "Never before in history has such an extensive secret network been established to shape the entire world's perception of a war."[23] As the 1990s unfolded, Rendon became Washington's leading marketing group on behalf of regime change, working closely with TV, radio, and print outlets to demonize Iraq and make the case for war. In other words, a vast propaganda apparatus was crucial to preparations for military aggression, part of a deliberate advertising and marketing strategy. Further, in the wake of invasion and throughout a protracted occupation regime, the Rendon campaign actually *intensified* as it strived to convince the American public that the "war" was being won (in this case with much less success).

The Rendon campaigns, waged with cynical disregard for facts, costs, and risks, give added meaning to the criminality of Bush's drive toward military action. If regime change was on the agenda as early as 1992, then issues revolving around WMD and terrorism, not to mention democracy, could not possibly have been decisive in the move to invade and occupy Iraq. The reasons invoked by

Bush were all simply a *pretext* for an illegal war that was, from the outset, based on resource and geopolitical agendas spelled out during the previous decade. It follows that "intelligence failures," moreover, had nothing to do with faulty decision-making: on the contrary, intelligence data was manipulated to serve policy ends, as insiders like Richard Clarke were able to demonstrate.[24] CIA analysts were repeatedly ordered to refashion their findings to suit phony Bush administration claims, as with Iraq's supposed nuclear program and its alleged ties to Al Qaeda.[25] Hell-bent on military action, Washington refused to allow any troublesome evidence to stand in its way.

The military occupation established a colonial regime that, with modest British help, the U.S. used to set about remaking the economic, political, and legal structures of Iraq—itself a violation of international law, contained in provisions of the fourth 1949 Geneva Convention (chapter III) governing conditions of foreign control. This convention stipulates that an occupying power is obliged to respect the laws, customs, and institutions of the nation it has taken over, but the U.S., motivated by its grand strategy of reconfiguring the Middle East, had its sights on transforming everything to satisfy its own objectives. Thus, according to Order 39 (September 2003), signed by L. Paul Bremer III for the coalition authority, the Iraq economy was to be privatized and opened up to foreign investment, with U.S. and British corporations having the inside track. Rather than safeguarding domestic laws and resources, the U.S. moved to secure its own economic priorities, assuming that its military could (with help from private contractors) manage the chaos and violence. As of early 2009 no Western political, military, or corporate leaders had been held accountable under the Geneva Protocols, even as Hussein and other former Ba'ath leaders were being tried, convicted, and (in some cases) executed for war crimes before the ad hoc Baghdad Tribunal.

U.S. criminality in Iraq has been all the more brazen given the deceit and cynical contempt for legality that accompanied the American drive to colonize the Middle East. Everything that took place grew out of longstanding U.S. economic and strategic aims in the region, a function in great measure of corporate globalization. The invasion and occupation—far from being a mistaken overreach by the clumsy Bush administration—occurred within a definite logic: to open up Middle Eastern economies to Western corporate penetration. As Antonia Juhasz writes, this was the Bush agenda from the outset: in the midst of bloodshed and chaos, U.S. companies were making billions of dollars in profits from the war, with more tens of billions and even trillions to be made in the future.[26] Following 2003, according to Juhasz, oil corporations were reaping all-time profits off the war, as were military-related firms like Bechtel, Halliburton, Chevron, Lockheed-Martin, and Raytheon. The year 2004 was Chevron's most profitable ever (at $13.3 billion) while Bechtel's gains reached a new high at $17.4 billion the same year. To sustain such profits, however, the U.S. would have to reshape the entire Iraqi infrastructure, including the government, laws, and social policies, to allow for maximum foreign investment—a goal that, while patently illegal, was embraced from the first days of the occupation. To this end the U.S. began to transform the whole political and economic terrain—banking, investment, taxation, copyright laws, trade, the media, even education. This agenda was already laid out in the 1992 Defense Planning Guidance document and reaffirmed later, establishing Washington's imperial supremacy in a post-Soviet world, with domination of Iraq a linchpin in the struggle for Pax Americana.

Although regime change was not originally central to a Bush agenda, Juhasz points out that it was Bush who finally "unified military and corporate globalization into one mighty weapon of Empire."[27] Perpetual war would be needed to confront actual and potential "threats"—such threats understood as challenges to U.S. global hegemony. In the build-up to war, Juhasz points out, the large oil and military companies were supporters of military action, hopeful of both super-profits from the campaign and an opening-up of the Middle East to further business investments. Although Iraqi oil reserves were listed at 112 billion barrels, some estimates anticipated discoveries of up to 400 billion barrels—which would amount to the largest deposits in the world. Hussein had excluded U.S. oil companies from bidding for lucrative contracts during the 1990s, preferring instead to deal with Russia, France, and China, and this was surely a major U.S. consideration in the drive toward regime change.[28] With occupation and the setting up of a puppet government, the U.S. was able to frame a new Iraq Constitution enshrining Bremer's Order 39, permitting continued occupation and new (mostly U.S.) licenses to "reconstruct" the economy and society. Here the Bush agenda worked to privatize state-owned industries and resources (including oil), opening up access to transnational corporations. The new government was "free" to sign huge contracts with such oil giants as ExxonMobil and Chevron. In 2004, the U.S., chronically short of combat troops and logistical supports, deployed 14,000 security guards to protect the Iraqi oil infrastructure against sabotage and insurgency.[29] After 2003, moreover, Iraq oil exports to the U.S. steadily increased, reaching more than one million barrels daily by mid 2006. Thus the occupation, in many ways a human catastrophe, eventually delivered lucrative benefits to Western corporations even in the midst of chaos, violence, and unpredictability.

The flagrant criminality of this project—its motivation sheer theft and exploitation—has been largely ignored within the American public sphere, as if the ends of that project were a matter of simple entitlement. The idea of U.S. domination over the Middle East has become an article of faith in Washington, virtually across the ideological spectrum—an updated sign of national exceptionalism. This view shaped the thinking of 2006 Iraq Study Group members, an ostensibly bipartisan gathering charged with arriving at an "alternative" war strategy to Bush's failed project. Their report amounted to nothing more than a refined blueprint for maintaining U.S. hegemony in the region. Recommendation 63, for example, calls on U.S. leaders to "assist Iraqi leaders to reorganize the national oil industry as a commercial enterprise" while "encouraging investment in Iraq's oil sector by the international community and by international energy companies"—as U.S. troops (in possibly smaller numbers) continue to occupy the country well into the future. The report echoed the ideas of such neocon think-tanks as the American Enterprise Institute (AEI) and the Heritage Foundation, which in March 2003 had called for full privatization of Iraq's oil economy. Although the Study Group looked to reduced American troop commitments, its hope was that Iraqi armed forces and law enforcement agencies (naturally with U.S. funding and cadres of "advisers") could solidify the Washington-installed power structure. The U.S. has built sprawling permanent bases around the country while the newly constructed American Embassy in Baghdad became the largest in the world—clear indications the Bush agenda (as of early 2009) was alive and well even with the transition to the Obama presidency, which largely carried forward the sentiments of the Iraq Study Group.

This agenda, as we have seen, is not confined to Iraq or even the Middle East; but is global in its aspirations. Goals spelled out in the crucial 2002 National Security Strategy document and reaffirmed in the 2006 version placed Iran squarely within the imperial agenda, its government targeted for regime change on the same pretext that justified war against Iraq: alleged possession of WMD, links to terrorism, tyrannical rule. Once again the world is being told that the U.S. must confront a fearsome, imminent threat to world peace. The pages of such neocon periodicals as the *Weekly Standard* were by 2006 promoting another war even at a time of mounting disaster in Iraq. In September 2006 Congress enacted and Bush signed the Iran Freedom Support Act, in the spirit of the 1998 Iraq Liberation Act, giving Bush (and later Obama) virtual carte blanche to carry out yet another war of aggression. Seemingly unthinkable just a few years ago, the supposed need to initiate military operations against Iran had by early 2007 gained new currency. Thus neocon Joshua Muravchik urged aerial bombardments of Iran, with or without U.N. approval, since Iran's "secret nuclear program" (never shown to be a *weapons* program) cannot be tolerated. He is convinced such attacks will undermine the Iranian government, but if that fails a ground invasion should be contemplated. Muravchik writes that "[Iranian leader] Ahmadinejad wants to be the new Lenin. Force is the only thing that can stop him."[30] Here, oddly enough, the current designated enemy is no Hitler on-the-move but rather a "new Lenin" ostensibly ready to launch world revolution.

As Scott Ritter argues in *Target Iran*, plans for regime change in Iran will predictably lead to even greater disaster than what has taken place in Iraq. He writes that American politicians have been propagandized into supporting possible military aggression against Iran, in the absence of evidence that the Ahmadinejad regime is a threat to U.S. national security.[31] The main problem, according to Ritter, is tenacious Israeli pressure to move before Iran acquires nuclear-weapons capacity—pressure simultaneously exerted mostly through the pro-Israel lobby in Washington. Thus: "The conflict currently under way between the United States and Iran is first and foremost a conflict born in Israel. It is based upon the Israeli contention that Iran poses a threat to Israel, and defined by Israeli assertions that Iran possesses a nuclear weapons program. None of this has been shown to be true."[32] As Ritter shows, it was the same pro-Israel lobby that influenced Congress members to support Iranian opposition groups working for regime change. (It is worth noting here that Iran, a signatory to the Nuclear Non-Proliferation Treaty, is completely entitled to explore and develop atomic energy, and no inspections process has found that the Iranians have a weapons program. The Israelis not only have such a program but possess a huge stockpile of nuclear weapons. The same is true of both Pakistan and India, the latter country receiving nuclear assistance from the U.S. despite not being an NPT signatory.)

As usual, U.S. geopolitical objectives are concealed beneath phony claims of threats to U.S. national security. Gestures toward military action (a violation of the U.N. Charter) have trumped diplomatic overtures—in this instance a willingness to even participate in direct talks with the Iranians—a curious behavior for leaders claiming to favor peace, democracy, and security. The U.S. has refused direct negotiations with the Ahmadinejad government while also rejecting Iranian efforts to secure a non-aggression pact. The push toward some form of warfare once again seems to follow the logic of necessity, obscuring efforts at political solutions. Unfortunately, as Ritter argues, "while the American public may be pre-programmed to accept the necessity of war with Iran, even if no such necessity exists, there has been no effort to prepare America, or even the world at large, for the awful reality of what a war with Iran would entail."[33] The potentially cataclysmic repercussions of U.S. or Israeli military intervention extend far beyond those of the ill-fated Iraq adventure, since Iran possesses the capacity to destabilize the global system.

DESCENT INTO LAWLESSNESS

As the Nuremberg precedent and the U.N. Charter both affirm, the first use of armed force against a sovereign state—except in cases of imminent self-defense—constitutes military aggression, a violation of international law. At Nuremberg, as we have seen, crimes against peace were considered the "supreme crime" for which Germany and Japan were held culpable during World War II. The Nazi regime was understood to be a criminal enterprise, its leaders guilty of deliberate and concerted plans to invade and occupy the territory of several European nations. If the entire regime was held to be a criminal entity, moreover, it followed that its top decision-makers as well as many of its functionaries should be prosecuted for their actions, and this indeed took place at both Nuremberg and Tokyo in the late 1940s. As Joseph Persico writes: "Not the slightest doubt could remain that Nazi Germany had planned and waged aggressive war, that it had fought that conflict with flagrant disregard for the rules of warfare, and that independent of any military necessity, it had committed mass murder on an inconceivable scale."[34] Precisely the same judgment could be rendered concerning U.S. actions in Iraq, but of course not only there. Yet neither the Nuremberg legacy nor the U.N. Charter—not to mention a long series of treaties and protocols—seem to have deterred U.S. leaders from following the path of war-making.

The U.S. has not only brazenly subverted international legality, its leaders have remained free of prosecution, beyond the reach of global rules, canons, and agreements. Meanwhile, the world descends further into a Hobbesian state of lawlessness.

The shameful reality is that, despite sharpening economic and political problems that have beset Washington, the legacy of U.S. exceptionalism remains very much alive—a subversion of legal universality in the absence of which efforts to solidify a regimen of peace and human rights become meaningless. In this context the U.S. intervention in Iraq has only exacerbated tendencies toward militarism and war, not to mention terrorism and the spread of WMD. U.S. contempt for the international law it professes to value so highly endows Washington with an outlaw status, mocking its lofty pretensions. By rejecting international conventions as too constraining or "obsolete" the U.S. has in effect embraced a superpower morality placing itself above the mundane concerns of other nations. By the early twenty-first century, U.S. global criminality had become so ordinary as to be taken for granted within the political culture. Where violations of international laws and norms become so routine and so flagrant they inevitably wind up as stable features of the political landscape.[35] Philippe Sands commented that "George Bush's America has become synonymous with lawlessness."[36] Long before the Bush presidency, however, the U.S. had become increasingly gripped by the ethos of war and aggression. Some academic theorists justified this state of affairs with rambling, obtuse treatises on the "limits of international law" since, as we know from historical example, imperial powers are expected (entitled?) to pursue nothing but their own selfish interests, by force where necessary. Any rival concept of global behavior, such as the accountability of *all* nations to contractual agreements and international rules, must be jettisoned as irrational if not utopian.[37]

Given the continuing legacy of American exceptionalism, this strident outlawry should hardly astonish any careful observer of the world scene. The Bush agenda for colonizing the Middle East is just one instance of U.S. foreign and military policy taking an aggressive turn, marked by a restlessness to throw away restraints on behavior. As Ritter observes: "The 2002 National Security Strategy of the United States represents a frontal assault on the basic framework of international law that had held the world together, however tenuously, since the end of World War Two. It also codified the doctrine of global hegemony on the part of the United States, replete with notions of preemptive war, unilateralism, and regime change."[38] Under these conditions Ritter sees U.S. willingness to honor international law as contingent on elite perceptions of national interest.[39]

Of course no U.S. political leader has ever believed that any facet of American global behavior could possibly be regarded as illegal or criminal; whatever occurs under the aegis of Washington decision-making is, by definition, noble, beyond the reach of ethical or legal condemnation. Mistakes are made, but the *ends* themselves simply cannot be questioned. Some opinion-makers insist that the U.S. represents an entirely new kind of empire, more benign and less exploitative than previous empires.[40] It follows that the actions of a benevolent empire demand more flexible criteria for judgment, as when global laws and treaties are broken in the service of higher purposes. Those standing in the way of U.S. power often find themselves depicted as impediments to human progress, as enemies of democracy and Western civilization, perhaps even as the reincarnation of Hitler and the Nazis. According to standard U.S. propaganda, Noriega, Milošević, and Hussein were all modern-day Hitlers who had to be stopped by (American) military force. Drawing on powerful myths of the 1940s "good war," the political and media establishment tends to portray domestic opponents of U.S. power as unpatriotic "appeasers," supporters of tyranny and/or terrorism. As in the case of the Japanese attack on Pearl Harbor, typical U.S. reactions to challenge are those of an innocent, wounded giant. Questions regarding the efficacy (much less morality) of U.S. military action under any conditions are dismissed as signs of weakness and cowardice, associated with liberals, feminists, and left-wing intellectuals who, if they had their way, would yield to every enemy of Washington. Atrocities and of course blunders do occur here and there, but American personnel and troops are dedicated patriots just doing their job, for better or worse, on the front lines of U.S. global interests. As during World War II, moreover, God is often recruited on the side of American power, endowing an imperial agenda with moral certitude. As Bush stated more than once in the lead up to the Iraq war, God had instructed the President to strike at the enemy with a mighty fist: even if illegal, the invasion and occupation would be entirely *legitimate*, affirming God's will in the epic struggle against Satanic Muslim terrorists.[41] Such embellishment of religious ideology was in fact always a linchpin of U.S. exceptionalism and colonialism. Today more than ever, the corporate media perpetuates every myth and deceit that contributes to a normalizing of U.S. outlawry within an elaborate political framework of imperial hegemony.

As for the Nuremberg principles, the hopes for binding international law and peaceful relations among nations that emerged from the rubble of World War II have been turned into nightmares. The late Walter Rockler, an American lawyer who prosecuted Nazis at Nuremberg, recently commented that the trials "had important symbolic value ... but no substantive impact." Criticizing the U.S./NATO military aggression against Yugoslavia, he said: "Wars and savagery have not been deterred, and I see no prospect that they will be deterred or punished in the near future." Military powers can always find reasons to violate international law, Rockler observed, adding "the rationale that we are simply enforcing international morality, even if it were true, would not excuse the military aggression and widespread killing."[42]

2
Warfare Against Civilians

Contrary to both official and popular mythology, civilian populations and related targets have always been the main victims of U.S. military ventures abroad and, more often than not, such victims were the result of deliberate military planning. If not always consciously intended, civilian casualties were nonetheless often a calculated element of armed-forces operations. Tariq Ali does not exaggerate when he writes that "the massacre of civilian populations was always an integral part of U.S. war strategy."[1] Nor does Edward Herman overstate the case when he observes that "U.S. military policy has long been based on strategies and tactics that involve a heavy civilian toll."[2] Yet one of the enduring residues of U.S. exceptionalism is the common belief that war crimes—including atrocities against civilians—are alien to the American tradition and character, owing to the presumably benevolent, democratic aims of U.S. foreign policy. War crimes are something committed by *others*—Nazis, Communists, terrorists, rogue tyrants, and the like. Common sense dictates that civilized democratic nations do not behave in such a fashion. Where U.S. savagery does come to light, as at My Lai in Vietnam and Abu Ghraib in Iraq, it is framed as the work of a few isolated thugs who will be punished by a system that holds them accountable. The idea that American leaders might be responsible for *recurrent* acts of mass murder is considered beyond the range of acceptable discourse. Given the lengthy and horrific record of U.S. war crimes, however, one must conclude that persistent collective denial remains an epidemic feature of the political culture.

We know that the history of European military assaults on Native peoples spans at least four centuries—what Ward Churchill refers to as a "vicious drive toward extermination" that has killed millions, a large percentage of which were defenseless civilians. Upon its founding the U.S. moved in the direction of exterminism at a time when its political and military leaders were proclaiming a civilized, enlightened agenda. Fueled by colonial expansion mixed with racist contempt for local populations, white massacres of Indian tribes were often systematic and planned, involving destruction of land and culture—war crimes by any reckoning, although such criminality was not yet internationally recognized or codified.[3] The later trajectory of American militarism was in great measure inherited from the Indian campaigns, given ideological articulation through such concepts as Manifest Destiny and the Monroe Doctrine. It was a tradition that, to varying degrees, gave permission for attacks on civilian targets.[4] As Caleb Carr writes, the U.S. was historically adept at constructing an "evangelical military" contemptuous of other nations and cultures that, once demonized, were ripe for targeting and possible destruction.[5] For more than a century the U.S. pursued imperial agendas by various means: wars of attrition, carpet bombing, free-fire zones, civilian relocations, local massacres, support for death squads, economic sanctions, attacks on public infrastructures, use of weapons of mass destruction. U.S. government and military leaders have consistently placed themselves beyond the reach of international laws and conventions, immune to established rules of engagement.

WORLD WAR II AND ITS LEGACY

Military assaults on civilian targets have been considered a breach of international law for more than a century. Such prohibitions are now a cornerstone of modern legality, regulating the behavior of all parties to armed conflict. By World War I the major powers had subscribed to certain rules of engagement, already outlined in The Hague Conventions of 1899 and 1907. It was generally agreed, for example, that warfare should be limited to actual combatants, with civilian populations immune from attack—although such norms, for the most part, were honored only abstractly. The Fourth Hague Convention in 1907, for example, stated (in Article 25) that "bombardment, by whatever means, of towns, villages, dwellings, or buildings which are undefended, is prohibited"; ("by whatever means" was meant to include aerial warfare, then only in its infancy.) The 1945 Charter of the International Military Tribunal defined war crimes as "violations of the laws or customs of war" that included wanton destruction and forms of armed assault that could not be defended as military necessity. At the Nuremberg tribunal, German leaders were charged with "the devastation of towns, not justified by military necessity, in violation of the laws of war." These violations were interpreted as wanton destruction of civilian targets but were never pursued since Allied leaders feared calling attention to their own (often more egregious) crimes that included far greater saturation bombing campaigns in Germany and Japan.

The World War II experience led to four Geneva Conventions in 1949 that arrived at international statutes to protect civilian populations in times of war, breaches of which were defined as war crimes. Expressly forbidden were willful killing, inhumane treatment, torture, extensive destruction not justified by military necessity or wantonly conducted, and mistreatment of prisoners of war. Both the U.S. and Britain fought hard, against efforts of the Red Cross, others groups, and many other nations, to eliminate or water down these Geneva protections, with limited success. Above all, they hoped to preserve maximum freedom to plan aerial bombardments, including atomic weapons, since this would become a fixture of military strategy. Additional Geneva Protocol One (1977) expanded earlier provisions to include a wider range of civilian objects. Thus Article 48 (Basic Rule) states that "Parties to the conflict shall at all times distinguish between the civilian population and combatants and between civilian objects and military objects and accordingly shall direct their operations only against military objectives," while Chapter II (Article 50) adds that "the presence within the civilian population of individuals who do not come within the definition of civilians does not deprive the population of its civilian character." Article 50 further states that armed attacks are illegal "which may be expected to cause incidental loss of civilian life, injury to civilians, damage to civilian objects, or a combination thereof, which would be excessive in relation to the concrete and direct military advantage anticipated." Article 54 prohibits attacks on objects indispensable to civilian populations, including foodstuffs, agriculture, livestock, water supplies, and irrigation works. Chapter IV (Article 57) concludes by stipulating that, "In the conduct of military operations, constant care shall be taken to spare the civilian population, civilians, and civilian objects." The U.S. is not a party to the Additional Protocols, but the statutes are binding on all states as an element of customary international law.[6]

During the twentieth century the international moral *Zeitgeist*, discussed in the introduction, has evolved to the point where perpetrators of war crimes and crimes against humanity could be tried before a tribunal. Moreover, beginning with Nuremberg and the U.N. Charter, the system of international law pertaining to war crimes had undergone progressive clarification, although bringing violators to justice would prove extremely difficult. When it comes to warfare against civilians, Nuremberg established the principle that no one, whatever their role in the decision-making hierarchy, is immune from prosecution—and no individual can avoid being charged on grounds of following superior orders. These precedents are now codified features of international law, imparting to rules of military engagement strong elements of continuity. The Nuremberg Charter defined four separate crimes: conspiracy to carry out aggressive war, the actual launching of aggression, killing, destroying, and plundering during a war not justified by military necessity, and crimes against humanity related to atrocities against civilians. While the Nazis were convicted mainly on the first two counts, the focus in this chapter is specifically on military attacks against civilian targets—violations that, in the language of Nuremberg and subsequent international statutes, extend to behavior under the heading "crimes against humanity." References to "ethnic cleansing" and "genocide," while often glibly applied to the actions of designated enemies, do not enter the picture here.

More recently, the 1998 statutes of the International Criminal Court (Article 8) define "serious violations of the laws and customs applicable in international armed conflict, within the established framework of international law," to include such behavior as "intentionally directing attacks against civilian populations" or "civilian objects, that is, objects which are not military objectives." The statutes add prohibitions against "launching an attack with the knowledge that such attack will cause incidental loss of life or injury to civilians or damage to civilian objects or widespread long-term and severe damage to the natural environment," as well as "attacking or bombarding, by whatever means, towns, villages, dwellings, or buildings which are undefended and which are not military objectives." The ICC further identifies as a war crime "employing poison or poisoned weapons" or devices "which are of a nature to cause superfluous injury or unnecessary suffering or which are inherently indiscriminate."[7]

Despite profound changes in the international moral *Zeitgeist* over the past several decades, however, sustained efforts to prosecute violators—that is, those responsible for planning and/or conducting warfare against civilians—have met severe limits and obstacles. The biggest problem has been refusal of the most powerful nations (above all the U.S.) to participate in or abide by rules and conventions having *universal* validity. In fact, international law, though vaguely formulated in many areas, was set up mainly for the benefit of the powerful. Later, its functioning tribunals (including Nuremberg and Tokyo) served largely as mechanisms of victors' justice, where everything was defined and arranged by the military winners. Global statutes themselves, moreover, are easily subverted where there is ambiguity and flexibility—reflected in the difficulty of separating military from civilian targets in the turbulence of armed conflict that, nowadays, blurs such distinctions in the context of guerrilla warfare and local insurgency. Questions regarding "military necessity" and "proportionality" of human costs relative to military ends become slippery in their concrete legal applications. Military units often justify assaults on civilian populations as a matter of strategic priorities: weakening enemy morale, impeding the workforce and industrial production, and undermining public infrastructures typically needed for both civilian and military activity. (While revenge can obviously be a factor here, perpetrators rarely admit this kind of motivation.) The very logic of counterinsurgency tactics— and in different ways, the "war on terror"—assumes that civilian casualties, clinically referred to as "collateral damage," will often be unavoidable, the inevitable by-product of violent warfare. What is legally or morally defensible under battlefield conditions can, admittedly, be difficult to establish with any degree of certainty. In most cases, however, claims of tolerable "collateral damage" are nothing more than flimsy justifications for going beyond commonly understood rules of warfare, while in other instances the death and destruction brought to civilians is so wanton and excessive as to render such arguments moot.

"COLLATERAL DAMAGE" OR MASS MURDER?

During the half-century since the end of World War II the U.S. has been easily the leading purveyor of violence on a global scale—the dark side of a political culture that champions freedom, democracy, and peace. No country qualifies as even a close second on this measure of barbarism. A rather conservative accounting of *civilians* killed by the U.S. military since 1945 would number in the vicinity of eight million, with higher estimates reaching double that figure. Add to this carnage the number of wounded, maimed, displaced, and imprisoned—more tens of millions, although no accurate figure is possible—then a more comprehensive picture of postwar U.S. militarism and its victims comes into focus. This picture reflects decades of U.S. warfare conducted against civilian populations and related targets, from Japan to Vietnam, from Korea to Afghanistan, from Laos to Iraq. It is an accounting, moreover, that should also include the massive (often permanent) environmental damage that

U.S. armed forces have left in their wake, as well as proxy warfare or secondary acts of violence financed and supported by the U.S. since the eighteenth century. Sadly, U.S. leaders have never faced moral, legal, or political accountability, either domestically or internationally, for wanton attacks on civilians fitting a long-established pattern of imperialism and militarism.

The rules of warfare have, with rare exceptions, never applied to U.S. global behavior. Had such rules ever come into play historically—as seemed to be the case during World War I, when civilians were spared the brunt of military carnage—they were mercilessly transcended by the final year of World War II, when large urban areas inhabited by millions of civilians became deliberate targets of military action. In the Pacific, this was scarcely limited to aerial terrorism (to be addressed later) but included ground and naval combat that appeared devoid of moral restraints on both sides. For its part, as John Dower explores in great detail, the U.S. carried out military operations with unbelievable savagery: prisoners were regularly tortured and shot, soldiers and civilians were massacred by the hundreds and even thousands, prisoners were buried alive in mass graves, survivors of sunken ships were strafed and killed at sea, towns and cities were annihilated with disregard for human life. Savagery of this kind was hardly isolated, nor was it always incidental to larger military strategies, much less the result of "collateral damage." It fitted an established *pattern*, accepted within the logic of the Pacific Theater operations. Thus high-ranking army officers were heard to say, for example, that "the 41st [unit] didn't take prisoners"—a sentiment that was frighteningly ordinary in the protracted conflict between the U.S. and Japan.[8]

The legacy of World War II, far from being the morally righteous "good war" handed down by U.S. propaganda, is one of militarism, racism, and imperialism on all sides, drenched in unlimited violence, including violence against innocent civilians. As Dower points out, for Americans "the Japanese were more hated than the Germans before as well as after Pearl Harbor ... They were perceived as a race apart—and an overwhelmingly monolithic one, at that." He adds:

The racist code words and imagery were often exceedingly graphic and contemptuous. The Western allies, for example, consistently emphasized the "subhuman" nature of the Japanese, routinely turning to images of apes and vermin to convey this ... Cartoonists, songwriters, filmmakers, war correspondents, and the mass media in general all seized on these images—and so did the social scientists and Asia experts who ventured to analyze the Japanese "national character" during the war.[9]

It follows that "such dehumanization ... merely facilitated the decision to make civilian populations the targets of concentrated attack, whether by conventional or nuclear weapons."[10] The Pacific War turned into one of the most barbaric conflicts in human history.

The Korean War of 1950–53, relatively hidden from history, took an even more horrendous toll of human life: aside from the torrent of bombs dropped by U.S. planes and massive offshore shelling by U.S. ships, American ground forces conducted themselves with extreme disregard for the rules of warfare in what became another ruthless war of attrition leading to possibly four million Korean deaths, mostly civilian. Referring to the entire Korean debacle, Stephen Endicott and Edward Hagerman write of a total war beginning in autumn 1950, when General Douglas MacArthur ordered his troops to destroy everything in their wake—factories, installations, means of communications, villages, cities, everything—from the Yalu River on the Chinese border to at least the 38th parallel. The authors observe that,

> as it had been in World War II, strategic bombing was extended to the mass destruction of civilian populations; and, as in World War II, the reservations that the United States had about the saturation bombing of Europeans in that earlier war were not extended to the Asians ... American military culture accepted the World War II standpoint that the mass destruction of civilians was a legitimate military target in an expanded war of attrition.[11]

Adamantly refusing any political settlement, MacArthur opted for a scorched-earth policy as his troops retreated and, with the frustrations of stalemate mounting, both he and President Truman considered using atomic weapons in Korea. General Matthew Ridgeway, Eighth Army commander, framed the conflict as an epic defense of God and Western civilization against godless Communist hordes. Driven by such fanaticism, the U.S. was prepared to extend the war to civilian populations and economic resources crucial to their survival. Thus eleven hydroelectric plants and other water resources were bombed in June 1952, and in August 1952 Pyongyang was destroyed as part of an assault, burning, and bombing campaign that was later extended to 78 other North Korean cities and towns. The U.S. decision to target civilians, to wage merciless war in disregard of international law and rules of engagement, was planned and systematic, going to the top of the power structure. The Chiefs of Staff in Washington directed U.S. military forces to wage war with contempt for all precedents.[12] Flagrant war crimes were committed by government and military leaders, as well as military personnel in the field, but no one was ever charged (much less convicted) in the aftermath of these crimes.

U.S. military policy and conduct in Indochina was even more brutal, involving another war of attrition this time spanning more than a decade (1961 to 1974) rather than three years, as in Korea. Horrendous death and destruction in Vietnam, Laos, and Cambodia resulted not only from sustained aerial bombardment but from ground warfare of varied types: strategic hamlets where civilians were thrown into enclosed compounds, free-fire zones, search-and-destroy missions, defoliation with chemical agents, deployment of hundreds of thousands of soldiers prepared to kill anything that moved. The war displaced more than ten million people, with hundreds of thousands relocated to hamlets serving as glorified concentration camps. By the end of this warfare the U.S. had destroyed 9000 out of 15,000 hamlets, 25 million acres of farmland, 12 million acres of forest, and 1.5 million farm animals. Towns and villages were bombed, torched, and bulldozed, their inhabitants often rounded up and slaughtered. Nearly one million orphans were left, along with 181,000 disabled persons and one million widows. More than 19 million gallons of toxic herbicides were dumped in the South alone, by far the greatest use of chemical weaponry ever. Vast regions of Vietnamese countryside were pulverized in the name of "pacification" and "nation-building," code words for the most ruthless counterinsurgency program ever undertaken.[13] In his lengthy exploration of the barbaric Phoenix Program, Douglas Valentine refers to an elaborate torture regimen that was well known in the field but largely kept secret from the American people. He writes that "prison conditions and interrogation practices in Vietnam were brutal—especially those taken out of sight." He quotes former Vietcong prisoner Tran Van Truong in his book *A Vietnam Memoir* as saying that an American interrogator told him "I have a right to beat you to death. You and all the other Vietcong they bring in here. There aren't any laws here to protect you. In here you are mine." Describing the locale of the Phoenix Program where he was taken, Van Truong added that "it looked like a medieval torture chamber. Iron hooks and ropes hung from the ceiling, as did chains and ankle and wrist rings."[14]

Massive long-term health, agricultural, environmental, and social harm to a poor third-world country will continue to be felt for decades, if not longer. Such criminal deeds, the product of carefully planned technowar waged across three presidencies, have never been officially acknowledged by any U.S. government official.

As in Korea, the standard *modus operandi* in Vietnam was to destroy virtually any impediment to military success in the field—to "kill 'em all," as the title of the BBC documentary on American war crimes in Korea suggests. "Search-and-destroy" meant attacking civilians along with combatants in the midst of guerrilla war where insurgents commanded overwhelming popular support, where boundaries separating fighters from noncombatants were inescapably blurred. Not only civilians but animals and the entire life-support system became part of the combat zone, fit targets in a war of attrition. In this setting, when troops arrived at any village or town they frequently began by opening fire, often supported by helicopter gun ships, on the sensible assumption that local populations harbored "enemy" forces (the Vietcong) involving anyone sympathetic to the resistance. Steeped in a military culture extending to the highest ranks, U.S. troops were rewarded according to the well-known calculus of "body count"—a "count" never limited to identifiable combatants, nor in reality could it have been. As one GI put it: "We're here to kill gooks, period." A common U.S. troop refrain in Vietnam went: "Bomb the schools and churches. Bomb the rice fields too. Show the children what napalm can do."[15] Still another refrain: "Kill one, they call you a murderer. Kill thousands, and they call you a conqueror. Kill them all, and they won't do anything."[16] One common viewpoint in combat areas was, if it's dead it must be VC (Vietcong). Pressures to record high body counts, to destroy everything that moved, automatically gutted any rules of engagement: whatever was stipulated in international law or the Uniform Code of Military Justice (UCMJ) became moot in the frenzied movement of battle. Units that routinely engaged in murder, rape, torture, and other atrocities did everything possible to ensure that no soldier would press charges, and of course few did, and even those who did were usually ignored or stonewalled at the higher levels. Under these conditions, moreover, prisoners were rarely taken, and those who were usually ended up tortured and/or executed. All such criminality was facilitated by a military culture in which the Vietnamese—like the Japanese and Koreans earlier—were viewed as subhuman savages, in a reprise of the Indian crusades. At the Dellums Committee hearings in April 1971 several veterans testified as to how military training itself prepared them for brutal, unrestrained killing in the field, for dehumanizing the enemy to the point that killing without mercy became possible, even celebrated, by armed-forces personnel at all levels.

As in Korea, U.S. forces pursued a relentless, total war—a war that spread from Vietnam to Laos and Cambodia—in a futile effort to quell a popular, intensely dedicated nationalist insurgency. "Victory" was impossible short of a full-scale nuclear assault that would have reduced the entire country to rubble. As it was, American firepower was nothing short of genocidal, dwarfing the combined bombardments of World War II and leading to the loss of at least three million lives (again mostly civilians). As William Gibson writes, U.S. war managers adopted a "production model of war" in Indochina, a commitment to technowar that, pushed to extremes, was bound to produce *systematic* destruction of the land and its people.[17] This lies at the very heart of the U.S. criminal legacy in Vietnam, insofar as crimes were on the whole *routine*, the product of imperial hubris, although no government officials or military personnel were ever charged—with the famous exception of Lt. William Calley for his role in the My Lai massacre of March 1968, when nearly 500 villagers were shot to death in cold blood. The problem (as we shall see) was that My Lai was no deviation from the norm; massacres of the sort were common but were either never reported or were simply covered up by the military. As the Bertrand Russell Tribunal reported at the time, American war crimes were of such magnitude and implicated so many high-level political and military officials that only a Nuremberg-style international court could have brought genuine justice. Since the perpetrators of mass murder and other war crimes were able to hide behind superpower status, there would be no repeat of Nuremberg and no justice. Indeed one of the leading war criminals of the period, President Richard Nixon, would seemingly have the last word: "When the President does it, that means it is not illegal"—a maxim that, in the case of Nixon, pertained only to foreign affairs.

Compared to the Indochina carnage, the U.S. invasion of Panama in December 1989 ended up as a relatively minor, brief episode resulting in moderate casualties. Sudden as it was, however, the operation (actually planned six months in advance) was intense, high-tech, and deadly, revealing again the contempt U.S. armed forces had for the welfare of local populations. With the ostensible goal of arresting Panamanian leader Manuel Noriega and protecting American lives, the invasion produced some 4000 civilian deaths and

50,000 homeless, according to the 1990 Independent Commission of Inquiry. Oppositional political groups were smashed or outlawed, with people arrested and detained for weeks, even months, with no formal charges, and many others (both military and civilian) winding up as "disappeared."[18] The Pentagon's strategy for rapid victory meant using heavy firepower over a small, densely populated territory, with predictable results. According to one eyewitness report: "Before reaching the street, we saw a group of some 18 U.S. soldiers coming down the street. We saw them entering each house and residents coming out followed by the soldiers and then we saw houses one-by-one going up in smoke. The U.S. soldiers were burning our houses."[19] Commenting on the fruits of technowar in Panama, Chu Chu Martinez said: "The volume of U.S. firepower and the refinement of their weapons is incredible. They did in Panama more or less what Hitler did in Spain, using it as a practice ground for the weapons he would use during World War II."[20] In this case, the dress rehearsal was for the first Gulf War little more than a year later.

As in most other instances of U.S. armed intervention, the pretext was entirely bogus and the action itself a violation of international law. There was no actual threat from Panama, and therefore no possible claim of self-defense. The real motives underlying the attack became widely known—to nullify President Bush's wimp image, to show the need for an increased Pentagon budget as the Soviet presence declined, to send a message to other third-world countries thinking of stepping out of line, to reaffirm the U.S. hold over the Panama Canal. Both the U.N. Charter and the Rio Treaty of the Organization of American States (OAS) permitted military attacks only as defense against foreign threat—which was obviously not the case here. The U.S. evaded these restrictions while the OAS repudiated Washington's flagrant intervention and its arrest of a foreign leader (Noriega), calling for immediate withdrawal of U.S. troops from Panama.[21] Referring also to the earlier U.S. attack on Grenada, Philip Wheaton writes: "When we put these items from U.S. invasions of Grenada and Panama together, they appear to be an outline for what we have called the *total war model*: the Pentagon's strategy for quick and decisive interventions against Third World nations when the circumstances are propitious."[22] The Iraq situation, of course, would bring this "model" into much greater relief.

It was during Desert Storm (winter 1991) that the U.S. military first unveiled technowar in its full glory: Iraq became another "free-fire zone" for armor, artillery, and air force, with minimal reliance on infantry. No less than 110,000 aerial sorties were flown, dropping some 88,000 tons of bombs in just a few weeks, on a country virtually bereft of air defenses. The USAF pulverized the Iraqi infrastructure while suffering few casualties of its own (until later, when illness and death from depleted uranium and other toxic agents used by the U.S. became visible). At the end of combat, with nothing left in doubt, American planes bombed and strafed retreating Iraqi troops, killing at least 20,000 on the "highway of death"—a gruesome diversion violating The Hague and Geneva conventions. Bombings, moreover, continued regularly after the main warfare had come to an end. The U.S. used thousands of artillery shells and bombs tipped with DU, ensuring that radioactive substances would remain in the water, soil, and food chain for decades.[23] In all, Desert Storm brought (by conservative estimates) 200,000 deaths to Iraq from direct military engagement, an estimated half of which were civilians.

Desert Storm was followed by more than a decade of harsh economic sanctions against Iraq, enforced mainly by the U.S. and Britain under U.N. auspices and giving rise to as many as one million civilian deaths. Sanctions were based on the hypocritical insistence that Iraq (alone) dispose of its weapons of mass destruction— with no proof, moreover, that it ever possessed a nuclear agenda. The embargo cruelly and deliberately blocked imports of medical supplies, water-treatment technology, even certain foodstuffs that, under an excessively broad definition of "dual use," might be considered valuable to the Iraqi military. Sanctions policies have been employed regularly by the U.S., which started using this economic weapon in the 1950s. As always, the main victims in Iraq were civilians, a large percentage of them children. The 1977 Additional Protocols to Geneva prohibit measures depriving the civilian population of goods indispensable to its survival, with Article 18 even mandating *relief* operations to aid a civilian population suffering "undue hardships owing to lack of support essential for its survival, such as foodstuffs and medical supplies" as a result of military destruction. The U.S. at one point had obstructed every humanitarian effort, initiated by NGOs as well as members of the U.N. Security Council, to lift sanctions against Iraq. Writing in *Harpers*, Joy Gordon characterized the sanctions as a "legitimized act of mass slaughter," adding: "Epidemic suffering is needlessly visited on Iraqis via U.S. fiat inside the U.N. Security Council. With that body, the U.S. consistently thwarted Iraq from satisfying its most basic humanitarian needs, using sanctions as nothing less than a deadly weapon."[24] More than a "deadly weapon"—in reality a weapon of mass destruction that, ironically, was supposedly used to get rid of the very WMD that never existed.

The U.S. invasion and occupation of Iraq constitutes one of the most extensive periods of war crimes in modern history, with still no end in sight (as of spring 2009). The initial "shock-and-awe" campaign offers a perfect case study in wanton violence against civilians, with indiscriminate death and destruction brought to densely populated urban centers. The campaign, modeled on the Nazi *Blitzkrieg* approach, converges with the larger carnage, following years of military action, occupation, and bloodbath of civil-war proportions that by late 2006 had cost an average of 3000 Iraqi lives monthly. The public infrastructure, including water supplies, health care, communications, electricity, and other basic services, was reduced to a shambles, a crisis exacerbated by a jobless rate of more than 50 percent. The society was riveted by violence and social dislocation, creating more than three million refugees scattered across bordering nations.[25] From Desert Storm through twelve years of sanctions, bombings, and covert operations paving the way toward more war and occupation, Iraq was overwhelmed by a cycle of death and destruction—a terrible criminal record by any accounting. In October 2006 a team of U.S. and Iraqi epidemiologists reported an estimated 655,000 people had died in Iraq following the March 2003 invasion—a report overseen by the Johns Hopkins School of Public Health and published in the journal *Lancet*.[26] As Nuremberg affirmed in 1946, those guilty of crimes against peace must be held responsible for everything that follows, in this case the ensuing atrocities, combat debacles, collapse of infrastructure, social breakdown, civil strife, torture of detainees, *everything*.

As in Vietnam, where U.S. soldiers were exhorted by commanding officers to elevate "body counts" as indicators of combat success, in Iraq such orders (usually carefully finessed) typically came from the upper ranks. For example, testimony in late 2006 was given to the effect that Colonel Michael Steele, commander of the 101st Airborne Division's Third Brigade and veteran of the 1993 Somalia campaign, issued orders to "kill all military-aged males" and handed out knives to his soldiers as a reward for kills.[27] Steele's attitude was understood to be rather common in the field. U.S. military culture in Iraq embraced a frenzied anti-Arab hatred that could, and did, lead to episodes of sadistic, random violence. As in Korea and Vietnam, rules of engagement seem to have little meaning in an environment where virtually *all* civilians (and not just military-aged males) are invariably treated as sinister demons—as terrorists now, Communists then.

The worst U.S. criminal behavior, however, involved military operations in urban centers, beginning with the famous "shock-and-awe" bombardments in March 2003 that kicked off the invasion. Such attacks on civilian targets (even where combatants might be located) are prohibited by the 1977 Geneva Convention (Articles 51, 52, and 57), referring to the destruction of public centers of life where even incidental (much less grievous) loss of civilian life can be expected. The targeting of dense population zones in Baghdad, Fallujah, Ramadi, and other cities with massive firepower was destined—and most probably *intended*, judging from results—to produce heavy civilian casualties. (There is in fact a certain military logic to such operations, as we have seen.) These tactics, relying on often concentrated bombardment from ground and air, not only marked the onset of invasion but were employed regularly throughout the occupation. Aside from the standard inventory of high-explosive bombs, missiles, and artillery shells, the U.S. arsenal has included weaponry tipped with DU, white phosphorous, napalm, and cluster bombs called "all-purpose air-delivered cluster weapons systems" designed to spread thousands of shrapnel pieces across large areas as it dismembers human bodies. The use of such weaponry was clearly meant to inflict maximum damage across a wide territory as the U.S. moved to crush popular rebellion. By late 2006, the consequences of prolonged occupation and civil strife had become acute: Baghdad, with a greater population of five million, was transformed into a shell of a city, its inhabitants victims of repeated troop home-invasions (up to 90,000 reported each month at the peak), strict curfews, round-ups, and other local atrocities— hardly the foundation of a U.S.-imported democracy.

The U.S. assault on Fallujah in November 2004 left a city of 350,000 people in ruins, with hundreds of civilians dead and most residents homeless—their food sources, water supplies, electricity, and medical services destroyed. The military purpose was to demolish a major center of the Iraqi resistance, with vengeance in response to local attacks on U.S. troops an added catalyst. Ground and aerial bombardment of the mostly defenseless civilian population came round-the-clock for several days while Marines cordoned off routes of escape and free-fire zones were exploited to maximum effect. In less than one nightmarish week, thanks to the power of technowar, a medium-sized city was turned into ruins comparable to Dresden or Stalingrad, as the U.S. military pulled out all stops to quell the insurgency. Desolate streets were filled with traumatized people, many of them children, seeking food, water, shelter, and medical services. Viewing the carnage, one Marine was quoted as saying: "It's kind of too bad we destroyed everything, but at least we gave them a chance for a new start." Others commented that Fallujah got just what it deserved for "harboring terrorists."[28] The real terrorism, of course, must be laid at the doorstep of U.S. militarism, its planners located at the Pentagon and White House.

The violence unleashed on Fallujah was indiscriminate, with few limits or restraints. Hundreds of homes were destroyed or badly damaged. Hospitals and other public structures were attacked, most of them destroyed. Cluster bombs were dropped by the thousands, along with containers of white phosphorous, both used as anti-personnel weapons. According to one observer, U.S. forces "shot all the sheep. Any animals people owned were shot. Helicopters shot all the animals and anything that moved in the villages surrounding Fallujah." Another resident said: "The rubble from the bombed houses covered up the bodies, and nobody could get to them because people were too afraid even to drive a bulldozer. Even walking out of your home was just about impossible."[29] To an extent greater than in Desert Storm, in Fallujah the U.S. planned assaults on facilities essential to civilian life and material production, which became a sort of microcosm of U.S. military behavior across Iraq.

The U.S. record of warfare against civilians spans many decades and geographical settings, in a context of extended military deployments around the globe. It is a record of endless *repetition*, an established pattern with civilian casualties simply part of the general calculus. The consequences of armed attacks are usually predictable and thus far out of proportion to any military end claimed as a legitimate outcome. Further, where the *aims* of military force can be shown to be in the service of imperial agendas, it follows that *no civilian casualties* are defensible within any reasonable ethical framework. (Nor, for that matter, are *military* casualties justifiable in such a case.) In cases where warfare is clearly defensible, as with U.S. entry into World War II, the usual criteria of proportionality still apply, as with the saturation and atomic bombing of Japanese cities at a time when the outcome of war had been decided. In any event, the extensive U.S. record of attacks on civilian targets reveals the bankruptcy of framing casualties as a strict function of combat miscalculations, tactical mistakes, and "collateral damage."

Despite the advertised benefits of "precision" high-tech warfare, the civilian toll resulting from U.S. military actions has been outrageously high throughout the postwar years—and indeed in much of the preceding century. Similarly, public callousness regarding foreign casualties seems to have declined little, if at all, over time, scarcely surprising for a militarized culture that has deepened across the past few decades.[30] The human lives of others—especially those with dark skins—continues to be devalued, written off as an inevitable cost of war. The global reach of U.S. military power is increasingly equated with a pervasive ethos of imperial arrogance, the logical expression of national exceptionalism and Manifest Destiny. As Phyllis Bennis observes: "This American-style law of empire [has] exuded extraordinary arrogance, the arrogance of absolute power unchallenged by any other global force."[31] This outlook became an accepted faith within post-Cold War neocon ideology that entered mainstream foreign policy-making, especially after 9/11. This has meant a valorization of warrior politics, merging with what Barbara Ehrenreich calls the "sacralization of war"—a "burst of nationalist religiosity" in which foreign populations are faceless, dehumanized, and demonized, nowhere more so than in the jingoistic mass media.[32]

Military training in the U.S. feeds on this ethos, generating a conversion process that Richard Rhodes calls a "brutalization ethos," marked by an easy willingness to kill, especially where the killing is depersonalized (as in the case of technowar). The act of killing, evident from many personal accounts in Vietnam, can bring pleasure and even excitement much as in the violent spectacles of ancient Rome.[33] In the boot camp the military is charged with preparing recruits for the transcendence of moral and social constraints; the actual consequences of the battlefield experience become normalized, acceptable. This is why instances of U.S. war crimes have been so widely ignored, denied, suppressed, and, where necessary, covered up. Even as Washington regularly denounces others for war crimes and human rights abuses, its own legacy encounters silence among religious leaders, government officials, intellectuals, and the popular media—a silence made all the easier when criminal behavior is perpetrated behind such enlightened claims regarding "democracy," "human rights," and "social progress."

AERIAL TERRORISM: FROM TOKYO TO BAGHDAD

Since the final months of World War II, the U.S. military has dropped tens of millions of tons of bombs on several mostly defenseless countries, with human casualties (the vast majority civilian) reaching well into the millions. Since the 1920s, war managers have placed increasing faith in the efficacy of aerial warfare: at that time planes were envisioned as awesome destructive machines capable of bringing military efficiency and order to the chaos and unpredictability of ground and naval operations. Bombing from high altitudes was a nascent form of technowar. By 1944 and 1945 this faith assumed new dimensions as first Britain and then the U.S. embraced plans for "strategic" or area bombing in Germany and Japan, ostensibly to end the war more quickly but in reality mostly for purposes of revenge, weapons testing, and sending political messages. With incendiary assaults on German cities (Hamburg, Berlin, and Dresden the most noteworthy) by the Royal Air Force, U.S. General Curtis LeMay saw a new model of aerial warfare with vast possibilities for striking the Japanese, with the idea of burning cities to the ground while minimizing American casualties. For U.S. military planners the likelihood of widespread violence and destruction seemed to open up exciting new opportunities for warfare. As Sven Lindqvist writes in *A History of Bombing*: "People between the wars had been afraid to be bombed back to barbarism—to filth, starvation, and the rats. But during the postwar period, especially for American men, barbarism began to look promising. The threat of destruction opened the door for male fantasies with roots in the old dreams of the wild west."[34] The strategy of technowar by means of aerial warfare remains a cornerstone of U.S. military power to the present day.

One problem with aerial bombardment is that it inescapably obliterates any distinction between combatants and noncombatants, between military and civilian targets—all the more so for strategic bombing which, by definition, rains death and destruction more or less indiscriminately across wide parcels of territory, often in urban centers. Boasts of "precision bombing" have always been greatly exaggerated, especially when "targets" themselves are hard to identify (as in guerrilla warfare) or when bombs or missiles explode across ever-widening zones. Article 25 of the Fourth Hague Convention in 1907 states that "bombardment, by whatever means, of towns, villages, dwellings, or buildings which are undefended, is prohibited"—still a valid principle of international law.[35] Efforts to deepen and further codify these statutes have been, predictably, fiercely resisted by the U.S. and Britain, nations that refused to prosecute the Germans and Japanese after World War II for bombing civilian populations, knowing they were even more guilty of the same crimes. Such rejectionism continued into the Geneva Convention proceedings of 1948, the U.S. being especially opposed to any restraints on its capacity to wage aerial combat (including the use of nuclear weapons). The two countries worked diligently to block any reference to aerial "war crimes" from the statutes. As Lindqvist notes: "The victorious powers could hardly forbid bombing of civilians without incriminating themselves for what they had already done and planned to continue doing."[36] Finally, in 1977 Protocol One of the Geneva Convention was signed by 124 nations, despite continued U.S. resistance to any laws guaranteeing protection to civilians. The basic rule states: "In order to ensure respect for and protection of the civilians population and civilian objects, the parties to the conflict shall at all times distinguish between the civilian population and combatants and between civilian objects and military objectives and accordingly shall direct their operations only against military objectives." Article 52 further states that "attacks shall be limited strictly to military objectives." Article 54, as mentioned earlier, contains additional references—for example: "It is prohibited to attack, destroy, remove, or render useless objects indispensable to the survival of the civilian population, such as foodstuff, agricultural areas ... crops, livestock, drinking water installations and supplies and irrigation works." Article 57 warns those planning military attacks to "refrain from deciding to launch any attack which may be expected to cause incidental loss of civilian life, injury to civilians, damage to civilian objects, or a combination thereof."[37]

If strictly adhered to, such provisions would rule out aerial warfare directed against populated areas or civilian infrastructures—the very methodology often favored by the Pentagon since 1945, and precisely why military planners vehemently objected to those provisions. In July 1945 American planes, with the Pacific War virtually ended, raided 66 mostly defenseless Japanese cities with no serious military purpose in mind, burning most of them to ashes and killing up to 500,000 civilians. On March 9–10, 1945, hundreds of U.S. planes attacked Tokyo with incendiary bombs, killing at least 100,000 people and making another one million homeless—again, without real military significance. As is well known, on August 6 and 9, 1945, the U.S. dropped atomic bombs on Hiroshima and

Nagasaki, unprotected urban centers with little military import, killing a total of at least 200,000 civilians. General Curtis LeMay and his aides celebrated these raids with enthusiastic testimonials to the awesome power of aerial warfare. General MacArthur's aide, General Bonner Fuller, on the other hand, described the raids as "one of the most ruthless and barbaric killings of noncombatants in all history."[38] From 1946 to 1948 the International Military Tribunal for the Far East tried Japanese government and military elites for war crimes, but in the actual course of events the U.S. was the far more serious offender. Of course, since the U.S. emerged victorious none of its officials were ever brought to justice, nor was the very *discourse* of U.S. war crimes ever broached (except by the Japanese themselves).

As A. C. Grayling writes in *Among the Dead Cities* (2006), the most extensive ethical and political treatment of these issues, "the area-bombing campaigns of the Second World War were as a whole morally criminal."[39] As he puts it, bombing civilians from the distance and anonymity of 20,000 feet is really no different from shooting innocent, defenseless people with guns at point-blank range. Whatever the specific rules governing aerial warfare—and they are deliberately ambiguous—there can be no denying that wanton attacks on civilian targets, no matter how conducted, violate established rules of proportionality; they cannot be morally or legally defended. Grayling concludes his exhaustive work by asking "Was area bombing necessary? No. Was it proportional? No. Was it against humanitarian principles that people have been striving to enunciate as a way of controlling and limiting war? Yes. Was it against general moral standards of the kind recognized and agreed in Western civilization in the last five centuries, or even 2000 years? Yes. ... Very wrong? Yes."[40] There is a further question as to whether such bombardments were even militarily *effective* much less necessary. The February 1945 saturation bombing of Dresden, a city of little strategic value, provides an illuminating case in point. The writer Kurt Vonnegut, whose novel *Slaughterhouse Five* was based on the horrors he experienced in Dresden at the time, commented:

> The firebombing of Dresden was an emotional event without a trace of military importance. I will say again what I have often said in print and in speeches, that not one Allied solider was able to advance as much as one inch because of the firebombing of Dresden. Not one prisoner of the Nazis got out of prison a microsecond earlier. Only one person on earth clearly benefited

and I am that person. I got about five dollars for each corpse [estimated to be as many as 260,000].[41]

In any event, if we can say that *all* nations, victors and losers and bystanders alike, adhere to principles of universality, then they have an obligation to face up to their own crimes—something U.S. leaders have never done.

In 2003, the Smithsonian National Air and Space Museum in Washington, DC, opened a new annex with its centerpiece a display of the Boeing B-29 superfortress *Enola Gay*, which dropped the first atomic bomb on Hiroshima. The museum provided an abundance of technical details regarding the plane but nothing about its bombing mission or the unspeakable consequences of that criminal mission. Such lack of information, of course, could hardly amount to an oversight. The museum director, retired General John Dailey, said at the opening that the public has no special need for such details: "We are displaying it in all its glory as a magnificent technological achievement ... Our primary focus is that it was the most advanced aircraft in the world at the time."[42] That the *Enola Gay* was responsible for the deaths of over 100,000 people, nearly all of them innocent civilians—surely one of the most egregious war crimes ever—struck Dailey as an irrelevant or trivial fact, but any rational judgment would have depicted the aircraft as a conduit of indefensible aerial terrorism—its mission unnecessary to end the war. Any display with even a modicum of professional competence and ethical sensitivity would have presented such information as a central feature of the exhibit. The remarkable absence of any meaningful contextual facts reveals not only an ethos of arrogant exceptionalism—the nation being so noble and democratic that anything it does must automatically be regarded as beyond criticism—but also the kind of war-crimes denial for which the U.S. has so frequently scolded other nations (including the *Japanese*).

The final months of World War II ushered in a new era in the history of military combat—aerial warfare with few limits. Strategic bombing with its inevitable destruction of civilian populations and related targets was now (above all for the U.S.) perfectly legitimate, indeed, was the *preferred* and embellished modality. If World War II served as a testing-ground for area bombing and use of incendiary weapons like napalm—and indeed for nuclear devices— the Korean War offered new opportunities for refining barbarism: aerial terrorism was pushed to new levels, even without nuclear weaponry. In just three months of 1951 the USAF used B-29s to systematically destroy every accessible North Korean city and town, not only slaughtering hundreds of thousands of defenseless civilians but creating vast regions of homelessness, starvation, and disease. Absolutely no laws of warfare were honored. By the end of the war the Korean death toll (North and South) reached nearly four million, mostly civilians and mostly resulting from U.S. aerial bombardments.[43] Visiting Korea in summer 1952, Supreme Court Justice William O. Douglas said: "I had seen the war-battered cities of Europe, but I had not seen devastation until I had seen Korea."[44] As in the case of Japan (and later Indochina), civilian populations were deliberately targeted, the unfathomable death and destruction celebrated by its militarily superior perpetrators. Referring to Korea and China, Lindqvist writes: "In American eyes, the yellow and red perils had now been united, and a half-billion people had suddenly become America's enemies."[45]

In Korea the U.S. campaign quickly developed into total war as the Pentagon set about bombing the country into oblivion, leaving virtually nothing untouched. As Endicott and Hagerman write, the result was that "Korea was pulverized. It is not easy to find words to describe the carnage. In a territory smaller than the state of Oregon, two and half million combatants fought on the battle lines for seemingly endless years; shells and bombs rained down in unmerciful torrents from naval vessels along the coasts and from aircraft overhead, setting new records for destruction."[46] As noted above, USAF attacks were extended in June 1952 to hydroelectric plants on the Yalu River, to population centers in North Korea, and finally, in May 1953, to irrigation dams on rivers—actions that by any definition were war crimes. U.S. pilots targeted their napalm, other incendiary, and fragmentation bombs on homes, shelters, vehicles, and horse carts, anything that moved.[47] Through all this the U.S. made few efforts to distinguish between civilian and military targets.

The USAF chose the North Korean capital, Pyongyang, as one of its special targets for saturation bombing. After June 1950 the city was visited by U.S. air attacks day and night, forcing most of the population of nearly 500,000 to evacuate or be killed. By December 1951, according to the Korean War-Crimes Tribunal, 64,000 homes were destroyed out of 80,000, nearly 5000 people were killed with several thousand wounded after bombardments hit schools, hospitals, and churches as a matter of military routine. The city was left in smoldering ruins.[48]

Two decades later, the U.S. had (between roughly 1965 and 1973) dropped eight million tons of bombs on Vietnam—by far the most intensive aerial bombardments in history, the sum total equivalent to 640 Hiroshima-sized atomic bombs. The goal was to conduct massive counterinsurgency operations mainly through saturation bombing by B-52s, again with little attempt to distinguish between civilian and military objects. To a degree greater even than in World War II and Korea, warfare would turn on technologically planned operations designed to leave no area untouched by the consequences of scorched-earth warfare. Vietnam marked the real beginnings of technowar based on a strategy explicitly intended to minimize ground combat and overall U.S. casualties, though this modality of war would achieve fuller expression with Desert Storm in 1991.[49] Except for nuclear weapons (considered at least once by Washington planners), the U.S. used everything in its arsenal, with the goal of bombing an underdeveloped country into total submission: saturation attacks with 2000-pound bombs, napalm, white phosphorous, cluster bombs, chemical defoliants like Agent Orange, sophisticated missiles, fuel-air bombs, and frightening amounts of regular ordnance. As Lindqvist writes, there were no limits in Vietnam: "The rule book said of course that civilians were not to be bombed. But for the military, rules were not norms to follow but problems to solve."[50] For U.S. leaders across the entire Indochina terrain international law had absolutely no relevance.

Waging merciless aerial terrorism against civilian targets, the U.S. manufactured new and improved napalm designed to adhere more closely to the skin, burn more deeply, and cause more horrific injury. During World War II the U.S. had dropped 14,000 tons of napalm, mainly on the Japanese. During the Korean War the total was 32,000 tons. But in Vietnam from 1963 to 1971 the total was about 373,000 tons of the far more debilitating napalm—eleven times the total used in Korea. Napalm was preferred by the military since it could destroy wide target areas while incapacitating human beings with only peripheral hits.[51] Its intimidating value must have been awesome. The air war in general left some ten million bomb craters in Vietnam alone, along with the aforementioned destruction of hamlets, towns, farmland, and farm animals, all part of a consciously planned war of attrition.

There can be no doubt that the U.S. air war was aimed directly at civilians: aside from the renovated napalm, new weapons were refined specifically for that very purpose—for example, CBU-24 cluster bombs that spread thousands of fragments across wide areas. Lindqvist writes: "When the B-52s carpet bombed, they often first dropped explosive bombs in order to 'open the structures', then napalm to burn out the contents, and finally CBU-24s to kill the people who came running to help those who were burning. Often time-released cluster bombs were dropped in order to kill those who did not come before the danger was over—or so they thought." Lindqvist reports that, after the war, the Pentagon conceded that nearly a half-million of these bombs were "directed only at living targets." The total was 285 million little bomblets altogether, "or seven bombs for every man, woman, boy, and girl in all of Indochina."[52]

Massive bombing campaigns were waged against North Vietnam, Cambodia, and Laos, especially after the Tet Offensive in early 1968. Nixon and Kissinger were dedicated to broadening the war of attrition by means of extended carpet bombing. That meant systematic destruction of farmlands, villages, towns, and civilian infrastructures such as dams, dikes, irrigation systems, and water-production facilities. According to Marilyn Young, the intensity of the bombing in Vietnam and Laos was so great that organized life was no longer possible in most of the villages. During peak attacks in 1969, U.S. planes conducted overflights daily, their goal to leave nothing standing—their purpose to annihilate the "material basis of civilized society." In late 1969 one observer stated that, "after a recorded history of seven hundred years, the Plain of Jars [in Laos] disappeared."[53] Throughout 1968 and 1969 some 230,000 tons of bombs were dropped on Laos, wiping out the livelihood of 150,000 farmers in the region. The U.N. observer George Chapelier reported that "nothing was left standing. The villagers lived in trenches and holes or in caves. They only farmed at night. All of the interlocutors, without any exception, had their villages completely destroyed."[54] These rank among the most horrific war crimes in modern history. As both material and psychological warfare, U.S. aerial bombardments often went far beyond their stated aim of interdicting supply lines. They were integral to a total-war strategy meant to demoralize the enemy, wreck the infrastructure, destroy the workforce, and simply convey a message of high-tech military supremacy.

The Indochina catastrophe was followed 15 years later by the first Gulf War, during which the U.S. flew 11,000 sorties dropping several million tons of bombs on Iraq, more than half of them on densely populated urban centers such as Baghdad and Basra. Here again we find a clearly deliberate plan to destroy the Iraqi infra-structure, with the stated objective of leaving the country in a state of pre-industrial crisis—a policy continued well after the Hussein regime vacated Kuwait. This meant destroying targets essential to human life: water and electrical plants, transportation, communications, agriculture, factories, various public structures. Racheting up its dedication to technowar in 1991, the Pentagon introduced 15,000-pound "daisy-cutter" bombs (their explosive power near that of mini-nukes), 2.5 ton superbombs, and a variety of missiles, bombs, and artillery shells tipped with DU along with the familiar cluster bombs. The human and ecological impact of such weapons of wanton destruction was a prelude to more bombing raids *after* 1991 that continued into the second Gulf War.[55] For its military aggression during Desert Storm the first Bush administration was charged with war crimes by an independent Commission for Inquiry for the International War-Crimes Tribunal. Indictment four states: "The U.S. intentionally bombed and destroyed civilian life, commercial and business districts, residential areas, historical sites, private vehicles, and civilian government offices." Indictment five adds: "The U.S. intentionally bombed indiscriminately throughout Iraq." Volumes of evidence were brought forward in support of these and several other charges.[56] The wanton aerial destruction carried out by the U.S. in Iraq violated established canons of international law.

As mentioned, in spring 1999 the U.S. and a few NATO allies conducted bombing raids over Yugoslavia that would last seven weeks, visiting massive destruction on Belgrade and other Serb cities, justified in Washington and a few other Western capitals as "humanitarian intervention." As in Iraq, these attacks—never involving ground operations—destroyed hundreds of public and residential buildings, water and electrical works, transportation, communications, bridges, hospitals, schools, and food production, as well as conventional military targets, leaving the Serb infrastructure in ruins.[57] All this was carried out against a nation posing no threat to the U.S. or any other country. It took place, moreover, against a nation virtually devoid of an air force or air-defense capabilities—that is, defenseless, as revealed by the fact U.S./NATO military forces suffered no casualties during the attacks. As in Iraq, of course, this was really no war but rather an organized, planned, criminal massacre orchestrated from the skies. In his lengthy account of the massacre, Michael Parenti writes in *To Kill a Nation* that "such massive aggression amounts to a vastly greater war crime than anything charged against Milošević."[58] At the end of the largely unrestricted bombing campaign, Belgrade officials reported that no less than 15 towns and cities were hit, resulting in large-scale casualties: 500 combat and more than 2000 civilian deaths, 6000 wounded, and many thousands made homeless. The use of DU-tipped ordnance and other toxic chemicals did permanent ecological harm.

In May 1999 a team of lawyers from Canada and Europe submitted a brief accusing U.S. and NATO officials of war crimes, including "wanton destruction of cities, towns, and villages, of devastation not justified by military necessity," but The Hague Tribunal set up by NATO to try war crimes in Yugoslavia chose instead to indict Milošević and ignored the U.S./NATO crimes of aggression and their consequences for the targeted population.[59] Later, in June 2000, a panel of 16 judges from eleven countries meeting in New York found U.S. and NATO leaders guilty of war crimes against Yugoslavia, based on extensive research and data collection along with testimony from eyewitnesses, historians, biologists, military experts, journalists, and others.[60] The findings of guilt applied to 19 charges, including "planning and executing the dismemberment, segregation, and impoverishment of Yugoslavia"; "destroying the peace-making role of the United Nations"; the "killing and injuring of a defenseless population"; "attacking objects indispensable to the survival of the population"; and "waging war on the environment." The tribunal called for "full reparations to be paid to the Federal Republic of Yugoslavia for death, injury, economic and environmental damage resulting from the NATO bombing, economic sanctions, and blockades."[61] In the end, of course, neither the U.S. political establishment nor the mass media paid attention to such findings and recommendations.

Following the events of 9/11, President Bush launched a bombing campaign against Al Qaeda and the Taliban regime in Afghanistan, producing initially an estimated 3000 deaths along with more thousands of homeless in the targeted areas. Despite the rhetoric of "precision bombing," it was civilians who suffered most of the casualties. After several years of intervention in Afghanistan, reports surfaced that U.S. planes frequently attacked civilian targets: bombers saturated large areas with devastating impact, while AC-130 gun ships armed with howitzers, cannons, and machine guns seemed to have carte blanche in many areas of the country. The main targets were Al Qaeda base sites, Taliban military positions, and bunker hideouts, yet civilian areas were commonly hit, with loss of life estimated in 2004 (by the Red Cross) at more than 3000. On December 29, 2001, U.S. aircraft destroyed an entire village, killing dozens of civilians and wounding many more, after flying several quick sorties in early morning darkness. Taliban leaders were said to be hiding out in the village of Qalaye Niazi, but most people hit were part of a large wedding party. According to U.N. reports, unarmed women and children were chased and killed by helicopters as they fled to shelter or tried to rescue survivors.[62] Previous efforts to bomb Al Qaeda were carried out by the Clinton administration in the Sudan and Afghanistan in 1998, with fewer casualties. Insofar as such actions might be justified as defensive operations against terrorist outposts, their status as war crimes is naturally more ambiguous—though deliberate assaults on civilian objects *under any circumstances* are clear violations of international law.

As for Iraq, the devastation visited by U.S. aerial bombardments after Desert Storm and especially after the "shock-and-awe" campaign of March 2003 has already been covered here. It is worth mentioning again that while media accounts have focused mainly on local atrocities and torture such as occurred at Abu Ghraib—generally framed as aberrant behavior—more noteworthy is the unfathomable carnage that high-tech American weaponry has brought to Iraq throughout many years of war and occupation. This larger pattern of warfare has been responsible for the vast majority of casualties. Aerial bombardment has devastated such urban centers as Baghdad, Fallujah, and Ramadi, much of it accompanied by cluster bombs and incendiary devices like white phosphorous and napalm. Under conditions of urban warfare that have existed in Iraq the assorted U.S. bombing runs and missile firings—no matter how much "precision guidance" is utilized—can rarely separate military from civilian targets.

A PATTERN OF ATROCITIES

The focus so far on wanton attacks against civilians and aerial terrorism—the cause of most casualties—calls attention to the *modus operandi* preferred by the U.S. armed forces in the differing conditions explored here. War crimes must be viewed as neither episodic nor isolated but as tied to specific military strategies and tactics. Turning to the local atrocities sometimes hidden from (U.S.) public view, there is always the question of whether such episodes are the rare, deviant outbursts of thuggish soldiers, as commonly thought to be the case in American discourse. The Uniform Code of Military Justice does in fact lay out rules of engagement that in theory are followed by personnel in the field. The problem is that, given the stress and chaos of battle—especially under conditions of guerrilla warfare—such rules are easily ignored or flaunted. Several factors are typically at work here: (1) commanding officers that emphasize high body counts or "enemy kills"; (2) vengeance as a human response to the loss of fellow soldiers to enemy fire; (3) outright racism and contempt for other groups and cultures; (4) a brutalizing psychology instilled in basic training and reproduced within a violent military culture; (5) lessened constraints with the breakdown of social norms and relations; (6) difficulty identifying military from civilian targets, above all in the context of local insurgency and guerrilla combat. An overarching factor is that where the U.S. carries out protracted warfare, as in Korea and Vietnam, the challenge of selecting only military targets becomes difficult if not impossible. The historical record shows that widespread local atrocities have occurred in every U.S. military venture, including civilian massacres, prisoner abuse and killings, and torture, and such violations can only be understood as part of a general *pattern* of imperial behavior. In those few instances where violations have come to light and the perpetrators tried for crimes, those held to account have been mainly lower level armed-forces personnel. Indeed no high-ranking military or government officials have *ever* been prosecuted, though many surely could have been brought to justice given the political willpower. Had accountability been affirmed, attention might have been focused on the institutional and policy *context* in which U.S. war crimes were committed.

In the Korean War, the strategy of "total war" deeply shaped U.S. battlefield conduct: local atrocities were remarkably common, especially as frustration over the stalemate mounted. The most horrific *well-known* episode occurred at No Gun Ri, but many other documented cases later came to the fore, though again few of these became known to the American public.

The criminality of U.S. military behavior in Korea has few parallels in the twentieth century or even before. The death toll reached perhaps four million, with some estimates much higher—totaling at least one-sixth of the entire Korean population. According to some reports, the U.S. military administration, working with the repressive Syngman Rhee dictatorship, killed roughly one million people and jailed more than 100,000 in crackdowns against popular opposition.[63] A postwar commission on U.S. war crimes in Korea revealed no less than 52 instances of large-scale atrocities.[64] American use of both chemical and biological warfare was demonstrated. The commission reported U.S. massacres of some 35,000 civilians in Sinchon during an occupation lasting from October to December

1950, where the entire population was designated as "reds" deserving of whatever terrible fate awaited them. Thousands of people were gunned down and thrown into mass graves, some while still alive, with hundreds burned to death reportedly on the orders of the U.S. army commander in charge.[65] At Sariwon on December 5, 1950, nearly a thousand civilians were rounded up, beaten, tortured, and then shot to death by U.S. troops.[66] In Anak during an occupation lasting from October to December 1950 U.S. troops reportedly murdered 19,000 civilians, more than 1000 of them buried alive.[67] On December 4, 1950 in Pyongyang, where most casualties were the result of bombing raids, U.S. army troops summarily killed some 3000 people, mostly women and children.[68] At Haiju during the same month more than 6000 civilians (suspected Communists) were taken into the countryside in small groups and machine-gunned to death, while others were beheaded with sabers. The list of such *major* atrocities goes on endlessly.

The most publicized U.S. massacre in Korea—the subject of a BBC documentary—took place in late July 1950 at No Gun Ri, where the First Cavalry Division leader ordered army units to shoot en masse a large group of retreating civilians, all women, children, and the elderly—all completely defenseless. Several hundred people were gunned to death under a bridge in a massacre lasting many hours and described by one survivor as "wholesale slaughter" and another as a sadistic mass killing where "American soldiers played with our lives like boys playing with flies."[69] Standing orders for the U.S. military in the area at that time were to kill everyone, as all persons were assumed to be "hostile" or "reds." The neighboring 25th Infantry Division commander, General William B. Kean, reportedly told his troops that "all civilians seen in this area are to be considered an enemy and action taken accordingly."[70] At No Gun Ri, Captain Melbourne Chandler told his machine-gunners to open fire, saying: "The hell with all these people. Let's get rid of all of them."[71] Never have any survivors or witnesses (including U.S. soldiers) indicated any legitimate reason for the onslaught—nothing such as gunfire directed at American positions or enemy combatants hiding among civilians. The U.S. military never acknowledged this or any similar episode in Korea, which means no apologies or reparations. When confronted with this information, a typical Pentagon refrain is that civilian casualties are an unfortunate by-product of combat, an inevitable part of warfare. In other words, "war is hell," so grounds for complaint are nonexistent.

In Vietnam, U.S. military operations were similarly geared to the "maximum production of death,"[72] to the wearing-down of a targeted population understood to be Communist savages, by means of relentless firepower. One vehicle of savagery was a pacification program designed by the Pentagon in 1962 and refined in 1967 as the U.S. became more deeply mired in protracted warfare. The Vietnam campaign evolved into a war without limits where "search-and-destroy" meant attacking everyone and everything that stood in the way of U.S. military control. Higher body counts were demanded as an increase in "enemy" killed-in-action represented progress for the technocratic war managers. Wanton attacks on civilians, mass killings, torture, rape, and abuse of prisoners was the *norm*, endemic to a criminal enterprise fueled by racism, imperial arrogance, and a cult of violence—an ethos permeating the entire structure up to the highest command levels. Cut off from Vietnamese society, Americans routinely made life-and-death decisions as they moved violently through the country. Gibson writes that "The Americans rarely knew Vietnamese language, Vietnamese culture, or Vietnamese history, but they were responsible for ascertaining who was a Vietcong and who was a civilian."[73] For the most part, these distinctions hardly mattered in a milieu where the combat imperative was to kill freely, and to kill without mercy.

Although it was one of dozens of civilian massacres in Vietnam, My Lai became a symbol of what the U.S. military presence meant in the field of action. In March 1968 U.S. troops of the 23rd Infantry Division carried out the deliberate and sadistic mass murder of about 500 unarmed civilians, shooting women and children repeatedly and piling up corpses as if going about routine duties, then reporting the massacre as simple Vietcong casualties. Army units entered the hamlet with guns blazing, ransacking everything, raping women, killing all of the livestock, burning all of the huts, and covering up all of the bodies. Troops machine-gunned helpless civilians without pause or, apparently, conscience (although a few did balk at the killing). For many soldiers the massacre was something of a spontaneous activity, but My Lai was mostly an *organized* military operation traceable to officer commands and consistent with the overall military culture.[74] This has been accurately described as a "sanctioned massacre" licensed by military orders that had the effect of reducing moral inhibitions regarding violence.[75] My Lai turned into a massive crime of obedience in which the victims were already fully dehumanized, enabling the perpetrators to murder with impunity. In fact the massacre, initially concealed by the military and only later brought to light by the journalistic work of Seymour Hersh,[76] was not investigated until 1969 and 1970. Charges were brought forward at a trial lasting well into 1971. Platoon leader Lt. William Calley alone was prosecuted (for murder) under Article 118 of the UCMJ and was convicted of killing 22 people. He was sentenced to life in prison, but the sentence was soon reduced to 20 and then ten years. Pleading innocent on the basis of following legal military orders, Calley wound up serving just three years under house arrest before being officially pardoned in 1975. The Vietnamese, however, have never forgotten: the massacre is kept alive by markers and plaques designating spots where villagers were killed, by a large statue, and by a My Lai Museum built in 1975.[77]

Historical evidence demonstrates a lengthy pattern of U.S. atrocities in Vietnam, as attacks on civilians by ground troops were especially widespread, later discovered to have taken place in almost every military unit. Soldiers murdered, raped, tortured, and abused prisoners with few restraints, seemingly as a matter of entitlement. Declassified Pentagon documents go into great detail concerning 320 such incidents in some 8000 pages of investigations, military reports, and sworn statements of participants and witnesses.[78] Among these, unfortunately, only 57 courts martial resulted, producing just 23 convictions and four jail sentences of any significant length. According to a *Los Angeles Times* story, "many substantiated cases were closed with a letter of reprimand, a fine, or in more than half the cases, no action at all." Military cover-ups and stonewalling were so frequent that witnesses often felt that filing reports was a waste of time. In one case, Medic Jamie Henry filed a complaint stating that, in February 1968, army troops rounded up and killed 19 civilians in Quang Nam province, after the company commander issued orders to "kill anything that moves." In the field Henry was denounced as a fabricator and traitor, and no one was ever indicted or prosecuted for mass murder. Upon returning to the U.S., Henry reported the incident to a Fort Hood legal officer but was told to keep quiet for his own good and was threatened with prosecution. His accusations were later proven to be true. Writing about the horrors in 1970, Henry related that "Incidents similar to those I have described occur on a daily basis and differ from one another only in terms of numbers killed."[79]

According to one comment in the declassified Pentagon files, "A battalion would kill maybe 15 to 20 [civilians] a day. With four battalions in the brigade that would be maybe 40 to 50 a day or 1200 to 1500 a month, easy."[80] In other words, the massacres were rather common to U.S. military operations in Vietnam, just as they had been in Korea. Killing parties, moreover, often carried out their deeds as a form of entertainment, while a code of silence was enforced across the entire battlefield. Of the relatively few reports that did finally surface—many long after the atrocities in question—their contents were rather graphic. For example, in September 1969, "members of a reconnaissance platoon swept through the Que Son Valley, burning homes, slaughtering animals, and clearing civilians. They killed an unarmed boy standing outside a cluster of huts and fired into one of the dwellings, killing three women and three or four children ... the soldiers then executed an elderly woman and a baby. The unit reported the victims as enemy killed in action." The investigation found sufficient evidence to charge seven soldiers with murder, rape, or dereliction of duty. By then, at least four of the perpetrators had left the service, and the army declined to pursue charges against them.[81]

Perhaps the most damning commentary on U.S. atrocities in Vietnam came from participants themselves, including hundreds of military personnel who later testified in such venues as the Winter Soldier hearings held in Detroit during 1971 (and released as a shocking documentary in 1972). The witness testimonies are powerful and devastating in their indictment of U.S. military behavior, in their emotional outpourings as a response to the death and destruction they observed first hand and in some cases initiated themselves. Referring to the carnage, one witness said: "It wasn't like they were humans. We were conditioned to believe this was for the good of the nation, the good of our country, and that anything we did was o.k. And like when you shot someone you didn't think you were shooting at a human. They were a gook or a Commie, and that was o.k."[82] The former soldier continued: "All Vietnamese were gooks ... and they were inferior to us. We were Americans, we were the civilized people. We didn't give a shit about those people." Said another former soldier: "If I'd go into a village and have to kill 100 people just to be sure there was no one there to shoot me when I walked out, that's just what I did." One Marine testified that "I had yet to be on an operation when I've gone through a village and that village was still left standing." At the hearings it was generally acknowledged that all atrocities—mass killings, torture, burning of villages—were understood to have been fully *endorsed* by military leaders in the field. According to one soldier, moreover, "Our minister [Chaplain] condoned everything that happened, all the horrors."[83]

The Winter Soldier hearings revealed that torture had become virtually a routine aspect of U.S. armed-forces behavior in Vietnam, motivated by revenge, intimidation, efforts to gain intelligence from POWs and inhabitants, and simple hatred. According to one witness, "we would go to torture very quickly ... We killed prisoners on the spot, with promises of rewards [and] officers always overlooked what was going on." Stated another: "I was told to elicit information by any means. He [the superior officer] told me I could use any technique I could think of, the idea being don't get caught. I could beat people, cut them, or shoot them ... just don't do it in the presence of a non-unit person. I personally used clubs, rifle butts, pistols, knives ... the important point here is that everything I did was always monitored." Such testimony corresponds to evidence gathered by a host of journalists and researchers in Vietnam across more than a decade.

Aside from My Lai, however, an episode taken up only belatedly and half-heartedly by the media and then the Pentagon, U.S. savagery in Vietnam drew little attention from the American media, politicians, government officials, and larger public. Even after it was revealed, the very behavior for which the Germans and Japanese were prosecuted after World War II was rationalized away or, more disturbingly, met with outright praise and honors. A case in point: former Senator Robert Kerrey, later to become President of the New School in New York, received a Bronze Star for leading a Navy SEALs operation into the village of Thanh Phong in Feburary 1969—an operation where 21 civilians were sadistically executed, at close range, in a free-fire zone, as part of the Phoenix Program responsible for at least 70,000 Vietnamese deaths. A member of Kerrey's team, Gerhard Klann, reported the massacre and was backed up by other witnesses, although Kerrey described the events as more complex than mass murder. When the atrocities later became known to the American media and public, the prevailing attitude was that Kerrey ought to be given the benefit of the doubt since he was just doing his job and, moreover, eyewitnesses in the heat of battle cannot be trusted. Incidents of this sort cannot be avoided since, after all, "war is hell." Politicians refused to investigate the matter and Kerrey was allowed to keep his New School post. The media was silent except for a long account in *Time* magazine (May 7, 2001) that whitewashed the episode, depicting Kerrey more as a sad victim of tragic circumstances than as the leader of a cold-blooded massacre. Barry Romo, National Coordinator of Vietnam Veterans against the War, observed that "everything is backwards. People shouldn't be looking at Kerrey as a victim but at the families of the Vietnamese who were killed. If Kerrey killed them by accident then he owed them some reparations. If he did line them up and shoot them, then you don't get away with murder because you wore a uniform."[84]

A number of U.S. assaults on civilians in Panama City—for example, the torching of dozens of homes in the El Chorillo district—have been duly noted above. Evidence of local atrocities in Afghanistan, where U.S. military action has been more limited than in Iraq but has continued for several years, has also surfaced. The U.S. military was reportedly involved in the mass murder of Taliban prisoners (estimated at more than 1000) rounded up by American and Northern Alliance troops near Konduz in late November 2001. According to reports from different sources, prisoners were herded into container trucks on a journey from Konduz to Sheberghan, condemned to a slow and painful death, and dumped into mass grave sites, all while U.S. Special Forces—working closely with ruthless General Abdul Rashid Dostum—remained in the area. As Red Cross and U.N. representatives expressed "grave concern" about the atrocity, the Pentagon stonewalled any investigation.[85]

In Iraq beginning in March 2003, local atrocities received more attention than had been the case in Vietnam, thanks to extensive reports and photos of torture carried out by U.S. troops at Abu Ghraib prison in Baghdad, which surfaced in 2004. For politicians and the media, however, these episodes were isolated, the rare outburst of a few overly stressed soldiers, although in Iraq as elsewhere such behavior is closer to the norm than gatekeepers of opinion want to admit. Military occupation has witnessed recurrent acts of murder, rape, torture, house raids, arbitrary detentions, and other abuses. In fact violence seemed rather ordinary in an atmosphere of chaos, strife, and insurgency, where social and political order had essentially collapsed. What has permeated everything, however, is the sheer oppression of American rule, making daily horrors nearly routine. Unit commanders have often encouraged troops to record maximum kills, with edicts to shoot all military-aged males in certain zones known to have been issued. As in Korea and Vietnam, the military culture has facilitated homicidal behavior. Dahr Jamail comments: "It's part of the dehumanization process. When you have a soldier who has—they call it light up—they've lit up a car full of civilians at a checkpoint and realized, oh, they've just killed a family. As a result, they dehumanize Iraqis, calling them hajis, ragheads, and other racist terms. Instead of killing a human being, now they've killed this less-than-human terrorist."[86]

One of the most devastating homicidal outbursts took place in November 2005, when U.S. Marines slaughtered 24 civilians in cold blood at Haditha, claiming revenge for the death of a fellow soldier. Using rifles and grenades, a unit from the Third Battalion of the First Marine Division mechanically killed men, women, and children in the setting of their own homes, including a 76-year-old blind man in a wheelchair. Soldiers rolled grenades into rooms crowded with children and babies. Unarmed residents were shot repeatedly, at close range, by troops going house-to-house. The Marines made return trips to the killing sites to finish people off. Witnesses said the men carried out deliberate executions and laughed about it. The episode was covered up but soon reached higher command levels, although no officer was willing to concede that anything unusual had taken place; the killings were simply business-as-usual.[87] Inquiries by reporters were dismissed as emanating from "terrorist propaganda" intended to "give aid to the enemy." A *Time* magazine report finally detailed both the massacre and the cover up, triggering new investigations. Reports drew a picture of U.S. troops confined to their fortress bases and cut off from Iraqi society by language, culture, and history—occupying forces willfully ignorant and filled with contempt for the local population.

A *Frontline* documentary on Haditha aired in February 2008 set out to present a balanced account of the events in question and their aftermath, based on eyewitness statements from both sides. Local Iraqis interviewed were shown emotionally revisiting a scene of execution-style bloodshed with innocent civilians murdered as they went about their normal daily routines—most at home, far removed from the scene of the initial Humvee attack.[88] It had become clear that, for the troops of Kilo Company, virtually anyone in designated combat zones (men, women, children, elderly) could be regarded as "threats" to be attacked and neutralized. In other words, rules of engagement were murky at best. Understandably outraged, Iraqis in Haditha viewed the unwarranted attacks as criminal and insisted on a full-scale investigation that Marines in the field considered unnecessary, an imposition, something of a terrorist propaganda ploy. In the documentary U.S. soldiers ventured forth to say that Haditha was a "very shady town" filled with people who didn't like Americans, who never appreciated U.S. sacrifices to bring help to their town. Others indicated that the killings were all in a day's work, an inescapable part of battlefield routine—"something that just happens." Still others argued the entire incident was blown out of proportion, especially since it was Americans who suffered the first roadside casualties. What became clear is that the Marines would likely have blocked any investigation into the atrocities were it not for the *Time* magazine report. As for the documentary, its purported "balance" left the impression that there were two equally valid sides to the narrative—that the familiar resort to self-defense might be a valid justification for the systematic murder of unarmed civilians. Even more puzzling, the *Frontline* program suggested that the Haditha episode provided a wake-up call, giving new impetus for American troops to win the "hearts and minds" of the Iraqi people. Nothing was mentioned about ending an illegal occupation where Haditha-style atrocities were common, indeed an inevitable part of the U.S. intervention.

A few months after Haditha, in the village of Ishaqi, army troops brutally murdered eleven civilians in one home, including four children under age seven, their corpses riddled with bullets.[89] A by-product of the U.S. pursuit of insurgents, this massacre (like others that came to light) was written off as "collateral damage," an unfortunate but necessary result of the war on terror—and no one was prosecuted. Such "escalation of force" incidents mounted as the U.S. occupation heightened Iraqi antagonism and resistance, although they have been rarely investigated much less punished. Haditha and Ishaqi represent only two of dozens, more likely *hundreds*, of similar atrocities in an environment where large-scale killing of civilians is the logical outcome of an occupation that breeds popular anger and hostility, where ordinary people become the enemy, and where rules of warfare have all but vanished.

With several years of war and occupation having brought sustained violence, chaos, and breakdown to Iraq—in a word, ruin—the burden has fallen overwhelmingly on the civilian population. As in the case of Vietnam, many Americans seemed to believe that "winning" (an elusive notion at best) requires maximum body count—that is, killing as many Iraqis as possible. One army Specialist, Michael Richardson, was quoted as saying: "There was no dilemma when it came to shooting people who were not in uniform. I just pulled the trigger. It was up close and personal the whole time, there wasn't big distance. If they were there, they were enemy, whether in uniform or not. Some were, some weren't."[90] It is important to repeat here that such murderous sentiments were from most reports (including those at Abu Ghraib) widely held among American military personnel—all the way to the top of the organizational hierarchy.

A CULTURE OF DENIAL

The U.S. government, media, and academic establishments have long either ignored or defended the U.S. record of war crimes detailed in this and other chapters of the present book. The culture of denial is so well-entrenched in American political culture as to be more or less invisible, accompanied by a remarkable degree of hypocrisy and double standards. After all, these are the kind of crimes for which American officialdom never tires of demanding that *others* be held accountable. The capacity for apologetics has been truly amazing, all the more so given that the record is hardly shrouded in secrecy. As mentioned, even on those rare occasions when U.S. military attacks on civilian populations are acknowledged, such attacks are usually rationalized away as a question of military imperative: destroying enemy morale, collateral damage, difficulty separating military from civilian targets, and so forth. A close look at U.S. military history quickly refutes such flimsy, self-serving apologetics. One result of this denial—that is, exempting Washington from responsibility for its criminal deeds—has been to subvert longstanding international attempts to establish legal and moral constraints on military behavior.

Contrary to prevailing mythology, civilian populations and related targets have always been strategically central to U.S. military operations. And there have been numerous of such operations just since the end of World War II. As we have seen, the civilian victims of U.S. warfare have often been *intended*—or at least the product of *indifference* on the part of armed-services personnel from top to bottom. The warfare has fit a *pattern* of ground, aerial, and naval action, with civilian victims having reached the tens of millions. According to the Nuremberg precedent, victims of war can be direct or indirect, immediate or delayed, in cases where military actions constitute crimes against peace, which commonly applies to U.S. behavior. Apologetics regularly surface across the political spectrum, and even outside it, reflecting widespread patriotic obedience often mixed with elements of ethnocentrism and racism. As Howard Zinn puts it:

> Our problem is the numbers of people all over the world who have obeyed the dictates of the leaders of their government and have gone to war, and millions have been killed because of this obedience. And our problem is that scene in *All Quiet on the Western Front* where the schoolboys march off dutifully to war.

Our problem is that people are obedient all over the world, in the face of poverty and starvation and stupidity, and war and cruelty... We recognize this for Nazi Germany. We know that the problem there was obedience, that the people obeyed Hitler... They should have challenged and they should have resisted; and if we were only there, we would have showed them... But America is different. That is what we've all been brought up on... But if we have learned anything [from history] it is that these lovely things about America were never lovely. We have been expansionist and aggressive and mean to other people from the beginning. And we've been aggressive and mean to people in this country... Now how can we boast that America is a very special place? It is not that special.[91]

Sam Harris, in his otherwise critically acclaimed book *The End of Faith*, notes a history of U.S. military atrocities but conveniently refers to them as "misdeeds"—departures from the norm—arguing that, in any case, atrocities committed in the past have nothing to do with contemporary world politics.[92] Attacking Noam Chomsky for "moral blindness" in equating U.S. war crimes with those committed by other nations and groups, Harris contends that even when the U.S. military has killed civilians such actions have been rarely if ever *intended*, in contrast to *deliberate* and planned atrocities of American enemies, for example Muslim terrorists. Referring to the U.S. as a "well-intentioned giant" facing a world of "genocidal sadists," he implausibly claims that evidence shows the U.S. operates at a higher level of "moral development" that rules out deliberate or indiscriminate attacks on civilians. Regarding Bush's intervention in Iraq, Harris writes "there is no reason to think that he would have sanctioned the injury or death of even a single innocent person."[93] Indeed the U.S. is really obsessed with minimizing or avoiding civilian casualties.[94] An immediate question emerges here: was not Bush as commander-in-chief of the U.S. military ultimately responsible for every (unprovoked) horror taking place in Iraq: the initial crime of aggression, shock-and-awe tactics, a bloody occupation, destruction of urban centers, massive civil strife, infrastructure collapse, torture of prisoners, routine atrocities endemic to occupying a foreign nation—in a word, ruin of an entire country? If not, then exactly who might be found most legally and morally accountable? Are we to believe that the poor beleaguered President of the most powerful nation in the world was simply trapped in a sad, unavoidable tragedy?

Recognizing such atrocities as My Lai in Vietnam, Harris contends "what distinguishes us from many of our enemies is that this indiscriminate violence appalls us."[95] How "appalling" could it have been when nearly every perpetrator involved, including high-ranking officers, was able to escape prosecution while the lone indicted mass murderer got a lighter sentence than most drug offenders? Observing that in an evil world the maiming and killing of innocent civilians will be regrettably unavoidable, Harris concludes: "Any honest witness to current events will realize that there is no moral equivalence between the kind of force civilized democracies project in the world, warts and all, and the internecine violence that is perpetrated by Muslim militants."[96] This is a puzzling claim from someone who resides in a country that "projects" by far the most violence in the world, that has built the largest war machine in history, that intervenes routinely around the world, whose global military reach has taken on the character of normalcy, and that is responsible for several million civilian deaths just since World War II. Harris' apologetics are noteworthy for their lack of historical contextualization, for their refusal to acknowledge far-reaching economic and geopolitical (i.e., imperial) objectives shaping U.S. foreign and military policy.

While somewhat extreme, Harris' uncritical repetition of standard fairy tales about U.S. global behavior is not far removed from standard discourse within the public sphere. Even where savagery is conceded, ideological platitudes veer toward apologetics, locating the violence in an epic struggle of modern civilization against barbaric Muslim terrorists—a more current recycling of familiar European colonial propaganda. It follows that only diabolical enemies of the noble U.S. imperium would ever deliberately attack civilians. Thus Christopher Hitchens, in *A Long Short War*, refers to Muslims for whom "the concept of a civilian casualty is meaningless"[97] and who, historically, "inflicted casualties of the kind that would be called barbaric if imposed by Westerners."[98] He writes that Muslims specialize in indiscriminate attacks on civilian populations,[99] one example being Saddam Hussein who used "tactics that [were] directed primarily at civilians."[100] Douglas Murray, in his book *Neoconservatism*, mockingly calls attention to Arundhati Roy's perfectly sensible comment regarding the absurdity of U.S. attacks on other nations for *allegedly* possessing nuclear weapons while the U.S. itself controls by far the world's largest nuclear arsenal (along with abundant other WMD) and, moreover, is the only nation to have carried out nuclear warfare (intentionally against civilians, no less). Murray smugly dismisses such criticism, noting that Hiroshima and Nagasaki are by now ancient history and that it is time people dispensed with such "inherited guilt."[101] The problem is that Roy, Chomsky, and every other "two-bit peacenik poseur" have refused to transcend the past and get comfortable with the vagaries of U.S. military power. Murray's book contains bits of endless wisdom along these lines drawn apparently from the worst civic textbooks. Of course had we substituted for Hiroshima and Nagasaki—well-known episodes of American barbarism—another evil committed by a U.S. enemy at exactly the same time (the Nazi Holocaust), Murray and other provincial apologists might have thought different about "transcending" the lessons of history.

Such flimsy rationalizations contain a recurring motif: the U.S. never attacks civilians or, if discovered to have somehow done so, the attacks are (a) relegated to a distant and forgotten past, or (b) deemed the unfortunate result of collateral damage, or (c) an isolated tragedy, the work of a few demented individuals deviating from the established military norm. The question of what constitutes legitimate military targets is, of course, a matter of longstanding debate with obvious gray areas here and there. But when massive civilian casualties resulting from an immense variety of combat operations fit an ongoing pattern across many decades, embedded in discernible military strategies and political aims, then gray areas vanish and war crimes must be the verdict of history. Any objective account would ultimately arrive at such a judgment. The legacy of indiscriminate U.S. attacks on civilian targets extends back more than two centuries, to the earlier period of the Indian massacres, so a judgment of war crimes hardly represents a shocking departure from historical traditions. Saturation bombing, the dropping of nuclear weapons, sustained attacks on urban centers, destruction of life-support systems, introduction of chemical warfare, widespread use of such inhumane devices as napalm, white phosphorous, depleted uranium, and anti-personnel bombs—all this amounts to a criminal legacy no other group or nation has even remotely duplicated. Harris rambles on about the significance of *intent*, as if such motivation could never apply to U.S. decision-makers but only to their wicked enemies. (How he arrives at this bizarre contention is never stated.) Of course no political actors admit to conscious intent when it comes to their criminal behavior, any more than the most hardened criminals are likely to concede guilt—yet for the U.S. military the *pattern* of criminal behavior is so lengthy, so repetitive, so obvious, so extreme, and so clearly tied to imperial aims that only Americans indoctrinated in the pervasive ideology of Empire might blindly overlook it. Surely the methodologies of aggressive warfare long embraced by U.S. leaders are a matter of undeniable historical record. So too are the unfathomable human consequences that go well beyond arcane and self-serving claims of collateral damage. No impartial legal process in the world would exonerate any individual or group under such conditions, whatever their proclaimed intentions.

Leaving aside silly claims about the obsolescence of history, Harris, Hitchens, Murray, and other apologists for U.S. war crimes might be advised to look more closely at present-day evidence—notably Iraq. They could have attended a reprise of the Winter Soldier hearings, this time concentrated on Iraq, held in spring 2008 at Silver Springs, Maryland. As in the case of Vietnam, the hearings presented dozens of testimonies from U.S. military personnel, earlier stationed in Iraq, regarding wanton killings of civilians, torture, destruction of property, and other mayhem. All agreed that rules of engagement were largely ignored in the field and met with indifference at the higher levels. One Marine said: "By the time we got to Baghdad, I could shoot at anyone who came close enough to make me uncomfortable." Others reported the widespread, deliberate killing of civilians and mutilation of the dead.[102] Chris Hedges interviewed 50 returning Iraq veterans and found the same evidence of criminal behavior. Interviewing medics, MPs, snipers, artillerymen, and others among both the officer corps and enlisted men, Hedges uncovered a terrible pattern of atrocities—civilians randomly killed at checkpoints, unprovoked beatings and arrests, widespread torture, midnight raids on homes, and repeated abuse of people thought to be hostile to the American presence. In an atmosphere of fear and hatred, U.S. troops essentially declared war on the entire Iraqi population, viewed as subhuman. Brutalization of civilians never generated military or other investigations, while senior officers were depicted as fully accepting of criminal behavior. Hedges concluded that this disturbing pattern of atrocities only gave rise to insurgency, terrorism, and hatred of the American occupiers.[103]

The general problem of war crimes is aggravated when the nature of modern warfare is taken into account. In particular the U.S. dedication to technowar that, combined with awesome firepower, inevitably exposes civilians to horrific military violence, as shown in Iraq. We should know by now that claims of "precision targeting" are a myth, especially where large civilian populations are located within zones of military attack. Modern armed conflict increasingly revolves around urban guerrilla warfare, local insurrections, and civil strife, conditions under which distinctions between civilian and military targets easily collapse in the midst of battle. Foreign occupation, moreover, ensures large numbers of civilian dead, wounded, and displaced. In this context any recourse to notions of military *necessity* by a superior military power rings hollow, a desperate attempt to cover up or rationalize criminal operations. (It is important to ask: "Necessary" for whom and for what?) Unfortunately, U.S. leaders have rarely charted adequate legal guidelines for rules of engagement in military *practice*, as documented in this chapter. Even more telling: the very thrust of U.S. imperial ambitions means that military interventions *as a whole* cannot be justified morally or legally. The death of any civilians resulting from the U.S. drive toward world supremacy, however finessed for public consumption, is impossible to sustain.

This last point deserves greater attention than it has typically received in studies of U.S. global behavior, for if the U.S. has been guilty of repeated crimes against peace then Washington is fully responsible for all the death and destruction growing out of its policies and actions—as the Nuremberg precedent clearly affirmed. The problem of U.S. criminality today, therefore, is the degree to which it is rooted in the very logic not only of the Bush agenda but of a larger U.S. imperial strategy going back to the nineteenth century. If Antonia Juhasz is correct in stating that in Iraq Bush "unified military and corporate globalization into one mighty weapon of Empire," it follows that the entire intervention is illegal and immoral from beginning to end.[104] All references to noble purposes, unintended consequences, and collateral damage will be patently insufficient, deceitful to the core. A long pattern of U.S. agendas and decisions illustrates a gross devaluation of human life in the many countries that have been subjected to its overwhelming economic, political, and military power. Even if U.S. global behavior could be justified on grounds of national security or military defense—rarely sustainable—government leaders and armed-forces personnel would still be culpable of indiscriminate attacks on civilian populations and their support systems.

3
War Crimes by Proxy

One of the most common U.S. violations of international law and human rights conventions has been its long history of support for tyrannical regimes, paramilitary groups, and myriad forms of distant warfare across the globe. Such outlawry, driven by economic and geopolitical agendas, has typically involved the setting-up of proxy wars, insurgencies, covert operations, and other forms of military conflict favored especially for intervention throughout the underdeveloped world. Brutal regimes, many guilty of terrible abuses and atrocities over years and even decades, have received substantial (often *necessary*) assistance from Washington in such countries as Colombia, Guatemala, Chile, Turkey, Indonesia, the Philippines, and Israel. Political rebellions have been not only aided and abetted but *organized* in Nicaragua, Yugoslavia, and Afghanistan, usually with deadly consequences. Local paramilitary or death squads have been created and financed in El Salvador, Guatemala, Yugoslavia, and Afghanistan for reasons having nothing to do with democracy or other high-sounding claims. Governments have been overthrown with the help of American covert and/or direct intervention, as in Chile (1973) and earlier in Iran and Guatemala (in the 1950s). In fact, proxy operations, where U.S. forces remain in the background or invisible while mayhem is created mostly by local actors, are the generally *preferred* method, one that was especially refined during the Cold War.[1] Support has taken multiple forms: direct material assistance, military equipment and weaponry, recruitment and training, logistics and intelligence, and political or diplomatic cover within international bodies like the U.N. For several decades the U.S. has trained thousands of military and law-enforcement personnel at bases within the country who would later become members of governments, armed-forces, the police, militias, and death squads complicit in horrendous war crimes elsewhere.

Government leaders and other figures who sponsor or otherwise support crimes by proxy—who knowingly and deliberately furnish perpetrators with resources to carry out murderous deeds—are just as guilty as the perpetrators themselves and must, in the end, be held just as accountable. Within international law this is known simply as the "aiding and abetting of war crimes."[2] This was a major charge brought against Yugoslav leader Slobodan Milošević at The Hague Tribunal, where he was accused (in effect singled out along with other Serb leaders) of assisting paramilitary groups in the Balkans, such as the notorious Arkan's Tigers, by means of financial aid, training, weapons shipments, and logistical supports. Prosecutors for the International Criminal Tribunal for the former Yugoslavia (ICTY) argued that Milošević was just as culpable of war crimes perpetrated by these groups as if he had taken over their formal leadership.[3] Whatever the degree of Milošević's guilt—and little was established at the ICTY before his death in 2006—this kind of proxy relationship to regimes and organizations has been a stock-in-trade of U.S. foreign and military policy since World War II, but no Washington political or military figure has ever been held legally accountable. Historical evidence shows that the very charges leveled against Milošević could be brought against U.S. leaders hundreds of times over, as they use massive economic, political, and military resources to wage extended proxy wars around the world.

A HISTORY OF AIDING AND ABETTING

U.S. proxy warfare is deeply embedded in its long imperial role in world politics, having extended to most parts of the globe—above all, to Latin America, Asia, and the Middle East. Washington has provided assistance and comfort to regimes, paramilitary groups, and sundry political organizations that, in advancing both their own and U.S. interests, have targeted civilian movements and individuals working for national independence, social reforms, labor interests, or human rights. This is surely one of the darkest features of American foreign policy across the twentieth century and into the present. In the decades just since the 1960s the U.S. has supported Central American oligarchs in their repressive agendas, death squads in Colombia, the Iraqi military during its brutal 1980s war against Iran, right-wing Muslim rebellions in Afghanistan and Bosnia, and dispersed local terrorist networks in Yugoslavia, not to mention the decades-long Indonesian military suppression of leftist and independence movements.

At the same time, Amnesty International found that the U.S. has been the major source of arms exported to nations most guilty of war crimes and human rights abuses, including Colombia, Indonesia, Turkey, Pakistan, and Israel. During the 1990s alone

U.S. arms shipments abroad totaled nearly $200 billion—nearly half of all world sales—to some 57 nations, with few if any ethical or legal guidelines taken into account despite some formal constraints. Between 2001 and 2005, U.S. annual weapons sales totaled as much as $13 billion, while in 2006 alone the Pentagon signed arms agreements amounting to $21 billion, including huge shipments of surface-to-air missiles. The U.S. military has further earmarked $90 million to *train* people in the use of these weapons. In recent decades the U.S. has been known as something of a warehouse for weapons-grade firearms made available to any buyer at the right price, few questions asked. A haven of the most developed (and fiercely defended) gun culture in the world, it is a nation aptly described as a convenient market for weapons of all sorts procured by dictators, terrorists, mercenaries, death squads, and criminals of all stripes, even as American leaders and media pundits preach human rights and nonviolence virtually non-stop. Even after 9/11, heightened concerns about terrorism, and the passage of the Patriot Act, the U.S. remains a prime conduit of military-style arms made relatively easy to purchase and transport.[4] Arms merchants, whether government, corporations, or smaller interests, must bear some responsibility for those criminal actions—entirely predictable in most cases—carried out by the recipients.

At the height of the Cold War, between 1965 and 1969, the Indonesian military regime under General Suharto massacred an estimated 500,000 people—virtually anyone associated with the left opposition and Communist Party (PKI)—with full U.S. economic, political, and military support. This was surely one of the most egregious criminal operations of the postwar years, but it was met with deafening silence in the Western media. To facilitate the Suharto regime's outlawry the CIA and State Department drew up lengthy death lists in which PKI leaders were especially targeted.[5] The bloodshed took place in the absence of any legal or political constraints. As early as the 1950s the U.S. and Indonesian militaries had become intertwined when the Jakarta general staff (more than 6000 officers) had been given training at several U.S. bases. A decade following the PKI annihilation, one of the deadliest Washington achievements of the Cold War, the regime moved against strong independence movements in East Timor, killing at least another 100,000 people whose sin was to be involved in the struggle for national sovereignty. As casualties mounted in the late 1970s the U.S. continued to provide Indonesia with massive financial and military aid while blocking U.N. measures to protest (and halt) the carnage. Given its geopolitical value, the Jakarta dictatorship was for many years a favorite of the CIA and Pentagon, all the more so owing to its ruthless efficiency in destroying leftist organizations. After the 1975 Suharto invasion of East Timor, U.S. weapons sales to the military regime increased steadily, reaching a peak of one billion dollars during the Reagan years 1982 to 1984. Meanwhile, the East Timor massacres, enabled by the spread of paramilitary squads, would continue on and off for least another two decades. U.S. leaders clearly share culpability for a legacy of mass murder that has few historical parallels.

The Washington proxy war in Afghanistan spanned roughly a decade (1979 to 1988), a bloody campaign that would be the final Cold-War salvo in fighting "Soviet aggression." The CIA and the Pentagon spent more than three billion dollars to train, equip, and support a large jihadic terrorist operation based in Pakistan and presented to the American public as "freedom fighters" waging heroic battles on the outpost of Western civilization. Islamic fundamentalists were mobilized to overthrow a regime said to embody a "Godless evil"—in reality a Soviet-backed reform government that set about getting Afghanistan out of the dark ages. It was a fanatical ideological crusade accompanied by unspeakable violence: rockets sent into densely populated areas, prisoners routinely tortured and killed, combat without regard for any rules of engagement. Financed almost entirely through drug trafficking and CIA largesse, the Afghan campaign represented the ultimate Washington Cold-War fantasy where Soviet power would be worn down without the loss of even a single American life. In the end the war turned one of the poorest nations in the world into a terrain of rubble, giving rise to unbelievable savagery: more than one million dead, three million disabled, and five million displaced. This extended proxy war also brought to power a fascistic Taliban regime—anti-Communist to be sure, but dedicated to turning Afghanistan into a traditional dictatorship bereft of basic human rights. The regime served as a launching pad for subsequent jihadic adventures in Chechnya, Bosnia, and North Africa, inspiring the rise and growth of Al Qaeda at the same time.

In the case of Turkey—a strong, nominally democratic ally of both the U.S. and Israel in the Middle East—we have yet another proxy relationship: brutal Turkish treatment of its large Kurdish population for decades while the nation has remained one of the biggest recipients of U.S. economic, military, and political aid. As government repression worsened during the 1990s with stepped up efforts to destroy Kurdish struggles for autonomy, the Turkish army moved to isolate and in some cases demolish local villages, forcing hundreds of thousands of civilians out of their homes and communities. As many as two million Kurds were left homeless while local paramilitary squads, with government blessings and support, murdered thousands. American-made planes dropped U.S.-produced napalm on villages, hitting mostly civilians. State terrorism became routine practice. Meanwhile, by the year 2000 Turkey had become the single largest importer of U.S. military goods, including F-16 fighter planes, M-60 tanks, Cobra gunships, and Blackhawk helicopters in vast numbers, all used against mostly defenseless Kurds—the very same ethnic population that Washington, driven by geopolitical aims, would champion as a great liberating force in Iraq.[6] Yet if in Iraq the stratagem dictated regime change, in Turkey it meant something altogether different—stabilization of a repressive government, whatever the cost in Kurdish lives.

The legacy of proxy wars—"wars" defined broadly to encompass multiple forms of political violence—has become profoundly embedded in contemporary U.S. foreign and military policy. Such operations have been a preferred strategy to secure global aims, as direct modes of intervention tend to be more costly. Through proxy relationships, moreover, Washington has been able to escape the close political and media scrutiny that inevitably follows direct military engagement, as in Korea, Vietnam, Iraq, and Afghanistan. Although proxy warfare was an integral part of U.S. Cold-War *strategy*, it has clearly outlived its origins, more recently visible in such widely diverse settings as Central America, the Balkans, and the Middle East.

CENTRAL AMERICA: SECOND-HAND TERRORISM

Among the most gruesome and sustained records of U.S. proxy warfare can be found in Central America—part of a legacy of military intervention going back to the nineteenth century and reaching its peak in the 1980s and 1990s. Throughout Latin America the U.S. supported decades of state terrorism as well as scores of deadly paramilitary groups created and sustained mostly by the CIA and the Pentagon. The final chapters of this history have, unfortunately, yet to be written, as the U.S. continues to protect its economic and geopolitical power in the region.

As in the cases of Indonesia, Afghanistan, and Colombia, U.S. engagement in Central America has included all phases of operations: training, arms and equipment, logistics, intelligence, financial aid. And the human consequences have been just as painfully far-reaching. At the infamous School of the Americas (SOA), renamed in 2001 the Western Hemisphere Institute for Security Cooperation, located at Fort Benning, Georgia, the Pentagon has trained more than 60,000 operatives in methods of counterinsurgency and guerrilla warfare across Latin America. SOA training manuals emphasized a wide array of methods, including assassination, commando raids, torture, mass executions, blackmail, and intelligence. Death squads were set up to wage proxy battles in defense of combined U.S. and local oligarchical interests, especially in Central America, since the 1960s.[7] Graduates of SOA include the notorious Roberto D'Aubisson, who organized a death-squad network in El Salvador during the 1980s, reportedly killing upwards of 10,000 people as part of a U.S.–Salvadoran campaign to crush popular insurrection and destroy leftist and civic movements. Massacres of defenseless civilians were common, with dozens of villages demolished, many of them burned to the ground. Death squads were recruited from both civilians and members of the armed forces and police, the vast majority trained and supported by the SOA and other bases in the U.S.

According to the U.N. Truth Commission on Salvadoran Death Squads, it was D'Aubisson and his corps of terrorist commandos who built and maintained a large network of paramilitary groups bringing together American interests, Miami-based exiles, and right-wing Salvadoran forces. They did their work in the name of combating Soviet subversion in Central America—the fear of another Sandinista regime was palpable—but in reality their agenda was to wipe out all domestic opposition to the Washington-backed power structure. In the period 1980–92 the U.S. spent six billion dollars to sustain one of the most ruthless proxy military campaigns ever waged in the Western hemisphere. That campaign produced a death toll estimated as high as 75,000, along with displacement of one-fourth of the population (mostly poor peasants) pushed out of their homes during sweeps by the army and death squads.[8] Abductions, torture, and mass executions were routine practices that never caused uneasiness in Washington. Air power too came into play, an instrument of bombing, strafing, and napalm runs in the countryside. In 1980 alone the Human Rights Office of El Salvador reported 8062 murders of people involved in opposition movements and civic organizations—a number that would increase to 12,500 in 1981.[9] Widespread reports surfaced during the 1980s of scorched-earth campaigns accompanied by mass torture and killings. The U.S. deployed hundreds of CIA agents, military "advisers," and other operatives in El Salvador as the terror escalated. Noam Chomsky writes that "It is notable that in El Salvador, as in Nicaragua, the level of atrocities, which rival the most gruesome in recent years, increased dramatically as U.S. involvement grew."[10]

In Guatemala a regime of U.S.-sponsored atrocities spanning at least four decades far exceeded what took place in El Salvador. The CIA and the Pentagon supported a reign of government repression and death-squad terrorism going back as far as the U.S.-engineered overthrow of the Jacobo Arbenz government in 1954, leading to a death toll reaching perhaps 200,000. The killings, presided over by a long line of Washington-backed dictators anxious to destroy all vestiges of political opposition and guerrilla insurgency, were made possible by a continuous flow of American weapons, equipment, and financial aid combined with SOA training and Pentagon logistical supports. Oppositional leaders, especially those connected to indigenous movements, were labeled "Communist" and executed by the thousands, many of them buried in mass graves. During 1966–68 alone Amnesty International reported a death toll of some 8000 attributed to the army, police, and paramilitary groups that roamed freely across the countryside. By 1972 the number of murdered was estimated at nearly 13,000 for that year alone—a figure reaching 20,000 by 1976.[11] Anyone involved in local organizing activity was subject to attack. In the early 1980s the Reagan administration renewed U.S. dedication to "peace and democracy" in Guatemala, to which end it backed the 1982 General Efraim Montt coup that brought an escalation of massacres to the rural areas, with several thousand peasants and Indians slaughtered in the first months after the coup. Assisted by both U.S. and Israeli military arms and equipment—Washington gave nearly $800 million between 1981 and 1990—atrocities were carried out with impunity.[12] A permanent state of terror existed throughout the nation, targeting even moderate forces of change. During the 1980s and 1990s Guatemalan death squads were organized primarily by two large groups, the G2 and Archivo, both funded by the CIA and run by CIA-paid Guatemalan military police officers trained at SOA and elsewhere in both the U.S. and Central America. According to witness accounts, the G2 maintained an extensive network of torture centers along with secret body dumps and crematoria.[13] Few if any of these atrocities were likely to have been unknown to the sponsors in Washington.

From 1979 to the mid 1980s the CIA recruited, trained, and armed a well-organized Contra network, a made-in-America insurgency set up to destabilize and then overthrow the reformist Sandinista government in Nicaragua. Based in Honduras, the Contras (numbering over 10,000) did everything possible to subvert and overthrow the system: economic sabotage, mining of harbors, political assassinations, and widespread killing of civilians with the aim of destroying public morale. During both the Carter and Reagan presidencies the U.S. claimed the Sandinistas were setting up a Soviet beachhead in Central America—a foothold allowing them to foment revolution elsewhere in the hemisphere. As part of their campaign, consistent with CIA instructional manuals, the Contras were to carry out hit-and-run raids across the border, attacking farmlands, homes, schools, and agricultural coops with remarkable savagery. Reagan's "freedom fighters" were encouraged to practice torture and did so with abandon.[14] CIA helicopters provided routine military cover and logistics in support of these criminal actions. When direct CIA management of the proxy Contra army was terminated by Congress in 1986, the Reagan administration secretly transferred authority to the National Security Council as terror operations continued, more sporadically, for another few years. When in 1984 Nicaragua protested U.S. mining of its harbors to the World Court—and was resoundingly vindicated—Washington simply ignored the Court's verdict, consistent with the larger pattern of U.S. double standards and national exceptionalism.

What occurred in Central America from the 1960s through the 1990s—a ruthless application of proxy warfare through state-engineered terrorism—was in fact no radical departure from past behavior. Bloody U.S. interventions in the region, both direct and indirect, go far back into the nineteenth century. The power structure responsible for such criminality, moreover, remains fully intact today, still prepared to advance U.S. economic and geopolitical agendas through a creative variety of police and military methods. Meanwhile, the conveniently renamed SOA retains its longstanding basic features and mission. Here as elsewhere U.S. proxy campaigns can be said to have been rather efficient and cost-free, largely outside the purview of government and media scrutiny, at least in the U.S. Reflecting on this context, Chomsky writes: "U.S. subversion, sabotage, and aggression are carefully plotted operations, as one would expect in the case of a terrorist state with unmatched power and only limited domestic constraints."[15]

YUGOSLAVIA: "HUMANITARIAN" WARFARE

The proxy-war campaign in Yugoslavia waged by the U.S. through NATO, going back to the late 1980s, intensified during the 1990s, culminating in the protracted spring 1999 bombing campaign. By the early 1990s the U.S. was busy recruiting, training, and equipping dispersed local rebellions and separatist movements in a nation increasingly under siege as Western powers moved to expand NATO eastward. With the end of the Cold War and collapse of the Soviet bloc these powers (notably the U.S. and Germany) sought control over the geopolitically vital Balkans. The aim was to strengthen right-wing oppositional groups including Bosnian Muslim fundamentalists, the fascistic Croatian government, the Kosovo Liberation Movement (KLA), and a variety of local paramilitary squads, hoping to destabilize the (elected) Serb government regarded by Washington as final holdover from the Communist era—one last impediment to the full marketization of Europe. While economic and geostrategic issues were mainly at stake, the Western media cast the Serbs and their leader, Slobodan Milošević, as an evil monster prepared to carry out "ethnic cleansing" and "genocide" to establish Greater Serbia—a charge that would later be filed against Milošević and other Serb leaders at The Hague Tribunal.

As the U.S. and other NATO powers set out to integrate the Balkans into a neoliberal Europe, the Federal Republic of Yugoslavia (FRY) was targeted for demolition, framed as an obstacle to democracy and progress. The Balkans, of course, occupy a crucial geographical zone linking Europe to the Middle East, a central preoccupation of Washington as it stepped up its resource agendas in the Persian Gulf and Central Asia.[16] In November 1990 the U.S. Congress passed the Foreign Operations Appropriation Law, withdrawing aid and credits from the FRY and calling for secession by each of the six republics. Both the World Bank and IMF were pressured to withhold financial aid at a time when right-wing secessionist forces were receiving an influx of U.S. and NATO funding. Strong centrifugal tendencies, bound to tear apart the FRY, would inevitably come to the fore. With abundant U.S. and German support, anti-Serb movements gained footholds in 1991 and 1992, first in Slovenia and then in Croatia and Bosnia. Separatist attacks predictably led to Serb military responses, denounced in the Western media as "genocidal," the product of Nazi-style expansionism and brutality. Meanwhile, the Franjo Tudjman (Croatian) and Alija Izetbegović (Bosnian) regimes were busy carrying out their own, far more ruthless and systematic, ethnic cleansing operations. In many instances Serbs, considered fair targets once they were demonized, were expelled from land their ancestors had occupied for centuries.

In 1992 the first Bush administration fought to push through economic sanctions against the FRY, succeeding as the U.N. moved to ban all exports and imports, resulting in financial and social chaos. Throughout 1992–95 the U.S. gave substantial economic and military aid to the Izetbegović forces in Bosnia while helping the Muslims gain nearly total control of a region inhabited by 30 percent Serbs—a campaign enthusiastically waged by a regime dedicated to Taliban-style governance. Most Bosnian military leaders were trained by the U.S. and fully equipped by the CIA. By 1995 the U.S. was calling for an extensive bombing campaign in Bosnia, having already deployed (through NATO) some 20,000 troops there, with the aim of essentially driving out the Serbs. Meanwhile, in Croatia the Tudjman regime initiated "Operation Storm"—fully backed by the U.S. and NATO—designed to aggressively evict Serbs from the Krajina region where they had deep historic roots, leading to the bloodiest episode of the decade-long Yugoslav civil wars. In August 1995 some 300,000 Serbs were forcibly removed from their homes and the area in an onslaught killing an estimated 14,000 people. Trapped Serbs pouring into Bosnia were massacred in large numbers by Croatian and Bosnian troops supported by the U.S. and Germany, an operation planned by Military Professional Resources, Inc. (MPRI), a Pentagon contractor made up largely of retired U.S. generals, many of whom had already been helping to train and assist the Croatian army. Despite its gruesome results, the offensive was unabashedly endorsed by Clinton's Secretary of State, Warren Christopher, who defined it as a campaign to fight "ethnic cleansing."[17] These efforts to destabilize and dismember the FRY were, not surprisingly, rather successful given the enormous resources behind them. Military actions of the Milošević regime, itself guilty of atrocities as it fought to preserve the integrity of the FRY, were conveyed in the Western media as simple acts of genocidal aggression, behavior devoid of political context and motive. But the historical context belied such simplistic propaganda: the civil wars were made possible by U.S./NATO proxy campaigns designed to overthrow a sovereign government that was never involved in military aggression.

By early 1995 the U.S./NATO destabilization efforts had centered increasingly on Kosovo, where the KLA was already operating freely in large numbers, thanks to abundant CIA support. Although Kosovo had been part of Serbia for 600 years, secession was now pushed hard from both inside and outside, reaching its peak in 1997–99, by which time the KLA had evolved into a military extension of NATO. The separatist movement carried out terrorist actions throughout Kosovo, killing hundreds of Serb officials with the blessing of the Western powers. Possessing a large network of foreign-supported operatives and a well-entrenched military apparatus, the KLA leadership chose to deal from armed strength, rejecting all negotiation offers while pushing full-speed ahead for total Albanian control of the province. The KLA goal was immediate, total secession to be achieved by means of military action.[18] Diana Johnstone writes that "Albanian separatists were able to capture the ear of the Empire because of their extraordinary eagerness to link their cause to the advance of NATO at the expense of a Yugoslav leadership still clinging to notions of national independence."[19]

In the U.S., meanwhile, a powerful Albanian lobby worked to secure Washington support for an ethnic cleansing of Kosovo, hoping to expel the 270,000 Serbs already victimized by daily mass evictions, beatings, torture, and other atrocities. These brutal actions were described in the Western media and related public-relations campaigns as a form of "humanitarian intervention." The Serbs and Milošević were presented, without evidence, as one of the last bastions of evil on the planet, totalitarian to the core and fully deserving of being forced out of the region. With the mounting casualties of Serbs in Kosovo, the harsh Serb military counter-response—predictable for any government challenged by militant secessionist forces—was quickly denounced in the U.S. and Europe as just another sign of "ethnic cleansing." As for the KLA, its terrorism was fully exempt from such condemnation since its leaders were, like the Contras in Nicaragua, another example of heroic "freedom fighters."

In the end, the U.S./NATO proxy war in the Balkans succeeded after many years of economic, political, and military subterfuge directed against the FRY, notably the Serbs, who were demonized as the reincarnation of Nazism. Right-wing and neo-fascist separatists emerged as heroic defenders of Western civilization struggling for freedom and democracy against unspeakable tyranny and "genocide." Liberals and Social Democrats joined conservatives in this holy crusade. In reality, naked geopolitical agendas were behind the intervention, facilitating NATO's eastward thrust. The end result, following protracted U.S./NATO aerial bombardments in early 1999, was foreign occupation of Yugoslavia and new opportunities for Western corporate expansion into the Balkans. For inhabitants of the former FRY, the outcome was nothing short of economic and political disaster. Here was a case of proxy warfare—and the crimes it perpetrated—conducted through a complex merger of interests: Pentagon, CIA, think-tanks, public-relations firms, the corporate media, local militias, and European powers. The cost in lives and resources to a relatively poor region was immeasurable. While The Hague Tribunal was quick to charge Milošević and other Serb leaders with a variety of war crimes, nothing was said about U.S./NATO military aggression against Yugoslavia in clear violation of international law, nor about the U.S. waging the kinds of proxy wars that would be laid at the doorstep of Milošević and the Serbs.

The U.S./NATO crusade for the break-up of Yugoslavia and subsequent erosion of Serb power in the Balkans culminated in the final move toward Kosovo independence in February 2008. Despite massive Serb protests inside and outside of Kosovo—and in direct violation of international law—Western powers gave lucrative assistance to the KLA and other right-wing secessionist forces in their struggle for a new nation grounded in overwhelming Albanian identity, but with no basis in any diplomatic or legal procedures. In reality U.S./NATO military forces had already taken control of Kosovo, with 16,000 troops in the field and a presence consolidated at the massive Camp Bondsteel compound, built in the aftermath of the 1999 aerial attacks. The effective result was continued U.S./NATO colonial occupation of Kosovo, destined to become a puppet state serving Western geopolitical interests. With unilateral recognition of statehood carved out of historic Serb territory, the U.S. and a few European allies won the "right" to dispose of the territory as they chose—but it was an outcome dictated by military and political power. And Kosovo, meanwhile, was turned into a dependent colony ravaged by violent conflict, massive unemployment, declining social services, and a growing mafia underground.[20]

ISRAEL: CLIENT–STATE OUTLAWRY

The Israeli occupation of Palestine, with its continuous acts of military aggression and human rights abuses over several decades, is surely the most visible (and no doubt most egregious) case of U.S.

war crimes by proxy. The state of Israel has in many ways served as an American imperial outpost in the Middle East, subsidized by every conceivable form of economic, political, diplomatic, and military backing—a relationship that is, indeed, *sui generis*. By the 1990s, thanks to U.S. largesse, Israel possessed the fourth largest army in the world that, over such a limited terrain, guaranteed a level of militarism appropriate to an occupying garrison state. Israeli militarism has helped to bolster an apartheid system marked by ongoing, flagrant violations of international law: forcible settlement of land, illegal arrests, torture, relocation of civilian populations, harsh curfews, killings, assaults on cultural institutions, wanton bulldozing of homes and property, depriving inhabitants of basic services needed for survival, and outright military assaults as in Gaza during early 2009. Such actions involve clear violations of the Fourth Geneva Convention, along with the U.N. Charter and other statutes of international law, but efforts to hold the Israelis accountable have been regularly blocked by the U.S., ensuring a worsening occupation of Gaza and the West Bank through repeated vetoes of U.N. resolutions. Further, as of 2000 there were some 5.5 million Palestinian refugees located in 59 camps, local inhabitants denied the right to return to their homes in contravention of U.N. Resolution 194 and general provisions of international law. Perpetual violence is the logical outcome of this horrid state of affairs. As Michael Neumann rightly points out: "Israel is the illegitimate child of ethnic nationalism. The inhabitants of Palestine had every reason to oppose its establishment by any means necessary."[21]

In November 1967 the U.N. Security Council unanimously passed Resolution 242, stating the "inadmissibility of the acquisition of territory by war" and called for Israeli withdrawal from occupied territories, that became the basis of an international consensus opposed only by the U.S. and Israel. Since 1967 the U.S. has been Israel's reliable weapons supplier and financial patron, accompanied by a fierce rejectionism regarding the establishment of a Palestinian state grounded on the universal principle of self-determination. Over several decades the U.S. has repeatedly vetoed any move toward a two-state arrangement, the only conceivable solution to the conflict. Palestinian resistance to Israeli occupation has been met with sustained force and repression, fully supported by the U.S. whether Democrats or Republicans were in power. Israeli leaders, from moderate to extreme, have set out to destroy any vestige of a Palestinian opposition viewed as nothing but savage terrorism. To solidify Israeli hegemony a settler movement has been allowed to flourish—the total number of settlers from abroad growing to more than 200,000 after 1993—while East Jerusalem was simply annexed. Palestinians were condemned to a life of brutal repression and poverty, with no viable alternative but violent insurrection. Local uprisings (intifadas) were met with ever more ruthless crackdowns, arrests, and violence. Meanwhile, Washington has furnished Israel with more than three billion dollars in aid yearly on average—the most generous U.S. allocation of foreign funds anywhere, all based on full, unconditional support.[22]

Beneath its celebrated "democracy," the Israeli state was historically founded on brute force and terrorism leading to an occupation regime in clear violation of international legality. The territory expropriated by Israel is stolen land, justified by Zionist ideology with its phony biblical claims and sustained by a fanaticism that views the local population as subhuman primitives. A racist system that degrades those it occupies inevitably rests upon force, terror, and expulsions—that is, on systematic violation of human rights. Since 1967 the illegal settlements have served to extend and deepen Palestinian dispossession, consolidating what has become the world's largest prison, all made possible by U.S. economic, political, and military support. To legitimate such criminality, Israel lays claim to ethnic and religious supremacy rooted in Zionism, an ideology that glorifies colonial theft of land, appropriation of resources, and military occupation denying even the most basic rights to Palestinians. Repeated U.N. votes demanding that Israel follow the precepts of international law have been repeatedly opposed by the U.S. and Israel, both nations totally cut off from standard global norms they so pretentiously champion.[23]

According to U.N. reports and comparable statements from Amnesty International along with other human rights organizations, the Israeli oppression of Palestinians amounts to an ongoing human catastrophe—destroying the lives of millions of people without much hope of political enfranchisement. As Norman Finkelstein concludes from his careful study of human rights in the region: "The consensus among human rights organizations ... is that Israeli security forces have resorted to reckless use of force in the Occupied Territories, showing callous disregard for human life."[24] The Israeli Defense Forces (IDF) have routinely employed U.S.-made helicopters in rocket attacks on civilian populations, part of a strategy of liquidating those involved in legitimate resistance. The Israelis have pursued assassination, extrajudicial executions, illegal detentions, and torture as regular practices all thoroughly documented by

Amnesty International and other groups.[25] Checkpoints have been set up to systematically control the local population, again in full violation of international law. Those arrested are often deprived of food and sleep, beaten, given electric shocks, exposed to extremes of heat and cold, and subjected to other creative methods of torture. Amnesty International reported thousands of such cases of inhumane treatment during the 1990s, a reality the Israeli legal system has come to view as normal.[26] Thousands of Palestinian homes have been demolished, mostly with U.S.-made bulldozers, to make way for Jewish settlements that further destroy agricultural land needed for human food consumption. Among many Israeli massacres were the indiscriminate assaults on unarmed civilians at Jenin in April 2002, producing hundreds of casualties including what Human Rights Watch found to be "unlawful and willful killings."[27] The Israel Supreme Court has consistently given legal approval to IDF operations that violated international law.

The issue of war crimes here cannot be addressed within mainstream currents of American politics or jurisprudence since, as Edward Said observed several years ago, "the systematic continuity of Israel's 52-year-old [now 60-year-old] oppression and maltreatment of the Palestinians is virtually unmentionable, a narrative that has no permission to appear." It is "the last taboo."[28] From 1949 to 2000, the U.S. gave more than $90 billion in foreign aid and other forms of assistance to Israel, including $5.5 billion in 1997 alone. There were 18 arms sales to Israel in just the year 2000 alone. Thanks to generous American aid, the Israelis have the largest fleet of F-16s outside the U.S., integral to their sophisticated war machine. The Ariel Sharon regime was fully backed by the U.S., although Sharon was held responsible for a series of atrocities against Palestinians, including the massacre of possibly 3000 unarmed civilians in the refugee camps of Sabra and Shatila in September 1982, when Sharon oversaw the mass killings carried out by the Christian Phalange. Sharon was obsessed with destroying Palestinian resistance, whatever the horrors brought to the targeted population. Not only was Sharon given reprieve from having to face any war-crimes tribunal, his subsequent election as Israeli Prime Minister was greeted (in both the U.S. and Israel) as a great event, said to be the triumph of a creative statesman and man of peace.

As defense minister in Menachem Begin's government, Sharon was the army commander who led the 1982 invasion of Lebanon with the intent of demolishing the PLO infrastructure and other vestiges of Palestinian political and cultural resistance. Toward that end the Israelis bombed civilian populations at will, took over nearly half the country, destroyed most of Beirut, and left the country in shambles. The invasion itself was, of course, a crime against peace. Outnumbering PLO fighters by twelve to one, the Israelis mobilized 172,000 troops, 3500 tanks, 4000 armored personnel carriers, and 602 combat aircraft—all reinforced by a constant infusion of U.S. funds and equipment.[29] In a bloody 67-day campaign dubbed "Peace for Galilee," Israel attacked urban centers, destroying homes, schools, hospitals, and whatever else could be targeted. The human toll: an estimated 20,000 killed, tens of thousands wounded, and 600,000 people driven from their homes. The Israelis attacked refugee camps with abandon for "harboring terrorists." Terror weapons were used, including incendiary devices and anti-personnel bombs.[30] During the siege of Beirut, moreover, Israel set up a blockade to cut off supplies of water, food, medicine, and energy sources—yet another crime against humanity. At the end of this one-sided "war," aside from the aforementioned refugee camp massacres, the IDF systematically targeted unarmed civilians in flight along roads of escape from the warfare.[31]

The U.S.–Israel client-state relationship is solidified and legitimated by the indefatigable and well-financed work of the Israel lobby comprised of groups like AIPAC, the Jewish Institute for National Security Affairs (JINSA), the Washington Institute for Near East Policy (WINEP), the Zionist Organization of America (ZOA), various Christian Zionist organizations, and the Israel Policy Forum (IPP) with crucial support from think-tanks like AEI, Project for a New American Century (PNAC), and the Hudson Institute—a political force massively documented by the work of John Mearsheimer and Stephen Walt in *The Israel Lobby* (2007). As the authors show, the lobby has powerful influence throughout American political culture, as illustrated by the fact that both Democrats and Republicans have adopted virtually identical policies on the Middle East. Above all this means unwavering and unconditional Washington support for Israel across the board: rejection of a viable two-state solution, tacit acceptance of new Jewish settlements in violation of international law, silence regarding the erection of barricades and walls, support for military aggression in Lebanon in 2006 and Gaza in 2009, willingness to go along with the unlawful occupation of Palestinian lands, refusal to deal with daily human rights violations such as home demolitions and the detention of thousands of prisoners without due process, and huge shipments of economic and military aid. As Mearsheimer and Walt further argue, it was this combination of powerful forces—Israeli leaders, the U.S. Israel lobby, and neocons within the Bush administration—that was probably decisive in Washington's move to carry out "regime change" in Iraq.[32] Although U.S. imperial maneuvers in the Middle East, widely understood to greatly benefit Israel's own power ambitions, have explosive implications for world politics, such maneuvers have achieved such a level of bipartisan support in American politics that debate is routinely closed off.

The power of the Israel lobby is such that it can push the U.S. into behavior that sometimes apparently conflicts with its own (American) strategic interests. Consistent support for Israeli oppression and disenfranchisement, for example, reinforces blowback across the Middle East and the world, fueling the very terrorism that the joint "war on terror" is supposedly meant to counter. Hypocrisy and double standards constantly visible at the United Nations only serve to undermine any pretense to democracy and human rights. While the U.S. pours tens of billions of dollars into the Israeli war machine, it vetoes dozens of U.N. Security Council resolutions condemning Israel—more than all other vetoes combined. The General Assembly has passed a similar number of resolutions condemning Israeli behavior, every one of them opposed by the U.S.[33] The U.S. has provided Israel with sophisticated high-tech weapons while helping cover for its "secret" nuclear-weapons program, all the while threatening Iran for its yet-to-be proven WMD enterprise. Israel operates active chemical and biological weapons projects that, as in the case of its nuclear stockpile, resist any external monitoring because the nation does not subscribe to any WMD treaties.

As for the ostensible *moral* basis of U.S. support for Israel, it is nonexistent—a point elaborated by Mearsheimer and Walt. Thus: "There is no compelling moral rationale for America's uncritical and uncompromising relationship with Israel ... Given Israel's brutal treatment of the Palestinians in the Occupied Territories, moral considerations might suggest that the United States pursue a more evenhanded policy toward the two sides, and maybe even lean toward the Palestinians."[34] Later in the text the authors take a sharper position: "if the United States were to choose sides on the basis of moral considerations alone, it would back the Palestinians not Israel."[35] Insofar as Palestinians have been victims of land theft, social oppression, political disenfranchisement, and military assaults from the beginning, U.S. participation in Israeli outlawry further subverts any possible moral case, instead making the U.S. fully complicit in ongoing criminal behavior. The idea that Washington represents some kind of "neutral arbiter," balancing the interests of two equally powerful and blameworthy sides, constitutes another preposterous myth: U.S.–Israeli collaboration extends to politics, economics, the military, and intelligence, with Washington most often serving as "Israel's lawyer" at the U.N. and other international venues. This cozy relationship simply reinforces blowback across the Middle East and represents by far the biggest source of terrorism in the world today. Sayyid Muhammed Hosayn Fadlallah, a Hezbollah leader, said in 2002: "I believe that America bears responsibility for all of Israel, both in its occupation [and] in all its settlement policies ... America is a hypocritical nation ... for it gives solid support and lethal weapons to the Israelis, but gives the Arabs and the Palestinians [only] words."[36] These sentiments have become nearly universal outside Israel and the U.S.

What further worsens this state of affairs has been the lobby's tenacious push for war against Iraq and Iran, both states having long been viewed as obstacles to Israeli power in the Middle East—a stratagem not to be confused with spreading democracy or even fighting terrorism, much less curbing WMD proliferation, as both the U.S. and Israel are perfectly content to strengthen their own nuclear presence in the Middle East.[37] Mearsheimer and Walt show how the drive toward war against Iraq and Iran has been a staple discourse of both Israeli political culture and neocon ideology going back to the early 1990s if not before. They differ with the conventional thesis that oil was the main catalyst behind U.S. intervention in Iraq—a point that would seem even more persuasive in the case of Iran. While it is easy to show that the Israel lobby and the neocons pushed hard for war against Iraq, evidence is more difficult to locate when it comes to the supposed role of fossil-fuel corporations, although without doubt many have benefited from the venture.[38] In any event, the joint U.S.–Israeli strategy for "transforming" the Middle East envisions joint domination of the region, a criminal project destined to cause immense human suffering and a further descent into lawlessness, militarism, and terrorism.

Given the sway of American global power, international bodies such as the U.N. and the International Criminal Court have been thwarted when it comes to legally confronting outlawry in the Middle East. Alvaro de Soto, a former U.N. envoy to the Middle East, warned in a report that the world organization had allowed itself to be "pummeled into submission" by U.S. pressure to favor Israel at every turn. He said efforts to deal with the Israel–Palestinian conflict were nothing but "side-shows"—fraudulent negotiations meant to go nowhere.[39] Among his many complaints, de Soto lamented U.N. orders blocking him from engaging Syria and the duly-elected Hamas government in Gaza as part of peacemaking efforts, a move generally seen as crucial to any success. De Soto wrote that the U.N. Middle East diplomatic process "has become strategically subservient to the U.S. policy in the broader Middle East, including Iraq and Iran."[40] He cited a "heavy barrage" of pressure from National Security Council official Elliot Abrams (a leading neocon), among others, to isolate Hamas or face prospects the U.S. would withhold its U.N. dues—a common blackmail ploy used by Washington at the U.N. De Soto concluded that the (illegal) economic sanctions imposed on the Palestinians owing to U.S.–Israeli pressure were myopic and "devastating" for the civilian population, and subversive of any peace process.

In summer 2006—having ended its occupation of southern Lebanon in 2002—the Israelis carried out yet another round of sustained military attacks on Lebanon, this time on the pretext that the militant organization Hezbollah abducted three IDF soldiers. This assault was equally fierce although of shorter duration, killing 1200 Lebanese (mostly civilians), displacing tens of thousands, and ruining much of the nation's public infrastructure. Israel waged a continuous air campaign and fired 160,000 artillery rounds into areas of concentrated population, destroying several villages—here with the intent of annihilating the core of Hezbollah opposition which, militarily speaking, far exceeded PLO power in the early 1980s. During the 2006 campaign Israel dropped cluster bombs on a vast scale, leaving some 100,000 unexploded devices scattered across the countryside. U.N. teams identified more than 700 cluster-bomb sites, about 90 percent of them hit in the final few days of warfare when the only purpose could have been punitive—an assault designed to punish local inhabitants for their support of Hezbollah.[41] In the midst of this brutal campaign the U.S. House passed a resolution offering unconditional support for Israel and praising its efforts to "minimize civilian losses," while also blocking all international moves toward a ceasefire. At the same time, Washington provided Israel with $200 million in jet fuel along with new supplies of bombs and missiles to reinforce its firepower. That this "war" turned out to be a miserable failure does not ameliorate its gross criminality.

Sadly, the horrors were destined to continue: in January 2009 the Israelis conducted a murderous assault on the Gaza strip lasting nearly a month, justified as retaliation for Hamas rocket attacks (mostly sporadic and harmless) into Israel. The attack produced nearly 7000 casualties, mostly civilians who could not escape the brutal, multi-tiered, round-the-clock operations of the IDF. One of the world's most powerful war machines battered a helpless population into submission, attacking homes, office buildings, schools, hospitals—anything that moved—while telling the world that painstaking attempts were being made to avoid civilian losses. The lengthy Gaza blockade had already reduced a poor, desperate population to further misery. The apparent Israeli goal was to destroy the social foundations of Hamas, a political organization that Israel and the U.S. had long defined as "terrorist" even after its fairly won election in early 2006. While Israel claimed to be exercising the right of self-defense, no such right was permitted Gazans long trapped in a miserable open-air prison—though resistance to an illegal occupation was entirely legitimate.

Using F-16 planes, attack helicopters, tanks, and armored bulldozers—mostly supplied by the U.S.—along with large-scale infantry units, the Israelis spared nothing in their drive to annihilate Palestinian resistance. Every possible civilian structure was attacked, including such "targets" as a United Nations food warehouse in Gaza City. A *Los Angeles Times* story from the small Gaza town of Khozaa reported such disturbing horrors as Israelis slaughtering groups of civilians who displayed white flags of surrender in open space. The IDF fired indiscriminately on civilians, including women and children, attacked ambulances and other medical emergency crews, conducted all-night barrages against residences, shot randomly at fleeing civilians, bulldozed dozens of homes, and used inhumane weapons, leaving in their wake three days of carnage visited on a population trapped, with nowhere to go. Reporters found noxious signs of white phosphorous throughout Khozaa, with scores of people seared and killed by the banned chemical. Everything was carried out with sadistic brutality. Observing one bulldozer demolishing homes, the reporter writes: "He picked up the side of the house like it was a box of matches ... We could see the bulldozer driver chewing gum and smiling like it was all a game."[42] Streets, buildings, and morgues were left with dead bodies. Emotional charges of war crimes came from even within the Israeli military, replete with accounts by soldiers of indiscriminate killing of civilians—many trapped in their homes, with nowhere to hide or run. In narrative accounts carried throughout the Israeli media, soldiers reported wanton assaults in densely populated areas of Gaza, saying the predominant Israeli attitude was that anyone in sight must be a "terrorist." Said one IDF member: "I call this murder. We were supposed to go up floor by floor [in an apartment building] and any person we identified, we were supposed to shoot." According to another soldier: "The attitude is very simple. It isn't pleasant to say, but no one cares at all. We aren't investigating this. This is what happens during fighting." Rules of engagement were apparently jettisoned altogether.[43]

The Gaza invasion came after nearly two years of another criminal Israeli operation—a military-enforced blockade depriving inhabitants of food and medicine along with the materials and equipment needed for infrastructural essentials like water, sewage, and electricity. According to international law, this was an act of war, all the more egregious in a situation where civilians end up as the deliberate targets. Thanks to the blockade, an already crowded, impoverished, oppressed population had been weakened and demoralized even *before* the Israeli invasion. Evidence suggests the Gaza population was being targeted simply for being Palestinian (and resisting), hardly surprising given that they were long ago reduced to subhuman status within Zionist ideology. The miseries of mass internment were given added barbaric dimensions by the Israeli leadership—the very context, incidentally, in which the (largely futile) Palestinian resistance was organized. This flagrant Israeli campaign, approved fully by Washington, received little if any attention within the American political and media establishment, where Israel's "right to self-defense" was the dominant refrain, while Hamas was demonized for its reliance on violence and "terrorism" at a time when Gaza residents were enduring thousands more casualties than Israeli soldiers, not to mention devastation of their communities. Following the bloodbath, the Israeli population, shifting ever rightward, expressed nearly unified support for the invasion: 94 percent were behind it, while right-wing nationalists scored dramatic gains in the February 2009 national election that resurrected the leadership of the militarist Benjamin Netanyahu.

The Israeli operation was criminal at several levels: civilian targets were attacked randomly and indiscriminately; inhumane weapons were used; collective punishment was meted out; obligations of an occupying power not to harm inhabitants under its control were flaunted; and clearly the entire campaign was a crime of aggression— all supported, indirectly and directly, by American power. And of course the cruel blockade and sanctions were equally illegal. After 27 days of carnage, calls for Israeli government and military leaders to be prosecuted for war crimes surfaced around the world, as facts of the carnage became widely known and outrage spread.

The International Criminal Court processed hundreds of requests to move against the Israelis, some of its leading jurists indicating the ICC would conduct an independent probe of the Gaza events. Luis Moreno-Ocampo, ICC chief prosecutor, seemed ready to bring the Israelis to justice despite the Palestinians' lack of statehood and the crucial fact that neither Israel nor the U.S. subscribe to the ICC, meaning that both theoretically retain immunity from prosecution. The Israelis, for their part, were desperately seeking to head off inquiries, promising to hold their own internal investigation while denouncing Hamas as a terrorist dictatorship (signifying, in effect, that the Palestinians should have no legal standing). As for the ICC, any rulings over jurisdiction regarding war crimes could take years as the Palestinians, in both Gaza and the West Bank, continue their saga of brutalized occupation.

PERPETUAL WAR

War crimes by proxy are the natural outgrowth of U.S. geopolitical agendas around the world that, in most cases, converge with the interests of local elites. The struggle is nowadays reinforced and legitimated by the war on terror and the persistent aftershocks of 9/11 likely to ensure an era of permanent warfare, with U.S. military engagement often likely to be *indirect*—that is, waged through proxy campaigns. These campaigns have less to do with national defense, the export of democracy, or even the fight against terrorism than with imperial goals shaped above all by mounting resource wars. American proxy interventions were widespread during the Cold War, although Washington support for Israeli militarism across several decades transcends the familiar anti-Communist or counter-insurgency politics. Eclipse of the Cold War has brought terrorism, especially that linked to the Middle East, into clearer focus. In any event, the U.S. has shown it will back virtually *any* government, party, movement, or group that can advance its geopolitical interests, regardless of ideology or human rights record.

Proxy operations can be set in motion to overthrow ruling governments standing in the way of U.S. interests (as in Nicaragua, Afghanistan, and Yugoslavia) or to support dominant groups seeking to eradicate oppositional forces (as in Palestine, Indonesia, Guatemala, and Colombia). Immense financial and military resources, often secretly allocated, have been poured into such operations. Targeted groups (in or out of power) are systematically demonized through efforts of government, the mass media, think-tanks, and public-relations campaigns, so that popular consent can be manufactured for any U.S. military operation that the elites decide to pursue. The overall thrust of U.S. proxy warfare, moreover, wherever it is carried out, has been to bolster authoritarian and militaristic elements against local popular forces; it has been manifestly *anti-democratic*. The methods of proxy warfare devised by Washington have been exhaustive: military and police training, arms sales, logistics, blockades and sanctions, covert action, combat "advising," general financial aid, a multitude of terrorist schemes (torture, assassination, death-squad massacres, etc.). Proxy campaigns include the kind of conventional battlefield activity that Washington is widely known to prefer. U.S. arms merchants have delivered untold tens of billions of dollars worth of equipment and weapons to actors responsible for mass atrocities, from Asia and the Middle East to Central America. In virtually *every* case, moreover, those involved in proxy operations must be judged just as guilty of war crimes as the immediate perpetrators themselves. (In the case of Israel, its illegitimate status as an occupying force already constitutes a violation of international law, which essentially dictates repressive and violent measures needed to sustain the occupation.) And the various combat and quasi-combat methods used for proxy warfare amount to war crimes as defined by international law, though rarely have the U.S. political and military leaders complicit in such violations been held criminally accountable.

4
Weapons of Mass Destruction

Nowhere is U.S. international outlawry more visible, more outrageous, and more destructive than in the arena of what is often misleadingly labeled "weapons of mass destruction." And nowhere are the fairy tales about noble intentions and righteous policies more outlandish. After the 9/11 terrorist attacks the Bush administration became obsessed with the supposedly imminent threat of WMD, manipulating that "threat" into a pretext for war against Iraq and possible ("preemptive") military strikes against North Korea and Iran. Amid this warmongering the U.S. remains by far the biggest champion of WMD in the world—producing, stockpiling, deploying, and indeed *using* more of this weaponry throughout the postwar years than all other nations *combined*. It is the only state to embrace WMD in its myriad forms (including nuclear) as a continuing linchpin of military strategy, a vital element in its goal of world supremacy.

Most historical definitions of WMD refer to warfare that involves both *indiscriminate* and *large-scale* attacks in which the destruction of civilian populations and targets is an inevitable, largely unmanageable, outcome of the military operations in question. The term was first adopted to describe German aerial bombardments of Guernica, Spain in 1937 that killed one-third of the civilian population. The idea of "mass destruction" was later meant to include distinctly *non-conventional* weaponry—chemical, biological, and nuclear—that was said by definition to kill indiscriminately and was, therefore, widely regarded as a violation of humane laws of armed combat. In a 1947 speech, J. Robert Oppenheimer, head of the World War II Manhattan Project, referred to the U.S. atomic bombings of Hiroshima and Nagasaki as the most horrible instances of mass-destructive force ever used in warfare. Since the late 1960s the arms-control community has regularly employed WMD phraseology, generally stressing nuclear weaponry that was understood to be an unthinkable military option. At the time of the first Gulf War—and then during the build-up to the 2003 U.S. invasion of Iraq—Washington resurrected the grave menace of WMD to legitimate its targeting of a Hussein regime said to be awash in chemical, biological, and nuclear weapons programs. In 1990 the supposed horrors of Iraqi WMD provided the foundation of a U.N. sanctions policy that would last until 2003. While there are no explicit prohibitions against nuclear weapons (either their production or use), WMD in general are regulated directly or indirectly by a long series of international laws and treaties: Nuclear Non-Proliferation Treaty (NPT), Anti-Ballistic Missile treaty (ABM), Chemical Weapons Convention (CWC), Biological Weapons Convention (BWC), Outer-Space Treaty (OST), and Comprehensive Test Ban Treaty (CTBT), along with relevant statutes in the Geneva Conventions.

The larger issue of just how to define weaponry with the potential for mass destruction, however, turns out to be more complicated than the label "WMD" presently suggests. It transcends the simple discursive framework preferred by the major powers and their opinion leaders. Using objective criteria, it would have to extend well beyond the familiar triad "nuclear, biological, and chemical." The U.S. military itself has defined WMD as "weapons that are capable of a high order of destruction and/or of being used in such a manner as to destroy large numbers of people. Weapons of mass destruction can be high explosives or nuclear, biological, chemical, and radiological weapons."[1] U.S. civil defense organizations have understood WMD to include explosive and incendiary weapons, as well as weapons that release radiation at levels dangerous to human life, while the FBI considers WMD to be any weaponry that results in "overwhelming local responders." In March 2006 jurors at the Zacarias Moussaoui death-penalty trial were told to define WMD to include "airplanes used as missiles." It follows that, according to these rather standard interpretations, not to mention any reasonable account of how warfare impacts human beings, our understanding of WMD must extend far beyond non-conventional weaponry. Thus "indiscriminate" and having a "high order" of consequences likely to "overwhelm local responders" must obviously include a wide range of generally regarded *conventional* methods of war, which indeed have produced casualties (both civilian and military) in much greater numbers than all non-conventional WMD used across history. Further, a broadened definition would have to include cases where economic sanctions have amounted to extraordinarily harsh warfare directed against targeted countries, such as the U.S. and Britain unleashed (under U.N. auspices) on Iraq between 1991 and 2003.

For our purposes, therefore, it will be useful to identify *five* distinctive types of WMD, all of which continue to pose major threats to local populations and, in some cases, to the planet itself. These instruments of war have awesome destructive power in at least three respects: the boundaries separating combatants and civilians are *by definition* obliterated; the potential for human casualties (again, both military and civilian) is typically massive; and the environmental impact can be devastating and longstanding. Of the five types of WMD—nuclear, biological, chemical, high-order conventional, and sanctions—to date only biological and chemical warfare have been explicitly outlawed; the use of nuclear and conventional weaponry (for example, saturation bombing), as well as peculiarly cruel instances of economic sanctions, violates international law specifically in the sense it can be deemed "wanton destruction," where civilians are either directly targeted or are likely to suffer harm disproportionate to any conceivable military objectives. Likewise, while such objectionable weaponry as ordnance tipped with depleted uranium (DU), napalm, white phosphorous, and anti-personnel bombs might not be strictly banned, their battlefield deployment can be viewed as illegal once the issue of wanton destruction is addressed.

The U.S. alone among nations has used all forms of WMD and, since 1945, is the only state to incorporate such awesome weaponry into its military *strategy*. Even today, while lecturing other nations, Washington is moving to upgrade and streamline its nuclear arsenal—a bulwark of Pentagon doctrine since World War II—as outlined in the 2002 Nuclear Posture Review.[2] This particular hypocrisy seems endemic not only to the Bush administration but to the larger requisites of Empire, a special privilege that comes with superpower status. U.S. exceptionalism, while deeply embedded in history, contains its own pervasive contradictions, one being that an ethos of hypocrisy and double standards works *against* national (and therefore global) security, undercutting prospects for international arms control. Geopolitical priorities dictate a U.S. obsession with WMD, meaning the production, stockpiling, and deployment of arsenals dependent on technological innovation, desire for military flexibility, preemptive warfare, and prospective militarization of space. Key to this approach, which transcends the war on terror, is the capacity of Washington to intimidate or repel by violence any challenger that might appear on the world scene.

This chapter focuses mostly on nuclear weaponry, with some attention devoted to chemical and biological warfare along with the sanctions policy imposed (under U.N. aegis) on Iraq. The wanton death and destruction caused by U.S. military operations against civilians was thoroughly detailed in Chapter 2 and requires little recapitulation here. We have seen, for example, how saturation or "strategic" bombardment has been a cornerstone of U.S. military actions since the final months of World War II, when American planes destroyed more than 60 Japanese cities using incendiary bombs and then, in the case of Hiroshima and Nagasaki, brought about the world's first (and so far only) nuclear holocaust—all with minimal significance for the military outcome. Since 1945 such aerial terrorism has evolved into a central instrument of U.S. air-force operations, used to devastating effect in Korea, Indochina, the Balkans, and Iraq, leaving a death toll of several million people. The Pentagon has frequently resorted across large swathes of territory to such high-impact conventional weapons as incendiary devices intended to burn humans, 15,000-pound fuel-air explosives (FAEs) that destroy nearly as much as tactical nukes without the radiation, and cluster bombs designed to kill and maim large numbers of people in a single blast. Such weaponry has been used in World War II, Korea, Indochina, Iraq, Yugoslavia, and Afghanistan, more or less with impunity.

ECONOMIC SANCTIONS: TERROR BY OTHER MEANS

Warfare by means of economic sanctions has been used extensively by the U.S. against such nations as Cuba and Yugoslavia but was later elevated into a far more deadly instrument against Iraq. While not traditionally regarded as a form of WMD, the brutal consequences of long-term sanctions for civilian populations can exceed anything so far attributed to chemical, biological, and even nuclear weaponry *combined*. In the case of Iraq, the U.S. managed to push through and then stubbornly enforce a cruel sanctions regime, legitimated by the U.N. between 1991 and 2003 basically as an extension of the first Gulf War—a continuation of warfare by other, supposedly more "refined," methods. For both Clinton and Bush the sanctions regime became a useful tool of geopolitical strategy in the build-up to war and the overthrow of the Hussein government. Already severely weakened by two wars, the Iraqi public infrastructure was devastated after years of sanctions that blocked imports needed for water facilities, electricity, food production, sanitation, and health care. The policy was overwhelmingly punitive, designed to weaken the material and social supports of the Ba'ath Party, ostensibly to force disarmament in accordance with U.N. resolutions—well after reports (in the mid 1990s) indicating that Iraq was largely disarmed and no longer posed a threat to its neighbors much less the distant U.S.

Despite pressure from around the world, including Security Council members Russia, China, and France, the U.S. refused to lift sanctions even after reports of the terrible civilian losses. In fact Washington pursued sanctions in conjunction with other instruments of warfare after 1990: recurrent bombings, sabotage, covert action, assassination attempts, surveillance, and so forth. With no justification beyond simple punitive zeal, the U.S. was able to impose the most debilitating sanctions regime in history, leading to economic collapse, massive unemployment, destruction of social services, terrible human casualties, disease, misery, and death. By 2002 the U.N. estimated that 5000 Iraqi children under five were dying on average each month, with the overall death toll reaching upwards of 500,000—mass murder of near-genocidal proportions by any reckoning. As Joy Gordon wrote: "U.S. policymakers have effectively turned a program of international governance into a legitimated act of mass slaughter."[3] Three U.S. administrations—under the two Bushes and Clinton—can share credit for the human catastrophe. A sanctions policy responsible for such unspeakable death and destruction clearly violates Article 54 of the Geneva Convention (1977 Additional Protocol) that prohibits devastation of objects vital to the survival of civilian populations—a point elaborated more fully in Chapter 2.

Looking at the case of Iraq, therefore, a deliberate program of ruination through economic sanctions must be understood as warfare by other methods, ostensibly more legitimate but in reality more horrific. When U.N. observers predicted, and later discovered, conditions of "unbelievable catastrophe," the Washington elites ignored everything and pushed ahead with their agenda of regime change, indifferent to the costs to the Iraqi people. Once in place the sanctions could not be lifted until the U.S. relented—something that sadly never happened. Long after Hussein's military had been severely weakened, the U.S. continued to block even the most obviously humanitarian needs under the guise of denying Iraqis "dual-use" imports that might conceivably be adapted to military purposes. Reviewing the documents, Gordon concluded that the U.S. "has fought aggressively throughout the last decade to purposefully minimize the humanitarian goods that enter the country. And it has done so in the face of enormous human suffering."[4] Here, in the guise of fighting the most terrible instance of WMD proliferation—a chimera from the outset—the U.S. carried out a sustained program of material and psychological ruination resulting in at least *triple* the human casualties produced by the two atomic bombings of Japan, a legacy that, as Gordon rightly observes, "is unlikely to be either forgotten or forgiven."[5] We now know, of course, that in the end sanctions worked quite efficiently for the U.S. war planners, paving the way toward the invasion, regime change, and occupation of a nation that had long before ceased to pose a credible threat to anyone.

THE NUCLEAR MADNESS CONTINUES

Within the historical rubric of WMD, the most awesome and planet-threatening weapons are beyond doubt nukes, first tested and used in 1945 and continuously refined by a growing atomic club ever since. We know that the U.S. dropped two atomic bombs on Japan at the end of World War II, just days before capitulation, producing entirely unnecessary wanton destruction of civilian targets. With the onset of the Cold War the U.S. rushed to further develop its nuclear capability and laid out a strategic doctrine tied to a first-strike option.[6] By the early 1950s the Pentagon shifted to a perpetual ready-alert status, prepared to rain more than 800 Hiroshima-type bombs on the USSR, embellishing its power to destroy human civilization on earth several times over. In March 1954 the U.S. detonated the hydrogen bomb "Bravo," with a force of 15 megatons—the explosive power of 1200 Hiroshimas—elevating the nuclear epoch to new levels of fright and horror and further obliterating any limits to modern warfare. In Sven Lindqvist's view, U.S. embrace of the threat of nuclear annihilation could in part be explained as a product of certain white-male ruling-class fantasies with roots in Wild West mythology.[7] In any event, the Armageddon-style policies established by Washington and followed by Soviet leaders during the Cold War remained in force throughout succeeding decades, backed by increasingly massive and flexibly deployed nuclear power.[8] There is evidence that the U.S. either threatened or seriously considered use of nuclear weapons numerous times in the postwar years—most notably to break the Korean stalemate and during the Cuban missile crisis.

In 1968 most nations of the world signed the Nuclear Non-Proliferation Treaty (NPT), but this did little to stop the U.S. from augmenting its warhead stockpile from 4500 to nearly 10,000 within a decade, an arsenal regularly modernized since. Far from renouncing nuclear warfare as unthinkable, as inherently barbaric, the U.S. (under all postwar presidents) has been fully dedicated to absolute strategic domination in this realm—one reason Washington is today increasingly rejectionist in its attitude toward antiballistic and other arms-control agreements at a time when it looks to militarize outer space.[9] Since the late 1940s U.S. leaders have fought consistently and strenuously against outlawing nuclear weapons although, in sweeping aside crucial distinctions between combatants and civilians—indeed in targeting civilian populations as such—nuclear weapons must be regarded not only as immoral but as illegal according to any sane rules of military engagement. Yet, as of 2009, the U.S. had manufactured and deployed more nuclear bombs and missiles than all other nations combined, still possessing at least 10,000 warheads. Meanwhile, the Pentagon has steadfastly adhered to the strategy of nuclear first-use while simultaneously embracing plans for the development of a new generation of mini-nukes designed for warfare in the age of global terrorism.

In the sphere of WMD, nuclear warfare stands alone in its unbelievable destructive power—at present it is the only form of military conflict that could place the entire planet in danger. It is the one truly doomsday threat, a superweapon capable of destroying "friends" and "enemies" alike. The U.S. from the outset insisted that nukes ought to be considered just another instrument of modern warfare. In 1945 President Truman apparently had no doubts about whether to use atomic bombs against Japan, relying almost exclusively on the advice of a committee chaired by Secretary of Defense Harold Stinson, which recommended using the weaponry against urban civilian populations without warning. For Truman the newly created nuclear devices represented a great superweapon that could destroy the enemy, bring peace, and deter future wars. As is now well known (though was kept secret at the time), the bombs were aimed at the heart of two cities possessing scant military significance, with immediate death tolls nearing 200,000 and later deaths from radiation adding several tens of thousands to that total. Although the Japanese had months before offered to surrender, Truman and Stinson argued that atomic warfare had to be unleashed in order to avoid a U.S. invasion of Japan and thus save perhaps a million lives. While Truman justified the bombings as necessary to pacify a "cruel and uncivilized nation of beasts," most armed-forces leaders had great misgivings. Thus Admiral William D. Leay, Chairman of the Joint Chiefs of Staff, said in late 1945:

"the use of this barbarous weapon at Hiroshima and Nagasaki was of no material assistance in our war against Japan. The Japanese were almost defeated and ready to surrender. In being the first to use it, we adopted an ethical standard common to the barbarians of the Dark Ages."[10] It was Truman, moreover, who once again threatened to drop atomic bombs to break the military impasse in Korea after 1950.[11]

The U.S. nuclear posture in the early twenty-first century has, amidst much self-righteous posturing about the evils of WMD, signaled a dramatic escalation of the world-wide nuclear danger.[12] The U.S. and Russia combined possess an estimated 20,000 atomic weapons, the vast majority directed at each other. (A strange reality: despite all the alarms heard in the media about rogue states, terrorists, and the famous "axis of evil," the U.S. in 2007 had more than 90 percent of its warheads targeted on Russia—one of the bizarre legacies of the Cold War nuclear standoff.) While fiercely opposed to the spread of WMD to countries designated as enemies—Iraq, Iran, North Korea—the Bush administration, following earlier U.S. policies, actually contributed mightily to nuclear proliferation, rendering its official policies and statements nothing short of fraudulent. It did so by (1) refusing to move toward any form of nuclear disarmament; (2) reinvigorating its longstanding plans for national missile defense (NMD), part of which augurs the heretofore prohibited weaponization of space; (3) continuing its own Cold-War established first-strike strategy; (4) developing a new generation of "bunker-buster" mini-nukes; (5) formulating several contingency options for use of nuclear weapons; and (6) aiding the nuclear programs of "friendly" nations (for example, India) through technological assistance and material transference. In virtually every one of these areas the U.S. stands alone in clear violation of the NPT as well as other treaties.

In 2002 President Bush and Russian leader Vladimir Putin signed the Moscow Treaty, ostensibly to control production and deployment of nuclear weapons by the two powers—heralded in the American media as a great move toward disarmament. The treaty, however, turns out to be illusory: as part of the agreement the U.S. wound up scrapping all *binding* arrangements that had involved strict limits and regular inspections in favor of one that is largely unilateral, *voluntary*, and devoid of monitoring provisions. With these accords all categories of nuclear warheads and delivery systems are left essentially uncontrolled—precisely what the Bush administration preferred. Meanwhile, the U.S. turned away from the CTBT provisions, possibly anticipating the need for future testing of its new cycle of nukes, and junked the 1972 ABM treaty that imposed limits on nuclear development. After 9/11 Bush deftly manipulated the "war on terror" and the menace of foreign enemies in order to expand the Pentagon's overall strategic (including nuclear) capabilities. The existing U.S. stockpile was modernized, funding for new programs was requested (though often turned down), new targets were identified, and first-strike options reaffirmed. Further, under Bush the U.S. moved to integrate nuclear weaponry into its broader strategic framework, marked by renewed flexibility that smaller, presumably more "usable," nukes would give the Pentagon in confronting a new era of warfare. Such flexibility (both standard and WMD) lies at the core of an increasingly aggressive, integrated global military strategy. As Helen Caldicott writes: "A huge conventional and nuclear arsenal allows America to do what it will around the world with impunity—it is the iron hand in the velvet glove of U.S. corporate globalization."[13] Whether an Obama presidency chooses to depart from this pattern remains to be seen.

Recognizing the limits of a nuclear strategy grounded in the postwar balance of terror, with its long-range delivery systems and mutually assured destruction (MAD), Bush and Secretary of Defense Donald Rumsfeld looked toward a more fluid, balanced stratagem mixing strategic and tactical, fixed and maneuverable, long-distance and battlefield, offensive and defensive systems within a paradigm of more viable nuclear options appropriate the current defense of Empire. This was the essence of the Pentagon's 2001 *Quadrennial Defense Review* and the subsequent Nuclear Posture Review, which in 2002 outlined new strategic and tactical departures for the post-9/11 global milieu. Not only did the Nuclear Posture Review stipulate a greater variety of nuclear alternatives, as part of its "Single Integrated Operational Plan," it also laid out conditions under which such alternatives might come into play. Military planners identified three "contingencies" possible at any moment—*immediate*, where the WMD of another nation might have to be destroyed; *potential*, requiring a military response to some imminent threat to U.S. security; and *unexpected*, where regime change somewhere in the world demands quick U.S. reaction.[14] It is clear from this very elastic schema that U.S. nuclear strategy presently adheres to few if any fixed restraints or boundaries—and there is no sign of imminent change. Unfortunately, a loosened nuclear policy of this sort, combined with general renewal of American imperial and military ambitions, has had the effect of encouraging other nuclear powers like Russia and China to enlarge or modernize their own arsenals and, more ominously, of helping trigger "lateral proliferation" by pushing weaker states (especially those targeted by the U.S.) to accelerate their nuclear programs. And no doubt it has sent a comparable message to terrorist groups. Reflecting on this dangerous state of affairs, former Secretary of Defense Robert McNamara wrote in the journal *Foreign Policy*: "I would characterize current U.S. nuclear weapons policy as immoral, illegal, militarily unnecessary, and dreadfully dangerous."[15]

The new "flexibility" of American nuclear doctrine has already made itself visible in two wars since 9/11—in Afghanistan and Iraq—where contingencies for nuclear attacks were openly discussed within the Pentagon and even mentioned obliquely by politicians and the media, bringing the threshold of usage to its lowest point since the Cuban missile crisis of 1962. Both countries were, and continue to be, regarded as havens of Muslim terrorists while strong remnants of both regimes (Taliban and Ba'athist) have been viewed as dire threats to U.S. regional aims. In both combat settings, moreover, the U.S. might easily confront nightmare scenarios where conventional weaponry appears to have exhausted its limits. Iraq, of course, was said to be in possession of huge stores of WMD, allegedly justifying a "preemptive" U.S. military response. Tactical bunker-buster nukes (the B6-11 earth-penetrating bomb with yields of between 300 tons and 300 kilotons) have recently been viewed by some as a quick way out of any protracted quagmire—fighting the Taliban and Al Qaeda in the mountains and caves of Afghanistan, fighting Iraqi insurgents in the difficult, endless, bloody urban warfare across a sprawling city like Baghdad. It was similar fears and calculations that prompted President Truman to drop atomic bombs on Japan and consider doing the same thing in Korea. While the U.S. has never used nuclear weapons in Afghanistan or Iraq, we can surmise that such devices were at some point integrated into military planning—at the very moment Bush and the neocons were lecturing the world about the perils of WMD. Quite clearly the dividing line between nuclear and conventional warfare has grown more blurred in recent years, in theory if not yet in practice.

Despite its self-congratulatory holy crusade against WMD, therefore, the U.S. has been doing everything possible to encourage proliferation of nuclear arsenals. While hostile to "evil" states that might want their own WMD for purposes of defense, the Bush administration obstructed attempts within the U.N. to create durable arms-control agreements binding on all states. The U.S. still fully reserves for itself the right to manufacture, deploy, and use nuclear weapons in violation of the NPT and other protocols. Washington has come to accept large WMD programs for friendly nations such as Israel, Pakistan, and India, even as Bush (in February 2004) called WMD "the greatest threat before humanity today." In fact the U.S. has tabled NPT amendments designed to place roadblocks to new nations acquiring nuclear devices. Israel, which possesses as many as 200 nuclear warheads, remains outside the NPT, firmly rejects any inspections process, and has never been the object of threats or inducements concerning the weapons it already possesses. As the only Middle East state with a nuclear arsenal, Israel—hostile to most Arab and Muslim nations in the region—clearly figures in the proliferation dynamic. In 1974 Egypt and Iran sponsored a U.N. resolution calling for a Middle East nuclear-free zone but Israel opposed it while the U.S., then as later, furnished political cover for the Israelis, who in 1981 attacked the lone nuclear reactor built by the Iraqis.

As for Pakistan, the U.S. rewarded the Musharraf regime in 2002 with a three-billion dollar aid package for its (marginal) assistance in the war on terror, indirectly giving the Pakistanis a green light to expand their nuclear capacity at a time when Bush and Rumsfeld were issuing dire warnings to Iran and North Korea about their nuclear plans. Actually Pakistan, like India and Israel, never signed the NPT or even the 1996 CTBT, which would have prohibited its nuclear testing in 1998. (The NPT was signed by Iraq, Iran, and North Korea, which later withdrew, and provides for the peaceful development of nuclear energy, which as of 2009 Iran claimed it was pursuing.) The fact that Pakistan and India, along with Israel, have been able to avoid U.N.-sponsored inspections—the very inspections demanded of both North Korea and Iran—has drawn nary a protest from the U.S. despite the long-simmering tensions between India and Pakistan over Kashmir not to mention the highly explosive situation within Pakistan itself. A crucial issue remains: if such nations as Israel, Pakistan, and India, following the pattern of major nuclear powers, can insist that atomic weapons are needed for their military defense, how can these nations credibly deny the very same motive to other, even weaker, states? Mohamed ElBaradei, director of the International Atomic Energy Agency (IAEA), recently asked pointedly why it is "morally reprehensible for some countries to pursue weapons of mass destruction yet [is] morally acceptable for others to rely on them for security while continuing to refine their capacities and postulate plans for their use."[16]

After calling WMD the "greatest threat to humanity," President Bush moved to establish a nuclear "strategic partnership" with India, a country firmly outside the NPT and seemingly intent on ignoring its provisions (including global inspections). In March 2006 the U.S. and India agreed to a long-term program of space and nuclear cooperation, in which Washington would sell advanced technology to India to enhance its status as a "democratic" and "peaceful" power in Asia—meaning as a counterweight to Chinese influence. According to the NPT, no country would be allowed to give assistance to India's outlaw nuclear program—in place with American blessings since 1974—but here as elsewhere the U.S. simply changed the rules to make an exception for the chosen nation. In opening up U.S. nuclear markets with this deal, the Bush administration was simply giving India an endorsement to produce as many nuclear warheads as it chooses. In October 2008 Congress approved the deal, thus rewarding a nation that flaunts the NPT and maintains eight nuclear plants still outside international scrutiny. Not surprisingly, this rogue arrangement, meeting with understandable outrage around the world, only served to further encourage WMD proliferation in countries aspiring to nuclear status. (By early 2009 there were some 35 states with the potential to reach nuclear status in coming years.) And the U.S. managed to pull off this deal at the very time it was threatening Iran, a member of the NPT with every right to develop non-military forms of nuclear energy. Given that U.S. leaders seem bound to enforce what has been called a "nuclear apartheid regime" dominated by the U.S. and its allies, the present NPT system would appear to be bankrupt.[17]

As for Iran (in early 2009), observers familiar with U.S. intelligence on Iranian military projects shared with the U.N. nuclear watchdog agency indicate that little if anything in that intelligence has proven to be true—a seeming replay of the Iraq situation in the build-up to war. The CIA and other agencies provided extensive information to the IAEA beginning in 2002, when Iran's nuclear program became fully public, but nothing has yet shown the presence of a weapons system, despite a constant barrage of claims, warnings, and threats emanating from the U.S. and Israel. The evidence so far indicates that Iran has worked within the parameters and guidelines of the NPT, though U.S. intelligence was described by many in the Bush administration as "cold" and totally "unreliable."[18]

Meanwhile, Bush unveiled plans to expand nuclear power globally, moving ahead with a U.S.–Japanese agreement to conduct joint research on a new generation of reactors and new type of nuclear fuel. The Department of Energy outlined a vigorous agenda to build nuclear power plants worldwide, part of a Global Nuclear Energy Partnership still in its infancy. A total of 222 new reactors were planned, with more than one trillion dollars in business potential for American corporations on the horizon. Under the global partnership, a new cycle of breeder reactors would burn reprocessed fuel stored at several domestic power plants. The U.S. was prepared to allow other nations to possess large amounts of nuclear fuel requiring enriched uranium—a move that could easily facilitate WMD proliferation. But the Bush administration was looking past that problem in favor of the huge economic and political advantages expected to accrue.

It follows that U.S. policy has had little to do with curbing the possession or spread of WMD, with arms-control agreements, or with honoring global treaties, and has had everything to do with enhancing American economic and geopolitical objectives. Here as elsewhere Washington seeks maximum freedom for itself and a few of its allies to expand and modernize their nuclear arsenals. Interwoven with this strategy is the renovated National Missile Defense (NMD) project, a spin-off of the Star Wars project undertaken during the Reagan presidency. One largely hidden facet of this program is the weaponization of space, with prospects for eventually deploying nuclear reactors and weapons hundreds of miles above the earth. In the 2001 *Quadrennial Defense Review*, the Pentagon laid out plans for a high-capacity, integrated, full-spectrum, global armed network to be coordinated from space, combining offensive and defensive modalities. If achieved, this would mean the full extension of American power into space—a revitalized Manifest Destiny for the twenty-first century—that would limit or deny access to other nations. To the degree that new forms of warfare demand sophisticated technology, information, surveillance, and flexibility, along with heightened nuclear capability, the U.S. space program could become a cornerstone of future military strategy, so that criticism of Star Wars and its spin-offs for presumed *defensive* inadequacies misses the central point. The space dimension furnishes the Pentagon with a high-quality "networked environment" integrated through satellites, military platforms, radar, laser technology, and infrared systems of the sort already found valuable in the Balkans, Afghanistan, and Iraq. Thus U.S. colonization of space greatly enhances its earthly military capacity to coordinate vast networks of ground, sea, and air operations, violating the spirit if not the substance of the 1967 Outer Space Treaty (discussed more fully later).

In the U.S. the permanent war economy has given rise to the largest and most sophisticated academic-scientific nuclear system ever assembled. Thanks to Pentagon and government largesse, this work has been centered in three large laboratories: Sandia and Los Alamos in New Mexico and Livermore in California. Research and development is overseen by the Pentagon, Department of Energy (DOE), and the University of California, Berkeley. Thousands of scientists are awarded scholarly status, generous salaries, and a patriotic niche in the social order, resulting in an elite community that Helen Caldicott refers to as a "scientific bomb cult."[19] In an atmosphere where production of nuclear weapons capable of killing hundreds of millions of people is viewed with great enthusiasm, signifying a mix of aesthetic beauty, scientific creation, and political obligation, even slight expressions of dissent are regarded as puzzling, reprehensible. It is a milieu in which untold numbers of civilian deaths are considered "collateral damage," a prospect shrouded in esoteric techno-strategic discourse and game-theoretical models embraced at major universities.

Inspired by the Bush administration's revival of nuclear politics, the three major nuclear labs entered into fierce competition over design and production of a new generation of atomic weapons, highly skeptical of well-known NPT stipulations requiring the nuclear powers to move toward *disarmament*. Teams of military, corporate, and scientific elites work virtually non-stop with the aid of supercomputers to design new bombs and missiles such as the "reliable replacement warheads" (RRWs) approved by Congress in 2005. In their drive to ensure overwhelming U.S. nuclear supremacy, these teams ridicule even the most ambiguous talk of arms control, their proponents seen as unpatriotic "crazies" and "wackos." International law is for utopian dreamers.[20] The weapons labs received a huge contract in March 2007 to develop a refined hydrogen bomb, projected to cost tens of billions of dollars—part of the RRW project.[21] The Pentagon wanted to employ sophisticated computer modeling exercises in order to sidestep the nuclear testing moratorium in place since 1992.

As Robert Jay Lifton observes, throughout the postwar years U.S. leaders set out to perfect a "godlike nuclear capacity" enabling them to shape history.[22] Despite a current fixation on "pragmatism" and "realism" in foreign affairs, the Pentagon has embraced apocalyptic visions of warfare involving massive levels of violence and destruction—visions going back to the 1945 atomic bombings of Japan. Washington long ago viewed the atomic age as a great revolution in the history of warfare, unleashing new fantasies and new possibilities that, it was hoped, could never be matched by any other nation. As an *ideology*, nuclearism therefore came to embellish a mode of warfare defined by life-sustaining power beneath which always lurked what Lifton calls a "shared psychological energy pressing toward cruelty and killing."[23] From the moment the first bomb was detonated at Alamogordo, nuclear weaponry was understood by its creators to be nothing short of "God's power unleashed"—a sentiment perfectly captured in Roland Joffe's 1989 film *Fat Man and Little Boy*. From this standpoint, the mission of the Enola Gay to obliterate Hiroshima fit God's historical mission. There is nothing especially aberrant about such notions when viewed against the backdrop of a deity-sanctioned Manifest Destiny.

Nuclear supremacy has endowed the U.S. not only with special military power and status—the ability to blow up the world many times over—but a certain *legitimacy* grounded in spellbinding scientific-technological progress. Nuclearism, moreover, seemed ideally designed for a world of infinite, perpetual warfare where rogues, terrorists, and other menaces inhabit the global landscape. As an unquestionable force for good, Washington can feel entirely justified in its role as historical agency of cataclysmic violence.[24] It follows that nuclear weapons are bound to persist as a vital element of superpower status in the minds of U.S. leaders.[25] Despite its self-righteous posturing about WMD proliferation, therefore, the U.S. retains a God-given right to develop, refine, and deploy atomic weaponry, with no willingness to entertain policies or agreements that might compromise that "right." Reinforced by such deeply ingrained nuclear ideology, Washington continues to resist any constraints on its global power or use of military force.

A LEGACY OF TOXIC WARFARE

In the realm of chemical weapons the U.S. has long been—contrary to general mythology—the world leader in the production, dissemination, and use of highly toxic liquids, sprays, gases, powders, incendiary devices, and radioactive explosives. The American military did not join the poisonous weapons parade in World War I, but at the end of World War II experimented with incendiary devices like napalm, which it refined for increased usage in Korea and later introduced on a murderous scale in Vietnam.

Napalm, along with horrific burning agents like white phosphorous, the poisonous herbicide Agent Orange, and radiation-spreading devices such as weapons tipped with depleted uranium, have to varying degrees been part of the U.S. toxic-warfare program ever since. It is well known that the U.S. military sprayed tens of thousands of tons of deadly herbicides over three million acres of Vietnam from 1965 to 1971, with the criminal intent of wiping out jungle foliage, crops, and other plant life deemed to be of use to anyone resisting American power. The use of Agent Orange and several other potent chemicals polluted Vietnam with 500 pounds of cancer-causing dioxin, leaving a devastating legacy for millions of local inhabitants as well as tens of thousands of U.S. troops. In a variety of military theaters since Vietnam—for example, Iraq, the Balkans, Afghanistan, Colombia—the Pentagon deployed and used, often indiscriminately, such weaponry as incendiary devices, defoliants, riot-control agents, and depleted uranium. Across this entire period Washington has refused, with just a few exceptions, to permit international laws and treaties to impose limits on its use of such weaponry.

At present the Chemical Weapons Convention (CWC) outlaws the production, stockpiling, and use of weapons considered poisonous, reflecting a growing international consensus, or *Zeitgeist*, around this specific type of armed engagement. According to Article II of the CWC, all munitions possessing highly toxic properties are banned—"toxic" here meaning "any chemical which through its chemical reaction on life processes can cause death, temporary incapacitation, or permanent harm to humans or animals."[26] After the CWC entered into force in April 1997—signed initially by 50 states and reaching a membership of 182 in 2007—all nations known to possess chemical weapons (including the U.S.) were directed to eliminate their stockpiles in four phases, a process that would involve systematic onsite inspections. The U.S. was expected to reach phase IV (disarmament) by the year 2014 but this was delayed to 2023, with prospects of further delays. In addition to napalm, white phosphorous, and DU, the Pentagon has been known to possess various nerve, blood, blister, choking, and riot-control agents, and has been reluctant to fully abandon these programs. (As of 2005 the U.S. was one of six nations to admit to having such chemical programs.) The U.S. is one of only a few nations to exempt itself from unequivocally condemning chemical warfare, and still denies inspection access to any external body. In fact, well before the CWC, major world powers (except the U.S.) signed The Hague Convention

(1907) outlawing use of chemical weapons in combat, reaffirmed at Geneva in 1925. And while some chemical devices might be regarded as technically beyond the reach of international law, the relevant measure here—as in the case of nuclear weaponry—is whether the device in question produces wanton destruction of civilian populations and objects. Where such destruction is the result, the form of warfare must be regarded as illegal.

By far the most horrendous U.S. resort to chemical warfare was its extensive and murderous use of defoliants in Vietnam, where the army deployed massive amounts not only of Agent Orange but such toxic chemicals as CS, DM, and CN gases, designated by the Pentagon as riot-control agents.[27] In the case of Agent Orange alone, the U.S. deposited so much dioxin in the soil, vegetation, food system, and water that several million people were exposed to its deadly effects for many decades: cancer, immune breakdowns, mental disorders, severe birth defects, and other afflictions. Setting out to destroy forests, jungles, and croplands as a deliberate method of warfare, the U.S. left behind unfathomable ecological destruction as well as countless human casualties. According to one in-depth report, the town of Ben Tre (population 140,000) alone suffered 58,000 victims of Agent Orange.[28] The Vietnamese landscape today remains littered with crippled and deformed human beings, with no end in sight to new casualties. According to the Hatfield Report, U.S. chemical warfare in Vietnam (even leaving aside napalm and white phosphorous) will leave its imprint for many decades into the future. In the late 1990s a Canadian study found extremely high levels of dioxin in Vietnamese soil, water, and food samples, with residents near Bien Hoa suffering at least 200 times normal amounts in their body—results U.S. officials have refused to acknowledge.[29] Further, based on the work of Le Cao Dai, Arnold Schechter, and others, it was found that the U.S. use of Agent Orange in Vietnam killed or maimed some 400,000 civilians, with another possible 500,000 children suffering defects such as retardation and spina bifida. Researchers also found that among the offspring of North Vietnamese soldiers who fought in the war and were exposed to Agent Orange, 5 percent were born with severe defects. Both Dai and Schechter were outspoken in their call for the U.S. to take responsibility for its chemical warfare campaign and to help with the enormous clean-up process needed in still-contaminated areas of the country. Said Schechter: "I believe the U.S. has a moral responsibility to help us clean up the contaminated areas."[30] But Washington has never responded to this problem at any level, insisting (with as many as one million cases now on the books) that no connection between Agent Orange and health problems among the Vietnamese population (or, for that matter, American troops) has ever been established.[31]

Thus neither the U.S. government nor corporations such as Dow and Monsanto that manufactured poisonous agents have ever offered apologies or reparations to the Vietnamese, and nothing for clean-up or health services. While American victims of chemical warfare have received some $180 million in judgments from U.S. corporations, the Vietnamese have been excluded from any such settlements.[32] In its lengthy treatment of chemical-weapons use as a violation of international law, the text *Crimes of War* scandalously omits any reference to the extensive history of U.S. chemical warfare, in Vietnam or elsewhere. The main culprit identified is Iraq, with Russia getting dishonorable mention.[33]

It hardly needs to be emphasized that chemical weaponry like that used on a massive scale by the U.S. in Vietnam brings death and destruction mainly to civilian populations. It is wanton destruction by definition, and was recognized as such at The Hague in 1907 and Geneva in 1925. The U.S. has usually paid formal attention to such prohibitions but, at least since World War II, has done little to actually abide by these global arrangements. Since 1945 the Pentagon has stockpiled huge amounts of chemical and biological weapons and has, for the most part, refused monitoring of its own facilities and inventories. The U.S. has deployed toxic devices in nearly every war it has fought since World War I. In January 1998 President Clinton said that the world must "confront the new hazards of chemical and biological weapons, and the outlaw states, terrorists, and organized criminals seeking to acquire them." Anticipating the later rhetoric of President Bush and the neocons, he castigated Iraq for developing weapons of mass destruction at the very moment Congress was passing the Iraq Liberation Act essentially giving the U.S. a green light to invade. Yet it was U.S. corporations that overwhelmingly furnished the Iraqis with a wide variety of chemical and biological agents, exported and licensed through the Department of Commerce—an arrangement going back to at least 1985. Shipments included materials related to anthrax and botulinum toxin that were vital to whatever illegal programs the Hussein regime was able to initiate.[34] Meanwhile, although the U.S. discontinued use of Agent Orange following the Vietnam revelations, it never shrunk from later use of chemical agents in both warfare and counterinsurgency operations—nor has it been reluctant to share scientific knowledge and resources with other nations. In Plan Colombia, for example, the U.S. has sprayed tens of thousands of square acres with chemical agents designed to defoliate coca plantations, in part to deny cover to insurgent groups, in part to carry on its ill-conceived "war on drugs." In certain rural parts of Colombia the U.S. deployed a new Monsanto-produced fungus, glyphosate, a herbicide causing lethal infections in humans and animals. Massive areas of targeted southern provinces were poisoned by fumigation, which drove thousands of peasants from their land.

In its November 2004 full-scale military offensive in Fallujah, intended to obliterate the core of the Iraqi resistance, the U.S. military is reported to have extensively deployed such chemical agents as white phosphorous—a charge the Pentagon first denied and then admitted as evidence mounted.[35] An Italian documentary aired in November 2005 showing that hundreds of Iraqi civilians had been indiscriminately targeted and killed by incendiary devices during the assault. Dubbed "Willie Pete" by troops, white phosphorous is a dangerous chemical that burns to the bone when it comes into contact with humans. Such incendiaries are universally regarded as inhumane weapons, and a 1980 U.N. convention established firm limits to their use, although the U.S. never signed the agreement. These are some of the very weapons that Washington so righteously accused Saddam Hussein of deploying against the Kurds in the 1980s. The use of incendiary weapons against civilians is unquestionably illegal, falling into the category of wanton attacks. Darryl Kimball, executive director of the Arms Control Association, said: "An incendiary weapon cannot be thought of just like any conventional weapon."[36] Whether or not the U.S. is obliged to follow rules set by the Chemical Weapons Convention, such indiscriminate attacks on civilians are clearly prohibited by the Geneva Conventions. In Fallujah, recalling the Vietnam experience, Iraqi doctors and local human rights organizations testified to hundreds of burned corpses resulting from white phosphorous as evidence of flagrant U.S. chemical warfare.

Since the early 1990s the most flagrant U.S. resort to chemical weaponry has been in the form of depleted uranium, used extensively in the battlefields of Iraq, Yugoslavia, Afghanistan, and again in Iraq. DU has been added to bombs, missiles, and artillery shells to enhance their explosive and penetrating force, since uranium has nearly twice the density of metals like lead, iron, and aluminum. Tanks, Bradley Fighting Machines, and Apache attack helicopters have routinely fired DU rounds in Iraq. When shells hit their target, they release the insoluble chemical agent uranium oxide, a form of radioactive dust that spreads rapidly. At the time of the Iraq invasion the Pentagon had more than one *billion* pounds of nuclear waste available, a by-product of processes used to make reactor fuel and nuclear weapons, much of it converted to reinforce conventional weapons in the Middle East, with deadly results. While the figures are not yet exact, reports indicate that the U.S. deployed some 350 tons of DU during the first Gulf War, followed by ten tons in the Balkans and more than 1000 tons in Iraq after 2003.[37] In each case the U.S. left behind a toxic wasteland with horrific consequences for people, crops, animals, and of course the general ecology.

Upon impact with a target, DU disintegrates into a widening mist of particles that, once inhaled or ingested, can produce cancer, kidney disease, genetic defects, and general immune-system breakdown. When one considers that the amount of DU used by the U.S. military in Iraq alone produced radiation levels equal to all previous nuclear testing worldwide *combined*, it is easy to see that the health effects are likely to be catastrophic. Iraqi doctors tried desperately to bring attention to the vast increase in cancer rates and birth deformities since 1991, with only limited success. Some reports indicate that the incidence of cancer skyrocketed by nearly 250 percent—with leukemia and birth defects found at similarly alarming rates. Many cancer and leukemia patients, especially numerous in southern Iraq, were under five years old. Meanwhile, tests conducted by Leuren Moret and others showed that DU emissions rose dramatically not only in Iraq but across the entire Middle East.[38] Moret argues that DU use amounts to a new form of chemical warfare the terrible consequences of which are just now beginning to surface in humans and the environment.[39] Dr. Ahmad Hardan, a special adviser to the World Health Organization, refers to the widespread dispersion of DU in Iraq as a new, more insidious mode of terrorism practiced uniquely by the U.S.

As in most cases of chemical and biological warfare, the perpetrator also turns out to be a *victim* of its own malfeasance— the architect of weapons of mass destruction often becoming its own enemy. Large-scale casualties among U.S. troops from DU poisoning are by now generally acknowledged by observers familiar with battlefield conditions in Iraq, although firm evidence so far remains elusive. It is believed by many close to the military that DU emissions in 1990 and then again in 2003 and later gave rise in part to Gulf War Syndrome among both Iraqi and American soldiers.[40]

Tens of thousands of troops have suffered immune disorders, kidney problems, cancer, mental breakdowns, and a variety of other afflictions that might generally be traced to radiation poisoning. As of 2004 the Veterans Administration had processed some 182,000 claims of disability related to battlefield experiences in Iraq—a number destined to surge as hundreds of thousands of U.S. military personnel continue to serve in Iraq. The Pentagon consistently denied that these symptoms and casualties have anything to do with DU, which military officials still regard as nothing hazardous, its radiation levels said to fall within "normal ranges." Indeed, at a Pentagon briefing by Colonel James Naughton in March 2003, the press was told: "Nobody goes into a war and wants to be even with the enemy. We want to be ahead, and DU gives us that advantage."[41]

This embarrassing problem has been stonewalled not only by the Pentagon but by U.S. political leadership across the board. There have been no serious investigations into the health and environmental consequences of large-scale DU emissions in Iraq or anywhere else. In fact the U.S. has never cooperated with research and testing carried out by foreign or international bodies on the harm caused by DU. In 1996 a U.N. subcommission passed a resolution condemning DU, but the U.S. simply ignored it, disdainful of any limits to battlefield options. In 2004 Representative Jim McDermott (D–Wash) sponsored a House bill merely to *study* the health and ecological impact of DU but the bill quickly died in the House Armed Services Committee. The Bush administration steadfastly refused to confront the issue even on the home front. Meanwhile, as of 2009, the U.S. still possessed several million DU-enhanced weapons, ready to be used against new targets susceptible to the same toxic horrors.

Whatever its codified status in law, the extensive military uses of DU—its long-term effects surely catastrophic—must be regarded as a criminal assault on humans, animals, and the environment, fitting the category "wanton destruction." Pentagon efforts to justify such chemical warfare fall short of any rational or humane defense. Since the powerful toxic effects of DU are so well known, the use of this weaponry is *prima facie* illegal according to international law established at The Hague and Geneva Conventions. And since DU emissions produce vast and indiscriminate harm to civilian populations as well as to their food and water sources, the weaponry clearly falls under the definition of "wanton destruction" covered in the 1948 Geneva Convention. In military theaters where the U.S. has deployed DU, the resultant dust, filled with poisonous radiation, encounters no limits or boundaries where health consequences are concerned; the spread is truly global and long-term, with particles lasting a half-life of 4.5 billion years. Increasingly regarded as a terror weapon, DU should fall under the rubric of the Chemical Weapons Convention that achieved full legal force in 1997, despite Washington protests to the contrary.[42]

The U.S. has possessed huge stockpiles of chemical weapons since World War II and today is one of six nations with known stockpiles along with production facilities. As mentioned, Washington has resisted any inspections of its facilities and has moved slowly and reluctantly toward dismantling even a small part of its arsenal—the size and character of which remain secret—being strongly opposed as ever to any infringement on the commercial freedom of American chemical and pharmaceutical companies. The U.S. still carries out extensive chemical weapons research at its Army Edgewood Biological and Chemical Center, and elsewhere. One investigation found that 113 university, government, hospital, and corporate laboratories are presently engaged in chemical research while refusing to disclose the nature of their work.[43] According to another report, the U.S. has stockpiled millions of pounds of methyl bromide, a pesticide with military functions that is extremely harmful to the ozone layer—an agent the Pentagon wants exempt from any global prohibitions.[44] Such research extends to a variety of agents: riot-control products, nerve gases, anesthetics, and psychoactive substances designed to put people to sleep. According to documents uncovered by the Sunshine Project, an international NGO that monitors issues related to biological weapons, the Pentagon remains interested in developing chemical weapons for use against selected targets, in the war on terror, and for counterinsurgency purposes where large-scale conventional weapons might prove futile.[45] The Pentagon and the corporations involved in such illicit programs recognize they are acting against the CWC, but they proceed in any case, while the U.S. government pays lip service to the idea of dismantling WMD. Meanwhile, Washington can afford to wait until at least 2023 before it must come fully to terms with its international obligations under the CWC.

THE BIOWARFARE OPTION

Fearing prospects of future biological warfare—seen by many as the most ominous type of WMD—nations of the world forged the Biological Weapons Convention (BWC), ratified by 22 states in

1975 and signed by 171 states as of 2007. Article I bans production and stockpiling of microbial and other biological agents or toxins, including delivery systems, while Article II directs all nations to destroy any existing biological arsenals. The problem with the BWC comes with Article VI, which empowers the U.N. to investigate any breaches of Convention statutes. The issue of verification procedures emerged in the 1990s, when attempts to establish ironclad protocols for monitoring were blocked by the U.S. At the Fifth Review Conference in 2001 the Bush administration declared that inspections did not coincide with U.S. national interests, infringing on sensitive military and commercial priorities. Thus, while the U.S. had long claimed its biological weapons programs were disbanded, suspicions remained that Washington was committed to developing arsenals in clear violation of the BWC.

As noted above, U.S. leaders have regularly intoned against WMD—but always with regard to *others*. In the case of biological weaponry, we have seen how American corporations, with government blessing, shipped off a wide assortment of materials useful for developing anthrax and botulinum toxin. Production and stockpiling of biowar agents has most likely continued throughout the postwar years, although shrouded in secrecy. In 2002, however, it was learned that the Pentagon had tested bioweapons in and near local civilian populations, off the coast of Hawaii, California, Florida, and Maryland, exposing millions of people unknowingly to deadly agents in the years spanning 1962 to 1973. The government conceded that 37 secret tests were held all told, for such toxins as sarin nerve gas, a form of bacterium (BG) related to anthrax, and MA, a deadly biological agent—all overseen by the Desert Test Center at Fort Douglas, Utah.[46] More recent reports indicated that similar testing is still being conducted today, at an army facility located in Fort Leonard Wood, Missouri. Such tests are said to focus on defensive weaponry, but offensive capabilities are surely built into those programs.[47]

The most frightening actual U.S. deployment of biological weapons occurred during the Korean War, a phenomenon recently documented with some degree of certainty.[48] Bioweapons were an officially sanctioned element of Pentagon strategy in the early 1950s and no doubt even later. Both Koreans and Chinese complained about significant death and illness tolls resulting from plague, anthrax, scarlet fever, encephalitis, and other diseases unleashed by bombs and artillery shells during American military operations in Korea. We know that the U.S. Medical General Lab, Far East, had become a major center for researching insect vectors that could carry such lethal diseases as smallpox, cholera, and encephalitis.[49] The Pentagon had been working to refine its bioweapons program so that it could occupy a niche alongside its nuclear capacity. Aside from the Far East lab, the U.S. army's Special Operations Division at Fort Detrick, Maryland, produced germ agents and delivery systems that received high praise for their effectiveness. Stephen Endicott and Edward Hagerman write: "It is significant that this was the first time in modern military history that biological warfare was incorporated into doctrine as a weapons system."[50] Needless to say, these aggressive and sophisticated programs adhered to no international laws, precedents, or limits outside the Pentagon's own dictates.

In Korea the U.S. extended its practice of unlimited warfare to not only strategic bombing and wanton attacks on civilians but also to WMD. As we have seen, the U.S. military strategy in Korea was to wear down and ultimately annihilate the enemy. Atrocities were routinely committed from the air and on the ground. USAF bombing campaigns, as earlier in Japan and later in Vietnam, were nothing short of barbaric. Cities were destroyed and prisoners of war were sometimes killed en masse, as at No Gun Ri and Pyongyang. As Endicott and Hagerman write: "These acts in Korea indicated again that the U.S. subscription to laws of war and treatment of prisoners was no check on its political and military leaders' use of whatever methods and weapons were considered necessary to achieve their goals."[51] Faced with a seemingly endless stalemate on the battlefield through 1951 and 1952, the Truman administration looked desperately for breakthrough solutions. One possibility was to expand the war further into civilian population centers and related targets, to which end the USAF demolished eleven hydroelectric plants along the Yalu River in June 1952. Another response, mercifully never followed, was President Eisenhower's resurrection of Truman's earlier threat to use atomic bombs in order to break the quagmire. A third response, evidently carried out with great vigor but minimal success, was biological warfare. In the words of Endicott and Hagerman:

> The U.S. had substantial stocks of biological weapons on hand. Moral qualms about using biological or atomic weapons had been brushed aside by top leaders, and biological warfare might dodge the political bullet of adverse public and world opinion if it were kept secret enough to make a plausible denial of its use.

If it were to be uncovered, a last resort could be to fall back on the fact the U.S. had not signed the 1925 Geneva Protocol on biological warfare.[52]

Evidence of U.S. biological warfare came not only from Korean and Chinese government archives, from an independent commission of scientists, and from extensive testimony on the ground, but also from confessions of American airmen (later recanted, apparently under pressure) and eventually from scholarly research. Disease-carrying vectors—fleas, beetles, flies, and mosquitoes, for example—were found in at least 15 Korean locations from late 1950 into early 1951. These insects, largely unknown to the area, were infested with plague, smallpox, cholera, encephalitis, and other epidemic diseases leading to at least 39 deaths and more than 7000 illnesses, traceable to the use of bioweapons.[53] An independent commission found that "the peoples of Korea and China had indeed been the objects of bacteriological weapons,"[54] many of them targeted at Pyongyang and several nearby provinces. The U.S. apparently hoped the rapid spread of deadly diseases would instill panic among Koreans and Chinese, resulting in a collapse of combat morale— but the outbreaks, while frightening, were quickly contained by systematic and effective public-health campaigns. It seems evident, moreover, that the biological attacks were so ineffective that the Pentagon decided to abort them within several weeks of the first attacks, and the military stalemate continued. In any event, the overall impact of the illegal U.S. biological warfare campaign on Korean–Chinese battlefield efforts was negligible.

One long-term result of the Korean failure was reduced pressure for the U.S. to sustain its bioweapons program and strategy— that is, to build huge stockpiles of toxins along with appropriate delivery mechanisms. In the end, biowarfare simply contained far too many limits and contradictions to be militarily efficacious. The program appeared to be largely, but not entirely, dismantled after 1953, although, as we have seen, testing did continue sporadically beginning in the early 1960s. We know that the Pentagon, whatever its anti-WMD rhetoric, has never abandoned contingency plans for the use of both chemical and biological weaponry. Today, in collaboration with a number of universities, it has expanded its biological warfare testing programs at such locales as the Dugway Proving Grounds—ostensibly for "defensive" purposes—in violation of the BWC. That the very *idea* of biological warfare, long regarded as barbaric and illegal, remained alive for the U.S. armed forces—in full violation of international law—speaks volumes about a military culture that recognizes few constraints on its battlefield options and has been perfectly willing, under particular conditions, to condone and practice these kinds of war crimes.

EMPIRE AND BARBARISM

Given the frightening and seemingly irreversible proliferation of WMD in the world today, despite all the international treaties and conventions, doomsday remains firmly on the horizon—brought ever closer by the U.S. development, stockpiling, and use of mass-destruction weapons, along with its scandalous disregard for global arrangements designed to avoid the horrors of total war. The protracted U.S. war and occupation of Iraq, along with new threats to Iran, can only further heighten conditions that could produce eventual military cataclysm. Delivering a speech in February 2007, Russian leader Vladimir Putin attacked U.S. militarism for its reckless policies and adventures, arguing that Washington was creating a world in which other nations would be driven to violate global restraints while expanding their own weapons systems. Putin said that "unilateral, illegal actions have not managed to solve any of the world's most urgent problems, but have in fact made them worse. Nobody feels secure anymore." Putin actually spoke these words in front of an American delegation visiting Moscow.[55]

Because weapons of mass destruction—including economic sanctions and extreme forms of conventional warfare—are now so strategically central to maintaining Empire, such weapons seem nowadays to represent a *non-negotiable* element of U.S. foreign and military policy. WMD are coveted and embraced by many high-level Pentagon officers like nothing else. It must be remembered that, for potential targets, the very *threat* of WMD constitutes an intimidating military reality. This helps explain why U.S. leaders, Democrats and Republicans alike, have strongly opposed even modest efforts to achieve treaties and conventions limiting or outlawing the production and deployment of nuclear weapons, though occasionally that kind of rhetoric can be heard even within the political establishment. Owing to its vast superiority in this area, moreover, the U.S. has arrived at greater flexibility than in the past to pursue its imperial ambitions. (Such flexibility, of course, could well be curtailed by other factors.) As the leading military power, Washington reserves for itself the right to unlimited global reach, and with it special license to own and project the most awesome

WMD imaginable. The political establishment knows fully the barbaric nature of such weapons, yet these very weapons when developed by the U.S. are endowed with civilizing virtues that come with the best democratic intentions and, for many, the force of God's will—that is, with the great blessings of American exceptionalism. In this way, Hiroshima, an unspeakable act of savagery, still hovers over the global landscape as the growth of U.S. imperial and military power subverts prospects for truly binding international laws, treaties, and rules of engagement.

POSTSCRIPT: THE WMD COMMISSION

In June 2006 Dr. Hans Blix, former chief United Nations weapons inspector, presented a report to the U.N. titled "Weapons of Terror," authored by the Weapons of Mass Destruction Commission with the intent of ultimately freeing the world of nuclear, chemical, and biological warfare.[56] The work of an independent project, the report asks nations of the world to address vital issues of WMD before it is too late—before, that is, some cataclysmic military event occurs. In focusing on issues of disarmament and non-proliferation, the Commission offered no less than 60 proposals that ask all countries, especially those in possession of WMD, to revisit and hopefully alter policies that over the past several decades have only worsened prospects for disarmament and non-proliferation. The report calls on nations to take international laws and treaties far more seriously than they have hitherto, implicitly (and in places explicitly) calling the U.S. to account for its actions in blocking arms control, disarmament, and moves toward curtailing proliferation. Here we explore several of the Commission's proposals (numbered according to their original location) with particular reference to questions of American outlawry raised in this chapter.[57]

1. "All parties to the Non-Proliferation Treaty need to revert to the fundamental and balanced non-proliferation and disarmament commitments that were made under the treaty and confirmed in 1995." Note: The U.S. retains nearly 10,000 nuclear warheads—the largest arsenal in the world—with a destructive power greater than at any point since the beginning of the atomic era. Since the NPT was signed in 1968 Washington has made no effort to reduce its arsenal, nor have its policies contributed in any way toward non-proliferation. The 2005 NPT review process ended without progress on the key issues,

with the U.S. being largely (though not only) to blame for the paralysis. At present, moreover, the U.S. is moving toward the manufacture of a new cycle of atomic weapons and seems ready to modernize its existing warheads.

2. "All parties to the [NPT] should implement the decision on principles and objectives for non-proliferation and disarmament, the decision on strengthening the [NPT] review process and the resolution of the Middle East as a zone free of nuclear and all other weapons of mass destruction." Note: The review process has been substantially weakened, as indicated by the 2005 failure, owing in great measure to American obstructionism. The idea of turning the Middle East into a nuclear-free zone has been proposed by Egypt, Iran, and others but consistently opposed by the U.S. and Israel, which together deploy hundreds of nuclear warheads in the region. Israel, moreover, has never signed the NPT.

6. "Negotiations must be continued to ... improve the outlook for the common aim of establishing a Middle East zone free of weapons of mass destruction. The international community and Iran should build mutual confidence through measures that should include: reliable assurances regarding the supply of fuel-cycle services; suspending or renouncing sensitive fuel-cycle activities for a prolonged period of time by all states in the Middle East; assurances against attacks and subversion aiming at regime change; and facilitation of international trade and investment." Note: Both the U.S. and Israel have failed miserably on every count here. Neither country—along with India and Pakistan—has moved toward halting fuel-cycle activities, nor do they allow monitoring of such activities. The U.S. demand that Iran suspend its nuclear program is both illegal and counterproductive insofar as Iran (in contrast to Israel and India) subscribes to the NPT and has full rights within it. Further, both the U.S. and Israel have continued to make armed threats against Iran while rejecting normal diplomatic and trade relations. There have been no guarantees against military attack or regime subversion despite repeated efforts by the Iranians to restore normal relations and agree to a treaty of mutual non-aggression. In this as in other spheres Washington has merely aggravated an already tense situation.

7. "The nuclear-weapon states party to the [NPT] should provide legally binding negative security assurances to non-nuclear-

weapon state parties. The states not party to the [NPT] that possess nuclear weapons should separately provide such assurances." Note: Clearly the only way to ensure that proliferation will be halted is for the leading WMD nations to extend security assurances to smaller and weaker states that rightly fear being attacked in the absence of a WMD deterrence. Neither the U.S. nor Israel (holding to secrecy about its nuclear program) has offered any such assurances.

11. "All [NPT] nuclear-weapon states that have not yet done so should ratify the protocols of the treaties creating regional nuclear-weapon-free zones." Note: The U.S. has resolutely and consistently rejected proposals for nuclear-free zones as they are viewed as impeding military freedom of deployment and action.

12. "All states ... in [the Middle East], including Iran and Israel, should commit themselves for a prolonged period of time to a verified arrangement not to have any enrichment, reprocessing, or other sensitive fuel-cycle activities on their territories." Note: Since Israel, backed by the U.S., refuses to either join the NPT or acknowledge its own nuclear enterprise, this admirable proposal is a complete non-starter, and it is hardly surprising to find Iran unwilling to move alone in this direction.

15. "All states possessing nuclear weapons should declare a categorical policy of no first use of such weapons. They should specify that this covers both preemptive and preventive action, as well as retaliation for attacks involving chemical, biological, or conventional weapons." Note: As is well known, the U.S. has long had a first-use doctrine in place, with no indication that change has ever been seriously debated at the higher levels of American power. And the U.S., of course, is the only nation ever to have used atomic weapons. As for Israel, its outlawry is so extreme that the issue of first-use has never been raised in any domestic or international forum.

16. "States deploying their nuclear forces in triads, consisting of submarine-launched missiles, ground-based intercontinental ballistic missiles and long-range bombers, should abandon this practice in order to reduce nuclear-weapon redundancy and avoid fuelling nuclear arms races." Note: This possibility has never been entertained by U.S. political leaders, who remain fully committed to the nuclear status quo and continue to regard the complete array of strategic options as vital to

national security. The Russians, for their part, retain the same nuclear options but have indicated a willingness to negotiate reductions based on Washington reciprocity.

17. "Russia and the United States should agree on reciprocal steps to take their nuclear weapons off hair-trigger alert and should create a joint commission to facilitate this goal. They should undertake to eliminate the launch-on-warning option from their nuclear war plans." Note: Nearly two decades after the end of the Cold War, neither Russia nor the U.S. has moved to defuse this frightening level of nuclear readiness, which places the entire world at the mercy of superpower technology.

20. "All states possessing nuclear weapons must address the issue of their continued possession of such weapons. All nuclear-weapon states party to the [NPT] must take steps toward nuclear disarmament, as required by the treaty and the commitments made in connection with the treaty's indefinite extensions. Russia and the United States should take the lead... While Israel, India, and Pakistan are not parties to the [NPT] they too have a duty to contribute to the nuclear disarmament process." Note: Not only have Russia and the U.S. failed to take the lead in pushing for nuclear disarmament, they have essentially refused *any* genuine initiatives, as show by the 2005 review fiasco. In this respect as in others, Russia and the U.S. have failed to live up to their obligations within the NPT, while Israel, India, and Pakistan continue blithely along their outlaw path, contemptuous of the NPT and the limitations it seeks to impose.

22. "Every state that possesses nuclear weapons should make a commitment not to deploy any nuclear weapons, of any type, on foreign soil." Note: For many years the U.S. has deployed nuclear weapons in Europe, Korea, and elsewhere—the only nation in the world that regards itself as entitled to such a global military presence. Any suggestion that Washington ought to reconsider this policy is rejected out of hand.

23. "Any state contemplating replacement or modernization of its nuclear-weapon systems must consider such action in the light of all relevant treaty obligations and its duty to contribute to the nuclear disarmament process. As a minimum, it must refrain from developing nuclear weapons with new military capabilities or for new missions." Note: The U.S. is presently relying on its three nuclear-weapons laboratories to develop new cycles

of weapons as well as to modernize the existing arsenal—plans that could easily aggravate international tensions and stimulate arms competition. In other words, Washington has totally ignored both the spirit and letter of the NPT.

27. "To facilitate fissile material cutoff negotiations in the Conference on Disarmament, the five [NPT] nuclear-weapon states, joined by the other states possessing nuclear weapons, should agree among themselves to cease production of fissile material for weapons purposes. They should open up their facilities for such production to IAEA safeguards inspections, building on the same practice of EURATOM inspections in France and the United Kingdom. These eight states should also address the issue of verifiable limitations of existing stocks of weapons-usable nuclear materials." Note: The U.S. has fiercely resisted any system of monitoring and verification since the very outset of the atomic age, reflected most recently in its stance at the 2005 NPT review meetings. In the absence of such moves from the leading nuclear state, other states have predictably refused to go along with NPT guidelines—except, as mentioned, France and the United Kingdom. The U.S. insistence that Iran subscribe to procedures that it refuses for itself and other states such as Israel and India reflects the ultimate hypocrisy.

28. "All states that have not already done so should sign and ratify the Comprehensive Nuclear-Test-Ban Treaty unconditionally and without delay. The United States, which has not ratified the treaty, should reconsider its position and proceed to ratify the treaty, recognizing that its ratification would trigger other required ratifications and be a step towards the treaty's entry into force." Note: The Commission has come forth with everything that needs to be said here.

30. "All states possessing nuclear weapons should begin planning for security without nuclear weapons. They should start preparing for the outlawing of nuclear weapons through joint practical and incremental measures that include definitions, benchmarks, and transparency requirements for nuclear disarmament." Note: Sadly, the U.S. has moved in precisely the opposite direction from this vital recommendation. In its National Security statements and nuclear posture reviews Washington has made it abundantly clear that nuclear weapons remain a central component of its global military strategy, embracing

thousands of warheads, proclaiming a first-use contingency, laying out a variety of nuclear options, and moving ahead with production of new, more sophisticated weaponry. Worse yet, there has been no indication of any willingness among U.S. political elites, despite some reported differences of opinion at the highest levels, to even *debate* a shift away from the current nuclear basis of national security.

While the threat of WMD, including nuclear proliferation, remains more acute than ever, U.S. failure to honor its NPT obligations could not reveal more clearly the extent of Washington outlawry and rejectionism on a world scale. As the Commission report makes clear, no progress on WMD containment, arms control, and proliferation—much less disarmament—will be possible so long as the U.S. maintains its current belligerent and militaristic posture. As Hans Blix, former chief U.N. weapons inspector, has written: "With accelerating independence, there is an increasing necessity to cooperate in order to protect the global environment, to manage the global economy, and to stop the spread of contagious diseases. Why not also cooperate to stop killing each other."[58]

Looking forward to the next NPT review in 2010, the U.S. as the world's supreme military power and repository of the largest WMD arsenal is morally and politically obligated to assume leadership toward achieving a post-nuclear globe. It should renounce its first-strike policy, drastically reduce its number of warheads, agree to setting up nuclear-free zones, pressure its allies to downscale their arsenals, junk plans for new weapons cycles such as the RRW, and retreat from its missile-defense schemes like those in Eastern Europe. Nothing is possible until the U.S. makes dramatic changes in its WMD orientation. While few elected American politicians favor such overtures—Representative Dennis Kucinich being the most notable—public opinion surveys reveal strong majorities in favor of significant nuclear reductions. Even the mainstream *Defense Monitor* could state: "At a time when the United States is understandably alarmed about other countries establishing military nuclear programs, it is hard to justify why Washington not only thinks it needs thousands of nuclear weapons, but is fighting to retain its gargantuan complex of nuclear weapons labs."[59] We face a stark and perhaps imminent choice—either move toward eliminating nuclear weapons or risk global destruction.

5
A Tale of Broken Treaties

If international law today has languished in its capacity to regulate behavior among nations—corrupted by double standards and too often honored in the breach—the major culprit in this sad trajectory has been the United States, determined since World War II to pursue its goal of world hegemony at virtually any cost. The major superpower has rejected or ignored global agreements that might impede the smooth functioning of its economic, political, and military imperium, including the U.N. Charter, independent tribunals, treaties, rules of engagement, Geneva Protocols, World Court verdicts. For more than a century international norms have been established to forge common global principles, hoping within the existing world (capitalist) order to constrain if not eradicate the worst excesses of modern warfare. But the U.S. virtually alone remains shamelessly and hypocritically outside these norms in a system increasingly reduced to lawlessness. American politics is infused with images of great-power exceptionalism linked to ever-greater reliance on military power. While politicians, media pundits, and academics pay lip service to democracy and the "rule of law," in practice they have been inclined to uphold a special American status within what is cynically referred to as the "international community." For decades Washington has violated or sidestepped treaties and conventions it regarded as obstacles to U.S. national pursuits—a tendency pushed to extremes during the Bush presidency, the neocon ascendancy, and the war on terror.

Enough terrain has been covered in previous chapters to dramatize the scope and gravity of U.S. outlawry. To briefly recapitulate the most egregious violations here, the supposedly benevolent and peace-loving superpower has:

- Routinely violated key provisions of the U.N. Charter, launching crimes against peace not only in Iraq but in such recent cases as Panama, Yugoslavia, and Afghanistan.

- Violated the Geneva Protocols (1948) regarding laws of occupation (in Iraq) that pertain to the disposition of property and the altering of domestic institutions.
- Violated several international conventions by carrying out wanton attacks on civilian populations, including in Japan, Korea, Indochina, Panama, Yugoslavia, and Iraq.
- Violated the Geneva Protocols by using weapons that are innately destructive to civilian populations and objects, involving biological and chemical warfare, depleted uranium, anti-personnel bombs, and other inhumane weapons.
- Violated international conventions prohibiting use of torture and extraordinary methods of interrogation—at Guantanamo, Abu Ghraib and elsewhere in Iraq, Afghanistan, and dispersed CIA detention sites.
- Violated the 1968 Nuclear Non-Proliferation Treaty that calls on the nuclear powers to move toward dismantling arsenals, forbids development of new weaponry, and requires a universal system of monitoring strongly opposed by Washington.
- Violated the NPT by assisting in the development of other nuclear programs, such as that of India.
- Refused to sign an international land-mines treaty calling for cessation of the production and deployment of such mines that remain dispersed around the planet in the tens of millions.
- Blocked global efforts to strengthen the 1967 Outer Space Treaty that would ban all weapons from space, while opposing U.N. resolutions urging strictly peaceful use of outer space.
- Undermined the Chemical Warfare Convention, which it signed, by blocking international attempts to monitor American corporate and military facilities.
- Undermined the Biological Warfare Convention, which it also signed, for precisely the same reasons.
- Refused to endorse the International Criminal Court, insisting on special exemptions for its own government and military personnel.
- Refused to sign the Kyoto Protocol designed to fight global warming, insisting that any restrictions on its own industrial growth will harm its national economy and security interests.
- Refused to sign the Genocide Convention until 1988, four decades after the U.N. set it in motion, and then demanded for itself special veto powers concerning legal initiatives within the framework of a series of "reservations."

- Refused to abide by decisions rendered by the World Court—for example, that brought by Nicaragua in 1986—while dismissing the body as irrelevant to U.S. interests and behavior.
- Consistently voted against U.N. Resolution 242 calling for Israel to withdraw from territories it illegally occupied in 1967, joining only Israel and a few other small countries in rejecting the longstanding international consensus.
- Opposed repeated U.N. General Assembly resolutions condemning Israel for systematic human rights violations in the West Bank and Gaza.
- Opposed (virtually alone) repeated U.N. General Assembly resolutions calling for nuclear test bans, cessation of the nuclear arms race, and nuclear disarmament. It withdrew from the 1972 Anti-Ballistic Missile treaty in 2001.
- Opposed (usually alone or with Israel) literally hundreds of U.N. General Assembly resolutions expressing an international consensus behind such issues as arms control, nuclear proliferation, and combating terrorism.

Many instances of U.S. outlawry are covered in other chapters. Several other violations—regarding the United Nations, the Genocide Convention, the Outer Space Treaty, and the Kyoto Protocol—are explored in the present chapter. Two other instances of American rejectionism (on treaties related to laws of the seas and tobacco regulation) deserve special elaboration here.

The U.N. Convention on Laws of the Sea has for decades furnished a basis for global agreements on marine boundaries, environmental and material resources, scientific research, and pollution controls—a sort of "Constitution of the Ocean" signed by 153 nations. A vital international agreement in an era of global warming, the U.S. refuses to lend its (obviously much-needed) participation. The U.N. has declared the oceans (covering 71 percent of the planet's surface) "the common heritage of mankind"—an ecological commons—but the U.S. is mesmerized by some trillions of dollars in wealth available to be exploited by corporations. During the Reagan presidency, Washington opposed any negotiations concerning the sea treaty, vowing never to "give away" deep-sea resources it said belonged to those with the necessary capital and technology to develop them. Later, President Clinton managed to win enhanced corporate access within the framework of the sea convention, but ratification was blocked in the Senate after Jesse Helms said he would reject any agreement in which the U.S. does not have preponderant voting power. That result was duplicated in 2004 when many senators expressed fears over potential loss of U.S. sovereignty—a familiar pretext for American rejectionism.

This failure takes on added meaning at a time when reports (in 2006) show that for years the U.S. military had been disposing of millions of pounds of dangerous chemical weapons at sea, part of an ocean-dumping program. The army alone secretly disposed of 64 million pounds of nerve and mustard gas, along with 400,000 bombs filled with chemical agents as well as thousands of land mines, rockets, and 500 tons of radioactive waste, off the East Coast of the U.S. Hazardous dumping, likely to bring terrible long-term devastation to vast regions of the ocean ecology, took place from World War II to at least 1970, with arrogant U.S. indifference to the welfare of human and marine life.[1]

As for the tobacco treaty—called the Framework Convention for Tobacco Control—Washington, under intense pressure from American tobacco companies, has repeatedly opposed an agreement now ratified by 144 nations. Developed by the World Health Organization, the treaty was intended to regulate worldwide sales of tobacco products expected to kill at least one billion people across the twenty-first century. Outside any regulations, major U.S. corporations like Philip Morris spent no less than $15 billion in 2006 to promote smoking worldwide. As the percentage of American smokers declined markedly, these interests looked to "replacement smokers" in foreign countries to increase their profits while the death toll escalates. The tobacco convention requires participating nations to regulate pricing, taxation, labeling, and advertising of tobacco products, but the tobacco lobby in the U.S. wants no part of such restrictions as the companies now sell roughly four times abroad what they can sell in the U.S. Meanwhile, the global capacity to regulate tobacco sales and use has been effectively gutted.

LAWLESSNESS: AN AMERICAN LEGACY

Beneath the familiar law-and-order mythology of U.S. history there is a long tradition of lawlessness—a condition with deep roots in the nineteenth century that continues into the present. Contrary to the prevailing wisdom today, the easy willingness of American leaders to break or ignore international agreements did not originate with the neocons or the second Bush administration, although with them the practice has surely been taken to new extremes. Here we focus on perhaps the saddest and most treacherous phases of this legacy:

the use and abuse of treaties to facilitate the violent conquest and destruction of Native American populations as part of "settling the West." Much of this history covers familiar terrain but some crucial (if often obscured) elements of it deserve renewed emphasis in the context of the outlaw trajectory explored in the present chapter.

The lengthy process of American nation-building, construed in mainstream texts as a noble, democratic, civilizing mission, became one of the most destructive episodes in human history—one justly deserving the label "genocidal." It could, without much exaggeration, be described as a sustained policy of extermination. An indigenous population numbering as many as 15 million at the time of Columbus was, by 1900, reduced to a mere 237,000 defeated, terrorized people forced onto mostly barren reservations.[2] This catastrophe followed many decades of conquest and forcible removal in which lawful treaties, negotiated with dozens of tribes occupying their own land, would be systematically abused and dismissed within a strategy of protracted warfare that white colonialists pursued as their God-given right. Having signed more than 400 treaties beginning in the late eighteenth century, the U.S. government broke virtually every one of them, justifying Vine Deloria's sad conclusion that "it is doubtful that any nation will ever exceed the record of the United States in perfidy."[3] This record is no arcane, distant memory but rather persists across the entire history of U.S. foreign and military policy.

As Deloria points out, the long trajectory of Indian population removals and physical destruction, punctuated with massacres, clearly shows the U.S. never intended to honor treaties it signed in actual practice, for they were simply another weapon in its vast arsenal of warfare.[4] The political foundation for displacing Indians was to be found in the discovery doctrine, first enunciated by Christian leaders, whereby the "rights of native tribes to their land would be taken away in favor of those Europeans who happened to 'discover' the land"—simply another rationale for theft and, in the process, mass murder. As more European settlers moved westward, treaties were signed between the U.S. government and retreating tribes with the supposed aim of ensuring peace on the frontier and security for tribal peoples in their (redesignated) homelands. Yet while the tribes generally held to their promises, the U.S. failed to do so, continuing its theft of land as changing conditions on the frontier provided new opportunities for property confiscation and resource theft. More than two billion acres of indigenous territory was stolen at the point of a gun, assisted by creative but duplicitous treaty-making. For example, between 1814 and 1824 the government signed a series of treaties with southern Indians (Creeks, Cherokees, etc.) as whites moved to take over what is presently Florida, Georgia, and Alabama, with Andrew Jackson playing a key role in the agreements. As Howard Zinn comments: "Every time a treaty was signed, pushing the Creeks from one area to the next, promising them security there, whites would move into the new area and the Creeks would feel compelled to sign another treaty, giving up more land in return for security elsewhere."[5] Indian resistance was met with swift and harsh military action. This same pattern would continue until the last bastion of Indian opposition was crushed, at Wounded Knee, South Dakota, in 1890.

While Native tribes believed they had an inalienable right to their sacred lands, the government and settlers viewed them as savages incapable of possessing rights, just as slaves had always been bereft of rights. Jackson, taking over the presidency in 1829, engineered this imperial crusade, setting out to expand inhabitable land for white settlers by means of forcible removal policies. In 1830 the Indian Removal Law was passed, abrogating existing treaties and pushing the tribes off the most fertile and resource-rich land, often relocating them to cold, barren territory far from their ancestral homes. Under Jackson new laws stripped away all Indian claims, including even the right to hold tribal meetings, while broadened federal treaties (imposed by Washington) gave Congress new powers over Indian communities. Many areas previously granted to the tribes "indefinitely"—in perpetuity—were now abruptly taken away. In many cases, after treaties were signed, new settlements would be followed by attacks carried out by the army or militias intended to push tribes out, where they often met with starvation, disease, and other miseries. In 1832 the government made extravagant promises to Indians in the Treaty of Washington, which forced them beyond the Mississippi River, but these promises (for peace, security, new homelands, etc.) were quickly and sadistically broken. The Indians had caved in to virtually every U.S. demand, but to no avail. A demonized population could be shamelessly violated at every turn, fully justified by politicians, theologians, and academics.[6]

As Robert Miller has shown in considerable detail, European white settlers were able to legitimate their colonial theft by means of the Discovery Doctrine, utilized well into the twentieth century.[7] This was nothing less than outright racist conquest codified and institutionalized within U.S. law. The principle was that the first Europeans to "discover" land occupied by Native populations could claim ownership on the grounds that they were in an elevated position to "develop" the property—a "principle" typically enforced through political coercion or military takeover. An 1823 Supreme Court ruling (*Johnson v. McIntosh*) established the Discovery Doctrine as basic to U.S. law, without the knowledge or consent of the Indian people.[8] The assumption, specified in legal documents, was that white colonizers were "civilized" while Indians were primitive "savages" incapable of improving the territory they had long inhabited. As Miller points out, Discovery ideology was closely linked to the idea of Manifest Destiny, which endowed the new American nation with special God-given rights and privileges. The white settlers would bring their unique virtues westward, clearing the terrain of all (human and natural) impediments to "progress." In Miller's words: "This kind of thinking could only arise ... from an ethnocentric view of one's own culture, government, race, religion, and country as superior to all others."[9]

One of the most disastrous betrayals of Native peoples occurred with the systematic displacement of the Choctaws, historically settled in the south-eastern regions. A series of treaties was signed between Washington and the tribes—one of the so-called "Civilized Tribes"—until the final treaty of Dancing Rabbit Creek (1830) forced them across the Mississippi onto the barren plains of Oklahoma. The Choctaws stubbornly resisted each encroachment while also clinging to new promises, but were eventually forced to make the long and difficult journey westward, defeated and impoverished.

Plenty of such episodes were later repeated. Thus in 1851 the Treaty of Fort Laramie was negotiated between the U.S. and representatives of the Sioux, Cheyenne, Arapaho, Crow, and other tribes, assigning specific territories to each tribe, guaranteeing peace and protection, and distributing $50,000 yearly to each group for supplies. Lands were promised to the Indians "forever." Immediately, however, tens of thousands of settlers poured across the territories, military forts were set up in the middle of tribal lands, and the U.S. wound up failing to comply with virtually every provision of this supposedly landmark treaty. Such duplicity gave rise to decades more of brutal war on the Great Plains, ending with the Wounded Knee massacre in 1890—in areas where the states of Montana, Wyoming, Nebraska, Kansas, Colorado, North Dakota, and South Dakota now exist.

In 1862 Congress passed the Homestead Act and the Pacific Railroad Act, effectively overturning earlier treaties and further opening Indian lands to white settlement, inspired by notions of "discovery" and Manifest Destiny as westward colonization took on a powerful "civilizing" mission. Homestead promised 160 acres to anyone (white) who claimed it and worked to improve it, while the PRA gave rail companies 174 million acres of land across the continent, mainly on Native territories.[10] In 1866—two years after the Sand Creek massacre of Cheyennes who had secured peaceful camping rights in Colorado—the government forced open the Bozeman Trail by military force, then called for a peace council at Fort Laramie to neutralize Indian resistance. The Oglala Sioux chief Red Cloud, upon learning of a planned chain of U.S. army forts in the region, said: "Why do you pretend to negotiate for land you intend to take by force? I say you can force us only to fight for the land the Great Spirit has given us."[11] The government response was simply more force, reflected in a *Montana Post* statement that, "If the Indians continue their barbarities, wipe them out."[12] Two years later Red Cloud did reluctantly sign the Fort Laramie Treaty of 1868, hoping furtively for some measure of peace, security, and homeland, but terms of the agreement (for undisturbed tribal stewardship of their lands) were soon violated by the government, validating the Oglala chief's earlier warnings about white duplicity and treachery.

In 1871 Congress declared that no further Indian treaties would be signed, no doubt concluding that, with weakened tribal resistance, the theft of land by force no longer required even minimal legal pretenses. As the remaining tribes were pushed onto mostly barren reservations, the U.S. military and settlers managed to wipe out the buffalo herds—an estimated 20 million—in little more than a century. Toward the end of this cleansing process General Sheridan told the Texas legislature that the buffalo slaughters "have done ... more to settle the vexed Indian question than the entire regular army."[13] The road was paved for the U.S. to run roughshod over the Treaty of Fort Laramie once gold was discovered in the Black Hills and other areas of the West. Indians could not be allowed to stand in the way of "progress," treaties or no treaties. In 1876 President Ulysses S. Grant issued an executive order dictating that all Sioux tribes must go to designated agencies or be killed, regardless of prior agreements. Congress passed the General Allotment Act in 1887, dissolving all tribal landholdings and dismantling all leadership structures. During the 1889–90 Oklahoma land rush, some two million acres of Indian territory was opened up to white settlers and speculators by edict of President Benjamin Harrison, at which time Thomas Morgan, Commissioner of Indian Affairs, said "the

Indians must now conform to the white man's ways."[14] According to historians like Frederick Jackson Turner, writing at the end of the U.S. annihilation of Native peoples, the colonial push westward reflected a triumph of the great American dedication to freedom, adventure, and private ownership.

The violation of Indian treaty rights did not stop with Wounded Knee, however. By 1934 another 86 million acres had been transferred from Indian to white owners. In the late 1940s vast resources were discovered under Indian reservations—uranium on Navajo, coal on Crow, oil and gas on Apache, and uranium along with coal on Laguna Pueblo lands—which, at the time of the Cold War, the government was anxious to mine for "national security" purposes. Efforts were underway in Washington to reshape or dismantle the reservation system as it had evolved. In 1950 Congress passed the Rehabilitation Act, providing Indians with resources to leave for cities and thus freeing the government to develop mineral-rich areas. In the 1950s some 13 tribes and hundreds of bands were simply terminated, from Wisconsin to California, while in northern Arizona thousands of Navajos were forcibly removed to allow for mining activities—all in violation of earlier treaties. Between 1952 and 1963 termination policy was carried out in earnest, as tribes progressively lost trust status and whatever other fragile official standing they had previously managed to negotiate. Little has changed in the political and legal culture since the 1960s. In 1972 the American Indian Movement (AIM) organized a Trail of Broken Treaties campaign—a four-mile procession of cars and trucks—to dramatize this long and sad U.S. history of broken treaties.

Treaties signed between Washington and the North American tribes were historically understood as contractual relations, meaning that each party had to agree to the terms of the agreement for it to be valid. The U.S. government was fully obligated to uphold treaties it had signed in good faith, but such legal responsibilities were never fulfilled; Indians were dismissed as serious contractual partners, despite rhetoric to the contrary. Tribes repeatedly went to court to confirm or uphold their treaty and property rights but typically lost as the federal judiciary consistently refused to recognize the legal validity of treaties signed with Indians. (At the same time, courts have generally upheld tribal claims of tax exemption, although these claims too have come under sustained political and legal challenge.) In the end tribes enjoyed no real leverage in federal courts, and no legal standing when it came to treaties. The government frequently justified their hypocritical stance by saying that whites "gave" Indians their land but the tribes had failed to "develop" it as required. In reality, as Deloria observes, "practically the only thing the white men ever gave the Indian was disease and poverty."[15] Of course the reverse of Washington propaganda was the actual case: Indians were routinely forced to "give" away their ancestral lands to the militarily superior white forces. Throughout this long process of fraudulent treaty making it was always possible, moreover, for Congress to pass legislation superseding earlier treaty provisions—and of course the tribes had no way to effectively fight back. Over the years, by signing and then breaking treaties, the U.S. was able to gain absolute domination over the lands and lives of Native Americans.

This record of betrayal and lawlessness established a strong precedent for subsequent U.S. behavior in the world. The legacy of national exceptionalism and colonial arrogance runs deep. As Deloria writes:

> The Indian wars of the past should rightly be regarded as the first foreign wars of American history. As the United States marched across this continent, it was creating an empire by wars of foreign conquest just as England and France were doing in India and Africa. Certainly the war with Mexico was imperialistic, no more or less than the wars against the Sioux, Apache, Utes, and Yakimas. In every case the goal was identical: land.[16]

One difference between the U.S. and the English or French, of course, is that U.S. imperial domination eventually became truly *global*. When the frontier was finally declared closed in 1890 it would be just a short time before U.S. militarism would take the country into the Spanish–American War—a watershed event for the development of twentieth-century American global expansion. "There has not been a time," Deloria writes, "since the founding of the republic when the motives of this country were innocent."[17]

SUBVERTING THE UNITED NATIONS

U.S. participation in the United Nations has a long, complex, and twisted history—one that evolved into a corrosive relationship generally indicative of American exceptionalism. In 1928 the U.S. and some European powers forged the Kellogg-Briand Pact with the goal of outlawing war as an instrument of foreign policy or, short of that, establishing a rules-based approach to warfare. The hope was that Kellogg-Briand might lead toward a new world legal order going beyond previous conventions and treaties. In 1942 the same countries signed the Atlantic Charter, an updated effort to create a framework of peaceful international relations, which eventually paved the way toward the U.N. Charter, framed in June 1945 to replace the defunct League of Nations (never supported by the U.S.). Benefiting from momentum created by the Nuremberg and Tokyo tribunals, the U.N. would be the first truly international body to ensure world peace: outlawing warfare, guaranteeing sovereignty and equal rights among nations, affirming a code of human rights, embracing the principle of universality. By the late 1940s, following the most destructive war in history, the U.N. Charter had emerged as a crucible of hopes and dreams for a world that might finally be liberated from the scourge of warfare and oppression. Toward this end the Universal Declaration of Human Rights was created under U.N. auspices in December 1948 and adopted by the General Assembly in August 1949.

From the outset, however, the U.S. (with a few of its allies) was able to dominate U.N. deliberations owing to its superpower status, preponderant military force, economic leverage, and veto rights as a member of the five-nation Security Council. As quickly shown by the U.S. intervention in Korea (1950–53), conducted as a legitimate U.N. operation, the U.S. was strong enough to pursue its own global interests through the world body despite the nuisance of occasional Soviet vetoes in the Security Council. (For the vote on Korea the USSR was mysteriously absent.) Over time, however, as U.N. General Assembly membership grew rapidly to include dozens of new (mostly third-world) countries—many at odds with Washington agendas—U.S. capacity to mobilize consensus behind its foreign-policy objectives grew more problematic. Its power to manipulate a majority of General Assembly members was so weakened that by the 1970s it frequently wound up among small minorities opposing General Assembly resolutions.[18] The U.S. increasingly found itself politically isolated despite its preponderant economic and military power. Since the late 1960s, the U.S. has taken the lead in vetoing Security Council resolutions, many of them condemning either U.S. or Israeli military actions. Thus, even where the U.S. was unable to bend the U.N. toward its own interests, it still retained enough power not only to block resolutions but to water them down in either the General Assembly or Security Council. By the turn of the new century, Washington had built such an enduring record of rejectionism at the U.N. that it effectively undermined the body as a global peacekeeping institution. The U.S. was doing more to *subvert* than to empower the very U.N. Charter it had helped bring into being.

In the case of the second Iraq war, the U.S. made several efforts to win Security Council support but in the end simply executed its plans for invasion and occupation with flagrant disregard for U.N. rules and deliberations. In the lead-up to military action Washington made clear its designs for regime change—in opposition to any U.N. or international consensus, if necessary—with Bush warning that Security Council refusal to endorse U.S. action would condemn the U.N. to irrelevance. In fact U.S. military operations had been planned months before March 2003, rendering the unprovoked war a crime against peace as defined by both Nuremberg and the U.N. Charter. Relying on an entirely bogus pretext for war—the imminent threat of the Hussein regime to U.S. security and world peace—the U.S. simply followed its own geopolitical agenda in brazen contempt for international law. The U.S. had already conducted sabotage, infiltration, and covert actions as a prelude to military intervention, much of it under U.N. cover. Paradoxically, at the very moment it was subverting or dismissing the U.N., the Bush administration shamelessly tried to justify its military aggression by invoking Security Council Resolution 688, passed in April 1991 to enforce Iraqi arms reductions, but the Hussein regime was never shown to be in violation of this resolution and, moreover, it never actually permitted unilateral military action.

If the Iraq debacle shows a U.S. readiness to violate the U.N. Charter—that is, if Bush could insist upon capitulation to U.S. military intervention, or else—this simply reveals the lengths to which Washington will resort to push its imperial objectives. Nor was this the first time Washington had launched a military attack without Security Council approval. The same contempt for international law was evident in U.S. military operations against Panama and Yugoslavia, for example, not to mention a series of earlier attacks on Iraq (such as the Desert Fox bombings in 1998), at times when U.S. leaders never bothered to so much as *consult* with the U.N. or any other body. (The U.S. vetoed a Security Council resolution condemning the illegal 1989 surprise attack on Panama.) Moreover, Bush was hardly the first President to invoke the need for "preemptive war," though using different language, to protect American global interests—the Truman Doctrine of the late 1940s being a case in point. We know, however, that Bush and the neocons have been more ideologically aggressive than most predecessors. Echoing the neocon approach, David Frum and Richard Perle could write: "When did the United States require the Security Council's permission to defend itself?"[19] They added that when the U.S. does not get its way it should "unashamedly and explicitly reject the jurisdiction of these [U.N.] rules."[20] What they had in mind, of course, was a strictly *offensive* military action to overthrow a sovereign government located some 10,000 miles from American shores.

U.S. subversion of the U.N. extends well beyond simple evasion or cloaking national schemes under the body's legitimacy: the use of bribes and threats to coerce pro-American votes has been widely employed, as for example in mobilizing Security Council backing for the 1991 Persian Gulf War.[21] Given a record of such power maneuvers, the carrying on of Washington politicians about other nations living up to their U.N. obligations seems vacuous.

U.S. exceptionalism and resort to double standards is, as we have seen, deeply ingrained in the political culture. Since the late 1970s Washington has opposed literally hundreds of U.N. resolutions favoring human rights, provisions of international law, disarmament, curbs on military intervention, and the like, and has consistently defended Israel against repeated U.N. resolutions condemning it for military occupations, illegal settlements, human rights transgressions, various atrocities, and crimes against peace. Despite self-righteous rhetoric concerning the horrors of WMD, the U.S. has fought off encroachments on its own sovereign "right" to manufacture, deploy, and even use such weapons, voting often against General Assembly measures to control WMD according to *universal* criteria, that is, agreements binding on *all* nations.

Since examples of U.S. rejectionist behavior are far too numerous to detail here, a brief survey will have to suffice. In December 1979 the U.S. opposed (with France and Britain) a resolution calling for negotiations to curtail the arms race; in December 1980 it rejected (with Britain) a call for cessation of nuclear testing; in December 1981 and again in December 1983 it alone refused to endorse prohibitions against chemical and biological warfare; in December 1982 it opposed (by itself) the idea of a comprehensive nuclear-test-ban treaty; and in December 1984 it rejected (alone) a resolution outlawing manufacture and development of WMD in any form.[22] Despite its adherence to the Outer Space Treaty, the U.S. in December 1983 opposed (alone) calls for space to be used for strictly peaceful ends. Meanwhile, rhetoric in favor of peace and democracy emanating from Washington was rarely translated into binding U.N. resolutions—witness its 1979 opposition (with Israel) to a ban on interventions in the affairs of sovereign states, and its 1983 refusal (alone) to put the U.N. on record as permitting all states to choose their own social order. Similarly, the U.S. stood completely alone in its failure to support resolutions (several in the late 1970s and early 1980s alone) condemning apartheid in South Africa.[23]

The international scourge of Nazism and terrorism? Historically, U.S. leaders have yielded to no one in their self-righteous opposition to political violence, and for at least two decades Washington claims to have been fighting a holy war against international terrorism. Within U.N. confines, however, the U.S. has turned a different face: in December 1985 it opposed (with Israel) a resolution calling for concrete measures against Nazi and neo-Nazi groups, while in December 1987 it rejected (with Israel) a series of proposals to prevent and combat terrorism. Further, despite its claims to uphold the ideal of national sovereignty, the U.S. has routinely opposed U.N. efforts (always joined by Israel) to repeal the decades-long harsh and senseless American embargo on Cuba—one typical vote (in 1998) being 157 to 2. Even modest humanitarian resolutions— for example, one in 1979 proposing a U.N. conference on the status of women—seemed too radical for Washington politicians: the U.S. and Israel alone rejected it. Far more obstructionist has been U.S. unwillingness to extend human rights to include health care, work, and education, provisions long ago enshrined in the Universal Declaration of Human Rights that the U.S. itself endorsed in the late 1940s. And the U.S. has been notably rejectionist in the area of environmental and health protections. Thus in October 1982 it opposed (alone) the idea of a World Charter to monitor and protect the global environment; voted in December 1982 (tally 146 to 1) against measures to protect humans from products deemed harmful to health and the environment; rejected in December 1983 (alone) a proposal to make health care a universal right endorsed by all nations; and opposed in December 1986 (alone) yet another measure designed to protect humans from production and sale of harmful goods.[24] More recently (in 2006), the U.S. has ardently opposed U.N. adoption of a Declaration on the Rights of Indigenous Peoples, a long-overdue measure supported by nearly 190 nations. Countries like the U.S. (including Russia and Canada), despite their human rights rhetoric, fear extending genuine freedoms to Native populations with access to considerable land and resources.

Yet nothing is more indicative of U.S. hostility to world consensus—and international law—than its unwavering support of Israeli violations across four decades. The belligerency of both nations includes rejection of dozens of General Assembly resolutions affirming Palestinian national rights and a two-state solution, along with demands for Israel to cease illegal settlements, vacate occupied territories, and discontinue its ongoing human rights abuses such as unlawful detentions and torture. Resolution 242, passed in November 1967, called for Israeli withdrawal from Gaza and the West Bank—illegally seized through military conquest—as the basis of any settlement. With strong U.S. backing, Israel has consistently opposed 242, a measure based on the principle of national self-determination and endorsed universally. In 1976 the U.S. vetoed a Syrian proposal for Security Council backing of a two-state solution based on 242, followed by U.S.–Israeli rejection of a General Assembly measure (December 1978) condemning Israel's systematic human rights abuses in the occupied territories and refusal to go along with another resolution demanding the right of Palestinians to return to areas from which they had been expelled (November 1979). In December 1980 the U.S. and Israel voted against a resolution calling for improved living conditions in occupied lands, and in October 1981 both nations opposed a resolution condemning Israel for its unprovoked military strike against Iraq. In 1988 the Palestinian National Council proposed a two-state settlement based on 242—supported by all nations except the U.S. and Israel, whose leaders argued that Jordan must be considered the true Palestinian state. Later, in December 1989, the General Assembly called for long-overdue progress toward a Palestinian state, again based on the 242 consensus, which the U.S. and Israel refused outright.

Since 1970 the U.S. has either formally or informally supported Israeli occupation in the West Bank and Gaza, new settlements, military aggression, and widespread atrocities while rejecting proposals for an international conference tied to the key provisions of resolution 242. The Israeli annexation of Jerusalem—illegal and condemned by the U.N.—has received U.S. endorsement since 1968. More recently, in December 2003, the General Assembly reaffirmed the Palestinian right of self-determination, denied only by the U.S., Israel, and a few tiny island-states. A January 2004 resolution calling for Israeli withdrawal from occupied territories and a two-state arrangement based on 242 met the same fate.[25] In August 2006, as mentioned, the U.S. blocked a Security Council measure condemning the Israeli military attack on Lebanon. Not only does such flagrant rejectionist behavior signal a dismissive attitude toward the U.N., international law, and basic human rights—not to mention Palestinian self-determination—it also reveals what should be obvious: the U.S.–Israeli preference for military force over diplomacy in resolving what is said to be an intractable conflict. This stands as perhaps the most egregious instances of lawlessness in the world during the postwar years.

With the ascendancy of Bush and the neocons, U.S. rejectionism at the U.N. turned even more strident and arrogant, revolving mainly around issues related to the Middle East: outright violation of the U.N. Charter, illegal invasion and occupation of Iraq, cynical use of the U.N. to conduct infiltration, surveillance, and covert action, refusal to endorse arms-control efforts, human rights double standards, unwavering support of Israeli outlawry, flagrant disregard for global treaties as in the case of the ICC. When John Bolton took over as U.S. delegate to the U.N. in early 2006, Washington took its bellicosity to new levels, threatening even to withhold American financial support in the absence of majority backing of U.S. initiatives. A hard-line neocon, Bolton injected a particularly abrasive style into his work, marked by a fierce antagonism toward any international body not fully subservient to American interests.

Such parochial views, predictably, have achieved widespread acceptance among the American public; national exceptionalism and its by-products have never been confined to elite culture. A 2005 German Marshall Fund survey found Americans far more willing than Europeans to dismiss the U.N. and other international organizations in situations where vital U.S. objectives might be compromised.[26] The poll revealed that Americans have less interest in global events and institutions than do Europeans and, by a large majority, believe U.S. leaders should not be required to seek U.N. approval for military action. Positive images of the U.N.—a body that Washington helped establish and which was once viewed as a bulwark of hopes for world peace—are presently held by fewer than half of the Americans surveyed.[27] No doubt many years of U.S. outlawry and rejectionism were destined to have this sort of impact on public opinion.

GENOCIDE ACCORDS: THE GREAT RETREAT

Since World War II, in the wake of unspeakable Nazi atrocities committed against Jews, Gypsies, Slavs, and assorted political enemies, the crime of genocide has become solidified in the global consciousness as the most horrible of offenses—one that can be charged against individuals, groups, or states. The concept of genocide was initially formulated by Raphael Lemke who, during the early 1940s, sought to define genocide as the crime of crimes—the destruction of an ethnic, religious, or national group by economic, political, cultural, or military methods (or some combination of these methods). According to Lemke, genocide could involve efforts aimed at undermining the capacity of a group to survive, as the perpetrator seeks to impose its own modes of existence on those it targets.[28]

With the Nazis defeated in 1945, one of the first orders of business for the victorious Allies—both at Nuremberg and at the United Nations—was to establish a legal precedent for trying and punishing those guilty of this ultimate crime, with hopes of preventing future occurrences. At Nuremberg many of the 21 defendants were charged with "crimes against humanity" understood to include atrocities against civilians—though not amounting to genocide as such—but only a few (Joachim von Ribbentrop, Herman Goering, and a few military leaders) were ultimately convicted as the tribunal focused mainly on crimes of aggression. In December 1946 the U.N. General Assembly passed resolution 96/II stating that "genocide is a denial of the right of existence of entire human groups, as homicide is the denial of the right to live of individual human beings," a crime contrary to the content and spirit of international law and the U.N. Charter.[29] In December 1948 the General Assembly unanimously adopted the Convention on Prevention and Punishment of the Crime of Genocide—a treaty that would become binding international law for the postwar era after a majority of U.N. member states ratified it by January 1951. (By 1990 more than 100 nations had signed on to this historic convention.) Despite areas of legal ambiguity, the Convention essentially carried forward the substance of Lemke's seminal definition of genocide.

Although the U.S. took the lead in prosecuting Nazis for war crimes, its politicians and lawyers eloquent in their moral denunciations of German monsters, Washington in fact had major reservations about the Genocide Convention from the outset, refusing to endorse it after trying to weaken its main provisions. To be sure, the agreement had at the time—and indeed continues to have—significant conceptual and legal problems. Yet what bothered U.S. delegates most was the ominous breadth of criminal offenses involved and the perceived threats to national sovereignty (namely possible restrictions on U.S. military operations) they seemed to pose. Then, as later, the U.S. feared institutionalization of truly global forms of juridical power, which the Genocide Convention sought to embrace and codify. At the time of a nascent Cold War, when the international fight against Communism was placed at the top of the agenda, Washington was in no mood to accept restraints on its exercise of economic, political, and especially military power. Some rather loose definitions of criminal accountability inserted into the Convention—for example, references to destruction of a group totally *or in part*—worried American negotiators, as did provisions for making perpetrators accountable for the *cultural* dimension of genocide. Many felt that genocide laws might in the future be applied to excesses of U.S. global behavior, a concern that would be later intensified with the onset of the Vietnam War. (Indeed the Russell Tribunal did charge the U.S. with waging genocidal warfare in Vietnam when the court issued its judgments in 1967.)

The U.S. fear of binding genocide laws persisted for decades after the first treaty was passed—a sentiment that politicians, the media, leading academics, and other opinion leaders all seemed to share. In 1970 the Genocide Convention was finally submitted to the Senate for ratification at a time when President Nixon apparently hoped to refurbish an American global image severely damaged by the Vietnam War. Still opposed by a majority of Washington elites, the treaty met with renewed hostility as senators raised familiar arguments about how the Convention might be turned against the U.S. Further, placing American military operations under stringent legal codes struck many senators and others as an unreasonable constraint on U.S. military activity abroad, some of which, after all, had already been extremely protracted and bloody. By 1985, however, as the Convention evolved into customary-law status, the U.S. appeared ready to accept legal protocols that were now part of an international consensus. The Vietnam War, meanwhile, was long over, even as the "Vietnam Syndrome" (referring to a heavy national mood of defeat and humiliation) remained very much alive.

The U.S. Senate eventually ratified the Genocide Convention in February 1986, but not until a "sovereignty package" was put together with the idea of minimizing potential negative consequences for American military behavior. With an elaborate set of Lugar-Hatch-Helms reservations firmly in place, congressional passage of the Genocide Convention Implementation Act, known as the Proxmire Act for the senator most aggressively pushing it, came in October 1988, achieving full legal status in February 1989—

four decades after the treaty was initially framed. But this was no great turning-point: modifications to the Convention demanded by Washington effectively gutted major provisions, at least where U.S. culpability might be at issue. Everything was arranged to give Washington maximum freedom to interpret the Convention as it chose, to protect itself against any possible charges. Thus Reservation I (2) states "that nothing in the Convention requires or authorizes legislation or other action by the United States prohibited by the Constitution of the United States as interpreted by the United States." A second reservation mandates that before any legal process can be brought before the International Court of Justice the U.S. has the right to give its specific consent. Finally, there is a provision stating that "acts in the course of armed conflicts committed without the specific intent required by Article II [of the Convention] are not sufficient to constitute genocide as defined by this Convention."[30] In other words, U.S. "sovereignty" reservations are broad and flexible enough to remove any possibility its citizens might be prosecuted for the crime of genocide. That charge, it turns out, is appropriate only for *others* lacking the benefit of such protective "sovereignty" clauses. Formal objections to these outrageous American exemptions were raised by many signatories to the Convention—exemptions widely regarded as a violation of international law—with Holland flatly refusing to accept U.S. ratification under these terms.

A prelude to later U.S. rejectionism in the case of the International Criminal Court, Washington's obsession here with immunity from prosecution would have a debilitating impact on the quest for global justice. Exempting the very nation most likely to be guilty of military-related crimes makes little moral, legal, or political sense. High-sounding rhetoric about Nazi genocide at the end of World War II would unfortunately never be translated into *universal* political discourses or legal codes, thanks to continued U.S. exceptionalism. The leading superpower insisted on the absolute freedom to behave as it chooses. The result has been a truncated Genocide Convention, leaving only ad hoc procedures created to punish those hostile to U.S. national interests. As Ward Churchill writes: "The upshot is that after a half-century of blocking implementation of the Genocide Convention, the United States has moved decisively to dominate it, harnessing international law entirely to the needs and dictates of American policy."[31]

Far from being systematically investigated, prosecuted, and punished, therefore, potential instances of genocidal behavior have been sidestepped or ignored, above all where U.S. culpability might be at issue. In at least three extended *postwar* cases the U.S. has been arguably guilty of genocidal behavior: Korea (1950–53), where the death toll reached up to four million; Indochina (1961–75), where as many as three-and-a-half million people were killed; and Iraq (1991–present), where a combination of two wars, sanctions, bombings, and military occupation has led to perhaps at least two million deaths along with millions of refugees. The massive casualties in each case were overwhelmingly civilian. And the military aggression was entirely planned and deliberate, conducted without provocation—entirely a function of U.S. imperial ambitions. Yet no charges have been filed against any U.S. government or military leader—or any related organizations—since the Genocide Convention was established. Other possible examples of genocide— Israel in Palestine since 1948 and the Indonesian massacres of the 1970s—have likewise never been brought before a tribunal. Only ad hoc prosecutions of genocide (in Rwanda, the Balkans, and Iraq, against *local* defendants) have made any legal headway.

Most careful observers agree that the Genocide Convention had serious flaws from the beginning—enough to undermine its capacity to be used to punish violators of this particular species of war crime. On the one hand, the offense itself was so vaguely defined as to be relevant to a wide variety of atrocities often committed during warfare or civil war—as reflected in the provision stipulating that genocide can extend to the destruction of a group entirely *or in part*, with no strict criterion as to what constitutes "in part." On the other hand, prosecutors had the burden of demonstrating *specific* intent on the part of decision-makers as shown by (usually absent) public statements and documents similar to the official Nazi accounts of the "final solution." Even so, some flagrant historical cases of what might generally be understood as genocide would seem to be morally and legally identifiable: the U.S. extermination of Native Americans; Turkish destruction of Armenians in 1915; the Nazi targeting of Jews and others during World War II; Pol Pot's Cambodian massacres of the 1970s; the Rwandan atrocities of the early 1990s. The postwar instances of possible genocidal criminality mentioned above might be added to this list. Yet rarely have any potential cases of genocide been investigated and prosecuted on a large scale; they have mostly been ignored and gone unpunished. A few Rwandan defendants were convicted of genocide at the International Criminal Tribunal for Rwanda (ICTR) in 1998. Attempts to win similar verdicts against Serbs at The Hague ultimately failed, while in Baghdad Hussein and his co-defendants were convicted (with some put to death) before they could be tried for the more serious crime. (Some Nazi defendants at Nuremberg, as mentioned, were found guilty of "crimes against humanity" rather than genocide.)

Whatever its flaws—and leaving aside the outrageous U.S. "reservations"—the Genocide Convention could have been invoked against American government and military leaders on at least three occasions: Korea, Indochina, and Iraq. Enough details of the massive death and destruction that Washington brought to these regions have been presented in other chapters of this book (much of it available from other sources) to substantiate charges of genocide, even given the requirement of having to prove specific intent. It can be shown that these offenses involved planned military aggression on behalf of specific global objectives, wanton attacks on civilian populations and related targets, and protracted operations across months and years. Whether these crimes qualify as "genocide" or simply "crimes against humanity," they surely merit investigation and prosecution at a level far exceeding charges leveled against Milošević, Hussein, Pol Pot, and others who were actually prosecuted. The fact that U.S. war planners have never been brought to justice has little to do with obvious flaws in the Convention and much more to do with superpower immunity from legal action. Ironically, the U.S. falls back on precisely the same rationalization invoked by the Nazis: national laws and priorities must take precedent over general moral and legal principles (which in fact are more effectively codified today than in the 1940s). Yet the thesis put forth by Jean-Paul Sartre at the Russell Tribunal—where he argues that imperialism logically produces genocidal outcomes—would appear even more compelling in 2009 as the U.S. continues its pursuit of world supremacy.[32]

The case against the U.S. in Iraq would seem to be especially compelling. Since 1991 Washington has started two bloody wars against the country, bombed it many times in between, imposed a harsh economic sanctions program, sponsored covert action, carried out wanton destruction of civilian targets, set up a military occupation regime giving rise to horrendous civil strife, decimated the public infrastructure, and practiced widespread torture at detention centers. As of early 2009, U.S. intervention had accounted for up to two million deaths and an estimated three million refugees—all in the interest of regime-change that, as shown in the historical documents, was carried out to serve American geopolitical interests. Evidence shows that the U.S. had planned these operations years in advance, visible in numerous reports and statements, the likely consequences well known before the first "shock-and-awe" military attacks took place. Iraqis involved in popular resistance to occupation have been demonized in the American media as "terrorists," common criminals, and thugs, just one reflection of imperial arrogance and racism surrounding the operations. Whether this barbarism amounts to genocide or crimes against humanity (along with assorted other war crimes) might be a matter for lawyers to debate, but U.S. culpability for the most horrific criminal behavior is hardly in doubt.

The Genocide Convention could also be applied to the Israeli occupation of Palestine and its brutal consequences for the population across six decades. If this ultimate crime is defined to include "deliberately inflicting on the group conditions of life calculated to bring about its physical [and cultural] destruction in whole or in part," then it would surely extend to Israeli behavior that has been extensively documented.[33] Indeed there is no example in the postwar era of such a protracted material, ideological, and physical assault on a civilian population, interspersed with recurrent military atrocities. Israeli leaders have justified ethnic cleansing on the basis of biblical claims to a "Greater Israel," a crusade permitting land to be stolen by armed aggression—a close parallel to the infamous Discovery Doctrine used by white American settlers to appropriate Indian land. For the Israeli leaders, local Palestinian inhabitants either "never existed" or were undeserving of the land they called home. In 1969 Israeli Prime Minister Golda Meir stated that "there was no such thing as Palestinians ... It was not as though there was a Palestinian people in Palestine considering itself a people and we came and threw them out and took their country away from them. They did not exist."[34] Whatever the case, Israeli claims to Palestine are rooted in Zionism, an essentially fascist ideology that the U.N. General Assembly referred to in 1974 as a virulent form of racism. It follows that in the historical example of Israel setting up a state in Palestine, as with the U.S. occupation of Iraq, the perpetrators have carried out genocidal policies easily traceable to official documents and statements—policies, that is, revealing both the "general" and "specific" intent to carry out genocide as laid out in the Convention.

That neither the U.S. nor Israel has been prosecuted, or even investigated, for genocidal behavior demonstrates the bankruptcy of the Genocide Convention in establishing a framework for the most serious offenders culpable. American and Israeli leaders have been spared indictments while others, the weak and demonized targets of these same leaders (Serbs, Iraqis), have been pursued with a vengeance. As for the U.S., its notorious "reservations" permit it to veto any legal action brought against it at the ICC. In the case of Israel—aside from claims that victims of its actions "never existed"—its own domestic laws state that genocide can only be a "crime against the Jewish people," meaning that Israel must be considered innocent by reason of its own national and racial exceptionalism. For both nations, in other words, "genocide" turns out to be an ideologically laden category, a criminal action for which only designated "others" can be held legally responsible.

IMPERIALISM IN SPACE

Interwoven with the U.S. pursuit of global hegemony is its renovated project of National Missile Defense (NMD), a spin-off of the Star Wars program launched by President Reagan in the early 1980s. Always integral to this ambitious military strategy has been the weaponization of space with its long-term prospect for introducing nuclear reactors and weapons—a scheme designed by the Pentagon to give Washington maximum *earthly* military flexibility and power. The Outer Space Treaty (OST), crafted by the major nuclear powers in 1967, specified that space should be reserved for entirely peaceful uses, the hope being to avoid a space-based arms race that could easily veer out of control. Nuclear armaments in space were completely forbidden to any country. While conventional weapons were not banned as such, the intent and spirit of OST (signed by the U.S.) was to short-circuit any military competition in space. Four decades later, the U.S. alone among nations has moved systematically to weaponize space, employing satellites and related technology for a wide range of military functions: combat, logistics, surveillance, intelligence gathering, and communications. More troubling, the Bush administration expressed its displeasure with even modest OST protocols and signaled its readiness to scrap this seminal treaty, perhaps anxious to reach the next (nuclear) level of space weaponization.

The U.S. colonization of space already goes far beyond "missile defense," a plan usually associated with the old Star Wars project, to embrace a global strategic capacity permitting full coordination of ground, sea, and air operations. In violation of at least the *spirit* of OST, the Bush administration earmarked tens of billions of dollars for NMD and related projects, a cost that could reach more than $25 billion yearly by 2010. As Karl Grossman observes, the U.S. set out to become the sole "master of space,"[35] giving it dramatic military advantages over all possible competitors—one signpost of revived American imperial objectives. Although (as of early 2009) the Pentagon had yet to introduce nukes into space, a future program could involve hundreds of nuclear-armed satellites orbiting the earth in multiple directions. Seeing both geopolitical and economic benefits to this, the Council on Foreign Relations—backed by the Heritage Foundation, the American Enterprise Institute, and several university think-tanks—has strongly pushed for a more expansive view of the space program combined with traditional missile-defense priorities. Corporations like General Electric, TRW, Lockheed-Martin, and Raytheon have developed vested interests in these projects, as have assorted university research and development programs.[36]

Weapons the Pentagon expects to be integral to the U.S. Space Command's "Vision for 2020" include laser-beam devices, particle-beam instruments, and other systems tied to orbiting nuclear reactors used for sources of power. This could signify not only weapons in space but nuclear devices deployed side-by-side with them. In its Project Prometheus the National Aeronautical and Space Administration (NASA) has laid out plans for nuclear-powered rockets. Already by 1999 these schemes had so alarmed government leaders, military officials, and scientists around the world that a U.N. General Assembly resolution aimed at short-circuiting an arms race in outer space was signed by 138 nations, with the idea of preserving space for strictly peaceful uses—just as the original OST intended. Ominously, both the U.S. and Israel (alone) refused to sign the declaration. Since then the Bush admin-istration has done everything in its power to subvert an arms race, but with different priorities in mind—by moving to solidify its own (unilateral, monopolistic) control of outer space. This stratagem, however, could well be frustrated as the Russians, Chinese, and others seek to counter American maneuvers, further compromising the intent of OST.

The threat of nuclear proliferation is likely to worsen, sooner or later, as U.S. space militarization intensifies, setting off global fears and responses. One problem is the atomic component of the space program itself: with reactors in place, how long will it take the Pentagon to nuclearize its military strategy? Another problem is the expansion of ground-based missile-defense systems that, as we have seen, bolsters U.S. *offensive* as well as defensive capabilities. The idea of a vast network of interceptor missiles designed to block incoming warheads might be a pipe dream in terms of effective armed national defense, but it has been taken seriously by other nations (notably Russia and China) as a move by Washington to enhance its first-strike capacity. As of 2009 few such missiles had been produced and tested, even fewer deployed. In fact by 2007 only ten or so missiles were fully operational, deployed within a new system called the Ground-Based Midcourse Defense (GMD), first established in July 2004 at Fort Greeley, Colorado. Despite repeated failure of intercept-missile testing, the Bush administration looked to deploy new ballistic devices while also moving, in the face of some external opposition, to set up new GMD sites in Europe and elsewhere. In this context Washington began to search for ways to supersede OST, increasingly viewed as a fetter on the Pentagon's outer-space ambitions.

After 2004 the Bush administration pursued a more aggressive space policy, accelerating weapons programs, expanding satellite-based surveillance and communications systems, and moving generally to integrate outer-space operations into U.S. global military strategy. In its quest for space hegemony Washington steadfastly refused any treaty banning weapons in space—against the grain of international consensus.[37] Its goal remains *military* domination of space, which entails blocking access, where possible, to other nations—a clear violation of OST intent. The U.S. appears to consider its monopolistic claims to space an inherent "right," similar to its earthly imperia entitlements. Toward this end the U.S. sought, between 2004 and 2008, to either scrap or "renegotiate" the OST, hoping to strip away limits to space-based military operations. (As of early 2009 the U.S. owned the vast majority of more than 1000 satellites in orbit.) In January 2007 Robert G. Joseph, Under-Secretary for Arms Control and International Security, outlined a national space policy affirming "free and total" American exploration and use of space, necessary to protect and advance "vital national interests." For the U.S., according to Joseph, development of its "space assets" was expected to proceed unilaterally, regardless of OST protocols, on the assumption that other nations might harbor duplicitous intentions.[38] (The incoming Obama administration, as of spring 2009, had yet to articulate new departures for the U.S. space program.)

The result has been an unfortunate gutting of OST agreements, meaning that opportunities for a global, cooperative, peaceful space regimen are rapidly vanishing. OST prohibits the full-scale militarization of space, its original intent being to negate an arms race possibly leading to nukes in space—but the U.S., as usual, stands virtually alone in its rejectionism. Efforts to preserve space for peaceful ends (scientific and commercial) depend on a comprehensive multilateral ban on testing and deployment of anti-satellite (ASAT) weapons, a system central to the Pentagon's NMD strategy.[39] Lacking such an agreement, the path toward accelerated space competition seems paved, accompanied by a potential arms race and new threats of a nuclearized outer space. In the absence of a strengthened OST, moreover, U.S. global *earthly* military supremacy will be easier to consolidate. Grossman already foresaw this dangerous trend several years ago in his seminal *Weapons in Space*, where he argued that the U.S. space agenda was destined to bring the world closer to expanded military conflict and, ultimately, nuclear catastrophe. He wrote then: "The military use of space being planned by the U.S. is in total contradiction to the principles of peaceful international cooperation that the U.S. likes to espouse. The aim is to develop a world in which it would literally be USA *uber alles* ... It pushes us—all of us—toward war in the heavens."[40]

GLOBAL WARMING: THE TRIUMPH OF CORPORATE PROFITS

As surely the greatest threat to planetary sustainability, the global ecological crisis presents a challenge more daunting even than the prospects of nuclear catastrophe. The crisis takes many forms, the most fearsome no doubt being severe climate change which, according to worldwide scientific consensus, would tip the world into environmental chaos, economic breakdown, and related social and political disasters. The consensus, moreover, stresses that global warming is a direct result of human economic activity: reliance on fossil fuels, deforestation, meat-based agriculture, over-use of chemicals, massive air, water, and soil pollution. Population growth, with its accelerating pressures on social infrastructures and fragile ecosystems, only compounds these trends. We are faced with severe impending changes in weather patterns, cycles of droughts and floods, melting ice caps, a dramatic rise of sea levels that could engulf the world's coastal areas, increased species extinction, and drastic shortages, of food, water, and other vital resources. If left unchecked (or countered with only modest reforms) global temperatures could rise by as much as 10 degrees Fahrenheit by 2100, a catastrophic possibility. The situation is so grave that, even with quick and extensive measures, the crisis could dramatically intensify within the next few decades—the expectation not of radical fear-mongers but of mainstream scientists, environmentalists, and government officials across the globe. Extreme warnings were issued by the U.N. Intergovernmental Panel on Climate Change, which in mid 2007 had released two of four reports based on the work of 2500 scientists from around the world.[41]

The U.N. panel urged immediate and far-reaching action that was supported by more than 100 nations, but, alas, the U.S. was not one of those nations. Proposals included charging polluters up to $100 for each ton generated, along with taxation policies and investment in alternative technologies. Without such counter-measures, the crisis would move along like a "runaway train." The reports concluded that agriculture could be decimated across large regions, leading to drastic food shortages while plunging the world into deep economic depression. Many scientists contributing to the research mentioned that, hard-hitting as it was, some of its conclusions and recommendations were watered down by a few governments anxious to forestall immediate action. Thus John Walsh, a University of Alaska scientist, commented that "the science got hijacked by the political bureaucrats at the last minute."[42] Predictably, it was American delegates who worked most diligently to soften the reports, President Bush stating that the U.S. "will not be stampeded into action" by warnings of doom. This was just one moment of obstructionism coming from the world's largest contributor to greenhouse gases.

Outside corporate boardrooms and right-wing think-tanks the idea that global warming needs to be fought with immediate, radical, and worldwide responses has become nearly universal. The broad picture is no longer a matter of debate. International efforts have mounted over the past two decades, beginning with furtive attempts at reforms during the 1992 Earth Summit in Rio de Janeiro and evolving further with the 1997 Kyoto Protocol—the first treaty based on binding limits to industrial pollutants. Regarded as a breakthrough of sorts, Kyoto demanded only the most limited reforms: after three years of negotiations, the agreement called on leading economic powers (responsible for about 85 percent of greenhouse gases at the time) to reduce fossil-fuel use by 2012 to 1990 levels, a target many thought realizable by means of technological innovation alone (thus requiring no decline in growth). Kyoto did point toward the long-term need for a fundamental shift in modes of production and consumption, especially for the most affluent nations, but this remained (then and now) a non-binding prescription. Later efforts to revisit the Kyoto Protocol have not produced significant forward steps even as scientific warnings grow louder each year. The struggles of many political leaders, NGOs, lobbies, and grassroots movements, along with the U.N., to forge new international *action* priorities have met with obstructionism, much of it emanating from Washington as well as other major contributors to the crisis, including Russia, India, and China.

The U.S. was obstinate on the issue of global warming from the start, and today remains the biggest obstacle to establishing a viable action regimen, on two levels—denial of the problem itself, and resistance to binding measures for capping emissions. (As of 2009 the U.S., with 4 percent of the world's population, accounted for nearly one-fourth of greenhouse gases.) With Presidents Clinton and Bush the stance was roughly the same: any forced reduction of fossil-fuel use would severely damage the American economy, retard growth, and generate tremendous job loss. U.S. politicians were fearful of altering a system of production and consumption that sustained lifestyles highly addicted to suburbia, cars, and mall culture. Under Kyoto, it was widely thought, the national economy would ultimately be forced to meet overall higher emissions standards, adopt new "green" technologies, make vast investments in research and development, shift toward sustainable agriculture, end fossil-fuel subsidies, and create more efficient waste-management systems—all indeed quite possible for the wealthiest nation on the planet, but obviously far beyond what U.S. government and corporate elites were for the most part willing to consider. Predictions of imminent global disaster made scarcely a dent in this fanatically capitalist worldview. The Bush administration rejected not only Kyoto but the idea of mandatory regulations, dismissing the science as bogus and turning its back on years of international negotiations to forge a global-warming treaty (although its views on the science softened by 2007). In this case, however, U.S. exceptionalism has been driven less by military than by corporate interests dedicated to growth and profits. As Sands writes in *Lawless World*: "The decision [to reject Kyoto] was seen as an arrogant step aimed at refashioning the global order, putting American lifestyles above foreign lives, American economic well-being above all other interests, and manifesting a refusal to be constrained by new international rules."[43]

Even before the unsettling U.N. reports surfaced, and with Kyoto basically languishing because of weak, uneven participation, delegates gathered in December 2005 for a Climate Change Conference in Montreal, hoping for a strengthened treaty. With new predictions of ecological disaster, the mood was set for agreement on binding emission caps and stiffer levies on industrial pollution exceeding those caps. More than 150 nations were ready to subscribe to these broad guidelines with even previously reluctant China and India willing to compromise for a U.N. treaty possibly more far-reaching than Kyoto. But the U.S. again held out, standing virtually alone in opposition to the international consensus, rejecting mandatory controls it claimed would harm the American economy and possibly send the global system into a downward spiral. (The downward spiral did in fact soon become reality, but not owing to implementation of strict emissions limits.) Denying both the science and politics underpinning the struggle against global warming, the White House refused calls for urgent action as the U.S. negotiator, Harlan Watson, walked out of the proceedings, creating an angry backlash. At that point the Bush administration still held to its view of global warming—indeed *any* environmental problem—as essentially a false alarm.[44]

The Bush approach to ecological crisis transcended mere denial: for years the White House did everything in its power to suppress information, discredit reports, and otherwise alter or manipulate facts it viewed as disconcerting—the very same *modus operandi* it used during the build-up toward the Iraq war. Scientific findings about the human contribution to climate change were dismissed as politically motivated, even when emanating from the U.N. Warnings about the need for drastic action were stonewalled. There were instances of studies conducted by the Environmental Protection Agency (EPA) and the National Research Council (NRC), among others, highly critical of the utility, coal, and oil industries, that were held back for many months and, when released, were often doctored to conform to Bush prejudices. The administration permitted corporate interests to get involved in research projects on the environment, including at the EPA where many Bush appointees were from fossil-fuel backgrounds. Scientists and officials within the administration going along with the international consensus on global warming might have found themselves out of a job. As Robert Kennedy, Jr. wrote: "Over the past two decades industry and conservative think-tanks have invested millions of dollars to corrupt science. They distort the truth about tobacco, pesticides, ozone depletion, dioxin, acid rain, and global warming." He added: "The Bush administration has so violated and corrupted the institutional culture of government agencies charged with scientific research that it could take a generation for them to recover their integrity."[45]

This problem, and with it U.S. refusal to join the fight against global warming, surely went much deeper than a small circle of obstructionist Bush Republicans. Some large corporations, along with their lobbies, think-tanks, media outlets, and sympathetic university research teams (often business funded) have also done a remarkable job trying to discredit work linked to climate change. Their main focus was to provide "scientific findings" showing that the overheating of the earth is a function of a long natural ecological cycle detached from human economic activity. For them, the international consensus revolves around fear-mongering that, if followed, would destroy the foundations of American efficiency and growth, the idea being that huge energy corporations—many of them lavish contributors to the 2000 and 2004 Bush campaigns—ought to be left alone, unregulated, free to conduct business-as-usual. Right-wing think-tanks like the American Enterprise Institute have advanced this ideological obfuscation, while lobbies of dozens of corporations have fought strenuously for their anti-regulatory agenda. Much lobby and think-tank activity has been funded by ExxonMobil, the world's largest oil company and the most aggressive force behind global-warming denial.[46]

The ExxonMobil-supported groups, recipients of tens of millions of dollars since 2000 alone, have relentlessly attacked global-warming research as "politicized science," often comparing it to what the Nazis and Soviets did with science in the 1930s and 1940s. They have framed regulatory efforts as a new threat to freedom and democracy and a violation of free-market principles. ExxonMobil has contributed not only to think-tanks like AEI but to such university research programs as Stanford's Global Climate and Energy Project (beneficiary of $100 million). An army of lobbyists has received $55 million from the oil giant since 2000. The larger picture is equally grim: Washington lobbying efforts between 2001 and 2005 received roughly $460 million from utilities, $283 million from oil and gas companies, $177 million from auto manufacturers, $56 million from mining firms, and $448 million from agribusiness.[47] Such vast mobilization of corporate resources demonstrates that U.S. business elites are not ready to sacrifice short-term profits even in the face of imminent ecological crisis.

The overriding thrust of such lobbying efforts, whether on melting polar ice-caps, deforestation, pollution, or species extinction, is that observable ecological changes have little or nothing to do with corporate behavior but instead are a function of "natural" causes. These bogus arguments are picked up and spread across vast networks of lobbyists, media outlets, local organizations, and academic researchers, giving rise to an atmosphere of uncertainty and confusion while sowing doubt in the minds of politicians. The main goal behind the investment of all this fossil-fuel largesse has been to undercut calls for action from the scientific community—and it has mostly worked at a time of growing corporate colonization of the American public sphere.[48]

Problems with the Kyoto Protocol, to be sure, remain significant, even leaving aside U.S. obstructionism. By mid 2007 only 40 nations had signed the treaty and the question of what to do about non-subscribers was yet to be resolved. Lesser-developed states remained outside the pact, but these included China and India, two large, rapidly growing economies that were already contributing substantially to global warming. (Within two decades China is expected to pass the U.S. as the leading producer of greenhouse gases.) No global body has been established to *monitor* and report on emissions, so that even signatories to Kyoto are essentially on the honor system. Equally problematic, Kyoto has given rise to a carbon-trading market whereby enterprises under the limit can distribute "credits" to the worst polluters. Thus, even should the U.S. enter into a renovated global-warming agreement, it can pay billions to purchase carbon credits from other countries while its corporate system moves blithely along the same trajectory.

At the June 2007 G-8 Summit in Germany, Washington made a few concessions to European demands for urgent measures and indicated the U.S. would "seriously consider" reducing emissions by half before 2050 within a new set of accords intended to include China and India. Still refusing mandatory emissions caps, Bush argued for a voluntary, free-market approach presumably compatible with the American growth-oriented neoliberal model. This attempt to have the best of both worlds—while relegating pollution-reduction goals to the distant future—was widely dismissed outside the U.S. as another corporate-driven illusion. The U.S. did finally grudgingly recognize global warming as a real challenge, but slighted that challenge by turning its back on any binding measures. In August 2007 Bush arranged for a summit to further address issues related to climate change, with emphasis on the development of clean technologies and energy conservation. It was clear, however, that U.S. opposition to mandatory curbs on greenhouse gases would be firmly upheld. Meanwhile, the

U.S. remained the only G-8 nation to refuse the Kyoto Protocol. Whether President Obama, far more committed than Bush to "green" development as a means of curtailing global warming, can break with the neoliberal model and corporate priorities to effectively face the new challenge—and join the global consensus—remains to be seen.

6
War-Crimes Tribunals: Imperial Justice

By the 1990s, after a full century of treaties, conventions, and tribunals designed to establish legal criteria for governing (and adjudicating) the military behavior of nations, no truly universal structure for this purpose has yet been created. Principles embodied in the various Hague and Geneva Protocols, along with the Nuremberg and Tokyo courts set up after World War II—many of which found their way into the United Nations Charter of 1948—have never become internationally binding, legally or politically. The great promise of Nuremberg to hold government and military leaders responsible for war crimes and crimes against humanity did not come to fruition. Finally, in 1998, the majority of nations (139 in all) met in Rome to ratify a treaty giving birth to an International Criminal Court (ICC) that would allow for effective global jurisprudence. The court would be a professional, independent body charged with bringing leaders and others to justice for assorted war crimes, genocide, and crimes against humanity. In July 2002 the ICC became a reality, confirming long-held hopes of human rights partisans around the world. Unfortunately, however, the U.S. took a fiercely hostile stance toward the court from the outset, first refusing to sign the treaty and then trying to sabotage the body's operations. The U.S. government, first under Clinton and then under Bush, insisted on guarantees that no American officials or military personnel could be brought before the tribunal. Emboldened by an inflated body of academic theoretical justifications, the nation with the only truly global military presence—and the one most inclined toward armed intervention—wanted total immunity.

THE NUREMBERG PRECEDENT—AND BEYOND

While efforts to codify and institutionalize global legal norms have been most visible in the last century or so, attempts to theorize the basis of international justice—notably with respect to the conduct of war—go back many centuries. The ideal of a community of interests based in common legal and moral sentiments that could regulate warfare was entertained by the Greeks, some Christian writers, Grotius, and Kant, among others searching for a world in which the power strivings of individuals, groups, and nations might be held in check. The establishment of a system of laws, principles, and procedures was embraced from time to time though never given concrete realization. The most coherent vision of a legal world order was formulated by the Dutch theorist Hugo Grotius in the wake of the Thirty Years War, but not until the 1890s at The Hague were the first steps toward such a vision put in place. Grotius envisioned something of a coherent, ordered world that would supersede perpetual chaos, anarchy, and bloodshed of the sort emphasized by Thomas Hobbes in his famous account of the state of nature. The problems then as today revolved around the possibility of great states and their leaders subordinating their own hegemonic or imperial aspirations to a Grotian (legal, moral) consensus of interests. Surely such international organizations as the League of Nations and the United Nations were thought to embody, in some form, ideals of global justice that would also entail rules of military conduct. Within this broad schema it was generally assumed that a system of international legality, to be fair and effective, would have to embody strong elements of universality.

The U.N., of course, was largely a product of World War II and its aftermath, which included the Nuremberg and Tokyo tribunals set up by the victorious Allies to prosecute and punish war crimes committed by the Germans and Japanese. (The idea of pursing crimes committed by *other* nations was never considered.) The legacy of Nuremberg has been invoked to legitimate and sustain the idea of a modern tribunal established for the purpose of trying criminals; it was to be the model for subsequent efforts toward binding principles of global jurisprudence. In reality the International Criminal Tribunal of Nuremberg was established by the U.S., Britain, France, and the Soviet Union and it was these countries that provided the prosecution and judges for bringing many leading Nazis to justice. There was at the time broad consensus for trying and punishing those (especially in Berlin and Tokyo) presumed guilty of the most heinous war crimes and crimes against humanity. This was accompanied by the dream of a world legal order making it unlikely such crimes would ever again be committed—that is, making barbarism a thing of the past. Yet by the idealistic standards of global justice embraced by earlier theorists both Nuremberg and Tokyo could hardly be judged as successful in laying the foundations of a truly *universal* system.

These tribunals were partial and biased—ad hoc mechanisms for victors to judge losers, according to a set of ex post facto criteria where most crimes were defined after the fact and, moreover, were prosecuted against just one side in a protracted warfare involving horrendous war crimes on *all* sides. As prime examples of victor's justice, Nuremberg and Tokyo might be regarded as poor beginnings of a viable international legal framework.

While the Nuremberg tribunal did manage to prosecute and sentence 21 leading Nazis for monstrous crimes, questions remained as to the fairness of the proceedings and, more significantly, as to the legacy that Nuremberg ultimately bequeathed. Several defendants were given the death penalty. The Nazi leadership, defined by the court as a "vast and malignant enterprise," was largely discredited and dismantled, in great measure because of proceedings that claimed to embrace a march toward global justice. Yet answers to the above questions, as historian Joseph Persico suggests, do not inspire optimism.[1] Persico argues that the entire IMT apparatus, despite its benign motivations, lacked legitimacy from the outset given its ad hoc, partial character. No trials at Nuremberg could be fair or independent, by definition. Both German and Japanese leaders were tried and convicted for committing crimes against peace—that is, waging military aggression against nations that had done nothing to provoke warfare. This was considered the "supreme crime" that led to and framed all the others. Here the Allied powers were clearly innocent of any wrongdoing. In most other areas of military behavior spanning several years, however, differences between the Allied and Axis nations were not such as to justify ad hoc jurisprudence; massive violations were attributable to all parties involved. Any legitimate tribunal would have put defendants on trial from *all* sides of the conflict. It could be argued that, for example, wanton attacks on civilian populations (already prohibited at The Hague Conventions) were far more widespread on the Allied (U.S., Britain, Soviet) than on the German or Japanese side. (Italians were not brought before either tribunal.) Surely the saturation bombing of major urban centers (Hamburg, Dresden, Berlin, Tokyo, and dozens of other Japanese cities), not to mention the atomic devastation of Hiroshima and Nagasaki, rank among the most egregious war crimes in history. Yet such crimes, as well as extensive abuse and killing of prisoners of war, were made totally off-limits by Allied prosecutors, so that the U.S., Britain, and the USSR could wind up fully immune to these and other possible charges. As such it is hardly surprising that Nuremberg has never led to any permanent, independent tribunal where war crimes and crimes against humanity might be tried and punished.

If the Nuremberg tribunal lacked legitimacy in this sense, it nonetheless established certain legal principles that might be viewed as compelling precedents for judging and punishing war crimes. The first, as mentioned, was the idea that crimes against peace—already codified in the 1928 Kellogg-Briand Pact—should be prosecuted as the "supreme crime," with violators responsible for all the mayhem and violence that follows. The second was the precept, still generally regarded as valid, that all individuals, whatever their status or degree of power, must be held legally and morally accountable for their actions, that illegal deeds cannot be justified on grounds of bureaucratic command or following military orders. Such principles were indeed enforced at the time of Nuremberg and have since generally been understood as integral to moral codes of individual behavior within or outside the context of warfare. Whether those principles have had any lasting global impact, however, is yet another story. Sadly, we encounter few postwar instances where the Nuremberg legacy has been applied in legal practice, despite its affirmation in the U.N. Charter. The historical record since 1945 has been one of repeated and flagrant horrors—wars, civil strife, insurrections, terrorism, etc.—marked by few prosecutions for war crimes committed by government and military leaders.

The Nuremberg precedent has done nothing to curtail, much less punish, those responsible for escalating levels of global violence. Tens of millions of lives have been lost to warfare and crimes against humanity, yet only rarely have the perpetrators been brought to justice in a court based on universal legal principles. The only judicial proceedings have involved local, ad hoc structures where, once again, victors (great powers) stood in judgment over the vanquished weaker parties, as in the cases of Yugoslavia and Iraq. In this context those most culpable of crimes against peace and war crimes—above all, the U.S. and its junior partners—have emerged scot-free, able to repeatedly carry out their criminal policies with impunity, subject neither to international law nor to the workings of any ad hoc tribunal. Persico writes: "As for crimes against peace, the likelihood of anyone being prosecuted for committing aggression has been even more remote than for committing atrocities. Aggression appears to be in the eye of the beholder."[2] As of the early twenty-first century, there were no laws or precedents that carry enough weight to supersede the interests and priorities of the world's lone superpower.

The issue of war-crimes tribunals and related bodies is today more crucial than ever as global violence intensifies and, moreover, the instruments of modern warfare grow ever more barbaric. The need for truly international procedures to try to punish crimes in accordance with the norms of international law cannot be ignored—first as a matter of official truth-seeking and, second, as a means of holding violators accountable for their behavior. Whether this process moves through global or local tribunals, special courts, or truth commissions—or some combination of these—its legitimacy (and therefore efficacy) will depend on norms of *universality* where legal procedures are no longer the sole province of dominant nations out to pursue nothing but their geopolitical agendas. A growing international consensus that human rights abuses and military atrocities ought to be legally, politically, and morally addressed has yet to be translated into institutional reality. The ICC represents a major step toward such an eventuality, as it embodies the spirit and content of the U.N. Charter. At this juncture, unfortunately, the U.S. and a few other nations stand resolutely opposed to such a tribunal, guided as always (in the case of Washington) by a fervent sense of exceptionalism. Since 1974 we have seen the appearance of some 30 truth commissions, instituted in such countries as Argentina, South Africa, Bolivia, and Panama, with the intent of revisiting the past and seeking full knowledge of past atrocities. A central theme here is that guilty parties will be forced to confront their criminal actions and, hopefully, offer apologies and reparations, a process that has taken place in South Africa and elsewhere but (except for recognition of World War II Japanese-American internment camps) never in the U.S. In the end, however, truth commissions have no power to convict or jail offenders. In any event, the future of global jurisprudence will depend on the capacity of nations to achieve universality, which means the current proliferation of ad hoc tribunals (usually set up and controlled by the leading powers) stands more as an *impediment* than an enabler of such prospects.

NATO'S HAGUE TRAVESTY

Even as the U.S. government refuses the jurisdiction of international law for itself, its leaders remain ever vigilant in seeking to bring *others* to justice—notably those (like Serbs and Iraqis) with the audacity to stand in the way of American geopolitical interests. The International Criminal Tribunal for the former Yugoslavia (ICTY), set up by the NATO powers in May 1993, was convened at The Hague explicitly to try Slobodan Milošević and other Serb leaders for crimes allegedly carried out during the decade of bloody civil wars in the Balkans. Milošević was formally indicted in May 1999, not coincidentally at the height of NATO military bombardments of Yugoslavia, on 61 counts including genocide, crimes against humanity, and war crimes associated with Serb policies of "ethnic cleansing" mainly in Kosovo but also in Bosnia and Croatia. Milošević was arrested in March 2001 and delivered to The Hague Tribunal in June 2001, after the U.S. first threatened the new Serb government and then bribed it with millions in cash. The Western powers, the U.S. in the lead, portrayed Milošević and the Serbs as modern-day Nazis intent on ruthless expansion and responsible for an unspeakable holocaust including acts of mass murder, mass rape, torture, and ethnic cleansing that left much of the region devastated. These atrocities were so broad in scope and so horrific as to demand urgent "humanitarian" intervention by NATO military forces. Once the 1999 bombings were finished, the NATO-financed Hague Tribunal would finally bring Serb leaders and their accomplices to trial.

In the U.S., the media and politicians eagerly championed the new war-crimes trials, celebrating the ICTY as an inspiring "triumph of the civilized world."[3] By holding Serb leaders accountable for their crimes the tribunal was said to open up a new era in the development of international law. Former Secretary of State Madeleine Albright referred to The Hague as the "mother of all tribunals," a site where it would now be possible to try, in the tradition of Nuremberg, some of the greatest monsters in European history.[4] Caricatured as a Hitler-like dictatorial figure obsessed with building an ethnically pure Greater Serbia, Milošević was deemed the kind of war criminal the world desperately needed to bring to justice in order to avoid "international anarchy." Serbs were routinely demonized in the media, referred to by columnist Anthony Lewis and others as "beasts" and "genocidal maniacs" for whom ethnic cleansing was a natural impulse. The mainstream text *Indictment at The Hague* (2002) is subtitled *The Milošević Regime and Crimes of the Balkans Wars*. In it, authors Norman Cigar and Paul Williams set out to present a case for war crimes against the Serbs, replete with arguments from The Hague Tribunal prosecutors and the U.S. State Department. There is no mention of any other party to the Balkans civil wars, nor of the role of NATO and the U.S. in their aerial terrorism directed against a sovereign nation. "No matter how he personally meets his end," wrote the authors, "Milošević shall remain one of the most villainous figures in the history of the South Slavs." They add: "The atrocities committed by Serbian forces were part of a planned, systematic, and organized campaign to secure territory for an ethnically 'pure' Serb state by clearing it of all non-Serb populations." The tribunal represents a historical breakthrough, they remind us, since by "attacking liability for war crimes [it] will serve as a reminder to other prospective war criminals that their actions will not be granted *de facto* immunity by the world community."[5]

Milošević was originally charged with "planning, ordering, or carrying out deportations and murders during the Serb forces' campaign to drive Kosovar Albanians from their homes, which killed thousands along the way." Other indictments linked to the conflict in Bosnia and Croatia were added later. By the time Milošević was brought to The Hague he faced charges of mass killings, rapes, expulsions, detentions, forced labor, torture, and looting of property among other violations. Other Serb political and military figures (along with a few Croatians and Kosovars) were brought up on similar counts.

Despite such grave indictments and all the overblown rhetoric denouncing genocidal Nazi Serbs on the march, it takes little effort to reveal the ICTY as an outrageous fraud from beginning to end. From the outset this tribunal was totally biased and one-sided, hardly the product of universal jurisprudence—an inevitable reality given that the tribunal was set up and financed by the NATO powers (above all the U.S.) and received the bulk of its investigative and informational resources from these same powers, the very powers that had carried out sustained military aggression against the Serbs. The fraudulence is quickly shown by the flagrant one-sidedness of the indictments: after so many years of civic strife involving not only Serbs but Croatians, Bosnian Muslims, Kosovar Albanians, and myriad paramilitary groups of varying ideological and ethnic make-up, not to mention the ongoing covert and armed interventions by NATO powers, we are told to believe that the Serbs alone were those overwhelmingly guilty of atrocities, that all others were simply innocent victims of a singular evil force, that others were victims *only* while Serbs themselves were *never* victimized. This scenario, constructed mainly by Western public-relations firms and mass media, defies all logic not to mention the historical evidence. Indeed, the Serbs could be said to have suffered *most* throughout the 1990s, especially when the U.S./NATO bombings are taken into account. Without doubt the Serbs were responsible for atrocities, but evidence from the field, unfiltered by propaganda, shows convincingly that atrocities were committed on all sides, and that Serbs were just as often on the receiving end of war crimes as they were culpable of them.

The Hague Tribunal completely ignored this complex history, dismissing instances where Serbs experienced the violence of civil war—for example, the several thousand killed and at least 200,000 displaced in Croatia alone and yet another 300,000 displaced in Kosovo in the wake of U.S.-backed KLA terrorism and NATO aerial bombardments. In August 1995, the U.S. and Germany assisted a bloody Croatian military offensive in the Krajina region of Croatia that produced some of the worst casualties in the Yugoslav civil wars.[6] Yet when looking at such atrocities, the great moral outrage over ethnic cleansing that consumed NATO elites and the Western media suddenly vanishes; the pursuit of justice turned out to be selective in the extreme. The failure of the ICTY to address this ridiculous anomaly, to investigate and prosecute war crimes across the board, to look impartially at *all* combatants involved in the protracted conflict, demonstrates ipso facto its moral and political bankruptcy not to mention its legal absurdity.

The ICTY proceedings grew out of a unilateral (U.S./NATO) claim to "humanitarian intervention" lacking any basis in the U.N. Charter or international law. The 1999 "war" was not only illegal—based on the fraudulent "precedent" of suspending the principle of national sovereignty (which none of the aggressors would be willing to waive for themselves)—but quickly turned into a humanitarian disaster of its own, producing new levels of military violence, civilian destruction, and social disruption. No evidence of "Serb genocide" or "ethnic cleansing" was ever uncovered, but even if it had been no justification for the U.S./NATO aerial campaign would have been established in the absence of U.N. backing. Such backing, in this case, was never even sought by U.S. and European leaders anxious to pursue military options. The Security Council did in fact approve humanitarian intervention four times during the 1990s (in Somalia, Haiti, Rwanda, and Bosnia) as a form of *collective action* under U.N. auspices, but the Kosovo intervention stemmed from a fictitious, entirely imperialistic notion that certain nations (the most powerful) have a rightful claim to act on their own authority, thus reversing decades of progress toward stigmatizing and outlawing crimes against peace. In this way the most powerful nations simply substituted their interests for those of the purported "international community" they claimed to represent.[7] Horrified by this precedent, which laid the basis of the U.S. invasion of Iraq, leaders of 133 nations condemned the move at the April 2000 South Summit, stating: "We reject the so-called 'right' of humanitarian intervention, which has no legal basis in the United Nations Charter or in the general principles of international law."[8] In the end, the ICTY was nothing more than a manifestation of this illegitimate scheme. As Mandel correctly notes, "the role that the ICTY was born to play came in the Kosovo war. This had nothing to do with trying and punishing criminals and everything to do with lending credibility to NATO's cause."[9]

As quintessential ad hoc victor's justice, the ICTY fit perfectly the ethos of U.S. exceptionalism: it would embody the rule of the most civilized and enlightened of states dedicated to bringing peace and order to an anarchic world infested with tyrants, rogues, and terrorists. While The Hague Tribunal was supposedly erected to purge evil monsters like Milošević from the world scene, in actuality it was the U.S./NATO elites, their military option grounded in familiar claims of moral supremacy, that ultimately most resembled the Nazis, mimicking Hitler's resort to higher values when he justified his invasions of Czechoslovakia, Poland, the Soviet Union, and other countries. The Kosovo war could indeed be viewed as fascist in substance, a view echoed by Nuremberg judge Walter Rockler, who referred to the U.S./NATO actions as "flagrant military aggression" comparable to what the Germans were prosecuted for and convicted.[10] Interestingly, the U.S. moved aggressively to ensure that statutes prohibiting crimes against peace would be excluded from the ICTY agenda.

The political effect of The Hague proceedings effectively concealed the long sordid involvement of the U.S. and its NATO allies in the Balkans, which became more evident nearly a decade after the saga was brought to a close as the U.S./NATO domination of the region was finally solidified. By 2007 the familiar self-righteous ruminations heard in Washington and other Western capitals concerning Serb ethnic cleansing and genocide started to ring hollow as the geopolitical agenda came more clearly into focus. The propaganda was stripped of its ideological power. Nowhere has it been shown that Milošević's supposed drive toward a Greater Serbia was motivated by goals of ethnic purity—or in fact was driven by anything beyond understandable efforts to preserve Yugoslav nationhood against external subversion and intervention. Was ethnicity more a factor for Serbs than for Croatians, Bosnian Muslims, or Kosovar Albanians? Belgrade itself was and remains today an extremely diverse, cosmopolitan city with Muslims, Albanians, and others by the hundreds of thousands living peacefully in close proximity. If the Serbs were such irredeemable ethnic cleansers, why was such a policy never undertaken in Belgrade? In no military operation of the civil wars was anything resembling a genocidal program ever actually designed or carried out by Milošević and the Serbs—and indeed even the ICTY, after years of "investigation," was never able to validate such charges. In fact no evidence was forthcoming from any source.

The non-stop Western propaganda crusade dwelling solely on Serb atrocities was in fact not too far removed from the narrative contained in Barry Levinson's film *Wag the Dog*, in which a U.S. President embattled by a sex scandal uses media experts to manipulate an international "crisis" in Albania. A one-sided, ahistorical moralism totally ignored the decisive role of Western powers in the post-Cold War disintegration of Yugoslavia, the U.S. role in supporting the fascist Tudjman regime in Croatia, horrors perpetrated by right-wing Islamic fundamentalist groups in Bosnia, and the rampant terrorism of the KLA and kindred secessionist forces that were organized and supported by Washington. Also conveniently ignored was the increased NATO *military* presence in the region after 1995, not to mention longstanding, and rather obvious, U.S. geopolitical interests in the Balkans.[11] To believe that only Serbs—or any other single party to the conflict—could have committed war crimes within such a labyrinthine historical matrix is so preposterous on its face that, for this reason alone, the credibility of the ICTY must be seriously questioned.

In fact the most egregious crimes in the Balkans—including above all the "supreme" crime against peace—can be laid at the doorstep of U.S./NATO military forces, guilty of carrying out 79 days of high-tech aerial terrorism in violation of the U.N. Charter and the Nuremberg precedent. The bombings brought extensive damage to civilian targets, including large sectors of the Serb public infrastructure. Belgrade alone suffered upwards of 10,000 casualties, with thousands more scattered across the country. The campaign was effective, destroying power plants, factories, apartment complexes, bridges, water facilities, roads, hospitals, schools, and communications networks. NATO targets in Yugoslavia were reportedly 60 percent civilian, including 33 hospitals, 344 schools, and 144 industrial plants.

This was of course no war but rather an aerial massacre of defenseless human beings, mostly civilians. Not only did the assault violate the U.N. Charter prohibiting military aggression against a sovereign nation, it willfully abrogated the tradition of The Hague and Geneva Protocols declaring illegal the wanton destruction of civilian objects—the very criminality that General Clark, unwittingly, was prepared to celebrate. Whatever the crimes of Milošević, they would pale in comparison with the U.S./NATO record of military atrocities not only during the aerial campaign but throughout the previous decade of proxy warfare. As mentioned earlier, NATO leaders were actually charged with an extensive list of war crimes in 1999, in a suit naming President Clinton, Defense Secretary William Cohen, Secretary of State Albright, and General Clark along with British leader Tony Blair as defendants. With massive evidence at their disposal, including stated intent to attack civilian targets, the plaintiffs took their case to The Hague Tribunal, hoping for a sympathetic audience before Chief Prosecutor Carla del Ponte—but the case was summarily thrown out after U.S. leaders protested vehemently, arguing for the mystical (but iron) principle of American immunity. As for Milošević, The Hague prosecutors were already conceding in September 2002 that the case against him—once affirmed with arrogant confidence—was more flawed than earlier believed, owing to difficulty in proving the Serb leader's actual connection to the atrocities in question. This was just a prelude to the further unraveling of the Milošević case.

As proceedings at The Hague Tribunal continued through 2003 and beyond, the political bias of the setup became increasingly transparent: U.S. and NATO interests were to be preserved at all costs. The mostly Serb defendants' right to an open, public, impartial trial, for example, was consistently violated by prosecutors and judges, especially when it came to Milošević—bias justified often on the vague grounds of U.S. national-security interests. Thus the vital testimony of General Clark before the tribunal, in December 2003, was held outside the reach of public and press, in closed sessions, a clear transgression of norms set up by the U.N. General Assembly. In this context Milošević's right to cross-examine Clark was severely curtailed, contrary to rules established by the ICTY itself. Clark, a public figure who later ran for the U.S. presidency, had been in charge of NATO military operations in Yugoslavia and admitted that the intervention was a "technical" violation of international law. He also embraced, as mentioned, the strategic targeting of civilian objects. It is difficult to imagine that Milošević and other defendants at The Hague could ever receive a fair hearing at such a thoroughly one-sided tribunal.

In its selective approach to justice, in its almost exclusive targeting of Serbs for criminal accountability, the ICTY exemplifies all the flaws of ad hoc tribunals. The entire legal process has been biased, partial, undemocratic, and politically charged. Its formation on the basis of Security Council resolution 827, moreover, has no legal foundation in the U.N. Charter, which was never established to create war-crimes tribunals. Court bias was evident from the outset when Richard Goldstone, the first ICTY prosecutor, declared that Serbs alone should be indicted as mass murderers guilty of genocide—well before evidence had been gathered. Not only did the U.S. provide most of the ICTY resources, it offered huge rewards for the capture of Serb "war criminals" (but nothing for the apprehension of Croatians, Bosnian Muslims, or others).[12] Defendants, often illegally kidnapped after indictments were brought, were typically presumed guilty as charged, giving rise to a legal milieu in which the rights of those charged were mostly ignored; due process was often simply tossed aside. Indicted war criminals languished in jail for months and longer, those in poor health often denied even basic health services. As an ad hoc body, the ICTY was essentially able to set its own rules of jurisprudence. And those rules were, more than anything, simply the rules of the military victors—that is, the NATO powers strong enough to bomb Yugoslavia into submission and then set the terms of postwar legality. It was a situation where the sheer exercise of power dictated the narratives of justice and criminality.

Meanwhile, the ICTY came to be regarded with contempt by the vast majority of Serbs, reflected in the fact that the status of Milošević and other leading defendants was enhanced despite the extremely serious charges. In the November 2003 elections, defendant Vojislav Seselj, representing the Serbian Radical Party from jail, won 28 percent of the vote—just one sign of popular opposition to the NATO agenda. Both Seselj and Milošević emerged as heroic figures for many in Yugoslavia, owing to their defiance of the U.S. and NATO, which had already begun to impose a neoliberal regimen on the Balkans that promised something akin to the "shock therapy" experienced by Russia and most of Eastern Europe in the 1990s. It was also the U.S. and NATO, as mentioned, that used financial inducements to get the Serb government to support the ICTY proceedings. In fact a central plank in Seselj's campaign was rejection of The Hague Tribunal as a kangaroo court set up to demonize the Serbs and legitimize Western military intervention.

The seemingly unending ICTY trial of Milošević for war crimes was concluded in February 2004, more than two years after it began, leaving some 500,000 pages of documents, 33,000 pages of trial transcripts, and 5000 video cassettes across 300 days of testimony. The court called no less than 298 witnesses. While this huge legal spectacle was meant to convey obvious guilt, the ICTY was never able to produce even a single item of evidence against Milošević. No connections were established between his actions or decisions and alleged criminal deeds. The NATO-led investigation itself was a total failure, resting as it did largely on myths and distortions of the actual historical record and events leading up to it. Further, Milošević and his defense team were able to turn the tables on the prosecution, showing not only the illegitimacy of The Hague Tribunal—Milošević was indicted in the midst of the NATO military intervention—but also the very criminality of unprovoked aerial terrorism. An impartial court would have thrown out the case against Milošević, but this was an ad hoc *political* tribunal destined to convict the Serb leader of crimes he was never proven to have committed. This being a politicized version of justice, Milošević was presumed guilty, was treated harshly in confinement, prevented from seeing his family, obstructed in his legal efforts, denied adequate medical treatment, and finally died in jail on March 11, 2006 before any verdict could be rendered. Milošević's demand that U.S. and NATO leaders be investigated and brought to trial for their own crimes was of course never realized.[13]

As mentioned, only a few non-Serbs have been indicted or prosecuted at The Hague—and the benevolent treatment they generally received, in stark contrast to that of the Serb defendants, only further reveals the tribunal bias. In 2006 Ramush Haradinaj, former Prime Minister of Kosovo and one-time KLA rebel commander, was indicted for crimes against humanity, but both U.N. and U.S. officials in the field and at The Hague regarded Haradinaj as one of the "good guys" deserving special consideration. The U.N. governor of Kosovo during 2004–06, Søren Jessen-Petersen, gave the defendant a ringing endorsement, describing him as a "man of dynamic leadership and strong vision" and urging (with U.S. backing) that he remain free until the start of his trial—a virtually unprecedented move. Haradinaj continued to be regarded in official NATO circles as a heroic fighter for liberation, valued as someone who gave the U.S. and NATO planes valuable logistical support during the 1999 attacks. Out of jail pending conviction, Haradinaj was given a gala farewell party in Kosovo before his appearance at the ICTY. The charges against him? No less than a 37-count indictment of mass murder, indiscriminate rapes, unlawful detentions, and torture of Serbs (and Kosovar enemies) throughout 1998–99. He was accused of leading a ruthless campaign of harassing, murdering, and forcibly displacing thousands of people in Kosovo. Along with a few co-defendants, he was indicted for a widespread campaign of terrorism marked by such grizzly forms of torture as cutting ears and noses off living persons, hammering spikes into people's heads, and numerous episodes of sexual assault. While Haradinaj was allowed freedom during preparations for trial, witnesses were killed, others disappeared, and still others were too frightened to testify. Given the highly selective nature of justice at the ICTY, perhaps the most salient question was why the NATO prosecutors chose to arrest and try Haradinaj in the first place.[14]

After Milošević's death the ICTY prosecutors moved to speed up the trials of other (mostly Serb) defendants, some 150 of whom had been indicted beginning in the late 1990s. Only a few political, military, and police figures were found guilty. Of significant interest was the February 2007 finding by the International Court of Justice (ICJ) that conclusively rejected charges of genocide against Serbia, citing lack of evidence, while dismissing Bosnian claims of reparations.[15] The ICJ decision, met with hysterical anger in the Western media, overturned the official U.S./NATO narrative for all Balkan atrocities in the 1990s. The ruling specifically refuted well-known contentions that the Serbs had planned and carried out atrocities at Srebrenica in 1994. Video materials, most of them later shown to be doctored or phony, were never admitted as evidence before the ICJ judges.

As in the first Persian Gulf War, in the Balkans there never was a bona fide war between two sides—rather simply a protracted, one-sided campaign of aerial bombardment carried out in violation of international law. In the end, this NATO attack simply brought more death and destruction to the Balkans than it claimed to prevent. One result was a Kosovo that became even more poverty stricken and filled with ethnic violence than before, occupied by NATO forces and ruled by a corrupt, authoritarian regime unable to furnish even basic public services. The U.S. military built Camp Bondsteel, a sprawling symbol of imperial domination. KLA fascist gangsters were free to continue their terror campaign against Serbs— all this in the name of democracy and "humanitarian" principles. It became clearer with the passing of time that the U.S. had targeted the Milošević government not because of crimes against humanity but because it was viewed in Washington as an impediment to U.S./ NATO domination of the Balkans, strategically close to the rest of Europe, Russia, the Middle East, and the Caspian Sea, a region rich in oil, natural gas, and other resources.[16] In fact U.S. plans were boldly laid out in a 46-page Pentagon document stating that Washington was prepared to militarily challenge any nation that stands in the way of U.S. policies and interests.[17]

In this context The Hague Tribunal ought to be seen as nothing more than a recycled form of victor's justice, the proceedings so politically charged and legally one-sided as to deny legitimacy. It represents less a new era of international law than a momentous step backward, a great retreat from the promises and hopes of global justice and a return to the earlier colonial ethos where the Western powers could dictate everything through military supremacy.[18] Reflecting on the partial and conflicted legacy of Nuremberg, Telford Taylor writes: "To punish the foe—especially the vanquished foe—for conduct which the enforcing nation has engaged, would be so grossly inequitable as to discredit the laws themselves."[19]

THE HUSSEIN TRIBUNAL: COUNTERFEIT JUSTICE

Long before the first trial of Saddam Hussein and seven co-defendants for assorted war crimes moved toward its preordained guilty verdict, the ad hoc Iraq Tribunal revealed itself as yet another naked U.S. exercise in one-sided punitive justice. The first court, convened in October 2005, found Hussein and six other former Ba'ath Party leaders guilty of war crimes for the killing of 148 people at the village of Dujail in 1982—a verdict rendered on November 5, 2006 and followed by the videotaped execution of Hussein in December. Two others, Awad Hamed Bandar (head of the Revolutionary Court) and Barzan Ibrahim Hasan (intelligence chief) were also sentenced to death, with others given long prison terms. (A second trial begun in August 2006—this one stemming from charges of genocide, war crimes, and crimes against humanity for the killing of Kurds during a 1988 military campaign—was set aside once the defendants were convicted of the Dujail offenses.) Not surprisingly, the verdicts were greeted by President Bush as a "great milestone" in the march toward global justice, a "turning point" in the achievement of peace and democracy in Iraq.[20]

Like Bush, the entire U.S. political and media establishment heralded both the Iraq Tribunal and its guilty verdicts as a wondrous exercise in international law, praised lavishly for its quick dispatch of one of the world's leading tyrants. In fact the Iraq Special Tribunal (later renamed the Iraq Higher Criminal Court, or IHCC) had been repudiated by the global community as a sorry effort by the Bush administration to cover its own more terrible crimes and simultaneously deflect public gaze from its costly and disastrous military intervention. As Washington politicians and the media pundits carry on about the virtues of international law and human rights, their carefully orchestrated legal processes have quickly turned into a mockery of juridical norms—for Iraq, as for Yugoslavia, we had a special tribunal set up to punish the designated enemy. All that surrounds and defines the Baghdad court, buried deeply within the high-security Green Zone—military occupation, puppet government, uncontrollable civil strife, and collapse of social order, not to mention full U.S. institutional, logistical, and financial support for the entire operation—has reduced the trials to comical farces, their procedures manipulated and outcomes predetermined.

Following the ICTY pattern, the Iraq tribunal was heralded by the Western media as a "triumph of international norms of legality," a "Grotian Moment" signaling a new phase in the history of war-crimes prosecution. Here as elsewhere imperial exuberance recognizes few limits: as the tribunal opened President Bush could say "this trial is indicative of the change that has taken place in Iraqi society ... Today there is a new system, a juridical system in place that will give Saddam Hussein a chance to make his case in court."[21] According to Christopher Reid, the U.S. regime liaison officer for the IHCC, "Saddam is on trial because the Iraqi people have chosen to embrace the rule of law and discard the methods of the former regime."[22] Vanderbilt law professor Mike Newton, who helped set up the tribunal, termed the proceedings an epic legal moment, "arguably the most important war-crimes proceeding since Nuremberg [with] the trial of Saddam Hussein likely to constitute a ... legal development so significant it carries the potential to create a new customary international law or radically transform the interpretation of treaty law."[23] Professor Ronald Sievert of the University of Texas, who worked tirelessly to train prosecutors and judges at the IHCC, indicated that the tribunal would bring together Iraqi and international law in a context where the entire world would be watching to see how the Ba'ath tyranny would be brought to justice.[24] International law scholar Christian Eckart of Cornell University embraced the tribunal as "a new start based on firm legal principles," adding: "The trial might hereby serve as another mosaic stone in establishing the rule of law and deter others from stepping over the lines of international agreements and custom in the area of international criminal law."[25]

Such "experts" are mainly propagandists for ad hoc justice shaped by U.S. geopolitical interests. They are specialists above all in disseminating mindless platitudes for public consumption, while the imperial architects of illegal war and occupation—those who should be *first* held criminally accountable—have had few worries about meeting their deserved fate, basking in their inflated self-images as bearers of liberation, democracy, and rule of law. Those who, like Bush, Cheney, Blair, and Rice, subordinate international law to their own grandiose power ambitions, who rudely dismiss the U.N. on those rare occasions when it fails to bend to their purposes, who routinely violate or ignore global treaties, who manage torture camps in Guantanamo, Afghanistan, Iraq, and other secret locations, who wage military attacks on civilian populations, are the same outlaws who refuse independent global jurisdiction at the World Court and International Criminal Court, fearing even modest constraints on their pursuit of imperial objectives. And these were the very architects of the IHCC, a prime example of imperial justice.

The trial leading to Hussein's conviction and execution was in fact upended by courtroom turmoil from the outset, its work conducted in a heavily fortified American enclave yet riddled throughout with security problems. Three defense attorneys were murdered execution-style, including lead lawyer Khamis Ubaidi, gunned down in Baghdad in June 2006—a severe blow to the defense. Anyone working for Hussein's legal team was vulnerable to periodic threats and harassment, a problem so acute it led to a series of boycotts and walkouts, including one organized by the Iraq Bar Association. The tribunal mood was overwhelmingly one of intimidation and fear, what one witness called "terrorism in the courtroom." At any respectable legal venue such collapse of legal norms, not to mention security, would be prima facie cause for mistrial, but in Iraq the juridical charade was simply allowed to move toward its programmed conclusion.

At the first IHCC trial, moreover, the defense was given little time to prepare its burdensome response to the charges: prosecution took all of five months, while the Hussein team had to squeeze its case into a few chaos-ridden weeks. Defense was repeatedly stonewalled in its motions—for delays, better security, adequate document-sharing, and so forth. (In fact the U.S. military refused to provide security for defense attorneys and witnesses.) Four defense attorneys were arrested soon after testifying on behalf of Hussein or co-defendants. Another defense witness accused prosecutor Jaafar al-Moussawi of trying to bribe him into giving damaging testimony against Hussein. Other witnesses said they were forced to testify under threat of punishment. Some tribunal proceedings were allowed without the presence of the accused in court. All of Hussein's prison interviews were monitored and recorded by U.S. intelligence. For Hussein's lawyers, access to vital documents was always problematic. Anyone found to have been in or close to the Ba'ath regime was disqualified from participating in the trial. On December 5, 2005 defense attorneys vacated the courtroom after questioning the legitimacy of the tribunal and requesting in vain access to papers seized by the U.S. army. Perhaps most troublesome, the proceedings did not require demonstration of guilt beyond reasonable doubt. In other words, judged by even the most lax juridical standards, no fair trial for the accused was possible.

Efforts to limit prosecutorial shenanigans made little headway since, after all, the Iraq tribunal was planned, set up, and largely subsidized by the Bush administration, which through its Pentagon liaison office provided a cadre of legal "advisers" from American universities to oversee every twist and turn in the case. One reason the U.S. insisted on an Iraq venue—the defense had always wanted to move elsewhere—was the obvious leverage it could exert by virtue of its military occupation, a vital concern after the disintegration of the U.S./NATO case at The Hague Tribunal, where Milošević and other Serbs were able to mount an effective defense. In Baghdad the U.S. poured some $128 million into the IHCC to maximize prospects for a guilty verdict that, it was hoped, would help legitimate the military occupation. Washington played a decisive role in training judges and prosecutors, building courtrooms, furnishing personnel and resources for investigations, providing funds for the tribunal staff, and setting legal ground rules. If Milošević had been able to turn the tables and publicly attack the U.S. and NATO for war crimes in the Balkans, there would be no replay in Iraq since the Ba'ath villains would be denied a forum in which to raise questions of *American* guilt for major war crimes. When the first hand-picked chief judge was deemed too "friendly" toward the accused, for a brief moment permitting Hussein and co-defendants freedom to denounce the invasion and occupation, he was rudely sacked in favor of Kurdish hard-liner Raouf Abdel Rahman in January 2006, following an impromptu visit to Baghdad by Arlen Specter, chair of the Senate Judiciary Committee, who warned that U.S. tolerance of "judicial balance" in dealing with evil monsters like

Hussein had exceeded its limits. The defense fought back within its limits, arguing that the U.S. military occupation hovered over and dictated virtually every phase of the trial, but such relevant objections were ruled out of order by the chief judge. Whenever Bashra Khalil, Hussein's lead attorney, sought to bring elements of political reality into the courtroom, Abdel Rahman denied every protest and motion. In early July 2006 the judge denounced Khalil as an ordinary gangster, unfit for legal duty, and had her dragged unceremoniously from the courtroom.

As the Hussein trial degenerated into theatrical chaos, criticism from legal observers outside Iraq (and the U.S.) intensified, little of it reaching the American media. U.N. Secretary-General Kofi Annan, usually quite congenial to U.S. interests, decided to bar assignment of U.N.-appointed lawyers and judges to the IHCC, pointing out that the tribunal failed to meet "relevant international standards."[26] The guilty outcomes were sure to be tainted accordingly, as another exercise in victor's justice—though of course not enough to save Hussein and other defendants from their fate. As for the death penalty that was handed out to Hussein and two others, it was repudiated by international courts and most legal systems outside the U.S., but this did not impede tribunal organizers from imposing it as a penalty for war crimes. Among other groups, Amnesty International harshly condemned the death sentences.[27]

As at The Hague, deeper problems marred the Baghdad tribunal, starting with its absence of legal and political legitimacy. How can a court established under foreign military occupation, itself the product of an illegal invasion, be considered remotely fair and independent? Neither the client Iraq government nor the war-crimes body could survive a single day without U.S. military power, which naturally lacks any international mandate. Tribunal statutes were created and imposed by U.S. armed forces, political and academic personnel, fully at odds with the requirement of an independent judiciary. The initial Hussein trial, limited to one relatively minor charge, was designed to show that the post-Ba'ath government was sovereign, efficient, and democratic—that is, a viable alternative to the Hussein regime—but in actuality the state system in place under U.S. occupation had no power over such crucial issues as taxation, investment, banking, trade, media control, and of course foreign policy. (In one parliamentary session during 2006 legislators passed just four minor bills over a span of five months.) The IHCC itself was a textbook violation of the Geneva Protocols that forbid an occupying power to dismantle domestic institutions in favor of alternatives chosen by the occupier. According to the 1949 Protocols (section III, article 53) an occupation force cannot destroy public or private property, alter national institutions, or take coercive action against public officials. Further, according to Article 64 of the Fourth Geneva Convention, an occupying power is first obliged to ensure public order and safety, but the U.S., far from satisfying this imperative, thoroughly exacerbated the violence and chaos through its very presence. Since the tribunal was created by the Coalition Provisional Authority (meaning the U.S.) with the Hussein trial alone in its sites, the American claim that this was an Iraq-controlled legal body allowing people to finally settle historical accounts with the Ba'athists is nothing but pure fiction. The Bush administration was concerned from the outset to prevent Hussein or any other defendant from using the trial to either attack its legitimacy or expose the complicity of the U.S. in the crimes that were charged against him.[28]

The historical aim of making government and military leaders accountable for war crimes always depended on efforts to codify universal principles of jurisprudence governing warfare. In the case of Iraq, however, even the pretext of universality is laughable; the entire legal operation was politically rigged from the start, dictated by the colonizing interests of the accusing party. For punishment to be legally and morally binding, to be valid before the norms of international law, the prosecution and judge cannot be selected, trained, and financed by the same interested party—in this case, with its own geopolitical priorities clearly at stake. Since the IHCC was from its inception little more than a U.S. enterprise (with only minor British and Australian involvement) the prosecution and judge were beholden to the very same interests, grounded not in valid legal foundations but in U.S. pursuit of domination over Iraq and the Middle East. The tribunal farce, moreover, could never be separated from ongoing societal turbulence just outside the Green Zone fortress, including a bloodbath of civil-war proportions, a public infrastructure effectively gutted, and a society torn by widespread militarized violence and social dislocation. From Desert Storm through twelve years of brutal economic sanctions, bombings, and covert actions leading to more war and occupation, Iraq was overcome by a cycle of death and destruction claiming possibly more than two million lives, mostly civilian—a monstrous criminal record by any accounting, with U.S. war planners surely the most culpable. As Nuremberg affirmed in 1946, those guilty of crimes against peace—that is, for unprovoked military aggression—must be held responsible for everything that follows, in this case the ensuing atrocities, infrastructure collapse, social breakdown, civil strife, torture of detainees, everything. Unfortunately, those responsible for the carnage are unlikely to be held accountable before legal proceedings set up by these very criminal offenders. (Washington and its allies were, however, identified as major war criminals at a series of "trials" conducted by gatherings of witnesses, researchers, and journalists at the World Tribunal on Iraq [WTI]—but this body, of course, had no effective legal powers.)

Given this historical backdrop, prospects for a renewed legal order, or "Grotian Moment," imagined by U.S. legal scholars and politicians is utopian in the extreme.[29] Both the IHCC and the long series of post-invasion atrocities—mass detentions, human rights abuses, wanton attacks on civilians, destruction of public services, torture, etc.—are integrally linked to the original act of military aggression, part of a planned, deliberate, and systematic U.S. agenda (with help from others) to reconfigure Iraq and the Middle East. In the end, the IHCC has served as yet another vehicle of military occupation in Iraq. International law scholar Leila Sadat, reflecting on the work of the Iraq tribunal, condemned the proceedings and the outcome alike as lacking credibility, another highly-politicized show trial.[30] In August 2006 Attorney General Alberto Gonzales, who earlier had dismissed statutes of the Geneva Conventions as "obsolete," visited Baghdad, proclaiming that the existing government and its war-crimes trials had ushered in a new era based in the "rule of law." But the laws of an occupied Iraq—like those internationally—have been too consistently subordinated to U.S. interests for such claims to be taken seriously. Those waxing eloquently about the "rule of law" turn out to be the most brazen and fearsome violators, whose culpability extends to the very top of a power structure that Gonzales represented. In Bill Van Auken's words: "the illegitimate persecution of Saddam Hussein and his associates only begs the question of when those in Washington who are responsible for far greater bloodshed will be brought to account for waging an illegal war of aggression."[31]

THE INTERNATIONAL CRIMINAL COURT

Beneath self-righteous rhetoric about defending human rights and prosecuting war crimes, the U.S. has fiercely opposed any genuinely independent criminal tribunal based on universal legal principles. Washington, as we have seen, prefers to work only through ad hoc courts designed to advance its own political interests. Dreading any loss of freedom to intervene militarily where and when it chooses, it endorses nothing beyond its own tailor-made tribunals—those where charges can be leveled against chosen villains while leaving itself, the accuser and prosecutor, fully immune. As of late 2008, the Bush administration continued to reject the only legitimate world tribunal, the International Criminal Court (ICC), founded on the Rome Statutes in July 2002 after initial ratification by 60 nations. (President Obama's approach to the ICC was, as of early 2009, still unclear.) The universal legality embraced by the ICC had the goal, never realized, of creating a system of global justice equally applicable to *all* nations, whatever their level of military power; legality would finally triumph over sheer power.[32] The Court was to have worldwide jurisdiction over individuals and states accused of war crimes and crimes against humanity (though not crimes against peace), but the U.S. refused to join when its outrageous demand for veto power over charges against U.S. citizens—requested by no other country—was unanimously disallowed. Secretary of Defense Rumsfeld's view of the ICC in 2002 typified the rejectionist attitude in Washington: "The United States will regard as illegitimate any attempt by the court or state parties to the [Rome Statutes] to assert the ICC's jurisprudence over American citizens."[33] No reason, aside from protecting maximum U.S. global power, seemed necessary.

Never especially interested in a truly global system of justice, the U.S. threatened to paralyze U.N. peacekeeping operations if it did not receive assurances that Americans would be granted immunity from criminal prosecution—a condition that backers of the Court found politically and legally untenable. Having refused to endorse the tribunal, the Bush administration then demanded special exemption from possible charges, arguing that the U.S. might be the target of "politically motivated" legal action. Despite broad global (and considerable domestic) support for the Court, Bush was able to affirm (in July 2002) that the U.S. would refuse to endorse the ICC. Within a week of that statement, the U.S. muscled through the U.N. Security Council a resolution granting U.S. troops and officials a renewable one-year exemption from investigation or prosecution by the Court. But the U.S. exemption turned out to be illegal, not to mention politically corrupt and riven with double standards. As one longtime U.N. observer remarked: "We do not think it is the business of the Security Council to interpret treaties that are negotiated somewhere else."[34] The resolution not only went against the world consensus, it also effectively validated the idea that the U.S. ought to be free to stand outside the canons of international law. Such exceptionalism, of course, renders the Court and its procedures a mockery, since, as noted, laws and processes demand universality to be legitimate and efficacious. At precisely the time all this was taking place, Rumsfeld outlined a series of sweeping proposals that would drastically weaken congressional oversight of the Pentagon—seeking greater military freedom to conduct domestic and global operations, a move largely justified by the war on terrorism. U.S. efforts to subvert an independent court coincided not only with Washington's preference for ad hoc tribunals it could easily manage but with Bush's overall aggressive foreign policy.

In summer 2002 the U.S. Congress passed the American Service Member's Protection Act, with the aim of intimidating nations that had ratified or were in the process of ratifying the ICC and empowering the President to fight the Court as a threat to U.S. sovereignty. The Act prohibits U.S. cooperation with the ICC for any purpose. It insists upon complete U.S. troop immunity from prosecution abroad—an implicit recognition that, with military forces scattered around the globe and intervention somewhere almost routine, the U.S. finds itself uniquely vulnerable to war-crimes indictments. Known as the "Hague Invasion Act," it bans the U.S. from giving military assistance to any state belonging to the ICC. As Sands writes in *Lawless World*, the topic of ICC jurisprudence is one that predictably reduces American politicians, the media, and normally tepid academic gatherings to fits of hysteria.[35]

U.S. disdain for ordinary canons of international law and human rights was further revealed by Bush's cavalier outlook on the torture of prisoners, long a staple of American intelligence practices in Iraq, Afghanistan, Guantanamo, and various secret CIA locations—and still defended, though more obliquely, in the wake of Abu Ghraib and related scandals. In February 2002 Bush, saying "I don't care what the international lawyers have to say, we're going to kick some ass," upheld harsh and abusive interrogation methods known to violate both the Geneva Protocols and the International Torture Convention (a position that was later softened). According to international law, detainees' rights can be challenged only in recognized courts of law but this did not stop Bush and Rumsfeld, emboldened by advice from their circle of neocon legal "theorists," from embracing coercive methods of interrogation, otherwise known as an "alternative set of procedures." In 2004 Bush called for drastic changes in the War Crimes Act through amendments that would retroactively protect U.S. leaders, military personnel, and ordinary citizens from criminal charges even where evidence of torture might be uncovered. Thus Americans would be immunized from past or future transgressions, an outright dismissal of Article 3 of the 1949 Geneva Protocols prohibiting "outrages upon personal dignity, in particular humiliating and degrading treatment." In September 2006 Bush proposed that Congress allow conviction of prisoners based on coerced evidence and hearsay testimony. (Neither of these moves succeeded.) Meanwhile, in August 2006 army Major General Geoffrey D. Miller, architect and overseer of illegal prisoner operations at Guantanamo and Abu Ghraib, was permitted a quiet retirement unencumbered by criminal prosecution or even disciplinary action despite the long cycle of atrocities he had set in motion. Upon retirement, Miller, said to be one of Rumsfeld's favorite generals, was awarded the Distinguished Service Medal for his work and praised by Pentagon brass for a "very, very distinguished career."[36]

THE U.S. ASSAULT ON INTERNATIONAL LAW

The norms and procedures of international law have evolved within a rapidly changing historical context of intensified economic globalization marked by the growth of corporate power and neoliberal policies. Even more significantly, such norms and procedures have unfolded at a time when U.S. imperial domination was being extended to new corners of the globe. Among critical issues posed by these developments is the fate of global justice: can the hopes of a universal legality for prosecuting war crimes and human rights violations be realized under present conditions? The compelling question here is: to what extent can government leaders, military personnel, and others be held accountable for their crimes in a legal forum that is independent, fair, and consistent in its functions? Can such a forum have *universal* efficacy in the transformed historical setting?

Since the end of World War II, as we have seen, there has been an evolving moral and political consensus—the moral *Zeitgeist*—in favor of holding those charged with war crimes legally responsible. The Nuremberg principles, in the main, soon entered the U.N. Charter, boosting efforts to achieve a rational foundation of global justice. Widespread hopes were that a new regimen of international law and human rights, properly enforced, could bring an end to the worst excesses of civil violence and warfare, perhaps an end to warfare itself. As some postwar architects of a renovated international law would argue, the political energy needed to reshape the global terrain would probably come from the West given its traditions of freedom, democracy, and rule of law. Indeed the U.S. itself became a major contributor to both Nuremberg and the Universal Declaration of Human Rights, a radical statement for its time (or indeed even for today). Many optimists in the West—liberals, social democrats, and other progressives especially—entertained hopes for a new global legal paradigm past the Cold War era and into the present. Thus Richard Falk would write: "From its modern origins in the Nuremberg and Tokyo trials of surviving German and Japanese leaders after the Second World War, international law has progressed to the point where such behavior is increasingly subject to indictment, prosecution, and punishment in various appropriate circumstances."[37]

While such optimism might appear well-grounded, Falk's view fails to take into account two crucial problems: the capacity of the lone superpower (or any superpower) to manipulate or subvert that consensus, and the requirement (so far frustrated) of a truly independent system that could perform legal functions that Falk mentions. The difficulties and obstacles have surely worsened in the wake of 9/11, the war on terror, the Iraq quagmire, and prospects for new heated military conflicts. Put concretely, the question remains—more salient now than ever—as to whether U.S. government and military leaders could be brought before a tribunal to face charges of war crimes that, as previously mentioned, have been abundant throughout the myriad U.S. imperial adventures. The answer so far is hardly reassuring. And in the absence of international legal procedures strong enough to hold those most guilty of criminal actions, it is impossible to take seriously Western claims about protecting human rights and ensuring the "rule of law." Frenetic U.S. efforts to subvert the ICC and many other treaties should alone be reason to question the validity of claims emanating from Washington and London, which reek of hypocrisy and double standards.

If there is indeed a widening commitment to norms of lawful international behavior—toward a system of commonly shared global rules—then the U.S. clearly occupies a hostile, outlaw relationship to such an agenda. One finds plenty of lip service in support of high-sounding ideals, but great-power dedication to a binding international system is feeble if not lacking altogether. U.S. global behavior remains steeped in a political culture of national exceptionalism, imperial arrogance, and glorification of military power. America's obsession with ad hoc tribunals, its rejection of independent legal processes, and its contemptuous attitude toward global agreements reflect this culture. International law continues to be subservient to the stratagems of a militarized imperial system.

The question of just who winds up indicted and prosecuted for war crimes—and precisely how and for whom legal processes are established—goes to the heart of the matter. As things now stand, the prevailing legal system is biased, inconsistent, and juridically indefensible. Washington has rushed to bring such political targets as Milošević and Hussein to trial, setting up specific political tribunals for the purpose, while overlooking the egregious crimes of a long list of American clients—Ferdinant Marcos in the Philippines, General Suharto in Indonesia, Rios Montt in Guatemala, and Ariel Sharon (among many others) in Israel. These U.S. "allies," all practitioners of brutal political repression and military atrocities, have been spared courtroom reckonings since their immune status is guaranteed by the major superpower. Thus Sharon was for many years a powerful force behind Israeli ethnic cleansing in Palestine, extending to his well-documented role in the 1982 Lebanon refugee camp massacres. Despite his dreadful record of waging deliberate attacks on civilians, Sharon has been toasted and feted in Washington, welcomed as a great statesman, a partisan of democracy, and a "man of peace." Far from having to face prosecution for many years of criminal deeds, Sharon was elected Prime Minister of Israel in 2001—an event duly celebrated in Washington as in Tel Aviv and Jerusalem. Meanwhile, the Belgian Supreme Court ruled in 2002 that Sharon ought to face war-crimes charges for his role in Lebanon, a move quickly denounced by Israel and the U.S. as anti-Semitic. How the Israeli public could elect a bona fide war criminal—and someone viewed as such around the world—to the nation's highest office raises still other questions. In any event, the legal and political message is unmistakable: mass murder is acceptable so long as the perpetrators are either Americans or their loyal clients.

Looking at the U.S. pattern of military intervention around the world since 1945, from Korea to Indochina, Central America, and the Middle East, the U.S. record of war crimes and human rights violations, including crimes of aggression, has no parallel. Nor does its abrogation of international laws and treaties. Virtually every postwar American President from Truman to Bush II could probably have been prosecuted as war criminals if the Nuremberg principles had been uniformly enforced. Any truly independent tribunal would have brought charges against these and a long list of U.S. government and military leaders. For the illegal invasion and occupation of Iraq dozens of Washington figures, including Bush, Cheney, Rumsfeld, Wolfowitz, Rice, and Powell along with high-level Pentagon officers and military leaders in the field, could have been indicted. The problem is that no tribunal has been created with enough power and legitimacy to challenge the major superpower: war-crimes trials are reserved for the weak and vanquished. Moreover, to date no U.S. political or military elites have been brought to trial for their criminal actions in Vietnam, Laos, and Cambodia—and indeed scarcely anyone in mainstream American public life has suggested such a prospect. Henry Kissinger, an architect of saturation bombing across Indochina (that is, the wanton destruction of civilian populations) remains free to conduct his life as a celebrity elder statesman, a regular on op-ed pages and the talk-show circuit. Kissinger was perhaps the leading war planner between 1968 and 1972, much of it involving massive chemical warfare, with the loss (in just this period) of perhaps two million lives. Reports indicated that Kissinger was even prepared to use nuclear weapons to destroy Vietnamese resistance.[38] One question posed by the genocidal Vietnam legacy is this: with major war criminals like Kissinger and Nixon (along with McNamara, Dean Rusk, and JFK before them) having evaded prosecution, what can be the legitimacy of *any* war-crimes proceedings that nowadays will be tarnished by (valid) accusations of double standards?

The International Criminal Court, as mentioned, has yet to achieve the efficacy needed to prosecute war crimes on a large scale—a major roadblock being U.S. rejectionism. The limits of ICC power were revealed in June 2007 when its chief prosecutor reported that the Sudanese government refused to cooperate with efforts to indict a senior official and a militia leader for war-crimes offenses in connection with ongoing attacks on civilians in the Darfur region.[39] Prospects for bringing anyone to justice amidst the carnage seemed bleak. So far, as we have seen, the only "successful" postwar trials of leaders (and others) for war crimes have taken place under the auspices of ad hoc tribunals arranged to suit U.S. geopolitical agendas at The Hague and in Baghdad. Aside from the ICTY and IHCC, the court receiving most attention—one promising to restore international justice and rule of law—has been the International Criminal Tribunal for Rwanda (ICTR), set up in Tanzania in 1994 and empowered to prosecute Rwandans for genocide and other crimes linked to a series of massacres beginning in 1994. One problem with the ICTR is that it quickly became a tool of Paul Kagame's corrupt Rwandan Patriotic Army dictatorship, backed by the U.S. and itself apparently immune from indictments despite considerable evidence of its own criminal actions. The pattern is typical of ad hoc tribunals. Indeed in the aftermath of protracted Hutu–Tutsi warfare only the Hutu massacres were prosecuted. Financed and provided expertise by Washington, the ICTR jailed hundreds of suspects without due process, often for lengthy terms. Legal operations were shoddy and one-sided from the outset.[40]

For the Darfur massacres the ICC indicted Ahmad Harun, in charge of the region's security at the time, for masterminding violent attacks on villagers leading to thousands of deaths and several million refugees during 2003 and 2004. Harun was charged with 42 separate crimes, including murder, rape, persecution, and forcible transfers among the population, but the Sudanese government refused to deliver him to ICC jurisdiction and, shockingly, he continued to hold the post of minister for humanitarian affairs.[41] Instead of being arrested and tried for his crimes, Harun retained enormous power in Darfur while the Sudanese government rejected any arrest warrants, saying the country was not a signatory to the Court and that the charges against Harun were false—claims viewed with great skepticism in the region. One Sudanese official said that "it is a matter for Sudan to decide and act upon. The prosecutor has no jurisdiction here. He is an intruder. Adds Harun: 'We are not signatories to the Court, and neither is the United States. When you [the U.S.] sign, we are going to follow. You go first.'"[42]

Other international procedures for trying war-crimes suspects have followed roughly the same pattern. For example, the trial of former Liberian President Charles Taylor in Sierra Leone and the proposed tribunal to prosecute those charged with the assassination of Rafik Hariri in Lebanon—both strongly backed by the Bush administration—contained all the defects of ad hoc legal bodies: selective prosecution, combined functions of prosecutor and judge, weakening of due process, capacity of a major power to shape outcomes, double standards. Meanwhile, the ICTY at The Hague was (in 2007 and 2008) urged to accelerate legal proceedings against mostly Serb defendants held after the Balkans operations ended. As in the case of every U.S.-supported tribunal, these judicial actions are championed in the Western media as giant steps toward global justice, their one-sidedness of little concern to opinion-makers claiming to be partisans of the "rule of law."

Other ad hoc or local structures for prosecuting war crimes have been adopted by some national governments and military forces including the U.S., for either domestic or foreign cases. As with most other armed forces, the Pentagon has set up court-martial processes mandated by the Universal Code of Military Justice (UCMJ) to try those accused of war crimes and related atrocities—for example, the bringing to trial of Lt. William Calley for his role in the My Lai (Vietnam) massacres. Such prosecutions, however, are few and isolated and typically deal with individual transgressions rather than broader military operations, planning, and high-level policy-making—all assumed to be guided by noble intentions. There have been a few scattered courts martial conducted in Afghanistan and Iraq, though the accused military personnel (in those instances where they are found guilty) usually receive lenient sentences, as in fact did Lt. Calley (a term of three years, later reduced).

As for enemy fighters, the U.S. apprehended hundreds of foreign combatants in Afghanistan and elsewhere in the wake of 9/11, many of them incarcerated in Iraq, Afghanistan, and at Guantanamo awaiting charges and legal proceedings in connection with the war on terror. President Bush initially classified such prisoners as "unlawful enemy combatants" (i.e., mere "terrorists"), meaning they would not be granted ordinary Geneva Convention protections as prisoners of war. Bush hoped to prosecute these detainees at special U.S. military tribunals in Guantanamo and other locations, but the Supreme Court ruled these bodies unconstitutional for such purposes. In 2006 Congress passed the Military Commissions Act giving the Pentagon jurisdiction over "unlawful alien enemy combatants" but in June 2007 a federal judge ruled against these legal bodies on grounds they lacked jurisdiction over prisoners of war. Reports indicate that Guantanamo detainees in particular have been treated harshly, often kept without being informed of charges for months or even years, deprived of due process, and subjected to forced confessions. Despite such legal setbacks the Pentagon (in summer 2007) vowed to push ahead with special prosecutions of detainees, isolating itself even further from the human rights community. According to Jennifer Daskai of Human Rights Watch, the Bush–Pentagon legal impasse "signals that these commissions need to be scrapped and the detention facility at Guantanamo Bay must be closed."[43] Whatever the future of these provincial bodies—and President Obama has indicated a new course—they surely offered a poor example of war-crimes courts that could gain wider legitimacy.

Other alternatives for the prosecution of war crimes have emerged in recent years—one of them, ironically, as an offshoot of the Military Commissions Act that Bush hoped would give the U.S. legal advantages in the war on terror. In November 2006 a group of lawyers and human rights advocates sought to bring war-crimes charges against leading figures of the Bush administration before a German court, employing the same doctrine of Universal Jurisdiction that was used to indict former Chilean dictator Augusto Pinochet before a Spanish court in 2002. In this case the doctrine was invoked on grounds that Bush's Military Commissions Act intended to provide retroactive immunity for Americans who might be indicted for war-crimes offenses. The case filed by the Center for Constitution Rights argued that, since under the Act no Americans could ever be charged within the United States, it would be legitimate (indeed *necessary*) to bring them to justice in another country. The widely accepted principle of Universal Jurisdiction allows for prosecution of war crimes, including genocide and crimes against humanity, in any locale where the principle has been officially enacted.

*   *   *

A consensual global jurisprudence rooted in universal norms consistent with an independent war-crimes tribunal remains today a distant hope. Experience shows the prevailing modalities—ad hoc, national, and military courts—offer no way out of the conundrum. The Kantian idea of ethico-political universality is no closer to realization in the early twenty-first century than it was at Nuremberg, despite claims of a new human rights era being on the horizon. The International Criminal Court, widely seen as a major step forward, has been sabotaged by the lone superpower. And the United Nations, previously thought to be a crucible of international law, suffers from failure to transcend the pressures of nationalism and imperialism. The U.S. and a few of its G-8 partners continue to hold sway over crucial U.N. decision-making, above all in the Security Council. The pursuit of global justice is inevitably blocked by great-power interests where norms of exceptionalism, claims of immunity, double standards, and easy resort to military force carry the day. This pathetic state of affairs has, unfortunately, been widely supported by the liberal intelligentsia in the West, above all in the United States. As Edward Herman and David Peterson observe referring to the workings of the ICTY, "this entire intellectual and moral construct was a fraud; and that it found as many advocates as it did tells us more about the grip of imperial ideology, ignorance, and potent propaganda in the West than anything about the new norms of the wished-for cosmopolitan order."[44] An emergent international consensus identified by Falk and others has little hope of being codified and institutionalized at a time when U.S. economic, political, and military power is determined to transcend all constraints. So long as Washington persists in its international outlawry, in its military aggression and refusal to support global agreements and treaties—and so long as it insists upon special immunity from war-crimes accountability—the struggle for truly independent mechanisms of justice will inevitably be frustrated.

The sad history of international criminal legality is that it has never moved beyond the realm of ad hoc, selective justice—that is, no authentic justice at all—despite moral pretensions to the contrary. International law embodied in various tribunals has been regularly superseded by dictates of political power that, in the postwar era, have meant above all American power. As Mandel aptly comments: "The only rational assumptions are that international criminal law will be firmly subordinated to power, that impunity will be a perk of economic and military hegemony, and that the usual suspects will continue to be rounded up while America gets away with murder."[45] The U.S. and a few of its allies or clients (notably Britain and Israel) have been the supreme criminals for many decades but have managed to escape legal accountability, a concept reserved for lesser offenders or, in some cases, the *victims* of U.S. imperial violence. Tribunals like those at The Hague and Baghdad are meant to give an appearance of justice, but in the end they do not serve the purposes of truth, justice, peace, deterrence, and punishment of wrongdoers. The outcome is nothing but fraudulent legality since, as Mandel notes, "if you study the theory of justice you will find no tolerance for selective justice. That's because justice is based on equality, and it is a serious violation of equality to voluntarily leave some wrongdoer unpunished."[46] The problem is compounded, moreover, when that wrongdoer happens to be the most prolific and horrendous criminal of all.

7
Torture and Other Atrocities

Throughout 2004, graphic revelations of systematic U.S. human rights abuses, including illegal detentions and torture, at Guantanamo Bay in Cuba and Abu Ghraib in Iraq shocked an American public that, for the first time, became aware of longstanding harsh and cruel CIA "rendition" programs. As clear violations of the Geneva Conventions and other international treaties, these practices were the topic of considerable media and political attention, giving rise to a stream of mainstream apologetics, pleas for reform, and legislative corrective measures—a rare outburst of establishment concern about an instance of American outlawry. The issue of torture in particular had seemingly touched a raw nerve in the political culture.

In the midst of embarrassing images of prisoner mistreatment and frenzied promises of change, however, government and military leaders were quick to affirm two comforting discourses—that the abuses were the product of a few wayward (and notably low-level) soldiers and were a radical departure from revered U.S. traditions and values. General Wesley Clark, former NATO commander and 2004 presidential candidate, gave a speech at UCLA in October 2006 in which he denounced torture and related practices, saying they go against the grain of American dedication to international rules and laws. "Law is sacred to the American system," pronounced Clark. "A retreat from Geneva means nothing less than abandoning American values."[1] In the aftermath of the Abu Ghraib revelations and publicity, President Bush said that prisoner abuse was a revolting exception to the norm, for "that's not the way we do things in America." Acknowledging the misguided actions of a few, Secretary of Defense Rumsfeld said in late 2004 that all detainees in U.S. custody are treated "humanely," consistent with the provisions of international law. A lengthier response came from Secretary of State Condoleezza Rice who, speaking in December 2005, stated: "With respect to detainees the United States government complies with its Constitution, its laws, and its treaty obligations. Acts of physical or mental torture are expressly prohibited. The United States government does not authorize or condone torture of detainees.

Torture, and conspiracy to commit torture, are crimes under U.S. law, wherever they may occur in the world." She described the atrocities at Guantanamo and Abu Ghraib (among others) as sickening aberrations from the norm, not likely to be repeated.[2]

References to U.S. obligations to the "rule of law" and international norms are, as we have seen, constantly invoked but rarely transcend ideological rituals detached from actual historical experience. Much the same can be said of the supposed power of American traditions and values. Viewed in the larger historical context, Bush-era human rights violations and other criminal abuses represent no deviation from earlier U.S. practices but rather their *extension* within a new paradigm of warfare. The act of torture itself can be viewed as part of the American legacy of imperialism and militarism, in many ways integral to the logic of geopolitical ambitions. A nation that has so often carried out military aggression, wantonly attacked civilian populations and targets, destroyed entire societies, used weapons of mass destruction, and deployed its armed might to crush oppositional movements around the world—killing millions and displacing tens of millions more in the process—cannot be expected to shy away from torture and similar atrocities as it routinely goes about its global business. Illegal detentions, denial of due process, kidnappings, assassinations, death-squad murders, and cruel interrogation methods are simply another expression of imperial power. (Whether the atrocities in question are carried out directly or through proxies is of secondary importance.) Viewed in this context, torture and kindred abuses must be understood as an outgrowth of U.S. militarism over time, sanctioned at the very top of the power structure (though usually not overtly). The ethos of death and destruction that inevitably accompanies U.S. efforts to achieve imperial aims has a long trajectory, first appearing well before international legal canons governing human rights were set in motion. Today, of course, prohibitions against torture and other atrocities have been systematically codified, part of global customary law concerning what are generally regarded as extreme criminal acts despite occasional attempts to justify them.

Torture and other comparable forms of inhumane treatment have been explicitly outlawed since World War II, first given full legal codification in the 1948 Universal Declaration of Human Rights (UDHR). Article 5 states that "no one shall be subjected to torture or to cruel, inhuman, or degrading treatment or punishment," while Article 9 states that "no one shall be subjected to arbitrary arrest, detention, or exile," and Article 10 affirms that "everyone is entitled to full equality, to a fair and public hearing by an independent and impartial tribunal." Additional rights are ensured by Article 12, which states that "no one shall be subjected to arbitrary interference with his privacy, family, home, or correspondence." These rights are unambiguously reaffirmed in the Geneva Convention III (1949), which states (Article 13) that "prisoners of war must at all times be treated humanely" and that "no physical or mental torture, nor any other form of coercion, may be inflicted on prisoners of war to secure from them information of any kind whatever" (Article 17). These rules are to be applied uniformly, with no exceptions, and extended not just to members of armed forces but to militias, volunteer groups, resistance movements, and insurgencies. The Convention Against Torture (1984) directs each state party to incorporate torture as an offense within its criminal law (Article 4), while the Rome Statutes of the ICC define torture and other abuses of prisoners as a war crime. The U.S. is a signatory to the UDHR, the Geneva Conventions, and the Convention Against Torture.[3] But this has not deterred Washington, as we shall see, from setting up its own outlaw regimen for treating prisoners and others under its control.

THE HISTORICAL LABYRINTH

For roughly two centuries military violence in myriad forms has been central to the expansion and defense of U.S. imperial objectives. Despite loud protestations to the contrary, torture and related abuses have always been a feature of this violence, part of a logic of perpetual warfare in which demonic enemies must be fought and contained. Atrocities become a routine, at times legitimated, aspect of the U.S. struggle for global supremacy as that struggle generates great reserves of hatred and contempt among the victims of targeted populations. These atrocities, part of a general ethos of lawlessness, have provoked relatively little outrage among either opinion leaders or the larger public in the U.S.

The best place to begin is with U.S. exterminationist policies directed against Native tribes throughout the nineteenth century (and earlier)—policies so horrific as to dwarf the many isolated atrocities carried out by the military and settlers during the same period. The history is one that fits the category of genocidal destruction. At the same time, those isolated atrocities deserve mention insofar as they were a prelude to the later pattern of lawless barbarism marking U.S. interventions in the Philippines, World War II, Korea, Vietnam,

Central America, and, more recently, the Middle East. The decades of Indian Wars brought not only well-known massacres—at Sand Creek, Washita, and Wounded Knee, for example—but unspeakable acts of individual brutality: beatings, scalpings, mutilations, sexual assaults, kidnappings, prisoner mistreatment, and shootings along with full-scale attacks on civilians. Captives were often summarily executed, including women, children, and the elderly. Dwellings were routinely burned to the ground, food stores destroyed, and both ponies and buffalo slaughtered by the thousands. Dying Indians were commonly tortured, killed, and mutilated. All of these atrocities took place, for example, when General George Armstrong Custer attacked a defenseless settlement of mostly Cheyenne women and children at the Washita River in Oklahoma in 1868, a massacre that solidified Custer's credentials as a heroic Indian fighter.[4]

At Sand Creek, Colorado, in 1864, the carnage wrought by the fanatically pious Colonel John Chivington had been even more barbaric, the individual atrocities even more gruesome. Reflecting on Chivington's God-ordained massacre, a lieutenant from the New Mexico Volunteers wrote: "Of from five to six hundred souls [killed,] the majority of which were women and children ... I did not see a body of a man, woman, or child but was scalped, and in many instances their bodies were mutilated in a most horrible manner—men, women, and children's privates cut out. I heard one man say that he had cut out a woman's private parts and had them for exhibition on a stick. I heard another man say he had cut the fingers of an Indian to get the rings on the hand."[5] According to this and many similar reports, soldiers used knives to rip apart bodies, and none were spared.[6] Torture, butchery, mutilation—there seemed to be no limits to barbarism on the frontier. Such atrocities, as it turned out, were hardly aberrant, but were repeated time and again, finally culminating in the Wounded Knee massacre of 1890, where more than 3000 defenseless women and children were slaughtered with most of the wounded tortured before they were killed. No disciplinary action was ever taken against U.S. military officers responsible for such horrors which, in the final analysis, helped pave the way toward unchallenged white-colonial power over the continent.

While international law has been steadily refined since the late nineteenth century, with prohibitions against torture and kindred abuses established and codified, in fact U.S. global behavior in this regard has changed very little—an apparent extension of what occurred during the Indian Wars. One obvious difference is that the newer regimen has been directed largely outside American borders, toward designated targets in Latin America, Asia, and the Middle East. It is not necessary here to detail all these historical episodes—that would require yet another book—but rather to identify general *patterns* of behavior in a few geopolitical settings. In the case of World War II, the fabled "good war," observers have often forgotten that the Allied Powers, while militarily victorious, were guilty of monstrous war crimes that in many respects matched or even surpassed those of the Axis nations. Torture is one atrocity that would surely fall into that category, especially in the Pacific Theater where the U.S. carried out a total war of attrition against the Japanese, replete with continuous saturation bombing raids and two nuclear infernos.

In the "war without mercy" that characterized the Pacific battlefield, we have seen how Americans viewed the Japanese as irredeemably evil, a monolithic race apart, so subhuman that even the most barbaric actions against them could easily be justified. Racial stereotypes of savage Asian hordes permeated U.S. media both in the military and on the home front, giving rise to a racially explosive milieu in which atrocities became routine and readily accepted by the public. Exterminationist language—for example, "kill Japs and more Japs"—was fueled by a racist hatred largely unknown to the European theater, at least in the context of U.S. motives. Revenge for Pearl Harbor could explain only a small part of this hatred leading to unrestrained savagery. Aside from the massive aerial bombardments of Japanese cities producing well more than a million civilian deaths, there was an abundance of local or isolated atrocities: shooting of prisoners, torture, lifeboat strafings, attacks on hospitals, civilian abuse, wounded buried alive, mutilated corpses.[7] When such atrocities became known within larger military circles and the general public, more often than not they were defended and even celebrated. The ideological atmosphere was one of vengeful racial hatred.

In July 1944—well before the U.S. bombing campaign against Japan—Charles Lindberg, a close observer of the Pacific War, wrote: "It was freely admitted that some of our soldiers tortured Jap prisoners and were as cruel and barbaric at times as the Japs themselves. Our men think nothing of shooting a Japanese prisoner or a soldier attempting to surrender ... these are condoned by almost everyone."[8] It was widely recognized that what would later be regarded as war crimes were committed virtually without restraint on both sides, despite rhetoric to the contrary. Both sides, moreover, viewed the imperialist conflict as a war to advance higher values. As Dower observes: "The civilization which both the Allies and Japanese claimed to be defending had failed to stem these [barbaric] impulses and World War Two simply witnessed new as well as old ways of carrying out mass destruction and individual violence."[9] In the case of the U.S., its great pretenses about a war being fought on behalf of democracy and the rule of law would turn especially sour, while for the world any notion that new rules and prohibitions would spell an end to war-related individual atrocities was indeed illusory.

During the Vietnam War era moral and social constraints operating within the U.S. military progressively broke down as the war dragged on, eroding rules of engagement and permitting some of the most horrendous war crimes in modern history. Guidelines included in armed-forces manuals deferred to international law, but soldiers in the field—as well as the pilots of air strikes—usually ignored them; rules were viewed as something to be eluded where possible. At the same time, there were informal codes: any Vietnamese running from combat, taking evasive action, or even having the appearance of being a fighter could be immediately detained, kept captive, and tortured—or simply fired upon. American troops often made little effort to distinguish civilians from combatants, a challenge that in any case was extremely difficult under conditions of guerrilla insurgency. The general idea was that, in the midst of combat and "free-fire zones," any Vietnamese encountered was a "gook" who, by definition, was the enemy.[10] And in Vietnam the atrocities inevitably resulting from this state of affairs were never-ending— burning homes, mass killings, torture, rape, murder of wounded prisoners, beatings, destruction of animals and life-support systems, all fueled by elements of revenge, sadism, combat stress, and in some cases sexual pleasure.[11] These practices were for some units virtually routine, informally tolerated or even encouraged in the battlefield as standard behavior to defeat an implacable enemy, and sanctioned at the very top of the command structure.

As the war intensified by the mid 1960s, military intelligence specialists had become thoroughly trained in methods of harassment, intimidation, and torture as they detained and questioned North Vietnamese and Vietcong troops in the field—methods often taught orally by instructors mindful of international-law violations. Methods included throwing people out of helicopters, electric shock treatment, severe beatings, and mutilation. Prisoners were often taken for "flying lessons" or "half a helicopter ride" as interrogators kept throwing people out until someone talked. Other creative modes of torture were employed to break down possible informants. When a captive proves stubborn, according to one U.S. soldier, "the answer is invariable, you take a field telephone, wire it around a man's testicles, you ring him up and he always answers. It's known as the Bell Telephone Hour. You won't find it in the curriculum."[12] Torture was applied to anyone, the assumption being that civilians in any case were likely to be "VC supporters" to varying degrees. Those captured were often tortured for information, then for revenge, then for sadistic or sexual pleasure. When American units came upon hamlets they would routinely engage in torture, rape, murder, and mutilation, generally without fear of being investigated or prosecuted. Any soldier reporting such crimes would likely be killed.

Wielding military power over local inhabitants, American troops often found great sexual pleasure in the process of carrying out these atrocities. Rape became a special means of bringing sex and violence together. According to one macabre account: "maybe four or five of us would go into a village and take a girl and bring her out to the jungle. ... Explain to her to lie on the ground and don't scream, otherwise she'll be killed immediately, and however many guys there are—well, they all do what they want. And if the guys are in a good mood, they let her go. If not they kill her."[13] Rape was often followed by torture, as girls and women ended up bleeding from their mouths, noses, and vaginas when further assaulted and beaten before being killed. According to reports, some women were burned to death after gasoline was poured over their body and troops stood around and sadistically watched.[14] Routine sexual encounters between GIs and Vietnamese women often grew violent, leading to rapes, beatings, and murder.

In Vietnam these atrocities were hardly isolated or aberrant acts carried out by a few demented, out-of-control individuals or groups, nor was the My Lai massacre in 1968 the horror set apart from standard U.S. troop behavior it was depicted as being in the American media. Recycling racist imagery that gave the wars against the Indians, Japanese, and Koreans added savagery, military leaders regularly called the Vietnamese gooks, thugs, and worse, with General William Westmoreland himself known to refer to them as "worthless termites."[15] These were the same "termites," presumably, who were to be brought the American blessings of freedom and democracy. Such bigoted attitudes permeated armed-forces units from top to bottom. Everyday violence against an evil force was not only tolerated but actively encouraged to the point where it became integral to the military culture. Veterans have repeatedly described their officers, comrades, and even chaplains as urging them to carry out blood revenge—acts made possible, as Rhodes observes, by a nearly total loss of restraint.[16] In the field, U.S. troops were "violently coached by their leaders, began beating up prisoners, torturing prisoners, executing prisoners—began, that is, expanding their range of violent performances." According to one participant in this barbarism, "the voices of authority in the company—the platoon sergeants and officers—acknowledged that [executing prisoners] was a proper way to behave. Who were the grunts to disagree with it? We supported it."[17]

Atrocities in Vietnam were the inevitable *modus operandi* of a ruthless U.S. war of attrition, planned by the liberal architects of technowar and counterinsurgency. Thus by the late 1960s the Phoenix Program set up by the CIA was already responsible for the illegal detention and torture of untold thousands of captives. Under this program, moreover, U.S. operatives assassinated an estimated 21,000 Vietnamese officials in the South. As the war expanded, Navy SEALs and other units mounted raids to destroy homes, capture and torture people, and conduct summary executions at random, devoid of any rules of engagement. By the end of the war many hundreds of thousands (mostly civilians) had been rounded up, detained, and subjected to unspeakable brutality—all of it condoned or at least ignored all the way to the top of the military and government leadership.[18] It was rooted in the very conduct of warfare. Many of these atrocities were revealed to the American public by the Winter Soldier hearings and testimony in 1971, but its impact on the political culture was sadly minimal. Indeed the hearings were barely covered in the mass media while politicians seemed inclined to dismiss the atrocities as just another unfortunate expression of modern (or any) warfare.

The record of U.S. criminal behavior in Central America hardly compares with that in Asia, but it covers a lengthier historical period during which the CIA, military, and proxy groups detained, tortured, and killed tens of thousands of people in Guatemala, El Salvador, Honduras, Panama, and Nicaragua. Such atrocities resulted from established operational procedures at times when U.S.-supported oligarchical interests were challenged or overturned by oppositional movements. As Jennifer Harbury shows in her well-researched study of torture across Central America: "A review of the materials leads relentlessly to just one conclusion: that the CIA and related U.S. intelligence agencies have since their inception engaged in the widespread practice of torture, either directly or through well-paid proxies."[19] Counterinsurgency campaigns involved regular kidnappings, detentions, torture, and executions. The U.S., often through the infamous School of the Americas and other domestic military bases, provided finances, training, logistics, and weapons—the work of mostly secret projects organized by the CIA.[20] In Guatemala, El Salvador, and Nicaragua local atrocities reach their peak during the 1980s as the linkage between the U.S. and Central American instruments of violence intensified, giving rise to a wave of abductions, torture, and murder, much of it directed against labor, civic, and religious leaders. Intensified repression, as during the Rio Montt campaign in Guatemala in the early 1980s, was usually accompanied by heightened U.S. financial and military assistance. After Reagan became President the Guatemalan army achieved the distinction of being the worst human rights violator in the Western hemisphere.

As in Vietnam, torture and related atrocities in Central America were hardly the product of excesses, mistakes, or a few renegade sadists; they were part of the logic of control and repression. What was understood to be necessary "dirty work" took years to plan and refine, much of it carried over from the Vietnam experience. Such methods as solitary confinement, beatings, electric shocks, stress positions, and sexual humiliation—to be replicated later at Guantanamo and Abu Ghraib—had been de rigueur in Vietnam. One difference in Central America was that the U.S. preferred to work through local military units and death squads, that is, by proxy, so that it would be more difficult to trace the atrocities back to the guilty Washington agents. Still, as Harbury points out, there were few doubts in the field as to who was calling the shots. Thus: "The Yankees in the torture cells were not working for local military officials at all. To the contrary, they were very much in charge, and had clear authority over the torturers themselves. The Americans were not taking orders, they were giving them. At times they were even supervising the entire torture session."[21] In such a brutal milieu, the idea that the U.S. somehow wanted to bring democracy and the "rule of law" to Latin America can only be greeted with ridicule.

Throughout the postwar years the U.S. routinely employed—directly or indirectly—illegal detentions, torture, assassination, and other forms of murder as valued instruments of imperial power. It has carried out or supported these actions across many geographical settings: South America, Indonesia, Iran, Central Asia, and the Balkans as well as the aforementioned Korea, Vietnam, and Central America. And the legacy continues on a regular basis, thanks not only to the CIA but to Special Forces units, Navy SEALs, Delta Force, and various regular military operations. In many cases Washington has been involved in repression directed against political, cultural, and intellectual opposition. Harsh interrogation methods are but one facet of this worldwide terror apparatus. As James Petras writes, for several decades the Israelis performed a complementary role in this process, their repression of Palestinians based on routine arrests, harassment, torture, and random killings— all with U.S. support and blessing. Thousands of Palestinians have been illegally detained at any given time. Torture practiced by the Israeli Mossad parallels methods used by the CIA: shackles, beatings, stress positions, stripping, and sexual intimidation.[22] Assassinations are often carried out by commando groups, helicopter gunships, F-16 fighter planes, and other techniques perfected since the early 1950s. The fact that all of these practices are flagrant violations of international law seems to have bothered neither the Israelis nor their American patrons.

We have plenty of history to show conclusively that present-day U.S. torture and other human rights abuses are deeply rooted in the past, now tied to an apparatus of control and repression integral to Empire. They constitute longstanding *patterns* rather than exceptions or departures from the norm. American militarism seems always to have been replete with criminal operations sanctioned, more often than not, at the very summit of government and military officialdom. The CIA torture network in particular, in place over several decades but only recently a focus of political and public concern, represents one cornerstone in the superpower efforts to maximize its surveillance, intelligence, and control capabilities.

In hundreds of pages of long-classified but recently disclosed files, CIA documents describe at length a wide variety of illegal actions: secret holding cells around the world, unlawful detentions without due process, vast surveillance functions, plots to assassinate foreign leaders. (Unfortunately, most of what was reluctantly released was blacked out.)[23] In *Ghost Plane*, Stephen Grey presents an exhaustive investigative report on CIA torture programs where, among other things, "ghost" prisoners are sent to secret locations around the world and held, typically without charges, outside any framework of international convention or law. Most detainees were sent to locales controlled by harsh regimes (for example, in the Middle East, Central Asia, and Eastern Europe) for "extraordinary rendition"—

that is, torture—ostensibly for purposes of obtaining crucial information. As part of the war on terrorism, these programs were strongly embraced by Clinton during the 1990s and then stepped up by Bush in the wake of 9/11.[24] At this point hundreds of CIA operatives were working more or less freely across the globe. In February 2007 an Italian judge indicted 26 Americans (both CIA and military personnel) for their role in plots to abduct targeted individuals. In one publicized case U.S. operatives abducted one Abu Omar off a Milan street in 2003, after which he was detained in Egypt for four years without charges, hooded and beaten, and tortured when he refused to become a CIA informant.[25] It was within such an environment that the U.S. torture regimen expanded its scope to include Guantanamo, Afghanistan, and Iraq with the war on terror and invasion of Iraq after 2001. Upon assuming office in January 2009, President Obama set out to limit abuses of detainees but also issued an executive order allowing the CIA to carry out its rendition programs so long as suspects were held only "short-term."

GUANTANAMO: THE NEW DEVIL'S ISLAND

The events of 9/11 set in motion new U.S. political and legal maneuvers that would overtly challenge basic provisions of international law, justified by the urgent need to fight global terrorism. By late 2001 the U.S. was already setting up detention facilities to house and interrogate hundreds (eventually thousands) of prisoners associated with the Taliban, Al Qaeda, and other Muslim groups thought to be involved in jihadic violence. According to the Bush administration, 9/11 ushered in a new kind of war requiring legal, political, and military flexibility in its pursuit—a radical departure from the familiar clash between rival nation-states. Toward this end Bush issued a secret executive order in late 2001 giving the CIA special power to detain and investigate prisoners, followed (in February 2002) by a broader executive order stating that, since terrorist suspects were not conventional prisoners of war but rather "unlawful enemy combatants," the U.S. was not subject to international legal provisions regarding treatment of detainees. These orders in effect opened the door to torture and other abuses of prisoners at Guantanamo Bay, a camp set up beyond the reach of American domestic jurisdiction, and elsewhere at mostly secret locations. Legal rationalizations (for such practices as torture and denial of due process) came from officials within the Bush administration, including Deputy Assistant Attorney General John Yoo, who contended that for a variety of reasons the U.S. should not be subject to the provisions of international law. For Yoo and others, the imminent threat of terrorism meant that Washington was now freed from legal restraints, including those set by the International Criminal Court where the U.S., in any case, was not a signatory. And torture itself was further given a peculiar American definition: it would apply only to the most extreme practices leading to outright organ failure or death.[26]

Legal opinions that the U.S. could operate outside international conventions in its treatment of detainees came from a series of memos sent to Bush by the Attorney General's office, culminating in Alberto Gonzales' report of January 25, 2002 indicating that Geneva Convention III does not apply in the war on terror where prisoners cannot be regarded as POWs but only as "unlawful combatants." Such prisoners were essentially stateless. Those suspected of being members of the Taliban or Al Qaeda were in any case operating within the context of a "failed state" (Afghanistan). Gonzales, moreover, argued that the President—and not international or domestic courts—should have exclusive power over any legal proceedings.[27] Bush's executive orders of November 2001 and February 2002 were grounded in Gonzales' opinions which, as it turned out, conflicted with prevailing readings of international law. Central to Bush's decrees was the establishment of military commissions ostensibly to try non-Americans on war-crimes and related charges. This rare maneuver, not employed since World War II, gave the President authority to set up ground rules for the conduct of strictly military proceedings whereby the prosecution and judges are answerable only to him while he alone is charged with reviewing the final verdicts. The commissions work in secrecy, the prosecution can rely on secret evidence and witnesses, and no appeal to civilian courts is possible. Defendants have no right of access to any domestic or international courts and cannot even select their own attorneys. Thus at Guantanamo a defendant could be given a harsh sentence without a public trial, presumption of innocence, right to appeal, or proof beyond reasonable doubt. In other words, Bush had created a juridical apparatus that flagrantly violated commonly held legal norms of due process. Both Human Rights Watch and Amnesty International denounced these attempts to bypass Geneva and other protocols as inconsistent with both human rights and criminal law.[28] The U.N. high commissioner for human rights, Mary Robinson, said the U.S. had no legal justification for dismissing Geneva III, after which her reappointment was blocked by the U.S.

While Bush's orders effectively snubbed the U.S. judiciary as well as international law, they served to immunize American government and military personnel from war-crimes charges where treatment of detainees was involved. The result was a green light for torture and denial of due process at detention centers in Afghanistan, Guantanamo, and (later) Iraq—despite a refusal to concede as much by top officials in Washington. The Pentagon spelled out a three-tier interrogation plan that would presumably be implemented first at Bagram Air Force Base in Afghanistan and at Guantanamo. Thus "Category I" would involve yelling, deception, and intimidation; "Category II" the use of stress positions, deprivation, hooding, isolation, use of phobias, and removal of comfort items; and "Category III" severe physical harm including temporary suffocation and exposure to extreme cold or heat. At least 24 of these methods were approved by Secretary of Defense Rumsfeld in April 2003, while CIA "rendition" measures at secret detention centers seemed to proceed with few if any constraints.

By early 2002, as hundreds of prisoners from Afghanistan were taken bound, shackled, and hooded to Guantanamo, stark images of human rights abuses began to surface despite the relative secrecy of the operations. Prisoners arrived from more than 40 countries. Whatever the stipulations of international law, the Bush administration was determined to squeeze information out of detainees—people that Bush, Cheney, and Rumsfeld had already concluded were evil threats to U.S. security—by any means necessary. Prisoners were stripped of all rights and detained indefinitely with no charges filed and no access to lawyers or courts, a state of affairs that for some persisted up to three years. A Red Cross inspection conducted in October 2003 found conditions at Guantanamo horrid, with physical and mental abuses rampant. The abuses recorded at that time were many: long-term solitary confinement, lengthy interrogation sessions, exposure to heat and cold, beatings, use of pepper spray, guns held to prisoners' heads, inadequate food, and stress positions, to name some.[29] Many cases of sexual and religious humiliation were reported as well. Prisoners had little or no privacy and were often denied exercise privileges. Harsh discipline was standard treatment, especially in cases where suspects were viewed as non-cooperative. Camp Delta, built in 2003 by KBR, came to be known as an American "Devil's Island" where prisoners were kept in maximum security. Such treatment was justified by U.S. officials who viewed detainees (already presumed guilty) as subhuman terrorists deserving of no legal or human rights. The detainees were also seen as vast sources of intelligence in the fight against terrorism, but these expectations turned out to be mostly illusory.[30]

While U.S. leaders invoked the war on terror as yet another pretext for national exceptionalism—here meaning special claims of immunity from war-crimes charges—the reality has been a systematic attack on global rules now well-established and part of customary law. Several problems were inherent in Bush's decrees from the outset. First, the notion that detainees as suspected terrorists could be labeled "unlawful combatants" and stripped of basic rights cannot be legally defended: international humanitarian law protects *all* human beings of all nations, whether civilian or military personnel, whatever the conditions leading up to their arrest. And no country has unilateral power to determine the status of detainees—that is a matter for independent courts to determine. Second, the indefinite incarceration of prisoners without charges, access to lawyers and courts, in virtual isolation from the world, clearly violates universal precepts of due process enshrined in the U.N. Charter and many treaties as well as the U.S. Constitution. Third, *any* form of torture under *any* circumstances is strictly prohibited by international law— by the UDHR, the Torture Convention, and several provisions of the Geneva Conventions, not to mention U.S. domestic and military codes. There are no exceptions to this law. Fourth, those in charge of detainees are not legally permitted to seek revenge or punishment against them, while interrogation is never allowed except for simple requests for personal identification. At Guantanamo and elsewhere, it must be remembered, any guilt regarding criminal charges was never initially determined.[31] Finally, Bush administration claims that "terrorists" were being held "outside U.S. territory" could not be sustained insofar as the naval station at Guantanamo was firmly under U.S. jurisdiction.

This unapologetic subversion of global rules was denounced by lawyers and politicians around the world, including many in the U.S., and by a series of media interventions including well-crafted books by David Rose (*Guantanamo*, 2004), Michael Ratner and Ellen Ray (*Guantanamo*, 2004), and Seymour Hersh (*Chain of Command*, 2004) that revealed the scandalous illegality of American prison operations.[32] Ratner's organization, the Center for Constitutional Rights (CCR), bravely took up the cause of the Guantanamo prisoners who, at least for the first three years, had no other recourse to the pursuit of justice. As Ratner writes in the preface to his book:

We believed strongly that the president, acting unilaterally, did not have the right ... simply to designate people for detention, hold them incommunicado, deny court review, and throw away the key. At that time we could not even imagine the abuses that have now [in 2004] been revealed. We began to round up other lawyers to work with us, but it was not an easy task ... And we got plenty of hate mail, especially early on, for our representation of the Guantanamo detainees.[33]

The CCR took its case through the American court system, first losing at the trial level and then at the district court before a surprisingly positive ruling was handed down by the Supreme Court (*Rasul et al. vs. Bush*) in June 2004. By a 6 to 3 vote the Court decided that U.S. federal courts had jurisdiction to determine the legality of prisoners held at Guantanamo, in effect restoring due process and declaring the military commissions illegal. This ruling, along with media revelations of the conditions at Abu Ghraib and Guantanamo, forced the Bush administration onto the defensive as the Pentagon and CIA moved to ameliorate some of its worst "detention methods."

In October 2006, however, Congress passed the Military Commissions Act (MCA), which essentially overrode the Supreme Court decision as it restored power to the executive in its empowerment of the commissions. All the previous claims—virtually every one a violation of international law—were restored through legislative action. Harsh methods of interrogation seemed to be validated within the vague and slippery language of the Act. More disturbing, the MCA gave the President authority to reconfigure both Geneva III and the War Crimes Act of 1996, presumably to give U.S. personnel immunity from prosecution under international law, including for charges of torture. The MCA received little attention in the American mainstream media.[34] In June 2007, however, as discussed previously, a federal judge ruled against the commissions on grounds they lacked jurisdiction over prisoners of war—again refuting the Bush–Pentagon contention that Guantanamo detainees were "unlawful combatants." Despite this legal setback, the Pentagon vowed to push ahead with its special prosecution of captives—a maneuver that further isolated the U.S. from the global human rights community, until President Obama issued an executive order in January 2009 closing down Guantanamo (to be implemented within a year).

In the end, the torture regimen set in motion at Guantanamo was counterproductive as well as illegal. Horrendous conditions and practices rarely produced useful information to U.S. interrogators fully convinced they could force valuable intelligence out of high-level terrorists. Some released prisoners said they were questioned up to 200 times and subjected to a variety of harsh and cruel techniques—beatings, stress methods, food and sleep deprivation, and so forth—but any statements they furnished under such pressure were typically worthless, either mundane or false.[35] By June 2004 only three of a total of 650 prisoners were actually charged with a crime and no one had yet been convicted. The White House and Pentagon believed that, by assembling hundreds of Taliban and Al Qaeda operatives at Guantanamo, enough intelligence could be gathered to decisively give the U.S. an upper hand in the war on terror, saving perhaps thousands of American lives. In spring 2004 General Geoffrey Miller, a veteran of Abu Ghraib, was sent to Guantanamo with the mission of pushing an aggressive interrogation regimen. But little was ultimately gained: it turned out that few upper-echelon fighters had been sent to Guantanamo and that, in any case, most information gotten by means of torture was simply fabricated. As Rose points out: "Multiple sources have confirmed that none of Al Qaeda's known leadership has ever been held at Gitmo."[36] And the supposed "confessions" and other responses, he added, uniformly turned out to be false.[37]

As of early 2009, fewer than 250 detainees were being housed at Guantanamo, and their cases were being reviewed in anticipation of the base closing. The Bush administration, as in its tenacious pursuit of the Iraq war and occupation, remained stubborn in its flagrant outlawry until the very end. The commissions, agencies of sham justice subverting even military law, had come under intensified opposition, much of it from Europe and even from within the U.S. political and military establishment. Sadly, for several years a number of American professions were seduced by this criminal enterprise, tainting their credibility: law, medicine, and psychology above all. Debates have raged within these professions. Doctors were involved in medicating and drugging prisoners at various locations. Ratner and Ray write: "It is terrible having the doctors play a part in this ... It smacks of what Nazi doctors did during World War II. It seems the medical profession has an obligation to speak out, to say that no doctor can ethically work with the people at Guantanamo."[38] Some medical people did indeed speak out, but not enough to overturn this sordid partnership. Many lawyers too denounced the entire

Guantanamo arrangement, as did some psychologists who sought to pass resolutions condemning illegal practices at their professional conventions, but with only limited success.

Meanwhile, Guantanamo has shattered the lives of many people—a good number of them probably innocent or guilty of minor crimes—since late 2001. Hundreds have been essentially kidnapped, kept in horrid conditions without due process, and quite often tortured in some way. The prisons have done plenty to generate more hatred of the U.S. while revealing once again the outrageous degree of U.S. criminality. An American lawyer who once sought to represent detainees and visited Guantanamo remarked: "There seems to be a new world order, an acceptance of utter illegality. You have all these wonderful treaties after World War Two—the Geneva Conventions, bans on torture—and all of them have been torn up. Effectively you are allowing international law to be rewritten."[39]

ABU GHRAIB: CHAMBER OF HORRORS

The shocking criminal abuses of prisoners at the Abu Ghraib facility outside of Baghdad first became known to the American (and world) public in April 2004, when the TV program *60 Minutes II* broke a story with photographs detailing torture and humiliation of Iraqi inmates during 2003. At about the same time Seymour Hersh wrote an article for *The New Yorker* (May 10, 2004) reporting essentially the same litany of abuses.[40] The astonishingly large number of acts, spanning many different types of abuses, were said to be committed by personnel of the 372nd Military Police Company, the CIA, and other U.S. agencies. On the *60 Minutes* program moderated by Dan Rather, Brigadier General Mark Kimmit, then deputy director of Coalition operations in Iraq, said: "I'd like to sit here and say that these are the only prisoner abuse cases we are aware of but we know that there have been some other ones since we've been here in Iraq." Former Marine Lt. Col. Bill Cowan was also interviewed, admitting: "We went into Iraq to stop things like this from happening, and indeed here they are happening under our tutelage."[41]

In reality the chamber of horrors at several Iraqi detention centers during the U.S. occupation had already become widely known to investigators—as had those in Afghanistan and Guantanamo. Reports surfaced of widespread criminal mistreatment, lack of due process, and harsh interrogation methods at least a year before the *60 Minutes* feature. Pentagon and CIA torture practices, many of them carried out at secret locations, were hardly a secret within the human rights community. Already in April–May 2003 the International Red Cross and other human rights groups were complaining about U.S. mistreatment of Iraqi, Taliban, Al Qaeda, and other detainees, many held incommunicado and/or without charges being filed against them. As early as January 13, 2004, a U.S. military policeman gave army investigators a computer disk containing graphic photos of abuse at Abu Ghraib. Information became available that torture and kindred abuses, some leading to death, had been practiced routinely at four other prisons aside from Abu Ghraib—abuses that most independent observers soon identified as war crimes. A report (in April 2004) by Major General Antonio Taguba concluded that Iraqi prisoners were subjected to "sadistic, blatant, and wanton criminal abuses."[42] Interviewed shortly thereafter, President Bush said the abuse was "abhorrent" and "does not represent the America that I know," but he never offered any apology nor did he move toward disciplining or removing high-level military officers whose commands extended to the detention centers in Iraq.[43]

By May 2004 terrible reports, photos, videos, and witness testimony regarding Abu Ghraib abuses continued to surface. According to this accumulated evidence, dogs had attacked and intimidated prisoners, naked prisoners were beaten and even shot for misbehavior, poisonous snakes were set on prisoners, and groups of naked detainees were forced into piles on the prison floor for the amusement of guards. Indeed the list of horrors was seemingly endless: pouring acid on captives, sodomizing prisoners with batons and other items, urinating on detainees, tying ropes on prisoners' legs and dragging them across the floor, jumping on detainees legs and other body parts, constant taunting of prisoners, deprivation of sleep and food, to name the most egregious. Many prisoners died of the horrific treatment while perhaps others wanted to die. According to the testimony of Ameen Saeed Al-Sheik, "They said we will make you wish to die and it will not happen ... They stripped me naked. One of them told me he would rape me ... and makes me stand in a shameful position holding my buttocks."[44] Prisoners were hooded, shackled, and forced into stress positions as part of regular procedures at U.S.-operated prisons, which housed thousands of detainees. In some measure this abuse was a product of harsh and coercive interrogation methods long practiced by the CIA and the Pentagon; they were scarcely novel, except perhaps for the scope. In 2004 a Red Cross investigation concluded that in military intelligence work at Abu Ghraib "methods of physical and psychological coercion used by the interrogators appeared to be part of the standard operating procedures by military intelligence personnel to obtain confessions and extract information."[45] The horrors inflicted at Abu Ghraib and elsewhere, however, more often seemed unrelated to strict interrogation processes but rather fell into the category of sadistic mistreatment and punishment. Thus in August 2004 a military investigator reported that soldiers charged with criminal activity said they were "joking around, having some fun during the night shift."[46]

The events at Abu Ghraib, of course, were ultimately just one episode within the larger pattern of U.S. military occupation, bringing several years of ongoing death and destruction to Iraq. Indeed prison abuse formed a logical part of the general mosaic, established in Washington and carried out with cruel rationality in the field where U.S. troops were perpetually surrounded by "enemies" viewed as terrorists and ordinary criminals. The atmosphere was pervasive: not only detention centers but homes, checkpoints, urban neighborhoods, and roadways became arenas of armed contestation, including arrests, beatings, home invasions, shootings, bombings, and massacres carried out routinely. Reports that U.S. military leaders ordered routine beatings of Iraqis were increasingly common from 2003 onward. Troops were ordered to "crank up the violence level" in the struggle to quell insurgency—all methods justified by an implacably evil opponent. Marine Corporal Saul Lopezromo said the general combat atmosphere permitted beatings, torture, and killings at random, both in and out of the prisons. Following a procedure called "dead-checking," moreover, it had become almost de rigueur for American troops to simply go ahead and kill the wounded according to the maxim "if somebody is worth shooting once, they're worth shooting twice."[47] Such atrocities were rarely covered by the press, suggesting an indifference born of a mixture of arrogance and adaptation to routine. Here the media and public outrage over torture at Abu Ghraib represents a departure from the norm.

At Abu Ghraib, although investigations revealed that abuses took place in a context of orders from above, media and political focus settled on lower-level military guards at the site—those who acknowledged guilt in most cases but who uniformly said they were following commands to "soften up" and otherwise intimidate prisoners, at least partly to gain intelligence. It was these lower-level personnel, moreover, who would receive the brunt of the punishment. One such guard was Specialist Charles Graner, considered a ringleader at Abu Ghraib, who had become a bible-thumping superpatriot after 9/11 and was a veteran of the 1991 Gulf War. Graner habitually left biblical scriptures engraved in his front yard at home in Pennsylvania. Described as a wonderful dad and husband by friends, Graner was viewed as "just an all-around good kid" by his fellow soldiers, another gung-ho patriot. Once back in Iraq, however, Graner's sadistic side apparently surfaced full-force as reports indicated that he loved to punch detainees and had a special preference for stacking up and taunting naked Iraqis.[48] In the end Graner was found guilty, in January 2005, on several counts: conspiracy to maltreat detainees, failing to protect prisoners from abuse, and cruelty as well as assault, indecency, adultery, and obstruction of justice. He was sentenced to ten years in federal prison.

Another instigator of the Abu Ghraib horrors was Pfc. Lynndie England, not quite as religious or superpatriotic as Graner but equally zealous in carrying out the mayhem. When first interviewed she was rather flippant, suggesting that the actions in question were "basically just us fooling around" and that "we thought it looked funny, so pictures were taken." Ultimately both England and Graner told investigators they were following orders to "soften up" prisoners. Convicted (in September 2005) of conspiracy, mistreating detainees, and an indecent act, England faced a ten-year sentence but was given three years and a dishonorable discharge. Other lower-level soldiers convicted included Sgt. Michael Smith (several charges), sentenced in March 2006 to 179 days in prison and a bad-conduct discharge; Sgt. Santos Cardona (assault and dereliction of duty), sentenced to 90 days hard labor and then transferred and promoted; Specialist Jeremy Sivits (several charges), sentenced in May 2004 to one year with a bad-conduct discharge; Sgt. Javal Davis (battery, dereliction of duty, making false statements), sentenced in February 2005 to six months with a bad-conduct discharge; Sgt. Ivan Frederick (several charges), sentenced in October 2004 to eight years and a dishonorable discharge; Specialist Sabrina Harman (several charges), sentenced in May 2005 to six months with a bad-conduct discharge. A few others involved in the abuses received lesser punishment while some (for example Corporal Joshua Lee Betts) were cleared of all charges owing to insufficient evidence.[49]

What then of the higher-level military officers in charge of operations in Iraq? What of the larger chain of command going all the way to Washington? As mentioned, both Graner and England—

along with several others convicted at Abu Ghraib—said they were essentially following orders. In fact military reports indicated that Colonel Thomas Pappas, commander of an intelligence unit at Abu Ghraib, and Lt. Col. Steven Jordan bore serious responsibility for the abuses but were "not directly involved" and therefore would not be prosecuted. Pappas was eventually relieved of his command in May 2005 after receiving non-judicial punishment for dereliction of duty (such as allowing dogs to be present during interrogations) and a reprimand that effectively ended his military career. Lt. Col. Jordan was the highest-ranking army officer to face charges—twelve in all, with eight of them dismissed—but in August 2007 he was acquitted and received only a reprimand for disobeying an order not to publicly discuss the prisoner-abuse investigations. Brigadier General Janis Karpinski, Abu Ghraib commandant during 2003–04, was removed from her position and demoted to colonel in May 2005, ending her chances of further career advancement. Both Karpinski and Pappas indicated that authority for the abuses came from General Ricardo Sanchez, the U.S. commander in Iraq at the time, and that those convicted were being used as scapegoats for policies that at least informally had encouraged harsh treatment to get information regarding the insurgency. These allegations were naturally denied by General Sanchez as well as by General Geoffrey Miller, in charge of all U.S. detention facilities, who said (quite rightly) that no official statements or memos traceable to prison abuses could ever be located. Neither General Sanchez nor General Miller was allowed to retire on the best terms, but at the same time they were given no punishment.

Karpinski and Pappas were obviously right in their contention, as were soldiers who said they were just following orders: as we have seen, torture and other forms of prisoner abuse had in fact become a staple of Pentagon and CIA detention programs, intensified after 9/11, while extraordinary methods (including what is generally considered torture) were justified at the highest levels of government and military. We have also seen how widespread abuses were practiced and defended at Guantanamo, in Afghanistan, and other locations where prisoners in the "war on terrorism" were held. In this charged environment it would be preposterous *not* to view the crimes at Abu Ghraib as part of a larger agenda congruent with the war on terrorism. It might well be that operatives involved in prison abuses were poorly trained and over-stressed, or were inadequately informed of Geneva III provisions, but that hardly furnishes a thorough view of the larger picture. A Human

Rights Watch report in April 2005 described Abu Ghraib as simply one facet of a much larger operation. According to HRW special counsel Reed Brody: "Abu Ghraib was only the tip of the iceberg. It's now clear that abuse of detainees has happened all over—from Afghanistan to Guantanamo Bay to a lot of third-world dungeons where the United States has sent prisoners. And probably quite a few other places we don't even know about." Brody added that, in the case of General Sanchez in Iraq, the fact widespread criminal activities went on directly under his command and he failed to halt them makes him legally culpable.[50] In the end, not surprisingly, the higher-echelon figures—from Sanchez to Rumsfeld, Gonzales, and Bush—were given the full benefit of the doubt and spared genuine legal, media, and political scrutiny.

Documents obtained by the American Civil Liberties Union (ACLU) and some media outlets reveal that General Sanchez did in fact authorize use of military dogs, temperature extremes, and sensory deprivation as part of ongoing interrogation methods at Abu Ghraib, apparently validating claims that guards were just following orders.[51] According to Karpinski, such orders went all the way up to Secretary Rumsfeld—a clear violation of Geneva III and the Torture Convention, if true. Predictably, both Sanchez and Rumsfeld denied such charges. But Rumsfeld at least accepted responsibility, saying he felt terrible about mistreatment of detainees and emphasizing "it was un-American [and] inconsistent with the values of our nation." His main complaint (on May 7, 2004) seemed to be elsewhere, however: "We're functioning in a ... wartime situation, in the information age, where people are running around with digital cameras and taking these unbelievable photographs and then passing them off, against the law, to the media, to our surprise, when they [the photos] had not even arrived at the Pentagon."[52] In any event, efforts to depict U.S. torture and other abuses as an aberration, as "un-American" as the product of a few out-of-control sadistic prison guards, could not be sustained given the broader context: policies formulated in Washington, similar practices carried out elsewhere, and the fierce hostility toward Iraqis generated by the occupation. The prolonged and effective insurgency, rooted in an urban-based guerrilla campaign, obviously caught the U.S. war planners off guard, giving rise to desperate military attempts (with limited troops) to crush the opposition with harsh methods. No one should be astonished to find that such methods would include the kinds of abuses prevalent at Abu Ghraib.

In the end, moral outrage over the Abu Ghraib events did not seem to reverberate very deeply across the political culture or within the military establishment. The general outlook appeared to be that the abuses were isolated, at odds with American traditions, and, however shocking, clearly understandable in the epic struggle to defeat the plague of terrorism. A common response was to minimize or deflect attention from the events. Thus Senator James Inhofe (R–Oklahoma), a leading member of the Senate Armed Services Committee, mocked the idea that the abuses deserved outrage: "I'm probably not the only one up at this table more outraged by the outrage than we are by the treatment [because they] are not there for traffic violations ... They're murderers, they're terrorists, they're insurgents. Many of them probably have American blood on their hands. And here we're so concerned about the treatment of those individuals." [53] Said radio host Rush Limbaugh, whose audience numbers several million: "This is not different than what happens at the Skull and Bones initiation and we're going to ruin people's lives over it and we're going to hamper our military effort, and then we are going to really hammer them because they had a good time. You know, these people are being fired at every day. I'm talking about people having a good time, these people, you ever heard of emotional release?" [54] Fouad Ajami, director of Middle East Studies at Johns Hopkins, commented that most of the anger over Abu Ghraib was "contrived anger" outside Iraq—most of it coming from people who never uttered a word about Saddam Hussein's atrocities. [55] As for the Pentagon, it spoke loudly when, in summer 2006, General Miller—supervisor of detainee operations at Guantanamo and Abu Ghraib—was allowed to retire without facing disciplinary action of any sort. On the contrary, Miller was awarded a Distinguished Service Medal and praised by Rumsfeld for an outstanding career at the very time HRW said he should be hiring lawyers for his defense rather than getting military awards.

In the documentary *Ghosts of Abu Ghraib* (2007), Rory Kennedy's interviews with participants in the events revealed a similar willingness to downplay or even justify the mistreatment. One or two of the guards expressed some contrition, as did Karpinski who, as in the case of others on the scene, framed the problem in more general terms: soldiers, fearful, stressed out, and vengeful were turned into robots simply following orders, or at least what they believed were expectations in a difficult war to defeat terrorists. Most interviewees justified the horrors which, regrettably, were unavoidable in dealing with a large assemblage of ruthless criminals bent on mayhem and violence. Others responded that the prison activities in question were simply a matter of business-as-usual, of troops behaving as might be expected in a frenzied combat situation; no moral criteria entered the picture. The fact that so many detainees were stripped naked, sexually intimidated or violated, beaten, hooded, shackled, handcuffed, and forced into stress positions—not to mention sleep-deprived—provoked little if any outrage at the scene. One of those convicted, Specialist Sabrina Harman, spoke at length about the atrocities as if she were describing a movie or tennis match: it was all in a day's work, nothing special. Photographed laughing next to an Iraqi corpse, she was totally unapologetic, explaining that she *always* liked to smile for photos. Another participant revealed that any soldiers publicly critical of the atrocities at the time—there were a few—had to be quickly sent back to the States before they too wound up as casualties. A few commentators argued that the events of Abu Ghraib could be traced back to a certain darkness in human nature which, if true, would at least morally exonerate those Americans culpable of war crimes. What emerged from *Ghosts of Abu Ghraib* was a bleak and depressing picture of military behavior, where moral and legal restraints had essentially vanished.

Media revelations of what took place at Abu Ghraib—as well as other U.S.-run detention centers—gave rise to a series of investigations, including one authored (in summer 2004) by Generals George R. Fay and Anthony R. Jones, which recommended charges against 41 people assigned to Abu Ghraib at the time of the abuses. A report by General Antonio M. Taguba (February 2004) identified command failures and wrongdoing by several military-police troops. Yet another investigation led by Lt. General Paul T. Mikolashek, army Inspector General, concluded that the problem was one of a breakdown of military procedures and that the abuses were "aberrations from the norm." These and later inquiries were *internal*—that is, conducted by the military itself—leaving only to outright speculation what an independent report might have found. Such investigations wound up sidestepping what had become obvious: the prison abuses in Iraq (and elsewhere) were systemic and far-reaching, going all the way to the top military and government leadership in Washington, symbolizing in many ways the general horrors of U.S. intervention in Iraq.

A subsequent episode of the protracted Abu Ghraib saga came in late 2007 with the farcical trial of Lt. Col. Steven Jordan, the highest-ranking officer actually living at the prison in 2003 and commonly referred to as the "mayor of Abu Ghraib." Since Jordan had effective oversight of all activities at the detention center, he was someone who ought to have been held fully accountable for the atrocities—and indeed he was the only officer the army decided to bring to court martial. He was charged with several counts of prisoner abuse but these charges were dropped as the prosecution opted instead to pursue a count of disobeying superior orders during the Abu Ghraib investigations that could have meant five years in prison. Found guilty, Jordan ultimately received only a mild reprimand and the conviction was eventually erased from his military record.[56]

Throughout his trial Jordan was treated with great courtesy, even by prosecutors, as the proceedings appeared set up to diminish the gravity of what had taken place at Abu Ghraib. Jordan's role in the events was deliberately made ambiguous, as if the superior officer had little knowledge of what was happening in his domain.[57] The defense team argued that the defendant was completely oblivious to the abuse which, in fact, had become increasingly routine by fall 2003. Investigations by General Taguba and others revealed that Colonel Jordan was responsible for ensuring that interrogation techniques would facilitate the "flow of data." According to one testimony, by Sgt. Sam Provance: "Col. Jordan and Capt. [Carolyn] Wood were the people running the show. They would be together. They would be like mom and dad. You had this feeling of family there. Everyone was so friendly and loving."[58] Why the army decided to let Jordan off with just a token punishment is difficult to fathom, and has never been adequately explained. One possibility is the sickening ethos of denial surrounding the Abu Ghraib events. Another is the willingness of people within the military culture to come to the defense of a colleague seen, in the final analysis, as just a good soldier doing the best job he could under trying circumstances. Testifying on Jordan's behalf, Colonel Robert Norton said: "He's a man I'd go to war with in a heartbeat. He was a team player." Also singing the praises of Jordan as just another hard-working army officer were representatives of Northrop-Grumman, ITT, General Dynamics, and other military contractors ready to protect a compatriot in the business of extending U.S. imperial power.

In summer 2007 a report of the International Committee of the Red Cross (finally revealed in early 2009) concluded that treatment of prisoners at the hands of the Bush administration involved repeated practices of cruel and degrading treatment—that is, "torture." The report was based on extensive interviews with U.S. detainees at Guantanamo and elsewhere, including infamous "black site" CIA locations. The brutality included beatings, people being slammed into walls, waterboarding, and exposure to extremes of heat and cold. In December 2008 the U.S. Senate issued a bipartisan report concluding that decisions made at the top of the chain of command—citing Secretary of Defense Rumsfeld in particular—were a "direct cause" of detainee abuses at Abu Ghraib, Guantanamo, and elsewhere. The Bush administration was blamed for creating a legal and moral climate in which sustained abuses, including physical pressures and mental degradation, could take place. This report, based on an 18-month investigation in which thousands of documents were reviewed and 70 people interviewed, went against the standard conclusions reached by most earlier *internal* military reports that rejected systemic interpretations while exculpating higher-echelon officials.

MERCENARY TERRORISM

The kind of atrocities committed at Guantanamo and Abu Ghraib, as previously in Vietnam, are no longer restricted to military units: the past two decades have seen the rapid growth of corporate warriors—referred to as Professional Military Corporations (PMCs)—that came into vogue with the Bush administration and its emphasis on a "Revolution in Military Affairs" (RMA). These "private soldiers," mostly highly paid support operatives, have come to perform a wide range of battlefield, security, and "reconstruction" activities at a time when the Pentagon has encountered ongoing recruitment crises. Now a $100 billion a year industry, PMCs like MPRI, DynCorp, Blackwater, and KBR draw from experienced combat veterans around the world to provide vital military and other skills. Over time the PMCs have developed a strong interest in war, in promoting aggressive military policies, and in pursuing combat ventures wherever U.S. geopolitical interests dictate. Their militarism stems from a mixture of profit-making and patriotism, infused with a love of battlefield combat. A major problem with PMCs, however, is their near-total immunity from legal sanctions in the countries where they operate—to some extent, indeed, from international rules of engagement. As of late 2008 there were an estimated 100,000 private warriors in Iraq alone (with some projections even higher), hired by the very companies involved at Abu Ghraib and other detention centers. Critics label the PMCs an outlaw force beholden to no domestic or global authority.

In September 2007 guards employed by the security corporation Blackwater USA were accused of shooting to death 17 Iraqi civilians while protecting a State Department motorcade in Baghdad. Angered Iraqi officials immediately moved to cancel Blackwater's license to operate in the country—the first effort of a government compromised by occupation to assert itself against foreign security contractors long accused of outlaw behavior in the streets of Baghdad and other cities. (Within a few days, of course, the license was reaffirmed.) Since 2003 the PMCs, crucial to the U.S. agenda in Iraq, had been subordinate only to their State Department employers, who gave them virtually free rein. The Iraq national security adviser, Mowaffak Rubale, said his government should use the September 2007 episode to begin overhauling private security guards' immunity from Iraqi jurisdiction, granted by Coalition Provisional Authority head L. Paul Bremer III in 2003 and later extended—a measure called CPA Order 17, passed outside any democratic process. While many Iraqis demanded that the Blackwater operatives be held legally accountable for murder, there were no procedures in place to do so. In fact the PMCs were not even subject to Universal Code of Military Justice rules, in Iraq or anywhere else.[59]

The September 2007 incident was only one of many where private security contractors employed by the U.S. shot and killed Iraqi civilians. Despite reports of these and other atrocities, including torture, no PMC employee was ever prosecuted in the U.S. or Iraq, although they are theoretically accountable to American domestic laws. Witnesses said 13 people were wounded along with the 17 killed when the security convoy came speeding by Nisoor Square at the edge of the Mansour district in western Baghdad. Although U.S. Embassy and Blackwater officials claimed the convoy had come under fire, Iraqi witnesses at the scene reported that no one had attacked the convoy.[60] Blackwater said their personnel were simply returning fire, part of a defensive response. Based in Moyock, New Jersey, and founded by a former Navy SEAL, Blackwater as of late 2008 hired nearly a thousand people in Iraq, being praised by the Pentagon as a vital partner of the U.S. military. The September 2007 killings were investigated by the Iraq Interior Ministry, which concluded that the armed guards fired on civilians without provocation. Yet the U.S. Embassy almost immediately agreed to allow Blackwater to resume its work, thumbing its nose at domestic authorities that, in any case, have no leverage in dealing with military occupation forces. In the aftermath of the incident Secretary of State Condoleezza Rice quickly defended Blackwater, saying "we have needed and received the protection of Blackwater for a number of years now."[61]

The State Department contended that Blackwater and other PMCs do not require a license from the Iraqi government to perform their security functions since their contracts are authorized directly by U.S. officials—a peculiar notion for those claiming to bring democracy to Iraq. Even American officials, however, admitted that previous PMC misdeeds in Iraq had been swept under the rug; there was never any criminal liability. "It's one of the big holes we've had in our policy, the lack of control, the lack of supervision over the security force," according to one U.S. diplomat in the field. "No one took on the responsibility of policing these units—neither the military nor the Regional Security Office [of the Embassy]. So many people, not just the Blackwater people, are there in Baghdad unsupervised with basically diplomatic immunity."[62] PMC operations in Iraq were described as "carte blanche," as in the Wild West, with armed mercenaries roaming the land freely. (Whether the term "mercenary" fits the PMCs is problematic insofar as few, if any, of the operatives are paid combat soldiers; they are support personnel.) The diplomat said that incident reports were a whitewash, and nobody did anything about them, adding that in a few cases Blackwater and other corporations fired workers for killing civilians, but those same workers could be back in Iraq with another firm in a few months, part of a "revolving door." Observed one security contractor quoted by the *Los Angeles Times*: "They are all untouchable. They've shot up other private security contractors, Iraqi military police, and civilians, often pushing themselves through crowded urban streets in the process."[63] The vast majority of these incidents went entirely unreported.

There is actually nothing new about U.S. reliance on corporate-funded mercenaries—the Pentagon, State Department, and CIA have employed some variant of PMCs for many years—but since the early 1990s their rapid growth in the field has deeply influenced military operations. Since 1994 the Pentagon alone has entered into 3600 contracts with twelve U.S. companies worth more than $300 billion.[64] One great advantage of PMCs over regular military units is loosened oversight and regulations, allowing for greater secrecy and latitude in dealing with rules of engagement. Since their work is often depicted as "humanitarian," the PMCs usually receive less political fallout when things go wrong—although revelations of the 2007 Blackwater atrocities in Iraq augured something of a change in this.[65] (By January 2009, in fact, Blackwater's license to operate in Iraq had been revoked.) In Saudi Arabia, MPRI, Vinnell, and DynCorp have trained security forces well known for their use of torture. Based in Falls Church, Virginia, DynCorp International has worked closely with the U.S. military in Afghanistan, Iraq, Bolivia, Bosnia, Somalia, Haiti, Colombia, Kosovo, and Kuwait, where it trains local police and military forces. In Colombia it helped the army eradicate coca crops and crush rebellions, often taking on direct combat roles. In most cases the PMCs had no legal standing but were highly potent armed units ready for action.[66]

As for DynCorp, which receives 96 percent of its two billion dollars annual revenue from the federal government, its employees have been implicated in the trafficking of women and children in Bosnia during the late 1990s, although no one ever faced criminal sanctions. In Afghanistan the firm has come under heavy criticism for aggressive tactics in its training and oversight of local police forces.[67] The situation in Iraq, predictably, has been even worse. In September 2005 General Karl Horst, deputy commander of the Third Infantry Division, complaining about DynCorp and other PMCs, said: "These guys run loose in this country and do stupid stuff. There's no authority over them, so you can't come down hard on them when they escalate force ... They shoot people, and someone else has to deal with the aftermath. It happens all over the place."[68]

In May 2007 the ACLU filed suit against a Boeing Company subsidiary accused of facilitating CIA programs involving torture and other abuses. Since 2001 Jeppeson Dataplan, Inc., of San Jose, was reported to have provided services to the CIA for its "extraordinary rendition" programs scattered across numerous locations. According to the suit filed by three plaintiffs, the firm assisted the CIA in carrying out more than 70 rendition activities, based on investigations conducted in Spain, Sweden, Italy, and Pakistan. The company was said to be involved in extracting "confessions" as part of the war on terrorism. The ACLU went to court under the Alien Tort Claims Act of 1789, which allows foreigners to file suits in U.S. courts for human rights violations.[69] In February 2009, however, the Obama administration urged the Federal Court of Appeals to throw out the lawsuit, invoking the infamous "state secrets" privilege that Bush had repeatedly used, insisting that all CIA programs should be kept secret as a matter of "national security."

In the case of Blackwater, its fortunes skyrocketed in the wake of 9/11, the war on terrorism, and the U.S. invasion of Iraq, giving rise to a reinforced "Praetorian Guard" presence in the Middle East and beyond. According to Jeremy Scahill, PMCs like Blackwater represent a dramatic new phase in Pentagon evolution where "privatization" and outsourcing of military activity permit greater strategic flexibility along with lessened political and legal account-ability—not to mention enhanced corporate profits.[70] Thus: "With almost no public debates, the Bush administration has outsourced to the private sector many of the functions historically handled by the military."[71] And: "Private forces are almost a necessity for a United States bent on retaining its declining empire."[72] In a context of military occupation as in Iraq, moreover, Blackwater and kindred contractors have provided crucial infrastructural and security functions, allowing the military to concentrate on combat operations, as the PMCs escape institutional and legal accountabil-ity. Since they are outside the law, operatives working for private contractors can often get away with all manner of anti-social behavior and human rights violations leading up to torture and murder. According to Scahill, Iraq witnessed a wave of abductions, torture, and killings at the hands of PMC operatives similar to the U.S.-sponsored death-squad horrors in Central America during the 1980s. By late 2006, when an average of nearly 1000 Iraqis were being killed every week, "the big-picture reality was that the country was quickly becoming the global epicenter of privatized warfare with scores of heavily-armed groups of various loyalties and agendas roaming Iraq."[73] In this setting it is hardly surprising to find PMC groups described as Storm Troopers, in this case possessing their own private aircraft, vehicles, weapons caches, and communications systems. Of course the people who run the PMCs see their work differently, as a vehicle of peace, democracy, and stability.

In February 2007, to cite another flagrant instance of PMC mayhem, a sniper killed three guards outside the state-run Iraqi Media Network office in Baghdad. An investigation quickly revealed that Blackwater was guilty, but no one was ever charged much less convicted of what was an attack on a news outlet considered less than friendly to the U.S. occupation. Everything was kept silent behind a great wall of secrecy. One American official even conceded: "Because they [contractors] are security, everything was a big secret. They draw the wagon circle. They protect each other."[74] There are massive efforts to protect the guilty, who already benefit from an immunity shield, answering (in the case of Blackwater) only to the U.S. Embassy security staff. Added one Iraqi government official: "They don't have car licenses. They don't have any names.

Nobody knows who they are. If they are asked anyway, they bully people."[75] Another Iraqi official referred to the PMC operatives, quite appropriately, as nothing but a pack of criminals.

The U.S. government does not count PMC workers as soldiers and therefore does not count those killed while on duty as part of overall casualty statistics, allowing this significant part of military engagement to be hidden from view. It is generally believed, moreover, that "privatization" augments the corporate potential for war-making profits. And since PMCs function mostly outside any system of legality, their capacity to commit atrocities of the sort attributed to Blackwater in September 2007 is heightened. Rules of engagement are thrown to the wind. It is for this and other reasons that such contracting work was declared illegal by the Geneva Conventions. At the same time, the oft-heard argument that PMCs constitute a fundamental remaking of the U.S. war machine or allow for a renovated combat force seems far-fetched. After all, the familiar military-industrial complex has always been just that, a tight, ever-expanding partnership between the Pentagon and huge corporations with consistently high profits accruing to dozens of major contractors. Viewed thusly, "privatization" hardly suggests a radical departure from the past but rather a different arrangement of priorities within the larger war machine. As for U.S. personnel in the field, while military forces are indeed subject to more rigid formal controls than workers at the PMCs, their record of war crimes and human rights abuses has nonetheless far exceeded that of the private contractors, even in Iraq. The PMCs, which have actually been deployed for decades, must therefore be seen as just an augmented extension of Pentagon operations instead of some new out-of-control monster.

OUTLAWRY AND DENIAL

What generalizations, then, can be set forth about the U.S. legacy of atrocities (including torture) of the kind explored in this chapter? What are the historical circumstances surrounding American global outlawry? We have already seen how practices of illegal detention, murder, assassination, torture, and myriad human rights abuses are neither isolated nor particularly novel but fit a longstanding pattern of behavior geared to imperial ambitions going back long before the Bush administration. Barbarism is not the product of mistakes or deviations from supposedly exemplary professional norms, much less the evil machinations of a few sadistic thugs. Such outlaw behavior perfectly coincides with U.S. imperial objectives that only became more aggressive with the rise of Bush and the neocons. We have seen how national exceptionalism, demonization of foreign targets, growth of military violence, and spread of U.S. global power have fed this logic. In the present context, it is easy enough to see how media and political stereotyping of Arabs and Muslims enters into American efforts to control, pacify, and remake the Middle East to suit its own economic and geopolitical ends.

At this historical conjuncture it is undeniably true that brutal practices have been carried out by ordinary soldiers and others driven by a combination of social and psychological forces—fear, conformity, revenge, egoism, hatred of the "enemy." Sadism too enters the picture, but in its absence the legacy of American battlefield crimes would surely be little different. On the other hand, the larger historical pattern suggests that moral and legal responsibility for the outlawry must extend all the way to the top leadership in the Pentagon and White House. We have seen how, in the contemporary situation, practices such as torture have been officially endorsed—or simply ignored—at the commanding heights in Washington, while the CIA is known to have carried out "extraordinary rendition" programs for decades. This means that military commanders in the field, their superiors at the Pentagon, and civilian leaders up to the President could be, indeed *should* be, held accountable for war crimes under provisions of international law and even the War Crimes Act of 1996. According to Nuremberg precedent, senior officials in the chain of command are to be prosecuted for criminal activity that takes place under their authority. In the case of Iraq, however, only lower-level soldiers at Abu Ghraib and elsewhere have been criminally prosecuted and punished; their military and government leaders, responsible for setting the broader agendas, have gotten off unscathed. The same can be said for every U.S.-initiated war in which battlefield atrocities are known to have taken place.

Further, despite a constant flow of rhetoric about human rights and "rule of law," Washington has shown relatively little interest in upholding basic principles of international law throughout the postwar years. As for the order of atrocities discussed in the present chapter, we have seen how the Bush administration not only escaped culpability but deliberately chose policies in direct conflict with international rules and norms. Constraints on action have been resisted at every turn, while secrecy, lies, and cover-ups have been the norm. Investigations into wrongdoing have been mostly *internal* affairs, with the Pentagon typically probing (and policing) its own domain. Penalties for violations have been shockingly few and mild, as detailed above, reflecting a pattern visible in Vietnam and elsewhere. No independent tribunals were ever set up. Meanwhile, Bush was until the end reluctant to abandon harsh and cruel "rendition" techniques long practiced by the CIA (and the Pentagon) and known to be illegal. For example, when the Senate in late 2005 passed a measure prohibiting the U.S. from using "cruel, inhumane, or degrading treatment" on any detainee, anywhere in the world, Bush, threatening a veto, managed to get CIA exemption. Later, in July 2007, Bush signed an executive order clearing the way for the CIA to continue its harsh interrogation methods, thus enabling the intelligence agency to operate according to special rules outside both domestic and international law. And Bush maintained his stance that "foreign terrorists" are not entitled to basic rights under the Geneva Conventions.

General outrage in the U.S. at revelations of torture and other abuses at Guantanamo and Abu Ghraib have been mostly episodic and muted, following the established discourse that such behavior is isolated and marginal, the product of a few renegade thugs. There is a pervasive mood in American society that "excesses" like torture might well be justified in fighting the war on terrorism. Not only law professors such as John Woo and Alan Dershowitz have argued as much, so too have editorials in leading newspapers like the *Wall Street Journal*. Taking a cue from Dershowitz, Mirko Bagaric and Julie Clark insist in their 2007 book *Torture* that such practices are not only permissible but obligatory where harsh treatment of "wrongdoers" might end up saving innocent lives. They argue: "Given the choice between inflicting a relatively small level of harm on a wrongdoer and saving an innocent person, it is verging on moral indecency to prefer the interests of the wrongdoer." They add: "It is indefensible to suggest that there should be any absolute ban on torture."[76] The atrocities explored in this chapter, however, go far beyond the limited examples that Bagaric and Clark have in mind, and the focus easily surpasses the question of information that *might* be gained by means of harsh and cruel "rendition." Further, the very social composition of "wrongdoers" in specific circumstances—for example, the U.S. in Iraq—will likely be just the reverse of what the authors glibly presume.

In the U.S., at least, both media and political culture have long been in a state of denial regarding the historical and systematic character of American outlaw behavior that has resurfaced in Iraq, Afghanistan, and Guantanamo. The issue of torture has never received anything resembling a full public airing much less thorough legal investigation within the framework of an independent tribunal. It has been more business-as-usual for an imperial power whose leaders (and supporters) believe they can set their own rules while engaging in criminal behavior with impunity—fitting the special claims of a great and noble superpower. The dominant belief appears to be that a nation embracing such enlightened goals as democracy, freedom, human rights, and peace ought to be granted broad latitude in its conduct of foreign and military policy, indeed that it should be exempt from precedents and norms routinely applied to other nations. Surveys reveal that more than half of all Americans are prepared to accept torture when it is used against designated enemies—that is, against those already demonized in the media as the "wrongdoers" mentioned above. That "humane treatment" ought to be extended to "terrorists" and kindred villains is frequently ridiculed in the media, especially in prevalently right-wing talk radio. Aside from lawyers and academics, other professionals have sometimes been complicit in an outlaw agenda—for example, psychologists assisting the military in refining its harsh interrogation techniques.[77] In the wake of the Abu Ghraib revelations, it is true, the media and politicians came forth to protest U.S. behavior, but their concerns revolved less around moral revulsion than fears the behavior would be counterproductive to American interests: it could hurt the U.S. "image" abroad and possibly lead to similar cruel treatment of U.S. captives.

In the end, while torture and related forms of violence might be counterproductive to some U.S. military agendas, they are best viewed as endemic to the far-reaching imperial operations of the permanent war economy and security state. As the pattern continues, however, the willful and often brazen use of torture reveals a wealth of insights into the *modus operandi* of an imperial power reluctant to concede limits to its geopolitical aims and international behavior. Integral to a sprawling Leviathan that stands outside all legality, such practices not only recall those of historical fascism but could signify revival of that ideology as the U.S. accelerates its pursuit of global supremacy.

Conclusion: Empire or Survival?

While the ideal of an orderly and peaceful international society grounded in universal norms goes back several centuries, efforts to forge a coherent legal framework—where, among other things, laws of warfare could be agreed upon and codified—began in earnest little more than a century ago. The Hague Conventions of 1899 and 1907 represented a major, though still partial, breakthrough on this terrain. The horrors of World War II, leading to the Nuremberg and Tokyo tribunals, the U.N. Charter, the Universal Declaration of Human Rights, and the 1948 Geneva Convention, gave new impetus to a system of international law that, it was hoped, would at the very least curtail the worst excesses of modern warfare. As we have seen, a new moral *Zeitgeist* evolved, its main premises being the equal standing of all sovereign nations, the principle of national self-determination, and the outlawing of military force except in cases of national self-defense. A new legal order would identify and punish war crimes, crimes against humanity, and human rights abuses while blocking the spread of weapons of mass destruction and, in time, the militarization of outer space. With the nuclear onslaught at Hiroshima and Nagasaki still in clear memory, world leaders were anxious to short-circuit possible doomsday scenarios. This *Zeitgeist* was upheld not only by the U.N. Charter and Geneva statutes but by a series of postwar multinational treaties, the work of Amnesty International and Human Rights Watch, and eventually by the Rome Statutes that gave rise to the International Criminal Court, the first truly independent global tribunal. Indispensable to hopes for a lawful global order were the normative ideals of universality and reciprocity, meaning that no state—regardless of its power and wealth—should be permitted to stand outside the legal consensus.

This postwar order, however, never achieved more than a partial, conflicted outcome in an era of international politics marked by deep conflicts endemic to the world system; the *Zeitgeist* failed to take hold. The promise of a binding legal framework, despite momentary breakthroughs, met with increasing defeat and futility. Over the past few decades the world has descended into a morass of lawlessness that, should it persist or worsen, could threaten future human survival. It would be tempting to identify the problem as that of an amorphous, *general* drift toward Hobbesian chaos and violence—the result of "globalizing," systemic forces at work beyond the control of any specific economic interests or political actors. The main thrust of this book, however, points consistently in another direction: the outlaw behavior of a militaristic United States bent on global domination. Superpower ambitions have inevitably clashed with the requirements of a lawful and peaceful world order, whatever high-sounding rhetoric Washington might invoke to justify its imperial projects. The militaristic outlook that actually *governs* U.S. foreign policy undermines both national and global constraints needed for the advent of genuine internationalism. While many prefer to think that present-day American lawlessness departs radically from the past, as reflected in the Bush Doctrine and the "preemptive" U.S. invasion of Iraq, in fact lawlessness has deep roots in a national exceptionalism that today, as before, extends across the ideological spectrum. The U.S. has been something of a rogue state since its formation—its definition, rationale, and scope having changed to fit new historical circumstances. Today this legacy is powerfully magnified by several conditions: the post-Cold War rise of the U.S. as the lone superpower, the increasingly effective global reach of its war machine, its virtual monopoly of WMD, and the capacity to invoke the "war on terror" in the service of expanded military force and endless war.

By the early twenty-first century, it would not be too far-fetched to depict the U.S. as the foremost menace to planetary survival. Washington has waged illegal warfare in flagrant contempt of the U.N., international law, and world public opinion; carried out indiscriminate attacks on civilians and life-supporting infrastructures; broken or disregarded many international treaties; perpetrated massacres and other atrocities; practiced torture; carried out crimes by proxy; planned the militarization (and possible nuclearization) of outer space; possesses by far the largest nuclear arsenal still encased in first-use "doctrine"; and imposed ruinous sanctions on nations designated as "enemies." This horrific legacy remains very much alive within a still-expanding imperial edifice tied to a permanent war economy, security state, hundreds of military bases scattered across the globe, and a growing presence in outer space. The U.S. military bases house what Chalmers Johnson calls a vigilant stratum of "armed missionaries" whose goal is not so much to spread "American values" as to help consolidate U.S. world supremacy in the shape of a neoliberal order.[1] Since the end of the Cold War the U.S. has built a geopolitical strategy around the resource-laden

Middle East and Central Asia, reinforced by military and support facilities in Qatar, Kuwait, Saudi Arabia, Oman, the United Arab Emirates, Tadjikistan, and Uzbekistan as well as Afghanistan, Iraq, Turkey, and the Balkans—bolstered through alliance with Israel. These bases appear more durable with each passing year, integral to economic and geopolitical agendas not likely to diminish for many decades, if ever. Within this Hobbesian milieu, as Johnson notes, "militarism and imperialism are Siamese twins joined at the hip,"[2] each thriving on the other. It is this pervasive, technologically sophisticated military presence rather than actual conquest of territory that now defines the modern American imperium—a ruthless system justified in the name of high-sounding virtues: peace, democracy, human rights, the rule of law. Yet it is these same "virtues," as we have seen, that American global power has so routinely and recklessly subverted.

For Washington elites the dictates of national power trump those of international legality, as they must for a military behemoth striving for ever-greater global advantage. The system, as I have argued throughout this book, draws its legitimacy from a complex ensemble of economic, political, cultural, and technological resources.[3] What is often called U.S. grand strategy is conceived as a means of creating a favorable balance of forces—that is, abundant space—in which Western corporations can dominate and shape the world economy. Such an industrial and military behemoth cannot function at existing (not to mention *higher*) levels of growth without aggressive pursuit of natural resources, cheap labor, investment options, and political leverage—a stratagem shared equally by Democrats and Republicans. A problem for American society, however, is that such imperial reach demands concentrated state power that is sure to undermine most of what remains of American democratic institutions and practices. As Johnson persuasively argues in his book *Nemesis*, the consequences of Empire predictably militate against a thriving, operational democracy.[4] At the same time, a growing *culture of militarism* has saturated American society as war (and preparation for war) dominates virtually every realm of public life. In a society addicted to war and beset with high levels of civic violence, where militarism approaches a kind of national mythology, legal and moral norms are all-too-often compromised. If, as Chris Hedges writes, "war breaks down long-established prohibitions against violence, destruction, and murder,"[5] then perpetual war and the culture of militarism surrounding it is likely to embolden those lamentable features of U.S. international outlawry and criminality addressed in this book.

Many optimistic Americans believed that the 2008 presidential campaign might signal dramatic changes in U.S. global behavior that would finally dispense with the cowboy image personified by George W. Bush. Of course the candidacy of Senator John McCain offered Republicans the prospect of even grander illusions of Pax Americana at a time when conservative platitudes (free market, family values, fiscal responsibility, reduced government) had lost much of their appeal. McCain relished tales of U.S. military heroics as he pressed for increased Pentagon spending, wider military deployments, and "victory" over "surrender" in Iraq, with a resulting U.S. occupation that could last many decades, perhaps "100 years." The Arizona politician, a Vietnam POW, staunchly backed every U.S. military intervention since World War II and seemed ready for military action against Iran, having famously sung "Bomb, bomb, bomb, bomb Iran" on several occasions. A McCain presidency surely would have heightened U.S. militarism and outlawry, which he (like Bush) justified as part of an endless "war on terrorism." Commenting on McCain's "lust for war," Matt Taibbi wrote: "All they [the Republicans] have left to offer is this sad, dwindling, knee-jerk patriotism, a promise to keep selling world politics as a *McHale's Navy* rerun to a Middle America that wants nothing to do with realizing the world has changed since 1946."[6] However, whether either viable Democratic candidate, Senators Hillary Clinton or Barack Obama, could steer U.S. foreign policy in new directions was always highly problematic. After all, like McCain, they were financially and political beholden to the same corporate interests, the same military-industrial system, the same security state, and the same Israel lobby. With only slight variations, they embraced identical visions of U.S. global supremacy. As mentioned earlier, an imperial Democratic agenda was visible in Obama's call for increases in military spending, more deployments abroad, escalation of the Afghan war, a stepped-up war on terrorism, and seeming willingness to keep U.S. troops in Iraq indefinitely. And Obama did not rule out using military force against Iran. Clinton, the new Secretary of State, also stated that American bases should be maintained in the Middle East without time stipulations and, regarding Iran, reiterated that the Islamic state "poses a threat to our allies and our interests." For these and the majority of Democrats any rejection of Bush's foreign policy was purely instrumental—that is, opposition based on tactics and effectiveness.

This book draws to a close by revisiting the nuclear issue as an especially defining, and fearsome, aspect of U.S. outlawry. As of early 2009 the Pentagon still had plans for a new generation of "usable" mini-nukes designed to meet specific "contingencies," all-the-while retaining its Cold War first-use policy. Despite a series of postwar arms-control measures, the U.S. still possesses an arsenal of several thousand warheads, far more than any conceivable military need. It is strongly allied with three countries—Israel, Pakistan, and India—that do not belong to the NPT and indeed stand in clear violation of its statutes. Ignoring the NPT, the U.S. has given India technological assistance to refine its outlaw nuclear program, while pretending not to notice Israel's even more threatening arsenal. Meanwhile, hypocritical threats from both the U.S. and Israel have been recurrently directed against Iran, an NPT member with a perfectly legal, non-military nuclear program. While officially opposed to WMD proliferation, in reality U.S. nuclear politics works mightily in just the opposite direction: above all, any hopeful nuclear power is bound to be emboldened by the double standards (and threats) emanating from Washington. Meanwhile, the U.S. moved to install "missile shields" in Eastern Europe, on the absurd rationale (invoked by Bush) that Iran posed an imminent atomic threat to Europe. These plans were predictably received by Russia as both threat and provocation—a response widely held across Europe where Iran is correctly viewed as having neither the intent nor resources to launch any long-range military attack. Although the shield was opposed (in 2007) by 70 percent of the Czech public, for example, it continued to be backed by Republicans and Democrats alike, with scarcely any debate or much awareness about the project in American society.[7] (By late 2009, however, President Obama indicated that a reassessment of the missile-shield project was in order, though as of this writing no decision had been made.) Little reflection is needed to see that it is neither Europe nor the U.S. but *Iran* which faces the larger military threat, as it is surrounded by U.S. armed-forces and faces continuous rumblings from U.S. and Israeli leaders about possible military intervention. One result is that both Russia and Iran have been thrust into a predicament where their own arms build-up makes abundantly good sense, especially at a time of perpetual NATO push eastward.

According to the 2007 National Intelligence Estimate (NIE) report, Iran had actually halted its nuclear-weapons program as early as 2003. Yet the Bush administration, determined to fix its military sites on Iran, went into large-scale denial, refusing the data of its own (supposedly reliable) intelligence agencies. For Bush, Iran was more than ever a serious "threat to world peace," a totalitarian menace to its neighbors and others, a source of aid and comfort to global terrorists.[8] (As of early 2009, none of these warmongering views had been disavowed by members of the incoming Obama administration.) For U.S. leaders the NIE report was an embarrassment, as were similar reports by the IAEA indicating that Iran was not close to developing nuclear weapons and, in any event, remained fully within the NPT framework. Ignored by the U.S. government and media was the undeniable fact that civilian nuclear projects had long flourished around the world, many with U.S. blessings and assistance even while some favored nations were permitted to build WMD arsenals entirely *outside* the NPT framework.

Meanwhile, beneath the radar, the U.S. has continued its drive toward military control of outer space, yet another program likely to accelerate global arms competition that could lead to nuclear weapons in space. In the Middle East, Washington's unwavering support of Israel means not only continued Palestinian oppression but endless warfare, spread of terrorism, and denial of a viable political solution—that is, more chaos and violence throughout the region. And nothing changed in the wake of the illegal and bloody Israeli assaults on Gaza in early 2009. More broadly, long before the advent of the Bush Doctrine, the U.S. proclaimed its "right" to militarily intervene anywhere in the world, on its own terms, even where that means violating international law. As for the U.N., Washington has for several decades veered from one extreme to the other—doing everything possible to manipulate the body to serve its own interests, subverting or ignoring it when those efforts failed.[9] Further revealing its disregard for a long list of international rules and agreements, the U.S. remains stubbornly and tragically outside the Kyoto consensus on global warming, obstructing the most hopeful worldwide initiative to reverse the ecological crisis—a dramatic case of the U.S. choosing to put its own industrial growth and corporate profits over environmental sanity.

Despite a widely expected historic turn toward international legality following World War II, therefore, several decades later the grounds for optimism are slim, and will remain so as long as the U.S. stands outside the moral *Zeitgeist* it so fervently championed in 1945 and that even now it ritually upholds as a watershed in the struggle for world peace. The sad reality is that, following Nuremberg, Washington has never supported an independent tribunal with jurisdiction over war crimes, crimes against humanity, and human rights abuses. Never has it departed significantly from its imperial *modus operandi*: local, ad hoc, victor's courts set up under U.S. (and sometimes NATO) aegis to punish its designated villains of the moment. Preferring an ethos of selective justice, the U.S. steadfastly ignored the International Criminal Court, justifiably fearful that such an impartial tribunal might be empowered to try *American* government and military personnel for war crimes. This is just one reason that hopes for prosecuting top Bush administration officials for war crimes in Iraq and elsewhere is now remote: as crude *Machtpolitik* dictates U.S. global behavior, moral and legal principles wind up as so much empty rhetoric. Addressing this superpower morality, Michael Mandel underscores this imperial logic, wondering how "a country so powerful as the United States [might ever decide to] submit itself to the democratic judgment of some impartial tribunal."[10]

Such unrepentant outlawry is no recent development, as we have seen, but grows out of a long tradition of national exceptionalism endowing U.S. global ambitions with an arrogant self-righteousness. The question here revolves around just how long the world can survive this unrestrained outlawry, especially as U.S. hegemony faces new challenges by powerful rivals, not to mention escalating blowback in the form of insurgencies, local movements, and terrorism. By the year 2050 the four largest economies will be China, India, Japan, and the U.S., with rapidly growing nations like Brazil and Indonesia on the horizon. The balance of global power is destined to shift, even as Washington is sure to do all it can to retain military supremacy, giving rise to powerful economic and political challenges to U.S. international leverage and, eventually, to a multipolar world order. In this context the world can look forward to mounting resource wars, renewed arms competition, spread of WMD, and struggles to control outer space—trends already set in motion. Faced with new threats to their hegemony, U.S. leaders might well resist any retrenchment or scaling back of imperial objectives, choosing instead a more defiant aggressiveness marked by Pentagon build-ups, warfare-state expansion, and new military interventions facilitated by the advantages of technowar designed, among other things, to minimize American casualties. (As the U.S. moves steadily toward reliance on a sci-fi battlefield—it currently deploys thousands of drone aircraft and many thousands of other unmanned vehicles, along with a sophisticated network of satellites—Pentagon intervention in remote areas of the globe will encounter fewer impediments, both strategically and ideologically.)

The Iraq venture by itself, projected by a Congressional committee in fall 2007 to cost more than $1.5 trillion, has simultaneously mirrored and exacerbated these trends. According to Joseph Stiglitz and Linda Bilmes, the fiscal drain of Iraq could run eventually beyond *three* trillion dollars—at least double what the Vietnam War cost Americans in taxes, deficits, and lost public services.[11] According to *The Defense Monitor*, the U.S. military budget for 2008 (counting *all* expenditures) was projected at a mammoth $927 billion.[12] This staggering burden will be felt for decades, not only in the U.S. but worldwide. War and occupation have bequeathed astronomic public debt, chaotic oil prices, social and political instability, and lopsided economic development favoring military over civilian priorities—all thanks to ironclad bipartisan support, as imperial Democrats ritually endorse every Pentagon deployment and allocation, their occasional timid reservations soon negated by the pressures of decision-making.

Today the world order faces mounting economic, social, and ecological crises reflected in sharpening class differences, the impoverishment of billions of people, escalating levels of violence, a shriveling of citizenship, and likely irreversible destruction of the global ecology. As these crises ultimately intensify, will the U.S. willingly abandon its drive toward world domination—or even its pursuit of military supremacy? The answer is sure to be: not likely. In that event, U.S. outlawry could reach frightening new levels, with no discernible global counterforce powerful enough to impose limits on the spread of WMD, space militarization, resource wars, crimes of aggression, and the cycle of militarism and terrorism. None of this bodes well for the future of international legality and peaceful relations among nations that just six decades ago was upheld as the great promise of Nuremberg, the U.N. Charter, and the Geneva Conventions.

Postscript:
The Routinization of Mass Murder

Long experience tells us that ordinary people from any background, especially after completing military training, can all too often calmly plan and/or carry out the killing of large numbers of unknown, faceless, innocent, and often defenseless human beings, whether by firing missiles, dropping bombs, shooting long-distance artillery shells, or simply engaging in high-tech ground combat. Many, from the upper-echelon officer to the lowest grunt, have been capable of participating in massacres of civilians. Only rarely are questions of morality and legality posed, much less brought into a political or institutional matrix where perpetrators might be held accountable. Once a wartime enemy is portrayed as a sinister and threatening monster, efforts to kill inevitably become a matter of organization, technique, and planning, part of the everyday routines of obeying commands, fulfilling assigned tasks, ensuring that everything fits properly into a bureaucratic procedure and discipline. In some cases (as at My Lai in Vietnam and Haditha in Iraq) killing sprees take on a spontaneous character—outbursts stemming from revenge, fear, hatred, and other psychological factors. U.S. history is replete with wartime circumstances where targets of military action are defined as subhuman, deserving of the most horrible fates: Native Americans, Filipinos, Mexicans, Japanese, Koreans, Vietnamese, Iraqis, Serbs. As on the American nineteenth-century frontier, mass killing—usually sanctioned from above—can be understood as necessary, a moral imperative to ensure survival and even save "civilization" or "democracy." Under such conditions behavior that on rational grounds might be considered immoral and criminal can be seen as natural, logical, perhaps desirable.

Within the postwar American culture of militarism, the killing of thousands and even hundreds of thousands of people—again, mostly authorized by government or military leaders—has taken on elements of the *ordinary*, where guilt and culpability are regularly eluded.[1] Actions viewed from outside this paradigm as criminal or barbaric may seem rather normal, acceptable, even praiseworthy *within* it, part of a taken-for-granted universe of meanings. Ethical discourses as such are roundly silenced, jettisoned from public view. Surveying the record of U.S. war crimes explored in this book, we can identify normalized criminal behavior such as the systematic bombing of urban centers, wanton attacks on civilians, use of weapons of mass destruction, free-fire zones, relocations of local inhabitants, massacres, the torture and killing of prisoners, and of course military aggression itself. The vast majority of these episodes have been planned and sanctioned at the highest levels of government and military; others have taken place within unwritten codes of regular armed-forces conduct in the field.

In technowar, as we have seen, the bulk of human activity is bureaucratic, rule-driven, and impersonal, transforming the end result into something "rational" where the carnage brought to victims has no physical, immediate, or emotional content. All personal initiative—and with it all human vulnerability—disappears within the organizational apparatus and the culture supporting it. The more developed the war machine, the more likely that the technocratic planners' ideology contains elaborate, specialized discourses with their own insular epistemology, devoid of ethical criteria. As Gibson argues in the context of Vietnam: "Technowar as a regime of mechanical power and knowledge posits the high-level command positions of the political and military bureaucracies as the legitimate sites of knowledge."[2] Here bureaucratic language conveniently serves to obscure the reality of militarism and its victims with familiar references to the primacy of "defense" and "national security," the need for "surgical" or "precision" strikes, the regrettable problem of "collateral damage" and "self-inflicted" casualties. Terms like "incursion" or "armed response" substitute for military aggression, "body counts" for mass slaughter, "civilian militias" for death squads, "rendition" methods for torture, and so forth. The very structure of language helps establish a moral and social gulf between perpetrators and victims, between war criminals and the crimes they commit. It seems to be a general rule, moreover, that those who plan do not kill, and those who kill are merely following orders—and they too are usually shielded from psychological immediacy by the mediations of technocratic warfare.

At the same time, not all war crimes are extensions of technowar: in Vietnam, Iraq, and other locales massacres and similar atrocities have been indeed authorized—formally or informally—by military personnel in the midst of ground combat. The My Lai horrors are well known, but others like them occurred with some frequency in countries where U.S. armed forces have intervened or set up proxy operations. My Lai itself was part of a much larger search-and-destroy mission by American troops, whose standing orders were to obliterate any resistance or "suspicious" activity and whose well-known incentives were to maximize "body counts" in a setting where GIs assumed that virtually everyone was VC, or enemy. After troops used machine guns, grenades, and hand guns to wipe out some 500 innocent people in the My Lai hamlet, the operation was defined as a "great victory" for Charlie Company by the army officers in charge. It is a matter of record that neither Lt. William Calley nor any of the other participants expressed much emotional angst over what they did, echoing previous responses of U.S. military personnel after episodes like the massacres at Sand Creek and Wounded Knee, the mass killings at No Gun Ri in Korea, and the bombings at Tokyo, Hiroshima, and Nagasaki that received the blessings of God. Said Calley: "I was just ordered to go in there and destroy the enemy. That was my job on that day. That was the mission I was given."[3] Calley's response duplicated that of the Nazis at Nuremberg almost word-for-word.

Referring to the "seduction of battle," Hedges argues that war itself quickly and often breaks down moral and social barriers to extreme violence; it serves to brutalize human behavior, often turning unspeakable horrors into the ordinary, the acceptable. If superpatriotism, ethnocentrism, and racism often furnish the ideological backdrop of war crimes, the battlefield itself (distant or immediate) provides the emotional context. Warfare typically weakens longstanding prohibitions against violence and destruction, permitting virtually anything: executions, mass killings, rape, torture. As Hedges puts it, "it takes little in wartime to turn ordinary men into killers," adding: "There are always people willing to commit unspeakable human atrocity in exchange for a little power and privilege."[4] When military forces are energized by the moral certitude of their own cause, normative codes easily disintegrate along with the social fabric itself. In a crumbling and atomized milieu, dominated by highly armed and well-trained killers, brutalization often reigns. Whether directly engaged in battle, supporting its myriad logistical activities, or watching as distant but emotionally partisan observers, people gain permission to unleash collective anger at the designated (and usually degraded) wartime target. And technowar facilitates these psychological dynamics as it renders the combat operations as such both more deadly and more efficient.

For human beings to reach the point where killing (and mass killing) can become a routine, orderly, sometimes even rewarding part of an assigned mission, they must undergo what Richard Rhodes calls a "brutalization process"—a psychological conversion typically begun in armed-forces basic training, or its equivalent, and then accelerated during combat.[5] The idea is to strip away moral and personal inhibitions so that troops will be prepared for a kill-or-be-killed environment. Individuals must be socialized into an intensely conflicted milieu where the darkest human behavior can seem "normal": violence, cruelty, hate, rage, traumas, insanity. From this point, the carrying-out of atrocities becomes all the more thinkable as the brutalization experience knows few limits. Participants come to view extreme violence as simply part of an organizational task—or in any event approved (formally or informally) by military superiors. After all, basic training instructs all personnel to follow orders, under all circumstances, and wartime conditions permit no exceptions. Yet if the military culture tends to produce a universal inclination toward extreme violence, the U.S. armed forces have nonetheless occupied a special place when it comes to war crimes. There are several reasons for this, including the constant pressures of maintaining imperial hegemony, the duration, scope, and severity of transgressions, the unprecedented levels of armed might wielded by Washington, and a long history of evading legal accountability.

Perhaps the best example of this special status is Vietnam: the U.S. brought more than a decade of death and destruction there to wage counterinsurgency warfare against the Communist enemy. Repeated war crimes were an inescapable outcome of this protracted campaign, as we have seen. Atrocities like My Lai represent not so much isolated episodes of barbarism as a microcosm of the entire catastrophe. There were many (though mostly smaller) instances of the sort, not to mention ongoing saturation bombing and chemical defoliation that in the end killed far more people than the accumulated local atrocities. As for My Lai itself, even before the massacre the leaders and soldiers of Charlie Company had been expanding their range of violent actions, one GI saying "it came to the point where a guy could kill anybody."[6] There was so much hatred of the Vietnamese that ordinary soldiers felt ready to empty their magazines into the heads of women and children without much thought or emotional response. Far from sheer madness, such behavior was closer to the "normal" category in Vietnam, so that My Lai came as no great shock to those in the field. One sergeant was quoted as saying "Before you leave here sir, you're going to learn that one of the most brutal things in the world is your average 19-year-old American boy."[7] When the My Lai massacre unfolded, reports were that troops were "shooting at everything in sight, children, men, women, and animals," all (with a few exceptions) ready to follow orders as civilians were lined up to be murdered. Reports indicated that many took great pleasure in the slaughter.[8]

Investigations into the My Lai massacre reveal that Charlie Company was indeed comprised of average soldiers who had become quickly integrated into the universe of search-and-destroy missions they were carrying out in early 1968.[9] As noted, standard orders were for soldiers to be aggressive and to maximize "body count"—orders that converged with a mood of revenge shared by GIs angry over VC attacks on their own units. Some men claimed that a superior, Lt. Col. Frank Barker, had issued commands to the effect that everyone in the hamlet (considered a VC stronghold) should be eliminated, a charge denied by Barker. What is known is that Charlie Company entered My Lai with guns blazing, shooting at everyone and everything, some soldiers following organizational discipline and other behaving more or less spontaneously. As for Lt. Calley himself, he would later say (at trial) that "all orders were to be assumed legal, that a soldier's job was to carry out any order given to him to the best of his ability."[10] Like other similar episodes, My Lai can be described as a "sanctioned massacre"— that is, a form of ruthless, systematic mass violence carried out within combat operations that at least appear to be legitimated by superior command.[11]

According to Kelman and Hamilton, sanctioned massacres ultimately depend on three interwoven organizational and psychological dynamics. First, they must be seen as *authorized* by superior officers, where questions of individual decision-making and moral choice appear decisively ruled out. As we have seen, military personnel are thoroughly trained in the practice of following orders—any failure to do so likely to be met, in wartime, with a summary court martial or worse. Such orders, moreover, do not always have to be formal; they can be informal, a function of implicitly understood expectations or even the mood of the moment. Second, they are a product of *routinization*, above all the strong social and psychological pressures brought to bear on the battlefield. Troops are trained to focus on the immediate tasks at hand, the details of a job they are programmed to complete at the highest level, no questions asked or even permitted to be asked. It follows that combat operations can easily morph into indiscriminate killings, fitting the standard bureaucratic model of discipline rooted in established norms, rules, procedures, and discourses involving "kill ratios" and the like. Finally, they depend on the capacity of actors in the drama to objectify and *dehumanize* an enemy to the degree that ordinary moral criteria no longer apply. This is largely a function of well-honed propaganda that ideologically underpins the war machine. When U.S. forces attack other nations, their view of the local population will be shaped by a national chauvinism and perhaps even racism that sets up human targets for easier destruction.[12] It is fair to say that all three of these mechanisms were at work during My Lai and indeed through much of the entire U.S. military *modus operandi* in Vietnam.

It is worth looking at the American public response to My Lai in the months following the massacre, for the aftermath speaks volumes about the ethnocentrism, double standards, and fetishism of violence embedded in the military culture—the same flaws Americans are quick to identify in other nations and cultures. At the outset, there is evidence that soldiers in Vietnam were versed in rules of engagement codified not only in international law but in the UCMJ itself, but combat troops up to the highest-ranking officers were commonly known to have laughed at such "rules," considering them arcane, out of touch, irrelevant to conditions prevailing during heat of battle. This was not so much a matter of ignorance, therefore, but rather of indifference. More than that: soon after My Lai the Americal Division (which included Charlie Company) actually celebrated the atrocity as a victory for its high body count, while the commanding officers rapidly initiated a cover-up.[13] Knowledge of the massacre in Vietnam became widespread, but few military personnel expressed outrage; it was simply another mission—bloody, to be sure, but just another mission. One solider talked of reporting the episode to his congressman but was met with immediate threats, with Lt. Calley's men deciding to place a bounty on his head.[14] There would be no references to American war crimes in Vietnam—at least until independent reporters like Seymour Hersh (himself quickly forced into hiding) could tell the story.

As Michael Belknap shows in his exhaustive treatment of the events surrounding My Lai, the mainstream news media in the U.S. had little interest in dealing with the massacres.[15] Little outrage was visible among politicians, many siding with the perpetrators. Public opinion shaded from mild indifference to outright support for Lt. Calley and other soldiers of Charlie Company. Most Americans seemed inclined to voice at least one of several rationalizations—

that My Lai was just a predictable outcome of war, that the enemy got what he deserved, that the VC itself was responsible because it hid amongst the inhabitants, that the Commies in any case were doing worse things, and so forth. According to one Gallop Poll survey in 1969, only 13 percent of respondents thought the GIs were guilty, the rest believing, no doubt, that Americans were not capable of such crimes. A *Time* magazine poll showed that a majority expressed sympathy for Lt. Calley.[16] President Nixon, calling My Lai an "isolated episode," expressed fear that giving too much public attention to the massacres would hurt the U.S. image and further erode popular support for the war (which was already ebbing). Rep. Don Fuqua (R–Fla) introduced a resolution giving Lt. Calley an opportunity to present his case before a joint session of Congress. Well after details of the massacre surfaced in the media, Lt. Calley enjoyed widespread backing by a public generally willing to give him every benefit of the doubt. When Tony Nelson's musical tribute to mass murder, "The Battle Hymn of Lt. Calley," hit the airwaves, it sold more than 200,000 copies. Many believed Calley himself was the main victim who should never have been tried for war crimes. When Calley was eventually found guilty at court martial, the verdict was overwhelmingly (by 78 percent) opposed by the American public.[17] The conviction brought outrage and protests, most urging that Lt. Calley be freed immediately or at least pardoned by Nixon. Several states passed resolutions favoring a pardon. In the two months following the trial, the White House received 200,000 letters in support of Lt. Calley, whose brief sentence for killing 21 civilians was served mostly under house arrest. Many media pundits and politicians argued (in part correctly) that Calley—a mere platoon leader—was being scapegoated for atrocities endemic to the whole Vietnam campaign and for which higher-level officers and even government officials should have been culpable.

The main argument here is that the vast majority of the American public, along with important sectors of the political, media, and military establishments, were little troubled by revelations of barbaric war crimes of which My Lai was only the tip of the iceberg. Instead of moral opprobrium, there was a facile willingness to forget and move on, often reciting the fashionable platitude that, in the end, "war is hell" under all conditions—a refrain rightly condemned at Nuremberg. While the evidence against Lt. Calley was as solid as it could have been (many on the scene attributed more than 100 killings to him), Americans preferred to look the other way, believing that in the final analysis he was a good soldier just doing the best he could under extremely trying circumstances. My Lai provides a fascinating case study, for it shows that the vast majority of Americans were willing to condone mass murder so long as it was committed by military personnel serving under the banner of their own country—that is, where the crimes could be overlooked because they fit a well-understood national agenda. In other words, when it came to a specific historical case moral values immediately gave way to the pull of superpatriotism and ethnocentrism. All respect for international law was thrown to the winds.

The example of My Lai—indeed the entire Vietnam disaster—hovers over questions of precisely who might be guilty of war crimes and, equally important, who of those responsible for such horrors should be deemed most legally culpable. As we have seen, there are no quick and ready answers to such questions for, among other considerations, wartime conditions are so often filled with chaos and ambiguity as to resist categorical definitions. We know that at Nuremberg the precept was established that following the commands of a superior could not be invoked as a defense—all individuals, whatever their rank, were held responsible for making their own moral choices. The Allied prosecutors assumed that all Germans involved in the Nazi system could readily distinguish right from wrong, and could behave accordingly. Yet this precept—that following orders is no justification for individual behavior—is far too simplistic and unrealistic as a basis for determining guilt. In fact the Allies essentially violated their own precept, choosing to prosecute only the highest echelon Nazis (top leaders of the "criminal enterprise") while sparing those lower on the chain of command owing to their supposed lesser accountability. That is, the tribunal recognized that "following orders," as opposed to giving them, could be a mitigating factor in determining culpability. At Nuremberg, therefore, only a small number of leading Nazis was convicted of war crimes—a pattern of identifying and prosecuting only the main decision-makers that would be repeated at Tokyo and subsequent tribunals.

This precedent makes abundantly good sense when one looks more closely at the conditions of warfare, as simple precepts and formulas about assigning guilt for war crimes quickly fall by the wayside. The first point to emphasize is the very chaos of most battlefield situations, where ordinary soldiers and even many officers are forced to make quick, life-and-death decisions at moments of great stress and where, as under conditions of guerrilla warfare, it might be impossible to easily distinguish civilians from combatants.

Chaos breeds rapid change, ambiguity, uncertainty, and of course fear. It is worth repeating here that all military personnel, whatever their rank, are trained first and foremost to follow commands—an iron rule during combat, where operations depend on quick, disciplined, and collective responses to battlefield threats. The deeply ingrained practice of following orders is nearly always a necessity impervious to time-consuming questioning or debate. Any failure to follow orders in wartime, moreover, will be met with swift and severe punishment: summary courts martial leading to dishonorable discharge, jail time, or even death. Even mild resistance to the unit's mission will typically produce ostracism, threats, harassment, and worse. The pressures to conform are overpowering.

At the same time, during battlefield operations ordinary troops have limited information and awareness about what is being planned or what, indeed, is even possible; the big-picture perspective of events is usually monopolized by a few superior officers. It would be unreasonable to expect average grunts—lacking experience, knowledge, and authority—to make rapid moral and legal judgments regarding combat tactics. Thus, in the case of the November 2004 U.S. attacks on Fallujah in Iraq, troops were mostly told they were pursuing small pockets of insurgents who would be quickly defeated, when in fact the entire operation turned into a massive operation directed against virtually the entire civilian population and its infrastructure. Information about this latter phase of the operation was no doubt available to leading military planners but almost certainly not shared with ordinary troops. If we compare the Fallujah campaign with, say, that at Normandy, it is fair to assume the average soldier will have encountered few if any differences regarding available options. Once combat orders are given to ordinary troops, those troops are scarcely in a position to challenge their all-powerful commanding officers (or even their peers). It is easy enough to suggest that military personnel are willing participants in a vast "criminal enterprise," but to expect individual or mass rebellion except under extreme conditions is far-fetched. Rebellion in the ranks has indeed taken place but it is rare, and those involved have always paid a heavy price. At My Lai, most personnel involved in the massacre, including officers, said they were just "following orders," but this defense could hardly be sustained once it was obvious the troops of Charlie Company were on a wild, bloody rampage against innocent and unarmed civilians that lasted for several hours. And indeed a few (but only a few) soldiers did refuse to participate, while the one soldier indicating he would report the atrocities was harassed and received death threats.

With My Lai as an obvious extreme case, the larger task of ascertaining who is guilty of battlefield war crimes—and to what degree—is not always as straightforward as the laws of warfare might indicate. (Indeed the laws themselves are often quite ambiguous.) This takes us back to an earlier question: who precisely ought to be considered a war criminal? One strong principle should be that, where violations have clearly taken place, culpability increases as we move up the chain of command. Hence those responsible for setting policy, or for implementing it at the highest levels, should be found most guilty insofar as they have greater access to power and information—and thus more capacity to determine another course of action. If we take Vietnam, for example, it was government and military leaders in Washington who initiated and prolonged the war, and it was the armed-forces commanding heights in the field that shaped the overall battlefield conduct. The pacification campaigns, bombing missions, search-and-destroy operations, emphasis on body counts, indifference to rules of engagement— all this was the domain of General Westmoreland and his staff, along with dozens of field commanders. In Vietnam the major war criminals were therefore Presidents Kennedy, Johnson, and Nixon, their Secretaries of Defense and State, other cabinet members, top Pentagon officials, and leading field commanders—a list of perhaps 100 people. The original architects of this catastrophe, including liberal policy-makers like Robert McNamara, Dean Rusk, Walt Rostow, and McGeorge Bundy, belong at the top of this list. A similar list could be compiled for Iraq, headed by Bush, Cheney, Rumsfeld, and Rice, and including top neocon figures like Paul Wolfowitz, Richard Perle, and Scooter Libby. Leading propagandists in both cases would likewise find places on the list—keeping in mind that Nazi propagandist Julius Streicher was tried and convicted at Nuremberg. Crucial to remember here is that both Vietnam and Iraq constitute flagrant crimes of aggression, so that war planners are guilty not only of that transgression but of the many crimes that followed. As for a savage episode like My Lai, we have blatant war crimes for which *all* participants ought to be prosecuted, whether they gave or followed orders. An extended massacre of unarmed civilians in any context cannot be defended on the basis of ambiguous circumstances, threats to survival, battlefield stress, or following commands from superiors.

A major problem with U.S. war crimes in general is that virtually *everyone* has managed to escape criminal liability, except in a few cases like My Lai and Abu Ghraib where lower-level personnel were tried, convicted, and generally given light sentences. Another problem is the extent to which repeated violations of international laws and rules take on the character of *normalcy* within American society and political culture. The prevailing discourse says that only other nations can be guilty of transgressions, while Japanese leaders (among others) are routinely chastised for ignoring or denying their criminal past. Such "normalcy" is a product of the way in which the long record of U.S. outlawry has become taken for granted as part of the national experience. Returning the example of former Senator Robert Kerrey, the revelations of war crimes hardly disturbed the established rhythms of his professional and daily life; he was viewed as just another dedicated, hard-working American citizen who had fought for his country and perhaps made a few mistakes along the way, but in no way could be regarded a war criminal. Indeed Kerrey, highly successful, looks and acts "normal" enough. So too do the vast majority of U.S. government and military elites who, in Nuremberg language, were "willing, knowing, and energetic accomplices in a vast and malignant enterprise."[18] The Pentagon war machine has been led and staffed by ordinary folks with typically good educations, solid family backgrounds, nice manners, elevated cultural tastes, and even good intentions. The Vietnam War itself was engineered and planned not by revolting sadistic thugs or Hannibal Lecter-type psychopaths—or even xenophobic right-wingers—but mostly by liberal, cultured, urbane, visionary government officials, many of them celebrated academics. Persico writes that the Nazi defendants at Nuremberg also looked and acted in every respect "ordinary," with the exception of the massive, gruff, red-faced Ernst Kaltenbrunner, a Nazi from central casting. In fact few Nazis looked like sadistic monsters: as Persico comments, "It would be hard to pick out most of these men as war criminals from a gathering of Rotarians or accountants."[19] Thus Albert Speer came across as just another intelligent, refined businessman, someone who could have been an executive at General Motors instead of a willing accomplice in a "vast and malignant enterprise."

Given the long history of U.S. militarism, along with the immense scope of American global power today, no one should be astonished to find the most terrible deeds engulfed and camouflaged by bureaucratic structures and legitimating ideologies that seem commonplace and rational enough on the surface. Nor should anyone be surprised to discover that such deeds have been planned and/or carried out by otherwise exemplary citizens. Obedience, violence, national chauvinism, even racism are built into the very logic of an imperial system. This recalls Hannah Arendt's famous commentary on the Adolf Eichmann trial and Nazism in general. The Nazis too were viewed internally as "normal" in their multiple criminal operations, and most indeed led "normal" lives. Writes Arendt: "The trouble with Eichmann was that precisely so many were like him, and that the many were neither perverted nor sadistic, that they were ... terribly and terrifyingly normal."[20] At the end of World War II the Army Air Force crews that brought atomic destruction to Hiroshima and Nagasaki, killing more than 200,000 innocent civilians, were comprised of highly competent, stable, dedicated military personnel all convinced they were doing the right thing. Said Paul W. Tibbetts Jr., pilot of the Enola Gay that bombed Hiroshima, "I never lost a night's sleep over it." As would later be the case in Korea, Vietnam, Iraq, and other theaters of U.S. war crimes, the people committing atrocities—from bottom to top, with few exceptions—believed they were doing the right patriotic thing, possibly even ordained by God, scarcely giving a second thought to their actions.

All this raises the fascinating question as to whether most people involved in committing war crimes might be labeled "psychopaths"—that is, psychologically deranged to the extent of being able to routinely or casually torture, rape, or kill other human beings. Nazis and other fascists were often believed to fit this category, as well as many tyrannical leaders like Stalin, Mao, and Saddam Hussein. Psychopaths are generally thought capable of carrying out the most heinous crimes, including genocide and ethnic cleansing, without feeling much if any guilt; in other words, such perpetrators lack a "normal" conscience. David Model identifies President Bush as a psychopath for his cruel and senseless Iraq venture.[21] Whether perpetrators of war crimes, including mass murder, are often psychopaths may be difficult to ascertain in particular cases, but what seems clear is that those involved— government and military leaders, troops in the field, propagandists, even supporters among the general population—typically rationalize those crimes within definite ideological frameworks: patriotic duty, a superior national mission, confronting perceived threats, and so forth. If such beliefs are strongly and frequently propagated within the political system, mass media, education, and other venues of opinion formation, they can provide an effective interpretive framework within which outlawry and criminality can be justified and legitimated. In this context the deeds are not really viewed as "crimes" so much as accepted praiseworthy behavior for which honors and medals are awarded. Where legitimating beliefs are internalized throughout a community of interests, as is often the case in the military, their psychological force on the individual will be all the more powerful and difficult to resist. In the midst of warfare, deeds typically regarded as abnormal or criminal might well be seen as routine, possibly heroic. While it might be tempting to blame "psychopaths" for monstrous atrocities and other crimes, American history reveals a more common, mundane source—the very patterns of activity that correspond to the requirements of an aggressive imperial war machine.

Notes

INTRODUCTION

1. Richard Dawkins, *The God Delusion* (New York: Houghton Mifflin, 2006), p. 267.
2. Ibid., p. 270.
3. David Chandler, *From Kosovo to Kabul* (London: Pluto Press, 2002), p. 153.
4. Ibid., p. 154.
5. Philippe Sands, *Lawless World* (New York: Viking Press, 2005).
6. Richard Falk, *Human Rights Horizons* (New York: Routledge, 2000), ch. 10.
7. David Chandler, "International Justice," *New Left Review* (November–December, 2000), p. 63.
8. Noam Chomsky, *Rogue States* (Boston: South End Press, 2000), p. 17.
9. See Michael Ignatieff, "Nation-Buidling Lite," *New York Times Magazine* (July 28, 2002).
10. Robert Jay Lifton, *The Superpower Syndrome* (New York: Nation Books, 2003), p. 112.
11. Robert Kagan, *Of Paradise and Power* (New York: Alfred A. Knopf, 2003), p. 27.
12. Ibid., p. 27.
13. Ibid., p. 76.
14. Ibid., p. 87.
15. Ibid., p. 99.
16. Chandler, *From Kosovo to Kabul*, p. 187.
17. Ibid., p. 191.
18. See Jack L. Goldsmith and Eric A. Posner, *The Limits of International Law* (New York: Oxford University Press, 2005).
19. Antonia Juhasz, *The Bush Agenda* (New York: Regan Books, 2006), p. 298.
20. For further elaboration of the argument that Republicans and Democrats have converged ideologically during the past two decades, see Carl Boggs, *The End of Politics: Corporate Power and the Decline of the Public Sphere* (New York: Guilford Publications, 2000), chs 1–4.
21. Edward Herman, "The *New York Times* Versus Civil Society," *Z Magazine* (December 2005), p. 54.
22. Ibid., p. 54.
23. Chris Hedges, *War is a Force That Gives Us Meaning* (New York: Public Affairs, 2002), p. 143.
24. Cited in Norman Solomon, *War Made Easy* (Hoboken, NJ: John Wiley and Sons, 2005), p. 26.
25. Sam Harris, *The End of Faith* (New York: W.W. Norton, 2004), p. 144.
26. Ibid., p. 143.
27. Sands, *Lawless World*, p. 48.
28. See Diana Johnstone, *Fool's Crusade* (New York: Monthly Review Press, 2002).

29. See Michael Mandel, *How America Gets Away with Murder* (London: Pluto Press, 2004) and David Model, *Lying for Empire* (Monroe, ME: Common Courage Press, 2005).
30. See Carla Del Ponte, *Madame Prosecutor: Confrontations with Humanity's Worst Criminals* (New York: Other Press, 2009).

CHAPTER 1

1. See William Blum, *Killing Hope* (Monroe, ME: Common Courage Press, 1995), and *Rogue State* (Monroe, ME: Common Courage Press, 2000).
2. On U.S. aggression in Korea, see Bruce Cumings, et al., *Inventing the Axis of Evil* (New York: The New Press, 2004), pp. 1–27; Blum, *Killing Hope*, pp. 45–55; and Stephen Endicott and Edward Hagerman, *The United States and Biological Warfare* (Bloomington: University of Indiana Press, 1998), pp. 88–106.
3. On President Kennedy's involvement in Vietnam war planning and escalation, see Bruce Miroff, *Pragmatic Illusions* (New York: David McKay, 1976), pp. 142–66, and Marilyn Young, *The Vietnam Wars* (New York: HarperCollins, 1991), pp. 60–105.
4. See Christopher Hitchens, *The Trial of Henry Kissinger* (London: Verso, 2001).
5. See Philip E. Wheaton, *Panama Invaded* (Trenton, NJ: The Red Sea Press, 1992), pp. 13–20.
6. Ibid., pp. 143–58.
7. The U.S. flew 110,000 air sorties against Iraq during Desert Storm, resulting in at least 200,000 deaths. According to the Red Crescent Society of Jordan, 113,000 civilians were killed in just the final week of the war. See Ramsey Clark, et al., *War Crimes* (Washington, DC: Maisonneuve Press, 1992), p. 15.
8. Anthony Arnove, ed., *Iraq Under Siege* (Boston: South End Press, 2000), esp. chs 1–3, 11, 12, and 13.
9. See Clark, et al., *War Crimes*, pp. 9–25. Nineteen charges in all were listed.
10. Dilip Hiro, *Iraq: in the Eye of the Storm* (New York: Nation Books, 2002), chs 5–9.
11. Wesley Clark, quoted in Michael Parenti, *To Kill a Nation* (London: Verso, 2000), p. 124.
12. See Mandel, *How America Gets Away With Murder*, pp. 176–200.
13. On the U.S. attack in Yemen, see the *Los Angeles Times* (November 5, 2002).
14. Quoted in Richard Clarke, *Against All Enemies: Inside America's War on Terror* (New York: The Free Press, 2004), p. 24.
15. On the Bush administration efforts to manipulate information concerning Iraq's supposed possession of weapons of mass destruction, see James Bamford, *A Pretext for War* (New York: Anchor Books, 2004), pp. 294–307.
16. On the illegality of the U.S. invasion of Iraq, see Sands, *Lawless World*, pp. 185–7.
17. Ibid., pp. 201–3.
18. See Hiro, *Iraq*, p. 82.
19. Ibid., p. 129.
20. Ibid., p. 88.
21. Ibid., p. 92.
22. See James Bamford, "How Public Relations Gave us the War in Iraq," *Rolling Stone* (December 1, 2005), p. 53.

23. Ibid., p. 61.
24. Clarke, *Against All Enemies*.
25. *Los Angeles Times* (July 1, 2004).
26. See Antonia Juhasz, *The Bush Agenda* (New York: Regan Books, 2006), pp. 6–8.
27. Ibid., p. 41.
28. Ibid., pp. 177–8.
29. Ibid., p. 252.
30. Joshua Muravchik, in *Los Angeles Times* (November 19, 2006).
31. Scott Ritter, *Target Iran* (New York: Nation Books, 2006).
32. Ibid., p. 208.
33. Ibid., p. 203.
34. Joseph Persico, *Nuremberg* (New York: Penguin Books, 1994), p. 261.
35. Noam Chomsky, *Failed States* (New York: Metropolitan Books, 2006), ch. 2.
36. Sands, *Lawless World*, p. 243.
37. See Goldsmith and Posner, *The Limits of International Law*, pp. 225–6.
38. Ritter, *Target Iran*, p. 141.
39. Ibid., p. 205.
40. On what is said to be the benign character of U.S. imperial power, see Michael Ignatieff, "The American Empire (Get Used to It)," *New York Times Magazine* (January 5, 2003).
41. Esther Kaplan, *With God on Their Side* (New York: The New Press, 2004), p. 10.
42. *Los Angeles Times* (October 29, 2007).

CHAPTER 2

1. Tariq Ali, *The Clash of Fundamentalisms* (London: Verso, 2002), p. 267.
2. Edward Herman, "'Tragic Errors' in U.S. Military Policy," *Z Magazine* (September 2002), p. 27.
3. See Ward Churchill, *A Little Matter of Genocide* (San Francisco: City Lights Books, 1997), p. 188.
4. Caleb Carr, *The Lessons of Terror* (New York: Random House, 2002), pp. 172–3.
5. Ibid., p. 255.
6. See Roy Gutman and David Rieff, eds, *Crimes of War* (New York: W. W. Norton, 1999), pp. 84–6, 372.
7. The reference to "poisoned weapons" in the International Criminal Court statutes is contained in Sands, *Lawless World*, p. 282 (Article 8, section xviii).
8. John Dower, *War Without Mercy* (New York: Pantheon, 1986), p. 69.
9. Ibid., pp. 8–9.
10. Ibid., p. 11.
11. Endicott and Hagerman, *The United States and Biological Weapons*, pp. 88–9.
12. Ibid., p. 188.
13. Young, *The Vietnam Wars*, pp. 144–8.
14. See Douglas Valentine, *The Phoenix Program* (New York: William Morrow and Co., 1990), pp. 156–7.
15. Quoted in James William Gibson, *The Perfect War: Technowar in Vietnam* (New York: Atlantic Monthly Press, 1986), pp. 141–2.
16. Quoted in ibid., p. 199.

17. The "production model" of war is discussed in ibid., ch. 5.

18. Wheaton, *Panama Invaded*, pp. 115–16.

19. Ibid., p. 31.

20. Quoted in ibid., p. 53.

21. Ibid., p. 147.

22. Ibid., p. 149.

23. See the collection *Metal of Dishonor* (New York: International Action Center, 1999), chs 1, 3, and 8.

24. See Joy Gordon, "Cool War," *Harpers* (November 2002), p. 43.

25. *Los Angeles Times* (January 17, 2007).

26. Johns Hopkins School of Public Health Report, in *Lancet* (October 2006).

27. *Los Angeles Times* (August 3, 2006).

28. *Los Angeles Times* (January 7, 2005).

29. www.dahrjamailiraq.com (February 3, 2005).

30. On the militarization of American political and popular culture, see Carl Boggs and Tom Pollard, *The Hollywood War Machine* (Boulder, CO: Paradigm, 2006), ch. 1.

31. Phyllis Bennis, *Before and After: U.S. Foreign Policy and the September 11 Crisis* (New York: Olive Branch Press, 2003), p. 104.

32. Barbara Ehrenreich, *Blood Rites* (New York: Henry Holt and Co., 1997), pp. 222–3.

33. Richard Rhodes, *Why They Kill* (New York: Vintage, 1999), p. 287.

34. Sven Lindqvist, *A History of Bombing* (New York: the New Press, 2001), p. 126.

35. Ibid., pp. 26–7.

36. Ibid., p. 121.

37. On Geneva Convention articles 52 to 57, see www.deoxy.org/wc/wc-proto. htm

38. Quoted in Dower, *War Without Mercy*, p. 41.

39. See A. C. Grayling, *Among the Dead Cities* (New York: Walker and Co., 2006), p. 272.

40. Ibid., p. 277.

41. Reported in the obituary of Kurt Vonnegut, *Los Angeles Times* (April 12, 2007).

42. *Los Angeles Times* (July 21, 2003).

43. Lindqvist, *A History of Bombing*, p. 131.

44. Quoted in ibid., p. 128.

45. Ibid., p. 121.

46. Endicott and Hagerman, *The United States and Biological Warfare*, p. 88.

47. Ibid., p. 101.

48. *Report on U.S. War Crimes in Korea* (Pyongyang: International Association of Lawyers, 1952), p. 23.

49. On the development of technowar in Vietnam, see Gibson, *The Perfect War*, pp. 433–59.

50. Lindqvist, *A History of Bombing*, p. 159.

51. Ibid., p. 162.

52. Ibid., p. 157.

53. Young, *The Vietnam Wars*, p. 235.

54. Lindqvist, *A History of Bombing*, pp. 158–9.

55. Arnove, *Iraq Under Siege*, chs 1, 4.

56. Clark, et al., *War Crimes*, parts 1–3.
57. Ramsey Clark, "Indictment of the U.S./NATO," in John Catalinotto and Sara Flounders, eds, *Hidden Agenda: U.S./NATO Takeover of Yugoslavia* (New York: International Action Center, 2002), pp. 33–45.
58. See Parenti, *To Kill a Nation*, p. 124.
59. Johnstone, *Fool's Crusade*, pp. 118–19.
60. Catalinotto and Flounders, eds, *Hidden Agenda*, pp. 318–21.
61. Ibid., pp. 320–1.
62. *Los Angeles Times* (January 4, 2002).
63. *Report on U.S. Crimes in Korea*, p. 3.
64. Ibid., p. 35.
65. Ibid., pp. 13–14.
66. Ibid., p. 15.
67. Ibid.
68. Ibid., p. 16.
69. Sang-Hun Choe, Charles J. Hanley, and Martha Mendoza, "The Bridge at No Gun Ri," *Dissent* (Spring 2000), pp. 39–41.
70. Ibid., p. 41.
71. Ibid.
72. Gibson, *The Perfect War*, p. 296.
73. Ibid., p. 183.
74. Herbert Kelman and V. Lee Hamilton, "The My Lai Massacre: A Military Crime of Obedience," in David M. Newman, ed., *Sociology* (Thousand Oaks: Pine Forge Press, 1997), p. 19.
75. Ibid., p. 24.
76. Seymour Hersh, *My Lai 4: A Report on the Massacre and its Aftermath* (New York: Vintage, 1972).
77. On the aftermath of My Lai and events surrounding it, see Michael R. Belknap, *The Vietnam War on Trial* (Lawrence: University Press of Kansas, 2002), chs 11, 12.
78. *Los Angeles Times* (August 8, 2006).
79. *Scanlans Monthly* (February 27, 1970).
80. *Los Angeles Times* (August 8, 2006).
81. *Los Angeles Times* (August 8, 2006).
82. *Winter Soldier Hearings* (film 1972).
83. All quotes are from the *Winter Soldier Hearings*.
84. Quoted in *Time* (May 7, 2001).
85. See *Newsweek* (August 6, 2002).
86. www.dahrjamailiraq.com (December 2005).
87. William Langewiesche, "Rules of Engagement," *Vanity Fair* (November 2006), p. 318.
88. *Frontline* documentary on Haditha (February 2008).
89. *Los Angeles Times* (June 8, 2006).
90. Quoted in Nafeez Mosaddeq Ahmed, *The War on Truth* (Northampton: Olive Branch Press, 2005), p. 294.
91. See Howard Zinn, "The Problem is Obedience," in Howard Zinn/Anthony Arnove, *Voices From a People's History of the United States* (New York: Seven Stories, 2004), p. 484.
92. Harris, *The End of Faith*, p. 140.
93. Ibid., p. 143.

94. Ibid., p. 146.
95. Ibid., p. 144.
96. Ibid., p. 146.
97. Christopher Hitchens, *A Long Short War* (New York: Penguin, 2003), p. 53.
98. Ibid., p. 96.
99. Ibid., p. 25.
100. Ibid., p. 20.
101. Douglas Murray, *Neoconservatism* (New York: Encounter Books, 2006), p. 117.
102. See the report on Winter Soldier hearings in *Z Magazine* (May 2008).
103. Chris Hedges' report is contained in *The Nation* (July 30, 2008).
104. See Juhasz, *The Bush Agenda*, especially chs 1, 2.

CHAPTER 3

1. For more details on this point, see William Blum, *Rogue State* (Monroe, ME: Common Courage Press, 2000), chs 4–10.
2. Thus, at the ICTY in The Hague, Serb leader Slobodan Milošević was charged with a series of war crimes that fall under the category of "aiding and abetting" criminal activity. Within Article 7 (1) of the Tribunal, Milošević was accused of participating in a series of "joint criminal enterprises," including providing financial, material, and logistical supports to various regular and irregular forces in Yugoslavia during the 1990s. Milošević was said to "share the intent" of other participants in joint criminal enterprises, fully aware of the consequences of *their* [others] actions. See Norman Cigar and Paul Williams, *Indictment at The Hague* (New York: New York University Press, 2002), pp. 292–8.
3. Ibid., pp. 96–7.
4. The U.S. has led the world in arms sales throughout most of the postwar years, reaching nearly 60 percent of the total by 2003. For an overview of global weapons sales, see Gider Burrows, *The No-Nonsense Guide to the Arms Trade* (London: Verso, 2002), ch. 1.
5. See Blum, *Killing Hope*, p. 194.
6. Between 1980 and 2000 Turkey received nearly $12 billion in U.S. military aid in addition to some $6.5 billion in combined grants and direct loans (www.fas.org/asmp/profiles/turkey). Turkey has been described as the worst human rights abusing state in the European region, its armed forces carrying out repression with sophisticated weapons supplied mainly by the U.S. See Burrow, *The No-Nonsense Guide to the Arms Trade*, pp. 55–6.
7. See Frederick H. Gareau, *State Terrorism and the United States* (Atlanta: Clarity Press, 2004), p. 23.
8. Ibid., pp. 37–41.
9. Noam Chomsky, *Turning the Tide* (Montreal: Black Rose Books, 1987), pp. 15, 18.
10. Ibid., p. 27.
11. Blum, *Killing Hope*, p. 232.
12. Gareau, *State Terrorism*, p. 62.
13. On human rights violations in Guatemala, see Chomsky, *Turning the Tide*, pp. 28–30; Blum, *Killing Hope*, pp. 229–39; and Jennifer Harbury, *Truth, Torture, and the American Way* (Boston: Beacon Press, 2005), pp. 32–40.

14. Blum, *Killing Hope*, p. 293.
15. Chomsky, *Turning the Tide*, p. 136.
16. See Michael Klare, *Resource Wars* (New York: Henry Holt, 2001), pp. 5–26.
17. Gregory Elich, "The Invasion of Serbian Kraijina," in Ramsey Clark, et al., *NATO in the Balkans* (New York: IAC, 1998), pp. 130–40.
18. Johnstone, *Fool's Crusade*, p. 228; Mandel, *How America Gets Away With Murder*, and Parenti, *To Kill a Nation*, pp. 95–107.
19. Johnstone, *Fool's Crusade*, p. 230.
20. Diana Johnstone, "Kosovo: Waiting for War, Dreaming of Diplomacy," *Z Magazine* (February 2008), pp. 9–12.
21. Michael Neumann, *The Case Against Israel* (Petrolia, CA: CounterPunch, 2005), p. 187.
22. See John J. Mearsheimer and Stephen M. Walt, *The Israel Lobby and U.S. Foreign Policy* (New York: Farrar, Strauss, and Giroux, 2007), pp. 23–30, on the trajectory of U.S. economic, political, military, and diplomatic support for Israel.
23. Ibid., pp. 81–91.
24. Norman Finkelstein, *Beyond Chutzpah* (Berkeley: University of California Press, 2005), p. 100.
25. Ibid., p. 142.
26. Ibid., p. 155.
27. Ibid., p. 103.
28. Edward Said, "America's Last Taboo," *New Left Review* (November–December 2000), p. 47.
29. Michael Jansen, *The Battle of Beirut* (Boston: South End Press, 1982), p. 3.
30. Ibid., pp. 30–5.
31. Ibid., p. 25.
32. See Mearsheimer and Walt, *The Israel Lobby*, pp. 229–62.
33. Ibid., pp. 40–1.
34. Ibid., p. 5.
35. Ibid., p. 80.
36. Quoted in ibid., p. 65.
37. Ibid., p. 235.
38. Ibid., pp. 238–55.
39. *Los Angeles Times* (January 12, 2007).
40. *Los Angeles Times* (January 12, 2007).
41. Ussama Makdisi, *Los Angeles Times* (October 21, 2006).
42. *Los Angeles Times* (February 15, 2009).
43. *Los Angeles Times* (March 21, 2009).

CHAPTER 4

1. www.en.wikipedia.org
2. U.S. Nuclear Posture Review (March 2002). For a larger overview of American nuclear policy, see Christopher Paine, "The Moscow Threat: Making Matters Worse," *Bulletin of Atomic Scientists* (December 2002), and Julian Borger, "U.S. Plan for Nuclear Arsenal," *Guardian* (February 19, 2003).
3. Gordon, "Cool War," p. 43.
4. Ibid., p. 44.
5. Ibid., p. 49.

6. See Robert Aldrich, *First Strike!* (Boston: South End Press, 1983), pp. 21–42.

7. Lindqvist, *A History of Bombing*, p. 126.

8. Aldrich, *First Strike!*, pp. 255–74.

9. Karl Grossman, *Weapons in Space* (New York: Seven Stories Press, 2001), pp. 9–17.

10. Quoted in Model, *Lying for Empire*, p. 70.

11. See Endicott and Hagerman, *The United States and Biological Warfare*, pp. 97–8.

12. David Model, "The Nuclear Peril," *Z Magazine* (July–August 2006). See also "The End of Arms Control," *The Defense Monitor* (December 2006). K. Gajendra Singh refers to the NPT as enforcing a global nuclear "apartheid regime" (www.uruknet.info). Mohamed ElBaradei, director of IAEA, has said that it is "morally reprehensible for some countries to pursue weapons of mass destruction yet morally acceptable for others to rely on them for security to continue to refine their capacities and postulate plans for their use" (*New York Times*, February 12, 2004).

13. Helen Caldicott, *The New Nuclear Danger* (New York: The New Press, 2002), p. 5.

14. *Quadrennial Defense Review* (Washington, DC: Department of Defense, 2001).

15. Robert McNamara, in *Foreign Policy* (May–June 2005).

16. *New York Times* (February 12, 2004).

17. See Fred Kaplan, "India's Summer," at www.slate.msu.com

18. *Los Angeles Times* (February 25, 2007).

19. Caldicott, *The New Nuclear Danger*, p. 15.

20. *Los Angeles Times* (June 13, 2006).

21. *Los Angeles Times* (March 2, 2007).

22. Lifton, *Superpower Syndrome*, p. 24.

23. Ibid., p. 41.

24. Ibid., p. 117.

25. Ibid., p. 130.

26. On the statutes of the Chemical Weapons Convention, see www.en.wikipedia/cwc.org

27. Blum, *Rogue State*, pp. 105–6.

28. See David Rose, "Weapons of Self-Destruction," *Vanity Fair* (August 2006), p. 110.

29. www.newsbbc.co.uk

30. *Los Angeles Times* (April 19, 2002).

31. See Rose, "Weapons of Self-Destruction," p. 112.

32. See Philip Jones Griffiths, *Agent Orange: Collateral Damage in Vietnam* (New York: Trolley, 2004).

33. Peter Pringle, "Chemical Weapons," in Gutman and Rieff, eds, *Crimes of War*, pp. 74–5.

34. Blum, *Rogue State*, pp. 121–2.

35. *Los Angeles Times* (November 28, 2005).

36. Ibid.

37. www.bushfash.com

38. See Stephen Lendman at www.globalresearch.ca/index (January 19, 2006).

39. See Peter L. Pellett, "Sanctions, Food, Nutrition, and Health in Iraq," in Arnove, *Iraq Under Siege*, pp. 151–68.

40. Michio Kaku, "Depleted Uranium: Huge Quantities of Dangerous Waste," in *Metal of Dishonor*, pp. 111–15.
41. Quoted in Rose, "Weapons of Self-Destruction," p. 111.
42. For an extensive account of the U.S. production, use, and justification of DU, see Caldicott, *The New Nuclear Danger*, pp. 153–7. See also *Metal of Dishonor*, introduction.
43. Carolina Ositore, "U.S. Biochemical Research," *Z Magazine* (March 2007). The U.S. has developed new grenades for use in biowarfare, in violation of the BWC. See, for example, the Sunshine Project report of May 8, 2003, at www.sunshine-project.org. The Sunshine Project has found that 113 university, government, corporate, and hospital labs have engaged in secret biochemical research.
44. *Los Angeles Times* (September 15, 2006).
45. Edward Hamoud, "The Pentagon's Secret Chemical Weapons Program," *CounterPunch* (September 25, 2002).
46. *Los Angeles Times* (October 10, 2002). There were no less than 21 tests at sea overseen by the Desert Test Center at Ft. Douglas, Utah.
47. *Los Angeles Times* (October 9, 2002).
48. See Endicott and Hagerman, *The United States and Biological Warfare*, ch. 6.
49. Ibid., p. 100.
50. Ibid., pp. ix, x.
51. Ibid., p. 103.
52. Ibid., pp. 103–4.
53. Ibid., pp. 148–51.
54. *Report on U.S. Crimes in Korea*, pp. 28-7 to 28-12.
55. *Los Angeles Times* (February 11, 2007).
56. See www.wmdcommission.org/sida.asp?id=1
57. The proposals are contained in Hans Blix, *Why Nuclear Disarmament Matters* (Cambridge, MA: MIT Press, 2008), pp. 75–95.
58. Ibid., pp. 61–2.
59. *The Defense Monitor* (September/October 2008), p. 13.

CHAPTER 5

1. *Los Angeles Times* (April 15, 2006).
2. Ward Churchill, *A Little Matter of Genocide* (San Francisco: City Lights Books, 1997), pp. 136–7.
3. Vine Deloria, Jr., *Custer Died for Your Sins* (Norman: University of Oklahoma Press, 1988), p. 28.
4. Ibid., p. 32.
5. Zinn, *A People's History of the United States*, p. 128.
6. Ibid., p. 140.
7. Robert J. Miller, *Native America, Discovered and Conquered* (Westport, CN: Praeger, 2006).
8. Ibid., p. 9.
9. Ibid., p. 3.
10. See Judith Nies, *Native American History* (New York: Ballantine Books, 1996), p. 268.
11. Ibid., p. 273.
12. Ibid., p. 274.

13. Quoted in ibid., p. 281.
14. Ibid., p. 297.
15. Deloria, *Custer Died for Your Sins*, p. 35.
16. Ibid., pp. 51–2.
17. Ibid., p. 51.
18. See Blum, *Rogue State*, pp. 184–99.
19. David Frum and Richard Perle, *An End to Evil* (New York: Random House, 2003), p. 267.
20. Ibid., pp. 271–2.
21. See Bennis, *Before and After*, p. 61.
22. See Blum, *Rogue State*, for these and related examples.
23. Ibid., pp. 186–92.
24. Ibid., pp. 191–6.
25. For extensive commentary on the evolution of Israeli outlawry, most of it carried out with full American support, see Mearsheimer and Walt, *The Israel Lobby*, pp. 49–77 and pp. 306–34.
26. See Andrew Kohut and Bruce Stokes, *America Against the World* (New York: Times Books, 2006), p. 18.
27. Ibid., p. 88.
28. On the original concept of genocide, see Raphael Lemken, *Axis Rule in Occupied Europe* (Washington, DC: Carnegie Endowment, 1944). According to Lemken, genocide is the coordinated and planned annihilation of a national, religious, or racial group by a variety of actions aimed at undermining the basis of survival of a group. This definition has been clearly watered down across the postwar years.
29. The text is contained in U.N. General Assembly Resolution 96 (I), passed unanimously December 11, 1946.
30. For an excellent discussion of the Lugar-Helms-Hatch "sovereignty" reservation, essentially reserving for the U.S. sole jurisdiction over its own actions, see Churchill, *A Little Matter of Genocide*, pp. 383–87.
31. Ibid., p. 391.
32. See the powerful statement by Jean-Paul Sartre (with Arlette El Kaim-Sartre), *On Genocide and a Summing of the Evidence and Judgments of the International War-Crimes Tribunal* (Boston: Beacon Press, 1988).
33. On Israeli oppression of Palestinians as genocidal behavior, see Churchill, *A Little Matter of Genocide*, pp. 73–5, and James Petras, *The Power of Israel in the United States* (Atlanta: Clarity Press, 2006), pp. 45–6 and pp. 115–17.
34. It is well known that Prime Minister Golda Meir remarked, in 1968, that in fact "there were no Palestinians," essentially dismissing *any* claims of Palestinian statehood—a view that continues to hold much currency within Israeli political culture. See Mearsheimer and Walt, *The Israel Lobby*, p. 96.
35. Grossman, *Weapons in Space*, p. 17.
36. Ibid., p. 61.
37. See Beth Dickey, "Bush Rethinking Space Treaty," at www.goveexec.com/dailyfed/2007
38. www.state/gov.htm/2007
39. See, for example, Laura Griego's Senate testimony of May 3, 2007, at www.ucusa.org/global/2007
40. Grossman, *Weapons in Space*, pp. 24–5.

41. The United Nations Intergovernmental Panel on Climate Change issued four reports in 2007. See www.ipcc.ch/ipccreports/assessments-reports.htm
42. *Los Angeles Times* (April 7, 2007).
43. Sands, *Lawless World*, p. 70.
44. *Los Angeles Times* (December 17, 2005).
45. Robert F. Kennedy, Jr., "The Junk Science of George W. Bush," *The Nation* (March 8, 2004).
46. See Chris Mooney, "Climate of Denial," *Mother Jones* (June 2005), p. 36.
47. On Washington lobbying efforts against measures to fight global warming, see *In These Times* (April 2007).
48. On the increasing closure of the public sphere, see Boggs, *The End of Politics*, and David Brock, *The Republican Noise Machine* (New York: Crown Publishers, 2004), chs 1–3.

CHAPTER 6

1. Persico, *Nuremberg*, p. 437.
2. Ibid., p. 442.
3. *New York Times* (February 11, 2002).
4. Quoted in Gary Jonathan Bass, *Stay the Hand of Vengeance* (Princeton, NJ: Princeton University Press, 2000), p. 282.
5. Cigar and Williams, *Indictment at The Hague*, pp. 17, 21.
6. On the Krajina massacres, see Gregory Elich, "The Invasion of Serbian Krajina," in Clark, et al., *NATO in the Balkans*, pp. 130–40. On the larger historical context, see John Catalinotto, "Washington's NATO Strategy," in Catalinotto and Flounders, eds, *Hidden Agenda*, pp. 153–64.
7. See Mandel, *How America Gets Away With Murder*, pp. 97–8.
8. Quoted in ibid., p. 112.
9. Ibid., p. 132.
10. John Loughland, *Travesty: The Trial of Slobodan Milošević and the Corruption of International Justice* (London: Pluto Press, 2007), p. 66.
11. On U.S. and NATO interests in the Balkans, see Catalinotto, "Washington's NATO Strategy," Sean Gervasi, "Why is NATO in Yugoslavia?," in Clark, et al., *NATO in The Balkans*, pp. 29–46; and Parenti, *To Kill a Nation*, chs 2 and 3.
12. Johnstone, *Fool's Crusade*, p. 101.
13. For a brief summary of Milošević's own statement regarding the ICTY proceedings, see his "Illegitimacy of the 'Tribunal'," in Catalinotto and Flounders, *Hidden Agenda*, pp. 59–74.
14. *Los Angeles Times* (July 12, 2007).
15. See Dimitri Oram, SWANS Commentary of February 26, 2007, at www.swans.com/library/artl3/doram03.html
16. See Gervasi, "Why is NATO in Yugoslavia?," pp. 30–33.
17. *New York Times* (March 8, 1992).
18. See Chandler, "International Justice," p. 65.
19. Telford Taylor, *Nuremberg and Vietnam* (Chicago: Quadrangle Books, 1970), p. 39.
20. *Los Angeles Times* (November 17, 2005).
21. *Los Angeles Times* (November 17, 2005).

22. See www.whitehouse.gov/government/reic-bio.html. Reid had been in Iraq since 2004, involved in "teaching human rights to Iraqi corrections officers in prisons around Baghdad" before heading the Regime Crimes Liaison's Office first field office, which investigated atrocities said to be committed by the Hussein regime. In March 2005 Reid became Deputy Regime Crimes Liaison.

23. For Mike Newton's comments and involvement, see www/law.vanderbilt.edu

24. See www.utexas,edu/law/news/2005/09140_sievert.html

25. On Christian Eckart's involvement with the Hussein tribunal, see www.Isr. nellco.org/cornell/lps/papers/13

26. Quoted in *Los Angeles Times* (March 6, 2006).

27. For the Amnesty International response, see www.globalresearch.ca/index. php?context=va&aid=3763

28. See the report of Peter Symonds, "Hussein Trial Descends into a Legal Farce," at www.wsws.org/articles/2006/jan2006/iraq-j31.shtml

29. On the notion of a "Grotian Moment," see, for example, the commentary of Mike Newton, who served as an adviser to Iraqi jurists, at www.law.vanderbilt. edu/about/news/2005/11_14b.htm

30. www.new-info.wustl.edu/news

31. www.wsws.org/articles

32. Sands, *Lawless World*, ch. 1.

33. *Los Angeles Times* (August 3, 2002).

34. *Los Angeles Times* (July 13, 2002).

35. Sands, *Lawless World*, p. 48.

36. *Los Angeles Times* (October 9, 2004).

37. Falk, *Human Rights Horizons*, p. 25.

38. Hitchens, *The Trial of Henry Kissinger*, p. 33.

39. *Los Angeles Times* (June 8, 2007).

40. See Ralph G. Kershaw, "Criminal Tribunal for Rwanda," *Covert Action Quarterly* (Fall 2002), p. 36.

41. *Los Angeles Times* (August 5, 2007).

42. Ibid.

43. *Los Angeles Times* (June 7, 2007).

44. Edward S. Herman and David Peterson, "The Dismantling of Yugoslavia," *Monthly Review* (October 2007), p. 47.

45. Mandel, *How America Gets Away With Murder*, p. 233.

46. Ibid., p. 235.

CHAPTER 7

1. *Los Angeles Times* (October 3, 2006).

2. *Los Angeles Times* (December 6, 2005).

3. The Convention against Torture (1984) is consistent with Article 5 of the UDHR, passed by the U.N. General Assembly without dissent in December 1948.

4. On the Washita River massacre, see Nies, *Native American History*, p. 276.

5. Cited in Churchill, *A Little Matter of Genocide*, p. 233.

6. Ibid., p. 234.

7. Dower, *War Without Mercy*, pp. 64–6.

8. Cited in ibid., p. 70.

9. Ibid., pp. 72–3.

10. See, for example, Gibson, *The Perfect War*, pp. 138–42.
11. Ibid., p. 149.
12. Cited in ibid., p. 184.
13. Cited in ibid., pp. 202–3.
14. Ibid., p. 203.
15. Ibid., p. 226.
16. Rhodes, *Why They Kill*, p. 300.
17. Cited in ibid., p. 303.
18. See Gibson, *The Perfect War*, pp. 300–1.
19. Harbury, *Truth, Torture, and the American Way*, p. 29.
20. Ibid., p. 30.
21. Ibid., p. 98.
22. Petras, *The Power of Israel in the United States*, pp. 88–9.
23. *Los Angeles Times* (June 27, 2007).
24. Stephen Grey, *Ghost Plane: the True Story of the CIA Torture Program* (New York: St. Martin's, 2006).
25. Mohamed Bazzi, "The CIA's Italian Job," *The Nation* (April 9, 2007).
26. See Sands, *Lawless World*, pp. 212–14.
27. See Michael Ratner and Ellen Ray, *Guantanamo* (White River Junction, VT: Chelsea Green, 2004), pp. 117–18.
28. Sands, *Lawless World*, pp. 156–7.
29. See David Rose, *Guantanamo: the War on Human Rights* (New York: The New Press, 2004), pp. 9–11.
30. On the tendency of U.S. operatives to elicit false information, see Ratner and Ray, *Guantanamo*, pp. 55–8.
31. Rose, *Guantanamo*, ch. 1.
32. Aside from the Ratner/Ray and Rose books cited above, see Mark Danner, *Torture and Truth: America, Abu Ghraib, and the War on Terror* (New York: New York Review of Books, 2004).
33. Ratner and Ray, *Guantanamo*, p. xvi.
34. Aaron Sussman, "The MCA," *Z Magazine* (January 2007).
35. Ratner and Ray, *Guantanamo*, p. 41.
36. Rose, *Guantanamo*, p. 114.
37. Ibid., pp. 121–2.
38. Ratner and Ray, *Guantanamo*, p. 46.
39. Cited in Rose, *Guantanamo*, pp. 38–9.
40. Seymour Hersh, "Torture at Abu Ghraib," *The New Yorker* (May 10, 2004). This article was followed in the next issues of *The New Yorker* by two more pieces, "Chain of Command" and "The Grey Zone," dealing with torture at Abu Ghraib.
41. www.en.wikipedia.org/wikiAbu_Ghraib_prisoner_abuse
42. General Taguba's damning report, never meant for public release, was completed in February 2004.
43. www.en.wikipedia.org/wikiAbu_Ghraib_prisoner_abuse
44. Ibid.
45. www.hrw.org/english/2005/04/27
46. www.cbc.ca/news/background/iraq
47. *Los Angeles Times* (July 15, 2007).
48. See *Los Angeles Times* (June 19, 2004).
49. www.en.wikipedia.org/wiki/Abu_Ghraib_prisoner_abuse

50. www.hrw.org/englishdocs
51. Ibid.
52. Ibid.
53. Ibid.
54. Ibid.
55. Ibid.
56. See JoAnn Wypijewski, "The Final Act at Abu Ghraib," *Mother Jones* (April 2008).
57. Cited in ibid., p. 40.
58. Cited in ibid., p. 35.
59. On the efforts of Blackwater and other PMCs to resist UCMJ legal jurisdiction, see Jeremy Scahill, *Blackwater: the Rise of the World's Most Powerful Mercenary Army* (New York: Nation Books, 2007), pp. xxi–xxii.
60. *Los Angeles Times* (September 18, 2007).
61. *Los Angeles Times* (September 22, 2007).
62. *Los Angeles Times* (September 18, 2007).
63. Ibid.
64. www.en.wikipedia.org/wiki/Private_military_contractor
65. See Ken Silverstein, *Private Warriors* (London: Verso, 2000), pp. 172–3.
66. www.en.wikipedia.org/wiki/Private_military_contractor
67. Ibid.
68. Ibid.
69. *Los Angeles Times* (May 31, 2007).
70. Scahill, *Blackwater*, pp. xvii–xviii.
71. Ibid., p xx.
72. Ibid., p. xxiv.
73. Ibid., p. 289.
74. *Los Angeles Times* (September 21, 2007).
75. Ibid.
76. See Mirko Bagaric and Julie Clark, *Torture: When the Unthinkable is Morally Permissible* (Albany: SUNY Press, 2007), pp. vii, viii.
77. *San Francisco Chronicle* (August 1, 2007).

CONCLUSION

1. On the spread of U.S. military bases around the world and development of the "new imperialism," see Chalmers Johnson, *The Sorrows of Empire* (New York: Henry Holt, 2004), ch. 1.
2. Ibid., p. 30.
3. See Carl Boggs, *Imperial Delusions* (Lanham, MD: Rowman and Littlefield, 2006), chs 1–4.
4. Chalmers Johnson, *Nemesis* (New York: Henry Holt, 2006), p. 278.
5. Hedges, *War is a Force That Gives Us Meaning*, p. 103.
6. Matt Taibbi, "John McCain's Lust for War," *Rolling Stone* (March 6, 2008), p. 34.
7. *The Defense Monitor* (March/April, 2008).
8. See Steve Rendell, "What National Intelligence Estimate?," *Extra* (March/April, 2008).

9. On the general U.S. record of obstructionism at the United Nations, see Blum, *Rogue State*, pp. 184–99. On U.S. efforts to manipulate the U.N. in the lead-up to the Iraq invasion, see Bennis, *Before and After*, pp. 106–36.
10. Mandel, *How America Gets Away With Murder*, p. 215.
11. See Joseph Stiglitz and Linda J. Bilmes, *The Three Trillion Dollar War* (New York: W.W. Norton, 2008).
12. *The Defense Monitor* (March/April, 2008).

POSTSCRIPT

1. See Henry T. Nash, "The Bureaucratization of Homicide," in E.P. Thompson and Dan Smith, eds, *Protest and Survive* (New York: Monthly Review Press, 1981), pp. 149–62.
2. Gibson, *The Perfect War*, p. 464.
3. Quoted in Kelman and Hamilton, "The My Lai Massacre: A Military Crime of Obedience," pp. 17–28.
4. Hedges, *War is a Force That Gives Us Meaning*, pp. 87–8.
5. Rhodes, *Why They Kill*, pp. 299–300.
6. Cited in ibid., p. 304.
7. Cited in Belknap, *The Vietnam War on Trial*, p. 49.
8. Rhodes, *Why They Kill*, p. 306.
9. See the analysis in Kelman and Hamilton, "The My Lai Massacre."
10. Cited in ibid., p. 24.
11. Ibid., p. 24.
12. Ibid., p. 27.
13. Belknap, *The Vietnam War on Trial*, p. 79.
14. Ibid., p. 87.
15. Ibid., p. 117.
16. Ibid., p. 135.
17. Ibid., p. 193.
18. Persico, *Nuremberg*, p. 440.
19. Ibid., p. 188.
20. Hannah Arendt, *Eichmann in Jerusalem* (New York: Penguin, 1963), p. 276.
21. Model, *Lying for Empire*, p. 301.

Index

Compiled by Sue Carlton